This book is due for return on or before the

d

g

d

Cloud Computing Explained

by John Rhoton

RP

Recursive Press

Cloud Computing Explained

By John Rhoton

Copyright © 2009, 2010, 2011, 2012, 2013 Recursive Limited. All rights reserved.

Recursive Press is an imprint of Recursive Limited.

The RP logo is a trademark of Recursive Limited.

Published simultaneously in the United States and the United Kingdom.

ISBN-10: 0-9563556-0-9

ISBN-13: 978-0-9563556-0-7

British Library Cataloguing-in-Publication Data

Application submitted.

Revision: 20130105183703

This book is dedicated to my son

—

Jeremy

Contents

Preface

Audience

This book caters primarily to consultants, architects, technologists and strategists who are involved with the planning and implementation of information technology at large enterprises. My background is heavily biased toward very large, international corporations and the challenges they face in implementing new technologies.

However, most of the contents of this book will apply to small and medium businesses too. Indeed, one of the effects of cloud computing is to remove some of the artificial segmentation barriers that differentiate larger and smaller organizations.

There are many stakeholders who are involved in implementing new projects and who might be affected by a completely overhauled service delivery model. The chief executive officers, and others on the executive board, may be concerned about the strategic impact of cloud computing. The IT managers must plan the portfolio. The architects need some background to design the end-to-end system. The technologists require a starting point for a deep technical analysis that will support them as they implement and support the actual infrastructure.

Each perspective is unique but, nonetheless, critical to the success of the overall objectives. I provide as much insight as I can for each vantage point. This may mean that some sections will be less interesting for some readers. But I hope there is some value for everyone.

Objectives (and non-objectives)

My overriding objective in writing this book is to provide a comprehensive picture of cloud computing. This is a challenging goal given the many different notions of the subject that are circulating in the press. However, precisely for this reason, I believe it is critically important for readers to be able to see how all the components fit together.

A wealth of information on cloud computing is readily available on the Internet. In fact, large amounts of my content are derived from fairly accessible sources such as Wikipedia and the results of obvious Google searches. However, the picture is fragmented and requires some effort to piece together clearly. I hope to make this task a little easier.

My second objective is to provide a practical framework for approaching cloud computing. I will not describe every detail of every step or each potential factor that an enterprise should consider. It is only a high-level structure and abstracts many of the specific obstacles that may occur in an actual deployment. It does, however, reflect the approach I have taken in implementing new technologies and some of the pitfalls and challenges that I have encountered.

Part of this framework includes a set of tools that are useful in working through each step. I identify and sketch these models. They do not necessarily change in a fundamental way as part of a cloud-based solution. Some are an obvious application of common sense. Nonetheless, I find it useful to present the whole chain in order to provide context for the individual cloud-based decisions.

Finally, I have tried to put as much substance to the concepts as possible by including a number of references to vendors and service providers that are active in cloud computing today. This is not an endorsement of any particular offering nor do I attempt to highlight any weaknesses in the solutions.

I may omit important information or not characterize and classify the services in the same terms as the vendors. Therefore I would encourage you to perform your own research before deciding on a particular service or eliminating it from your list of options.

It is also not an exhaustive survey of the products that are on the market. Given the volatile nature of the cloud landscape, I cannot even imply a guarantee that companies mentioned in this book will still be in business when you read about them or that they will offer the same functionality.

Nonetheless, I believe that you will get a better picture of what is happening in cloud computing with some actual examples and rough descriptions of the services currently on offer in the market place – if for no other reason than to give you a starting point for your own analysis.

Organization and Structure

This book is structured as thirty chapters divided unevenly into ten parts:

1. Define
2. Assess
3. Design
4. Select
5. Integrate
6. Implement
7. Operate
8. Control
9. Adapt
10. Evolve

Each one of the parts represents a step in my approach at examining a new technology. This does not mean that each chapter follows the preceding in a completely chronological process.

The general theme is sequential, at least in my mind, but the steps are not discrete. I've tried to minimize forward references, since it isn't practical to read all chapters in parallel. However, there are still a few, which I hope do not present a significant distraction, especially for readers who already have some familiarity with the subject matter.

I've also tried to make the parts as independent of each other as possible since they tend to target different stakeholders. Depending on your focus you may want to skip some chapters. You may even rely primarily on the text as a reference and not read it at all except to research specific questions. The general outline is as follows:

Define: The first five chapters are probably relevant to all readers. Those who have already spent some time in the field may be familiar with most of the concepts. However, many differences in terminology and approach are represented in the press. There is nothing wrong with the other perspectives; but if you are familiar with my usage of the terms, it will help to put the rest of the discussion in context.

This entails, above all, a common definition of what cloud computing actually means. It also includes a common view of how cloud components fit together. I walk through each layer of the SPI (Software, Platform, Infrastructure) model to give an introductory view of what a cloud architecture looks like.

Assess: The second part examines the impact of cloud computing on corporate business and other areas that are likely to affect readers of the book. The first question to tackle is whether the new technology is appropriate at all and, if so, for what purposes. I then look at the impact from three different perspectives: company strategy, risk and finance.

Design: The third section covers the design of a cloud solution. Given the wide range of participants, it is vital that the methodology used incorporate all relevant requirements. It is then necessary to put together a design that can be mapped to cloud-based components.

Select: The next three chapters describe the selection process. This involves identifying the most suitable applications for cloud deployment and then finding the best candidate services to fulfill them. It also involves determining which users will be using which services and how they will use them.

Integrate: Once you have all the parts, the next challenge is putting them together. You need to make sure you have an end-to-end design that includes all the components. And then you need to make sure that the service you have built has all the necessary connectivity, provides the required business continuity and guarantees sufficient security to meet all your requirements.

Implement: After the design and planning is complete, we will begin to put everything in place to go live. This means assembling the right project team, setting up the required infrastructure, migrating all the applications and data and taking care of all user concerns that arise in the process.

Operate: Getting the services running is just the beginning of the lifecycle. Once they are live, someone needs to manage them, which involves administering changes and new releases as well as monitoring the services to ensure that they continue to run satisfactorily. It also entails providing full support to both end-users and all IT personnel involved in the service delivery.

Control: The fact that there are multiple stakeholders involved in the service delivery and consumption inevitably leads to control issues. This section looks at the topics often referred to as GRC (Governance, Risk and Compliance).

Adapt: Although there is very little cloud-specific in systematically refining every service in the portfolio, it would be an unpardonable omission to neglect it. Over time the business and its context change. A successful organization will leverage these changes and incorporate any feedback that it has accumulated. This is an ongoing process, which should start immediately after the implementation.

Evolve: Cloud computing itself is also a very dynamic topic as are many of the other technological trends currently underway. It is important for architects, technologists and business executives to be aware of what changes we might expect over the coming years. This doesn't mean that we need to predict the future. There are many options, so it is difficult to know which are most likely to develop at which speed. However, we should at least be familiar with any likely changes so that we are prepared to address and leverage them if required.

Enterprise Focus

In addition to readers who represent enterprises potentially adopting cloud computing, there may be some who represent service providers, small businesses or non-profit organizations. As mentioned above, the focus of this book is on the enterprise and my terminology reflects that perspective.

Nonetheless, there should be some benefits for other readers too.

Service providers require a solid understanding of their customers in order to optimize their services.

I do not differentiate between large or small organizations so I expect that much of the discussion will apply to small and medium businesses as well as multinationals.

A profit-driven charter is a central focus of most corporations and this is reflected in the financial calculations. Other organizations may balance their priorities differently but even governments and charities have budgetary constraints that make the analysis relevant.

I do hope that everyone who reads this book finds the value that they expect but, to keep the discussion simple, I have placed the enterprise at the center of all my explanations. This means that when I mention customers and suppliers without any further qualifications I mean enterprise customers and suppliers.

Print on Demand

This book is printed on demand through a company called LightningSource. I deliberated for some time before deciding to take this path. I've previously authored four books distributed through traditional publishing companies. In addition to printing, they provide valuable services in editing and marketing the book. On the other hand, print on demand gives the author much more control, cuts the time-to-publish cycle and facilitates more frequent updates.

I believe that the publishing industry will undergo radical changes over the next few years as the ability to print is extended to the masses at ever decreasing costs. Whether we have already reached the tipping point for self-publishing is hard to say except in retrospect. Nonetheless, I feel that a book on cloud computing would be hypocritical if it didn't leverage distributed and on-demand printing services to their maximum.

Feedback

A direct consequence of the print-on-demand model, and actually one of its primary benefits, is the flexibility it gives the author and publisher to incorporate incremental changes throughout the lifecycle of the book. I would like to leverage that advantage by drawing on the collective experience and insights of my readers.

As mentioned above, I have ambitious objectives for this book. There is the risk that my vision may exceed my talent. You may also find errors and omissions. Or you may actually find some parts of the book very useful and interesting. Regardless of your feedback, if you have something to say then I'd love to hear from you. Please feel free to send me a message:

john.rhoton@gmail.com

I can't guarantee that I will reply to every message but I will do my best to acknowledge your input!

Acknowledgements

I am grateful to the following reviewers who provided critical input that help me refine the content of this book: John Bair, Samy Benzekry, Jamie Erbes, Rowan Evans, Giuliani Giovanni, Walt Lammert, Rick Morley, Peter Put, Tony Redmond, Royce Resoso, Juha Sallinen, Martin Visser and Yong Jun Yi.

I would also likc to acknowledge the many technologists in HP whose insights I leveraged as I put together the structure and substance of my analysis. In addition to the internal discussion groups at HP, I also drew on numerous Internet sources ranging from bloggers to Wikipedia entries. I am constantly amazed at the wealth of information on every topic that has been created and shared by the technical community on a voluntary basis.

I would like to thank those who have assisted me in the development of my manuscript and the publication process. In particular, Elisabeth Rinaldin offered assistance with the layout and cover and Gill Shaw provided excellent proof-reading and copy-editing.

Finally, I'm thankful that my family was generous enough to grant me the time and effort that I needed to write and produce this book.

Define

Chapter 1

What is a Cloud?

So, what is "Cloud Computing"? As we shall see, the experts disagree on its exact definition, but most concur that it includes the notion of web-based services that are available on-demand from an optimized, and highly scalable, service provider. Despite the technical sound of its characterization, it has not only garnered excitement from technologists but has captured the attention of business leaders around the world.

2009 may long be remembered as the year of the worldwide economic downturn. The impact across many industries, including IT, was devastating. And yet, even then, there were bastions of hope in the midst of all the turmoil. One of the most prominent IT analysts, Gartner, identified cloud computing as the primary source of growth in IT spending, increasing over 20% year-on-year to global revenues of $56B in 2009 and surging to over $130B by 2013[1]. Experts from IDC, Forrester and Yankee Group painted a similar picture (Simonds, 2009).

In other words, while IT managers saw their budgets decimated in the course of intense scrutiny over any uncritical or non-urgent costs, they actually received permission to spend more in a completely new area that didn't even appear in any of their proposals a few years before.

Hype Cycle

It is easy to make technology predictions, but difficult to make accurate ones. In the case of cloud computing, however, the estimates have been corroborated and the trends appear to continue.

According to Gartner's 2012 IT spending report, the public cloud services market hit $91.4B in 2011, is expected to reach $109B in 2012 and grow to $206.6B

---

[1] Gartner estimates are expressed in U.S. dollars. Gartner, Inc., 56 Top Gallant Road, Stamford, CT 06904 USA, +1 203 964 0096–www.gartner.com

in 2016 (Gartner, 2012). At the same time, over 75% of enterprises polled plan to pursue private cloud computing by 2014.

While it is always difficult to predict the future, the signs are appearing that cloud computing is poised for a breakthrough. Before you bet your business on it, however, it's worth investigating the relationship between the excitement around new technologies and actual investment.

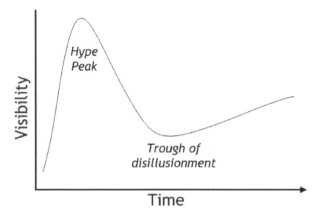

Figure 1-1: Cloud Hype Cycle

Industry analysts use a "Hype Cycle" (originally developed by Gartner and loosely depicted in Figure 1-1) to describe the tendency for new technologies to attract an excess of interest long before they are mature enough to be deployed in production environments. The disappointment that many advocates feel when their initial zeal is frustrated leads them into a "Trough of Disillusionment". During this phase many lose heart and redirect their focus toward other promising ventures. However, as the underlying problems are resolved and aligned with user needs, the systems become ready for the mainstream and interest picks up again.

There is an element of subjectivity around the precise positioning of any technology in the cycle. Gartner placed cloud computing in the middle of the initial slope in 2008 and advanced the position to the peak of the hype curve in 2009. Other analysts loosely concur with this assessment – there is little disagreement on the level of enthusiasm around cloud computing, even if it may already be seeing some signs of the onset of disillusionment in 2013.

A more objective, albeit not necessarily extremely reliable, way to gauge the excitement around any given topic is to use Google Trends (Figure 1-2)[1]. You can enter a search expression and Google will provide a graphic representation that illustrates the relative frequency of search of this specific expression over time.

---

[1] http://www.google.com/trends

DEFINE

For instance, the figure below illustrates the popularity of the phrase "Cloud Computing" over the past five years. Until the middle of 2007, the term was virtually never used in search queries nor did it appear in news references. Since then, the user requests have grown dramatically. We can now see signs that the generic searches are tapering off, particularly as users become more familiar with the term and more specific in their enquiries.

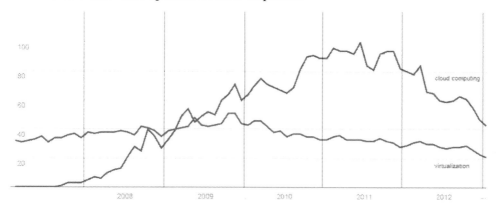

Figure 1-2: Google Trends: "cloud computing" and "virtualization"

Needless to say, it is obvious from the above that there has been a major shift in interest toward cloud computing over the past five years. I have not shown them here, but if you compare these results to the graphs generated for other topics such as "Grid Computing", "Web 2.0", "P2P", "Wireless" you will see a stark contrast in the shape of the curves.

Implementation Gap

While it is very interesting to understand the hype around a new technology, it is also helpful to examine the historical implementation cycle of new technologies. I find it very useful to describe adoption in terms of Geoffrey Moore's model presented in his best-selling book: "Crossing the Chasm" (Moore, 2002).

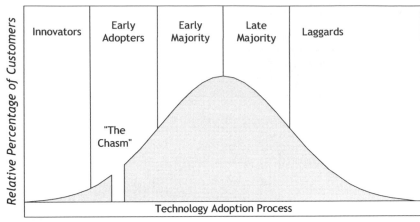

Figure 1-3: Moore's Implementation Chasm

Moore segments the target market according to the speed with which they adopt new technologies (Figure 1-3). He uses five categories (Innovators, Early Adopters, Early Majority, Late Majority, Laggards) to designate these segments. While being at one extreme or the other may give cause for some concern, there is not necessarily any value associated with being earlier or later in the adoption curve. Some companies can gain competitive advantage by leveraging and showcasing the newest technologies. Others may risk their business if they pursue areas outside their core competency too early.

Moore's salient observation is that there is a significant barrier to overcome between the Early Adopters and Early Majority. Technology enthusiasts often embrace new developments before the commercial business case becomes compelling. A generally applicable business case, alongside a reliable and easily deployable technological foundation, pave the way to widespread adoption, which will be recognized and further refined by an Early Majority.

An interesting twist that cloud computing brings to the adoption model is that, in some ways, the propensity to adopt may be reversed from other technologies. Typically, technologically savvy organizations prefer new developments while those who like to remain distant from technology also tend to keep the status quo as long as possible.

In the case of cloud computing, an increased trend to outsourcing shifts large portions of the information technology systems outside the company control and responsibility. This can be attractive to those Luddites who would prefer to concentrate on non-technical aspects of their business and are glad to see their fixed IT costs reduced and their computer departments, which they never considered to be contributing to the bottom line, minimized.

Common Definition

We have established that "Cloud Computing" has been one of the most popular IT buzzwords of the past few years. Everyone wants to know more about it. All the vendors are rebranding their products to indicate alignment with the cloud. And still the most common question I hear when I mention the topic is "what does it actually mean?"

It makes sense to start this discussion with the same question. After all, you will have trouble building a solid architecture if you are unsure what you are trying to build.

In the simplest sense, a cloud represents a network and, more specifically, the global Internet. Cloud computing, by inference, is the use of computational resources that are hosted remotely and delivered through the Internet. That is the basic idea underlying the term. It may be sufficient for your non-technical friends and colleagues, but shouldn't be adequate for anyone reading this book.

If you have ever tried to isolate the core meaning of "Cloud Computing" by looking for an authoritative definition, you will have quickly discovered that the term entails many different notions. There is some disagreement among the experts as to what constitutes the essence of this fundamental shift in technology. Some are able to articulate their perspectives more elegantly than others, but that doesn't mean they are accepted any more universally.

For instance, some definitions that have circulated in the blogosphere include:

The 451 Group: "The cloud is IT as a Service, delivered by IT resources that are independent of location"

Gartner: "Cloud computing is a style of computing where massively scalable IT-related capabilities are provided 'as a service' across the Internet to multiple external customers"

Forrester: "A pool of abstracted, highly scalable, and managed infrastructure capable of hosting end-customer applications and billed by consumption"

Wikipedia: "A style of computing in which dynamically scalable and often virtualized resources are provided as a service over the Internet. Users need not have knowledge of, expertise in, or control over the technology infrastructure "in the cloud" that supports them."

The most commonly recognized definition in use today was articulated by NIST (2011):

Cloud computing is a model for enabling convenient, on-demand network access to a shared pool of configurable computing resources (e.g., networks, servers, storage, applications, and services) that can be rapidly provisioned and released with minimal management effort or service provider interaction.

Unfortunately, neither the NIST formulation, nor the interpretation of what it means, is universally accepted. In "A Break in the Clouds: Towards a Cloud Definition", a White Paper published for the ACM Computer Communication Reviews, the authors found over twenty distinct definitions of cloud computing in their research (Vaquero, Rodero-Merino, Cáceres, & Lindner, A Break in the Clouds: Towards a Cloud Definition, 2009).

They assembled some of the main notions into:

A large pool of easily usable and accessible virtualized resources (such as hardware, development platforms and/or services). These resources can be dynamically reconfigured to adjust to a variable load (scale), allowing also for an optimum resource utilization. This pool of re-sources is typically exploited by a pay-per-use model in which guarantees are offered by the Infrastructure Provider by means of customized SLAs.

This is a comprehensive definition but it hides the primary discovery of the paper that no single theme seemed to permeate all of the definitions. This observation may be somewhat discouraging, but before you concede defeat you might consider that, although the definitions are not identical, or in some cases even very similar, they are still not contradictory. They simply emphasize different aspects of a complex and multi-faceted notion.

If there is one element of cloud computing that can be considered a core concept, it is that of resource pooling. Generally, resources are shared across customers in a public environment and across departments or cost centers in a private implementation. The increased scale allows for better allocation and utilization, which contribute to additional benefits.

A pragmatic approach to understanding more specific interpretations of the term is to examine the assortment of attributes of typical cloud solutions. This doesn't imply that every cloud attribute is essential to cloud computing, or that any combination qualifies a given approach as fitting the cloud paradigm. On their own, they are neither necessary nor sufficient prerequisites to the notion of cloud computing. However, the more of these attributes apply to a given implementation, the more likely others will accept it as a cloud solution.

One popular analogy is an old Indian story of six blind men who encountered an elephant and used their hands to determine what it was. One felt a leg and compared it to a pillar. Another felt the tail, which he likened to a rope. The trunk felt like a tree branch, and the ear like a hand fan. The belly was like a wall while the tusk felt comparable to a pipe. Each description held an element of truth and yet fell short of a complete description.

Similarly, most definitions of cloud computing include elements of the complete description and yet they typically do not address every single aspect that anyone has associated with cloud computing.

I won't add to the confusion with another attempt at perfecting the definitions that are already available. For the most part, they all do a good job at giving an idea of what is involved; and it's not obvious to me that there is any particular value in having an authoritative definition.

The most important consideration for any IT manager is not whether a potential solution satisfies the definition of cloud computing but rather whether it adds value to the business. A cloud-based solution that does not increase revenue or decrease costs is of little interest. And a completely non-cloud-oriented solution that does unambiguously improve the bottom line should be implemented regardless of the name you use to label it.

Metaphorical Interpretation

Even if a universally accepted and precisely expressed definition doesn't appear to be possible, it is still necessary to come to some consensus on what typically makes up a cloud computing solution. If you allow anything at all to qualify as cloud computing, you open the door to very unscrupulous rebranding and misleading advertising.

One obvious place to start is the cloud metaphor itself. After all there is a reason why the term cloud computing has established itself rather than other conceivable terms such as forest computing or ocean computing. A cloud has long been used in network diagrams to represent a sort of black box where the interfaces are well known but the internal routing and processing is not visible to the network users. A cloud, by nature, is opaque. It is also typically very large and distant.

The metaphor applies elegantly to cloud computing where not only the internal substance is opaque but also the boundaries are blurred; clouds may be overlapping; they may dynamically intersect or split.

Attributes

The key to understanding common interpretations of the term "Cloud Computing" is to examine the assortment of attributes of typical cloud solutions. This doesn't mean that every cloud attribute is essential to cloud computing or even that there is necessarily any which qualifies a given approach as fitting the cloud paradigm. On their own, they are neither necessary nor sufficient prerequisites to the notion of cloud computing. But typically, the more of these attributes that apply, the more likely others will accept it as a cloud solution.

Some key components include:

DEFINE

Off-Premise: The service is hosted and delivered from a location that belongs to a service provider. This usually has two implications: The service is delivered over the public Internet and the processing occurs outside the company firewall. In other words, the service must cross both physical and security boundaries.

Elasticity: One main benefit of cloud computing is the inherent scalability of the service provider, which is made available to the end-user. The model goes much further in providing an elastic provisioning mechanism so that resources can be scaled both up and down very rapidly as they are required. Since utility billing is also common, elasticity can equate to direct cost savings.

Flexible Billing: Fine-grained metering of resource usage, combined with on-demand service provisioning, facilitate a number of options for charging customers. Fees can be levied on a subscription basis or can be tied to actual consumption, or reservation, of resources. Monetization can take the form of placed advertising or can rely on simple credit card charges in addition to elaborate contracts and central billing.

Virtualization: Cloud services are usually offered through an abstracted infrastructure. They leverage various virtualization mechanisms and achieve cost optimization through multi-tenancy.

Service Delivery: Cloud functionality is often available as a service of some form. While there is great variance in the nature of these services, typically the services offer programmatic interfaces in addition to the user interfaces.

Universal access: Resource democratization means that pooled resources are available to anyone authorized to utilize them. At the same time, location independence and high levels of resilience allow for an always-connected user experience.

Simplified management: Administration is simplified through automatic provisioning to meet scalability requirements, user self-service to expedite business processes and programmatically accessible resources that facilitate integration into enterprise management frameworks.

Affordable resources: The cost of resources is dramatically reduced for two reasons. There is no requirement for capital expenditures on fixed purchases. Also, the economy of scale of the service providers allow them to optimize their cost structure with commodity hardware and fine-tuned operational procedures that are not easily matched by most companies.

Multi-tenancy: The cloud is used by many organizations (tenants) and includes mechanisms to protect and isolate each tenant from all others. Pooling resources across customers is an important factor in achieving scalability and cost savings.

Service-level management: Cloud services typically offer a service-level definition that sets the expectation with the customer as to how robust that service will be. Some services may come with only minimal (or non-existent) commitments. They can still be considered cloud services but typically will not be "trusted" for mission-critical applications to the extent that others (which are governed by more precise commitments) might.

DEFINE

All of these attributes will be discussed in more detail in the chapters to come.

Related Terms

In addition to the set of characteristics that may be associated with cloud computing it is worth mentioning some other key technologies that are strongly interrelated with Cloud Computing.

Service-Oriented Architecture

A service-oriented architecture (SOA) decomposes the information technology landscape of an enterprise into unassociated and loosely coupled functional primitives called services. In contrast to the monolithic applications of the past, these services implement single actions and may be used by many different business applications.

The business logic is then tasked with orchestrating the service objects by arranging them sequentially, selectively or iteratively so that they help to fulfill a business objective. One of the greatest advantages of this approach is that it maximizes reusability of functionality and thereby reduces the effort needed to build new applications or modify existing programs.

There is a high degree of commonality between cloud computing and SOA. An enterprise that uses a service-oriented architecture is better positioned to leverage cloud computing. Cloud computing may also drive increased attention to SOA.

However, the two are independent notions. The best way to think of the relation between them is that SOA is an architecture, which is technology independent in nature. Cloud computing may be one means of implementing a SOA design.

Grid Computing

Grid Computing refers to the use of many interconnected computers to solve a problem through highly parallel computation. These grids are often based on loosely coupled and heterogeneous systems, which leverage geographically dispersed volunteer resources. They are usually confined to scientific problems that require a huge number of computer processing cycles or access to large amounts of data. However, they have also been applied successfully to drug discovery,

DEFINE

economic forecasting, seismic analysis, and even financial modeling for quantitative trading, including risk management and derivative pricing.

There may be some conceptual similarity between grid and cloud computing. Both involve large interconnected systems of computers, distribute their workload and blur the line between system usage and system ownership. But it is important to also be aware of their distinctions. A grid may be transparent to its users and addresses a narrow problem domain. Cloud services are typically opaque and cover a wide range of almost every class of informational problem using a model that decouples functionality from the user.

Web 2.0

The term Web 2.0 is also often closely associated with cloud computing. Darcy DiNucci first used the expression in 1999 (DiNucci, 1999) to refer to radical changes in web design and aesthetics. Tim O'Reilly popularized a recast notion in his Web 2.0 conference in 2004 (O'Reilly & Batelle, 2004). This term has evolved to refer to the web as not only a static information source for browser access but a platform for web-based communities that facilitate user participation and collaboration.

There is no intrinsic connection between cloud computing and Web 2.0. Cloud computing is a means of delivering services and Web 2.0 is a class of services that may be delivered in many different ways. Nonetheless, it is worth observing that Web 2.0 is one of the fastest growing areas for new applications and that it typically involves little infrastructure other than the computers and networks needed to make the services available to users on the public Internet. These requirements, and the absence of legacy dependencies, make it optimally suited to cloud platforms.

History

Cloud computing represents an evolution and confluence of several trends. The ultimate objective has been on the radar screen of many IT companies (such as Sun, HP and IBM) for several years. But the first commercially viable offerings actually came from other sectors of the industry.

Amazon was arguably the first company to offer an extensive and thorough set of cloud-based services. This may seem somewhat odd since Amazon was not initially in the business of providing IT services. However, they had several other advantages that they were able to leverage effectively.

As most readers will recall, Amazon started as an on-line bookstore in 1995. Based on its success in the book market, it diversified its product portfolio to include CDs, DVDs, and other forms of digital media, eventually expanding into computer hardware and software, jewelry, grocery, apparel and even automotive parts and accessories.

DEFINE

A major change in business model involved the creation of merchant partnerships that leveraged Amazon's portal and large customer base. Amazon brokered the transaction for a fee thereby developing a new ecosystem of partners – and even competitors.

As Amazon grew, it had to find ways to minimize its IT costs. Its business model implied a very large online presence[1], which was crucial to its success. Without the bricks-and-mortar retail outlets, its data center investments and operations became a significant portion of its cost structure.

Amazon chose to minimize hardware expenditures by buying only commodity hardware parts and assembling them into a highly standardized framework that was able to guarantee the resilience they needed through extensive replication. In the course of building their infrastructure, their system designers had scrutinized the security required to ensure that the financial transactions and data of their customers and retail partners could not be compromised.

The approach met their needs. However, it was not inherently optimized. Amazon and partners shared a common burden or boon, depending on how you look at it, with other retailers in that a very high proportion of their sales are processed in the weeks leading up to Christmas. In order to be able to guarantee computing capacity in December, they needed to overprovision for the remainder of the year. This meant that a major share of their data center was idle eleven out of twelve months. The inefficiency contributed to an unacceptable amount of unnecessary costs.

Amazon decided to turn their weakness into an opportunity. When they launched Amazon Web Services in 2002, they effectively sold some of their idle capacity to other organizations who had computational requirements from January to November. The proposition was attractive to their customers, who were able to take advantage of a secure and reliable infrastructure at reasonable prices without making any financial or strategic commitment.

Google is another player in cloud computing history that is worth examining, given the success of Google Apps and Google App Engine. Their story bears some resemblance to Amazon's. They also host a huge worldwide infrastructure with many thousands of servers worldwide. In order to satisfy hundreds of millions of search requests every day they must process about one petabyte of user-generated data every hour (Vogelstein, 2009).

However, their primary business model is fundamentally different. They do not have a huge retail business that they can leverage to easily monetize their services. Instead, Google's source of revenue is through advertising and their core competence is in analytics. Through extensive data mining, they are able to iden-

---

[1] Amazon.com received unique 76 million visitors in March 2011 (Compete, Inc, 2011)

DEFINE

tify and classify user interests. And through their portals, they can place advertising banners effectively.

I will not go into detail on the different implications of these two approaches at this point but it will be useful to keep in mind as we discuss the various cloud platforms in the next chapters. Also keep in mind that there are several other important cloud service providers such as Salesforce.com or Microsoft. Each has its own history and business model. The two above are merely two notable examples that I feel provide some insight into the history of cloud computing. Nonetheless, it could be completely different players who shape the future.

Innovation or Impact?

I hope I have clarified some of the mystery surrounding cloud computing and provided some insight into how the new service delivery model has evolved. However, there is still one very important question that I have not addressed:

What is so novel about cloud computing?

I've listed a number of attributes that characterize the technology. But which of those has made significant breakthroughs in the past few years in order to set the way for a revolutionary new approach to computing?

Timesharing (multi-tenancy) was popular in the 1960s. At the same time, IBM made a successful entry into virtualization with their VM/370 series. A utility pricing model is more recent but also preceded the current cloud-boom. The same can be said for Internet-based service delivery, application hosting and outsourcing.

Rather than answering the question, I would challenge whether it is essential for there to be a clear technological innovation that triggers a major disruption – even if that disruption is primarily technical in nature. I will make my case by analogy. If you examine some other recent upheavals in the area of technology, it is similarly difficult to identify any particular novelty associated with them at the time of their break-through.

Simon Wardley pointed out at the O'Reilly Open Source Convention in 2009 (OSCON 09) that we still lack a common definition of the Industrial Revolution, which began two hundred years ago (Wardley, 2009). Nonetheless, historians tend to agree that its influence on the economy and society was fundamental.

More recently, the PC revolution saw a shift of computing from mainframes and minicomputers for large companies to desktops that small businesses and consumers could afford. There were some advances in technology, in particular around miniaturization and environmental resilience, but these were arguably incremental in nature.

The Internet is a particularly clear example of a technological transformation that caught the industry and large segments of business by surprise, but was not primarily a technical breakthrough. Although Tim Berners-Lee's vision of the World Wide Web brought together many components in a creative, and certainly compelling manner, the parts were invented long before the web made it into the mainstream.

For example, the fourth version of the Internet Protocol (IPv4, RFC 791), which is the most common network protocol today, was specified in 1981. The Hypertext Transfer Protocol (HTTP; RFC 1945) leans heavily on SMTP, NNTP, FTP, Gopher and WAIS, which predated it. The Hypertext Markup Language (HTML) was developed as an application of the Standard Generalized Markup Language (ISO 8879:1986 SGML).

Even the notion of hypertext isn't new. In 1945 Vannevar Bush wrote an article for The Atlantic Monthly about a device, called a Memex, which created trails of linked and branching sets of pages. Ted Nelson coined the term hypertext in 1965 when he developed his Hypertext Editing System at Brown University in 1967.

And yet, the impact of these technological shifts is hard to oversee and all those who contributed to their initial breakthrough deserve credit for their vision of what could be done with all of these parts.

The innovation of the Internet, from a technical perspective, lies in identifying the confluence of several technical trends and visualizing how these can combine with improving cost factors, a changing environment and evolving societal needs to create a virtuous circle that generates ever-increasing economies of scale and benefits from network effects.

Cloud computing is similar. It is difficult to isolate a single technological trigger. A number of incremental improvements in various areas (such as fine-grained metering, flexible billing, virtualization, broadband, service-oriented architecture and service management) have come together recently. Combined, they enable new business models that can dramatically affect cost and cash flow patterns and are therefore of great interest to the business (especially in a down-turn).

This combined effect has also hit a critical threshold by achieving sufficient scale to dramatically reduce prices, thus leading to a virtuous cycle of benefits (cost reduction for customers, profits for providers), exponential growth and ramifications that may ripple across many levels of our lives, including Technology, Business, Economic, Social and Political dimensions.

Technology

The impact of cloud computing is probably most apparent in information technology where we have seen the enablement of new service delivery models.

New platforms have become available to developers, and utility-priced infrastructure facilitates development, testing and deployment.

This foundation can enable and accelerate other applications and technologies. Many Web 2.0 applications take advantage of a cloud-based infrastructure. There is significant potential to offload batch processing, analytics and compute-intensive desktop applications (Armbrust, et al., 2009).

Mobile technologies may also receive support from the ubiquitous presence of cloud providers, their high uptime, and reduced latency through distributed hosting. Furthermore, a public cloud environment can reduce some of the security risks associated with mobile computing. It is possible to segment the data so that only non-sensitive data is stored in the cloud and accessible to a mobile device. The exposure of reduced end-point security (for example with regard to malware infections) is also minimized if a device is only connected to a public infrastructure.

By maximizing service interconnectivity, cloud computing can also increase interoperability between disjointed technologies. For example, HP's ePrint service facilitates an interaction between mobile devices and printers.

As cloud computing establishes itself as a primary service delivery channel, it is likely to have a significant impact on the IT industry by stimulating requirements that support it in areas such as:

- Processors: Processor virtualization and memory management
- Network adapter and router/switch: network virtualization
- Discs: storage virtualization and improved capacity scaling
- Network adapter: better wireless broadband access

Business

Cloud computing also has an undeniable impact on business strategy. It overturns traditional models of financing IT expenditures by replacing capital expenditures with operational expenditures. Since the operational expenditures can be directly tied to production, fixed costs tend to vanish in comparison to variable costs thus greatly facilitating accounting transparency and reducing financial risk.

The reduction in fixed costs also allows the company to become much more agile and aggressive in pursuing new revenue streams. Since resources can be elastically scaled up and down, they can take advantage of unanticipated high demand but are not burdened with excess costs when the market softens.

The outsourcing of IT infrastructure reduces the responsibilities and focus in the area of IT. This release can be leveraged to realign the internal IT resources with the core competencies of the organization. Rather than investing energy and managerial commitment to industry standard technologies these can be redirected toward potential sources of sustainable competitive differentiation. The primary role of IT is therefore shifting from "Plan – Build – Run" functions to a focus on "Source – Integrate – Manage".

Another form of business impact may be that the high level of service standardization, which cloud computing entails, may blur traditional market segmentation. For example, the conventional distinction that separates small and medium businesses from enterprises, based on their levels of customization and requirements for sales and services support, may fade in favor of richer sets of options and combinations of service offerings.

As a result of the above, it is very likely that there will be market shifts as some companies leverage the benefits of cloud computing better than others. These may trigger a reshuffling of the competitive landscape, an event that may harbor both risk and opportunity but must certainly not be ignored.

Economic

The business impact may very well spread across the economy. The reduction in capital costs eliminates entry barriers for many industries which can lead to enhanced startup speed and ultimately a larger number of smaller companies entering the market.

Knowledge workers could find themselves increasingly independent of large corporate infrastructure (Carr N. , 2009, p. 146). Through social productivity and "crowdsourcing"[1] we may encounter increasing amount of media, from blogs and Wikipedia to collaborative video ("Live Music", Yair Landau).

The Internet can be a great leveling force since it essentially removes the inherent advantages of investment capital and location. However, Nicholas Carr (2009, p. 149) contends that the acceleration of volunteer labor may very well polarize the economy, increasing the returns of only the very successful, and therefore erode the middle class. At this stage it is difficult to predict which influences will predominate, but it is likely there will be some effects.

As the cloud unleashes new investment models it's interesting to consider one of the driving forces of new technologies today: the investment community. Most successful startups have received a great deal of support from venture capitalists. Sand Hill Road in Palo Alto is famous for its startup investments in some of the most successful technologies businesses today ranging from Apple to Google.

---

[1] Crowdsourcing is a neologism that refers to a distributed participatory design that leverages the community through a public request to perform tasks traditionally executed by employees or contractors.

DEFINE

On the one hand, small firms may be less reliant on external investors in order to get started. If someone has a PC and Internet connection, they can conceivably start a billion-dollar business overnight. On the other hand, and more realistically, investors are able to target their financing much more effectively when they can remove an element of fixed costs.

Social

You can expect some demographic effects of cloud computing. By virtue of its location independence, there may be increases in off-shoring (Friedman, 2007). There may also be impact on employment as workers need to re-skill to focus on new technologies and business models.

Culturally we are seeing an increasing invasion of privacy (Carr N. , 2009, pp. 164, 190) and possibly even more alarming an increased tolerance for these invasions. While the individual impact of privacy intrusions is rarely severe, there are disturbing ramifications to its use on a large scale. Carr alerts us to the potential dangers of a feedback loop which reinforces preferences and thereby threatens to increase societal polarization.

From a cognitive perspective, we can observe the blending of human intelligence with system and network intelligence. Carr (2009, p. 219) illustrates this notion with Google's page rank algorithm, which effectively aggregates human individual decisions (clicks) to determine composite societal preferences. While there are certainly benefits from the derived information, it begs the question of our future in a world where it is easier to issue repeated ad hoc searches rather than to remember salient facts.

Political

Any force that has significant impact across society and the economy inevitably becomes the focus of politicians. There are many increasing regulations and compliance requirements that apply to the Internet and information technology. Many of these will also impact cloud computing.

At this point, cloud computing has triggered very little legislation of its own accord. However, given its far-reaching impact on pressing topics such as privacy and governance there is no doubt it will become an object of intense legal scrutiny in the years to come.

Chapter 2

Cloud Architecture

Physical clouds come in all shapes and sizes. They vary in their position, orientation, texture and color. Cirrus clouds form at the highest altitudes. They are often transparent and tend toward shapes of strands and streaks. Stratus clouds are associated with a horizontal orientation and flat shape. Cumulus clouds are noted for their clear boundaries. They can develop into tall cumulonimbus clouds connected with thunderstorms and inclement weather.

The metaphor quite aptly conveys some of the many variations we also find with cloud-like components, services and solutions. In order to paint a complete and fair picture of cloud computing we really need to analyze the structure of the offerings as well as the elements that combine together to create a useful solution.

Stack

One characteristic aspect of cloud computing is a strong focus toward service orientation. Rather than offering only packaged solutions that are installed monolithically on desktops and servers, or investing in single-purpose appliances, you need to decompose all the functionality that users require into primitives, which can be assembled as required.

In principle, this is a simple task but it is difficult to aggregate the functionality in an optimal manner unless you can get a clear picture of all the services that are available. This is a lot easier if you can provide some structure and a model that illustrates the interrelationships between services.

The most common classification uses the so-called SPI (Software, Platform and Infrastructure as a Service) model (NIST, 2011). Amazon Elastic Compute Cloud (EC2) is a classic example of IaaS (Infrastructure as a Service). Google App Engine is generally considered to be a PaaS (Platform as a Service). And Salesforce.com represents one of the best known examples of SaaS (Software as a Service).

DEFINE

The SPI model is a simple taxonomy that helps to present a first glimpse of the primary cloud-related services. However, as is often the case with classification systems, the lines are not nearly as clear in reality as they may appear on a diagram. There are many services that do not fit neatly into one category or the other. Over time, services may also drift between service types. For example, Amazon is constantly enhancing its AWS (Amazon Web Services) offering in an effort to increase differentiation and add value. As the product matures, some may begin to question if it wouldn't be more accurate to consider it a platform service.

Nonetheless, it is easiest to begin with a conceptual distinction. The three approaches differ in the extent of sharing they imply for their consumers. Infrastructure services share the physical hardware. Platform services also allow tenants to share the same operating system and application frameworks. Software services generally share the entire software stack.

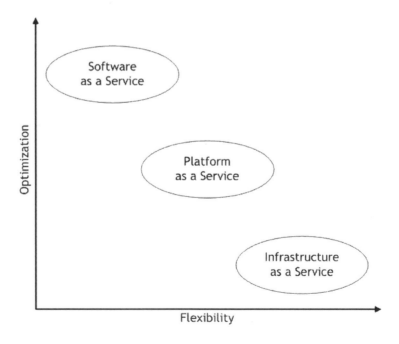

Figure 2-1: Software, Platform and Infrastructure services

As shown in Figure 2-1, these three approaches represent different tradeoffs in a balance between optimization, which leverages multi-tenancy and massive scalability, on the one hand, and flexibility to accommodate individual constraints and custom functionality, on the other hand.

Software services are typically highly standardized and tuned for efficiency. However, they can only facilitate minor extensions. At the other extreme, infrastructure services can host almost any application but are not able to leverage the benefits of economy of scope as easily. Platform services represent a middle ground. They provide flexible frameworks with only a few constraints and are able to accommodate some degree of optimization.

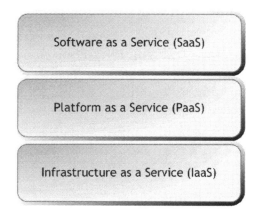

Figure 2-2: SPI Model

The classification illustrates how very different these services can be and yet, at least conceptually, each layer depends on the foundation below it (Figure 2-2)[1]. Platforms are built on infrastructure and software services usually leverage some platform.

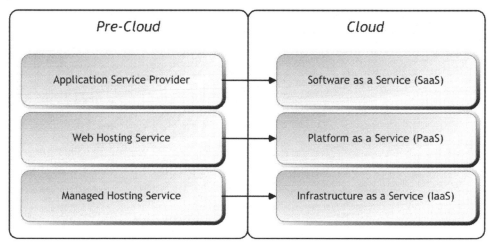

Figure 2-3: SPI Origins

---

[1] This doesn't mean that the implementation of any given service necessarily decomposes precisely along these lines.

DEFINE

In terms of the functionality provided at each of these layers, it may be revealing to look at some of the recent precursors of each (Figure 2-3). SaaS offerings bear a strong resemblance to the hosting services delivered by Application Service Providers (ASPs) in the past. PaaS is a functional enhancement of the scripting capabilities offered by many web-hosting sites today. IaaS is a powerful evolution of co-location and managed hosting services available from large data centers and outsourcing service providers.

The conceptual similarity of pre-cloud offerings often leads to cynical observations that cloud computing is little more than a rebranding exercise. As we have already seen, there is some truth to the notion that the technical innovation is limited. However, refined metering, billing and provisioning, coupled with attractive benefits of scale, do have a fundamental impact on how services are consumed with a cloud-based delivery model.

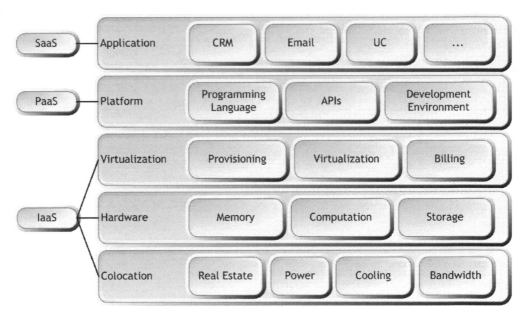

Figure 2-4: Extended Model

We will examine each of the layers in more detail in the next three chapters. But to give you an idea of what each represents, it's useful to take a look inside (Figure 2-4).

Software Services represent the actual applications that end-users leverage to accomplish their business objectives (or personal objectives in a consumer context). There are a wide range of domains where you can find SaaS offerings. One of the most popular areas is customer relationship management (CRM). Desktop productivity (including electronic mail) is also very common, as well as forms of collaboration (such as conferencing or unified communications). But the list is

DEFINE

endless with services for billing, financials, legal, human resources, backup and recovery, and many other domains appearing regularly on the market.

Platforms represent frameworks and common functions that the applications can leverage so that they don't need to re-invent the wheel. The offerings often include programming language interpreters and compilers, development environments, and libraries with interfaces to frequently needed functions. There are also platform services that focus on specific components such as databases, identity management repositories or business intelligence systems and make this functionality available to application developers.

I have divided infrastructure services into three sublevels. I don't mean to imply that they are any more complex or diverse than platform or software services. In fact, they are probably more homogenous and potentially even simpler than the higher tiers. However, they lend themselves well to further segmentation. I suggest that most infrastructure services fall into three categories that build on each other.

There are providers of simple co-location (facilities) services. In the basic scenario, the data-center owner rents out floor space and provides power and cooling as well as a network connection. The rack hardware may also be part of the service, but the owner is not involved in filling the space with the computers or appliances that the customers need.

The next conceptual level is to add hardware to the empty rackspace. There are hosting services that will provide and install blade systems for computation and storage. The simplest options involve dedicated servers, internal networking and storage equipment that are operated by the customer.

There are also managed hosting providers who will take over the administration, monitoring and support of the systems. Very often this implies that they will install a virtualization layer that facilitates automated provisioning, resource management and orchestration while also enforcing consistency of configuration. In some cases, they will leverage multi-tenancy in order to maximize resource utilization - but this is not strictly required.

Management Layers

In addition to the software and applications that run in the SPI model, and support a cloud application in its core functions, both the enterprise and service provider need to address core challenges, such as Implementation, Operation and Control, in order to successfully keep the solution going (Figure 2-5).

DEFINE

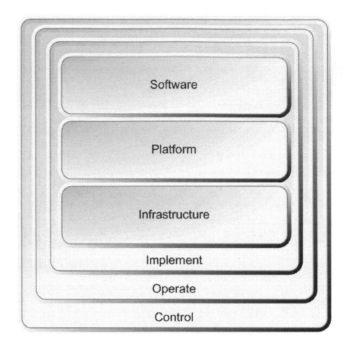

Figure 2-5: Implementation, Operation and Control

Implement

It is necessary to select and integrate all the components into a functioning solution. There are a large and ever increasing number of cloud-based services and solutions on the market. It is no simple task to categorize and compare them. And once that is done, it would be naïve to expect them all to work together seamlessly. The integration effort involves a careful selection of interfaces and configuration settings and may require additional connectors or custom software.

Operate

Once the solution has been brought online, it is necessary to keep it running. This means that you need to monitor it, troubleshoot it and support it. Since the service is unlikely to be completely static, you need to also have processes in place to provision new users, decommission old users, plan for capacity changes, track incidents and implement changes in the service.

Control

The operation of a complex set of services can be a difficult challenge. Some of the challenge may be reduced by working with solution providers and outsourcing organizations who take over the operative responsibilities. However, this doesn't completely obviate the need for overseeing the task. It is still necessary to ensure that service expectations are well defined and that they are validated on a continuous basis.

Standards and Interoperability

There are software offerings that cover all of the domains from the previous sections, ranging from SPI layers to integration, operation and governance. One of the biggest challenges to cloud computing is the lack of standards that govern the format and implied functionality of its services. The resultant lock-in creates risks for users related to the portability of solutions and interoperability between their service providers.

The industry is well aware of the problem. Even though it may be in the short-term interests of some providers to guard their proprietary mechanisms, it is clear that cloud computing will not reach its full potential until some progress is made to address the lock-in problems.

The problem is quite challenging since it is not yet exactly clear which interfaces and formats need to be standardized and what functionality needs to be captured in the process. There is also some concern that standards will lead to a cost-focused trend to commoditization that can potentially stifle future innovation.

Nonetheless, there is substantial activity on the standards front, which is at least an indication that vendors realize the importance of interoperability and portability and are willing to work together to move the technology forward.

The Open Cloud Manifesto established a set of core principles in 2009 that several key vendors considered to be of highest priority. Even though the statement did not indicate any specific guidance and was not endorsed by the most prominent cloud providers (e.g. Amazon, Microsoft or Google), it demonstrated the importance that the industry attaches to cloud standardization.

Since then several standards organizations have begun to tackle the problem of cloud computing from their vantage points:

The *Distributed Management Task Force (DMTF)* has a focus on interoperable management of enterprise computing and cloud computing.

The *Storage Networking Industry Association (SNIA)* has defined a Cloud Data Management Interface (CDMI) and hosts a working group that is examining container capabilities, lifecycle management and storage security.

The *Object Management Group (OMG)* is modeling deployment of applications and services on clouds for portability, interoperability and reuse.

The *Organization for the Advancement of Structured Information Standards (OASIS)* has taken responsibility for extending WS* standards, SAML, XACML and KMIP key management infrastructure to be cloud friendly.

The *Open Group Cloud Work Group* is collaborating on standard models and frameworks aimed at eliminating vendor lock-in for enterprises.

The **Open Cloud Consortium (OCC)** supports the development of standards for cloud computing and frameworks for interoperating between clouds. They develop benchmarks and support reference implementations for cloud computing.

Evidently, the amount of standardization effort reflects the general level of hype around cloud computing. While this is encouraging it is also a cause for concern. A world with too many standards is only marginally better than one without any. It is critical that the various organizations coordinate their efforts to eliminate redundancy and ensure a complementary and unified result.

To protect customer investment and reduce the risk of lock-in, there is a strong and growing demand for convergence across the entire software stack used for cloud computing. The best-known initiatives include Eucalyptus, CloudStack and OpenStack.

Cloud Delivery Models

The previous section classified services according to the type of content that they offered. It can also be useful to examine the types of providers that are offering the services. In an ideal world, designed according to a service-oriented architecture, this distinction would not be meaningful. A service description should cover all relevant details of the service, so the consumer would be independent of the provider and therefore have no reason to prefer one over another.

Sadly, however, this is not the case. There are many implications in the choice of provider relating to security, governance, invoicing and settlement. It is therefore still very relevant to consider if the provider should be internal or external and the delivery should include an outsourcing partner, a community (such as the government) or a public cloud service.

In the earliest definitions of cloud computing, the term referred to solutions where resources are dynamically provisioned over the Internet from an off-site third-party provider who shares resources and bills on a fine-grained utility computing basis. This computing model carries many inherent advantages in terms of cost and flexibility, but it also has some drawbacks in the areas of governance and security.

Many enterprises have looked at ways that they can leverage at least some of the benefits of cloud computing while minimizing the drawbacks by only making use of some aspects of cloud computing. These efforts have led to a restricted model of cloud computing that is often designated as "Private Cloud", in contrast to the fuller model, which by inference becomes a "Public Cloud".

NIST (2011) have expanded on these two deployment options with the notion of Community Cloud and Hybrid Cloud. Most experts would still consider Public Cloud as the quintessential paradigm for cloud computing. Nonetheless, the oth-

DEFINE

er options merit some discussion, particularly as they appear to be rising in importance.

Private Cloud

The term "Private Cloud" is disputed in some circles as many would argue that anything less than a full cloud model is not cloud computing at all, but rather a simple extension of the current enterprise data center. Nonetheless, the term has become widespread and it is useful to also examine enterprise options that fall into this category.

In simple theoretical terms, a private cloud is one that only leverages some of the aspects of cloud computing (Table 2-1). It is typically hosted on-premise, scales "only" into the hundreds or perhaps thousands of nodes, connected primarily to the using organization through private network links. Since all applications and servers are shared within the corporation the notion of multi-tenancy is minimized.

From a business perspective you typically also find that the applications primarily support the business but do not directly drive additional revenue. So the solutions are financial cost centers rather than revenue or profit centers.

	Private	Public
Location	On-premise	Off-premise
Connection	Connected to private network	Internet-based delivery
Scale direction	Scale out (applications)	Scale up (users)
Maximum scale	100-1000 nodes	10 000 nodes
Sharing	Single tenant	Multi-tenant
Pricing	Capacity pricing	Utility pricing
Financial center	Cost center	Revenue/Profit center

Table 2-1: Private and Public Clouds

Common Essence

Given the disparity in descriptions between private and public clouds on topics that seem core to the notion of cloud computing, it is valid to question whether there is actually any commonality at all. The most obvious area of intersection is around resource pooling. As mentioned earlier, resources are shared across customers in a public environment and across departments or cost centers in a private implementation. The increased scale allows for better allocation and utilization, which contributes to additional benefits.

Virtualization can also play a central role in both scenarios. By enabling higher degrees of automation and standardization, it is a pivotal technology for many cloud implementations. Enterprises can certainly leverage many of its benefits without necessarily outsourcing their entire infrastructure or running it over the Internet.

Depending on the size of the organization, as well as its internal structure and financial reporting, there may also be other aspects of cloud computing that become relevant even in a deployment that is confined to a single company. A central IT department can just as easily provide services on-demand and cross-charge the business on a utility basis as could any external provider. The model would then be very similar to a public cloud with the business acting as the consumer and IT as the provider. At the same time, the security of the data may be easier to enforce and the controls would be internal.

Cloud Continuum

A black-and-white distinction between private and public cloud computing may therefore not be realistic in all cases. In addition to the ambiguity in sourcing options mentioned above, other criteria are not binary. For example, there can be many different levels of multi-tenancy, covered in more detail in Chapter 18.

There are also many different options an enterprise can choose for security administration, channel marketing, integration, completion and billing. Some of these may share more similarity with conventional public cloud models while others may reflect a continuation of historic enterprise architectures.

What is important is that enterprises must select a combination that not only meets their current requirements in an optimal way but also offers a flexible path forward encompassing the ability to tailor the options as their requirements and the underlying technologies change over time. In the short term, many corporations will want to adopt a course that minimizes their risk and only barely departs from an internal infrastructure. However, as cloud computing matures they will want the ability to leverage increasing benefits without redesigning their solutions.

Regardless of whether the cloud is hosted internally or externally, it needs to leverage a great deal more than virtualization in order to achieve maximum value. There are a host of other improvements related to cloud computing ranging from fine-grained metering for usage-based cost allocation to rigorous service management, service-oriented architecture and federated access controls. An organization that implements these systematically has the most flexibility in selecting from private and public offerings or combining them for their business processes.

Partner Clouds

The distinction between internal and external delivery of cloud computing is not always clear. Depending on whether these delivery modes are determined on the basis of physical location, asset ownership or operational control, there may be three different perspectives on the source of a cloud service.

For the sake of completeness, it is also important to mention that there are more hosting options than internal/private versus external/public. It is not imperative that a private cloud be operated and hosted by the consuming organization itself. Other possibilities include co-location of servers in an external data center with, or without, managed hosting services.

Outsourcing introduces an additional dimension. Large IT providers, such as HP Enterprise Services or IBM Global Services, have been in the business of running data center operations for large customers for many years. They can manage these services in their own facilities, on customer premises or on the property of a third party.

In some ways, you can consider these "partner" clouds as another point on the continuum between private and public clouds. Large outsourcers are able to pass on some of their benefits of economy of scale, standardization, specialization and their point in the experience curve. And yet, they offer a degree of protection and data isolation that is not common in public clouds.

Community Cloud

Another delivery model that is likely to receive increased attention in the future is a community cloud, also often called a "vertical" cloud. It caters to a group of organizations with a common set of requirements or objectives (Figure 2-6). The most prominent examples are government clouds that are open to federal and municipal agencies. Similarly, major industries may have an incentive to work together to leverage common resources.

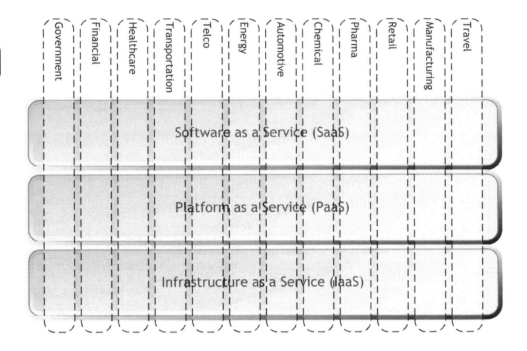

Figure 2-6: Community Clouds

The value proposition of a vertically-optimized cloud is initially based on the similarity of requirements. Companies operating in the same industry are generally subject to the same regulations and very often share customers and suppliers who may impose additional standards and interfaces. A provider that caters to these specific demands can offer platforms and infrastructure with default service levels that meet all participants' obligations at a reasonable price.

Furthermore, a large part of most industry-specific IT solutions fails to generate a sustainable competitive advantage. Reservations systems, loyalty programs, logistics software are easily replicated by competitors and therefore represent wasted intellectual and administrative effort that could be channeled much more effectively into core competencies. Thus, there is a compelling argument for sharing common platforms that have been optimized for collective use.

However, the real benefits begin to accrue when a critical mass of industry players build a co-located ecosystem. When providers and consumers of software and information services are protected behind common security boundaries, and are connected with low-latency network links, the potential to share resources and data is greatly improved. The synergy that develops in this kind of cloud can spawn a virtuous cycle that breeds both additional functionality and efficiencies, and thereby allows the industry to advance in concert.

One area where there has been significant progress is the development of a government cloud. Terremark has opened a cloud-computing facility that caters spe-

cifically to US government customers and addresses some of their common requirements around security and reliability (Terremark, 2009). It offers extensive
physical security ranging from elaborate surveillance, including bomb-sniffing
dogs, to steel mesh under the data center floors.

As long as the governments involved belong to the same political entity there is
less need for elaborate financial incentives. Furthermore, the concerns around
multi-tenancy may be somewhat reduced compared to enterprises sharing infrastructure with their direct competitors.

Hybrid Cloud

The categorization of cloud providers in the previous section into private, partner and public is a great simplification. Not only is there no clear boundary between the three delivery models but it is very likely that customers will not con-
fine themselves to any given approach. Instead, you can expect to see a wide
variety of hybrid constellations (Figure 2-7).

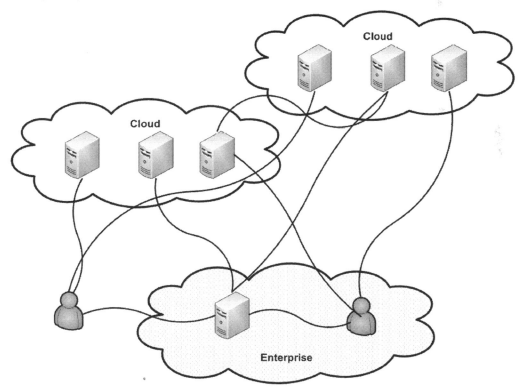

Figure 2-7: Multi-sourcing Options

Hybrid models can implement sourcing on the basis of at least four criteria.

Organizational: The simplest distinction would be that some business units use one source and other parts of the organization use another. This might be the case after a merger or acquisition, for instance.

Application: Another point of segregation would be the application. CRM, Email, ERP and Accounting may run from different delivery points for all applicable users in the organization.

Service: It is also possible that some services, such as Identity Management or a monitoring tool, are not immediately visible to the users but are transparently sourced from disparate cloud providers.

Resource: Virtual private clouds offer a means of extending the perimeter of the organization's internal network into the cloud to take advantage of resources with more elastic capacity than the internal systems. This extension is also invisible to end users.

Multi-sourced delivery models are inherently complex and therefore require careful planning. A framework such as eSCM (eSourcing Capability Model), developed by ITSqc, can be useful to ensure the design is systematic. It defines a set of sourcing life-cycle phases, practices, capability areas and capability levels as well as their interrelationships and suggests best practices both for the service providers and the customers who consume the services.

Cloud Maturity

While a hybrid model is the most likely end-point for many enterprises, a realistic look at the industry today reveals that we still have a way to go before we achieve it. It is not uncommon to find small startups today that are fully committed to cloud computing for all their service requirements. Large organizations, on the other hand, have been very cautious, even if they recognize the value that cloud computing can bring to them.

Corporate reluctance comes as no surprise to anyone who has followed the adoption path of emerging technologies over the past few years. Legacy applications, infrastructural investment, regulatory concerns and rigid business processes represent tremendous obstacles to change. Even if there are obvious early opportunities, the transition is likely to take time.

However, this doesn't mean that enterprises are completely stationary. In their own way, most of them began the journey to a private cloud years ago and they are gradually evolving in the direction of a public cloud. We can break down this path by identifying three steps, which are each associated with an increasing level of efficiency.

Resource efficiencies are usually the first objective of a private cloud implementation. Standardization of components sets the scene for data-center consolidation and optimization. Each level of resource abstraction, from server virtualization to full multi-tenancy, increases the opportunity to share physical capacity, and thereby reduces the overall infrastructural needs.

Operational efficiencies target human labor, one of the highest cost factors related to information technology. Ideally, all systems are self-healing and self-managing. This implies a high degree of automation and end-user self service. In addition to a reduction of administration costs, these optimizations also enable rapid deployment of new services and functionality.

Sourcing efficiencies are the final step and represent the flexibility to provision services, and allocate resources, from multiple internal and external providers without modifying the enterprise architecture. This agility can only be attained if all systems adhere to rigorous principles of service-orientation and service management. They must also include fine-grained metering for cost control and a granular role-based authorization scheme that can guarantee confidentiality and integrity of data. On the plus side, the benefit of reaching this level of efficiency is that applications can enjoy near infinite elasticity of resources, and costs can be reduced to the minimum that the market has to offer.

Once the businesses have full sourcing independence, they are flexible in terms of where they procure their services. They can continue to obtain them from IT or they may switch to an external provider that is more efficient and reliable. However, this independence can work in both directions (Figure 2-8).

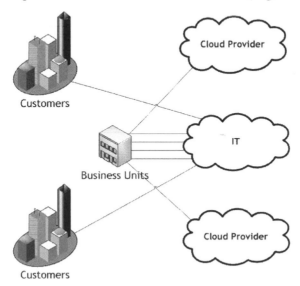

Figure 2-8 : Multi-source and Multi-target Services

If IT develops its services in a generic and modular form, then the organization also has the flexibility to offer parts of the functionality on the external market, and therefore monetize the investment in ways that were not possible before.

Topology

Over the past half century, we've seen the typical computer topology shift from the mainframe in the 1960s to the client-server computing in the 1980s. The 1990s popularized the notion of N-tier architectures, which segregate the client from the business logic and both from the information and database layer (Figure 2-9).

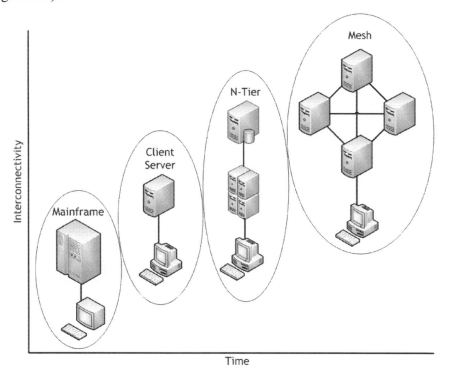

Figure 2-9: Connectivity Evolution

We are now seeing an increase in mesh connectivity. For example, peer-to-peer networks leverage the fact that every system on the network can communicate with the others. Data processing and storage may be shared between systems in a dynamic manner as required.

Cloud computing can facilitate any of these models but is most closely associated with a mesh topology. In particular, it is very important to consider the client device as part of the complete cloud computing topology. Desktop virtualization can have a fundamental impact on cloud computing and can also leverage cloud services to provide content on the terminal.

However, Moore's law continues to apply. We may have reached limits in transistor density but processing power is still advancing with multi-core processors. Therefore it is not realistic to think that cloud equates to thin client computing.

Some functionality is simply easier to process locally, while other functions, particularly those that are collaborative in nature, may be more suitable for the cloud.

The key challenge ahead will be the effective synchronization and blending of these two operating modes. We may also see more potential for hybrid applications. Desktop applications, such as MATLAB and Mathematica, with high computational requirements, may seamlessly extend into the cloud.

Content Delivery Model

One way to look at topology is to trace the content flow (Figure 2-10). There are many possible options for delivering content on the Internet. These do not necessarily change through cloud computing, but it is important to be aware of all actors and their respective roles since they are an integral part of the complete cloud offering.

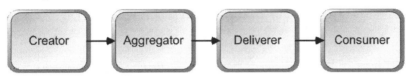

Figure 2-10: Content Delivery Model

There are at least three different players in many solutions. The entity that creates the content, or provides the ultimate functionality, may be hidden from the user. It is inherent in a service-oriented architecture that the end-user not be explicitly cognizant of the individual component services. Instead the user interacts primarily with a content aggregator who bundles the services and content into a form that adds value to the user.

In some cases, the user may then receive the content directly from the solution provider but, particularly for high-volume and latency/bandwidth sensitive content, it is often the case that the provider partners with a content delivery network, such as Akamai or Limelight. These network providers have extensive global presence and very good local connectivity. They can replicate static content and therefore make it available to end-users more quickly, thereby improving the user experience and off-loading the hosting requirements from the aggregator.

Value Chain

Although there is some correlation, the path of content delivery is quite distinct from the payment and funding model (Figure 2-11).

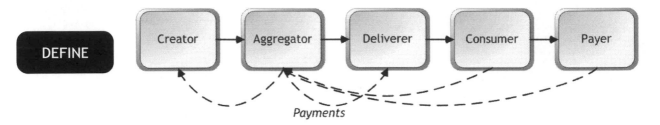

Figure 2-11: Payment Ecosystem

The simple part of the payment model is the flow from the aggregator to the delivery network and content creator. This is intuitive and merely reflects a means of profit sharing toward those who facilitate the end-to-end service.

The source of the funding model is the bigger challenge for all investors who would like to capitalize on the excitement around cloud computing. There are at least two ways to monetize Internet services.

- Direct consumer billing
- Advertising

In a case where the value of the service is explicitly recognized by the end-user, there is the opportunity to charge the consumer. Most users have an aversion to entering their credit card details on the Internet unless it is absolutely required. This typically means that the user must be convinced the content has a value that covers both the transaction costs (including risk and effort) and the actual billed costs. Services from Amazon and Salesforce.com appear to be very successful with this model.

For small items, the transaction costs may actually exceed the perceived value. This makes direct billing virtually impossible. However, Google has popularized another way to monetize this value: through advertising. This business model means that an advertiser pays the content provider in exchange for advertising exposure to the end-user.

Ecosystem

In reality, the roles of the value chain are more complex and diverse than just described. An ecosystem ties together a fragmented set of cloud computing vendors.

There are two key parts of the cloud computing ecosystem that you should keep in mind as you look at different offerings.

- It is extremely large. The hype surrounding cloud computing, combined with the lack of entry barriers for many functions, has made the sector extremely attractive in an economic downturn. There are literally hundreds of vendors who consider some of their products and services to relate to cloud computing

- It is very dynamic. This means there are many players entering the market while some are exiting. Many are dynamically reshaping their offerings on a frequent basis, often extending into other cloud areas. Even the delivery mechanisms themselves are changing as the technologies evolve and new functionality becomes available.

As a result, it is very difficult to paint an accurate picture of the ecosystem which will have any degree of durability or completeness to it. The market is changing and I can only provide a glimpse and high-level overview of what it looks like at this point in time.

Total Cloud

There are many parts to cloud computing and each of these components can be technically delivered in many different ways using a variety of different business models. A direct outcome of this diversity is that we can expect the effects of the technology to cross many boundaries of influence. A less obvious form of impact is that each of the functions needed to implement cloud computing can, itself, be delivered as a service.

Slogans such as "Anything as a Service" or "Everything as a Service" are becoming more popular to indicate that we not only have software, platforms and infrastructure as services, but also components of these, such as databases, storage and security, which can be offered on-demand and priced on a utility basis. On top of these, there are services for integrating, managing and governing Internet solutions. There are also emerging services for printing, information management, business intelligence and a variety of other areas.

It is unclear where this path will ultimately lead and whether all computational assets will eventually be owned by a few service providers, leveraged by end-users only if and when they need them. But the trend is certainly in the direction of all functionality that is available also being accessible on-demand, over the Internet, and priced to reflect the actual use and value to the customer.

DEFINE

Open Source and Cloud Computing

Richard Stallman, a well-known proponent of open source software attracted significant publicity for his skepticism of cloud computing (Ricciuti, 2008). His concerns around loss of control and proprietary lock-in may be legitimate. Nonetheless, it is also interesting to observe that cloud computing leverages open source in many ways.

Self-supported Linux is by far the most popular operating system for infrastructure services due to the absence of license costs. Cloud providers often use Xen and KVM for virtualization to minimize their marginal costs as they scale up. Distributed cloud frameworks, such as Hadoop, are usually open source to maximize interoperability and adoption.

Web-based APIs also make the client device less relevant. Even though some synchronization will always be useful, the value proposition of thin clients increases as the processing power and storage shifts to the back end. Time will tell whether enterprises and consumers take advantage of this shift to reduce their desktop license fees by adopting Linux, Google Chrome or other open-source clients.

Many SaaS solutions leverage open-source software for obvious cost and licensing reasons. For example, SugarCRM is one of the most common platforms for cloud-based CRM. In some ways, SaaS is an ideal monetization model for open source since it facilitates a controlled revenue stream without requiring any proprietary components.

In summary, there is the potential that cloud computing may act as a catalyst for open source. Gartner has projected, in one of their Strategic Planning Assumptions, that through 2013, 90% of market-leading, cloud-computing providers will depend on open-source software to deliver products and services (Gartner, Inc., 2008).

Chapter 3

Infrastructure as a Service

In the beginning there was the Data Center – at least as far back in time as cloud computing goes. Data centers evolved from company computer rooms to house the servers that became necessary as client-server computing became popular. Now they have become a critical part of many businesses and represent the technical core of the IT department. The TIA-942: Data Center Standards Overview lists four tiers of requirements that can be used to categorize data centers ranging from a simple computer room to fully redundant and compartmentalized infrastructure that hosts mission-critical information systems.

Infrastructure as a Service (IaaS) is the simplest of cloud offerings. It is an evolution of virtual private server offerings and merely provides a mechanism to take advantage of hardware and other physical resources without any capital investment or physical administrative requirements. The benefit of services at this level is that there are very few limitations on the consumer. There may be challenges including (or interfacing with) dedicated hardware but almost any software application can run in an IaaS context.

The rest of this chapter looks at Infrastructure as a Service. We will first look at what is involved in providing infrastructure as a service and then explore the types of offerings that are available today.

Infrastructure Stack

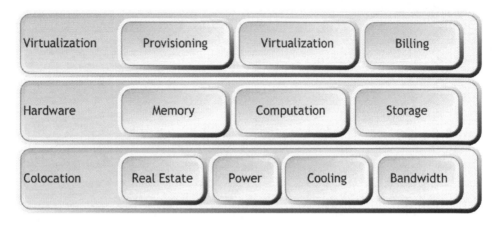

Figure 3-1: Infrastructure Stack

In order to understand infrastructure services it is useful to first take a look behind the scenes at how an Infrastructure Service provider operates and what it requires in order to build its services (Figure 3-1). After all, the tasks and the challenges of the provider are directly related to the benefit of the customer who is able to outsource the responsibilities.

Co-location

This section describes a co-location service. Note that services at this level are available from many data centers. It would be stretching the notion of cloud computing beyond my comfort level to call them cloud services. However, they are an essential ingredient in the infrastructure services described in this chapter.

At the lowest level, it is necessary to have a piece of real estate. Choice locations are often re-purposed warehouses, or old factories, that already have reliable electrical power, but it is becoming increasingly common to take a barren plot of land and place container-based data center modules on it. Some of the top cloud service providers scout the globe in search of cheap, large real estate with optimal access to critical infrastructure, such as electricity and network connectivity.

Power and cooling are critical to the functional continuity of the data center. Often drawing multiple megawatts, they can represent over a third of the entire costs, so designing them efficiently is indispensible. More importantly, an outage in either electricity or air conditioning can disrupt the entire operation of the facility and cause serious damage to the equipment.

It is very important for the data center to have access to multiple power sources. Points of intersection between the electrical grids of regional electricity providers are particularly attractive since they facilitate a degree of redundancy should one utility company suffer a wide-spread power outage. In any case, it is necessary to have uninterruptable power supplies or backup diesel generators that can keep the vital functions of the data center going over an extended period of time.

Another environmental requirement is an efficient cooling system. Over half of the power costs of a data center are often dedicated to cooling. As costs have sky-rocketed there have been numerous advances in cooling technologies and techniques. Most recent cooling designs leverage outside air during the colder months of the year. Subterranean placement of the data center can lead to better insulation in some parts of the world. The interior of the data center is often designed to optimize air flow, for example through alternating orientation of rows of racks, targeted vents (using sensors or log data) and plenum spaces with air circulation underneath the floor.

One other area of external reliance is a dependency on network connectivity. Ideally the data center will have links to multiple network providers. These links don't only need to be virtually distinct – they need to be physically distinct. In other words, it is common for internet service providers to rent the physical lines from another operator. There may be five DSL providers to your home but only one copper wire. If you were looking for resilience, having five contracts would not help you when someone cuts the cable in front of your house.

Whoever owns and operates the data center must also come up with an internal wiring plan that distributes power and routes network access across the entire floor wherever computer hardware or other electrical infrastructure is likely to be placed.

Other environmental considerations include fire protection systems and procedures to cope with flooding, earthquakes and other natural disasters. Security considerations include physical perimeter protection, ranging from electrical fences to surveillance systems.

Hardware

The next step for an infrastructure provider is to fill the rented (or owned) data center space with hardware. These are typically organized in rows of servers mounted in 19-inch rack cabinets. The cabinets are designed according to the Electronic Industries Alliance EIA-310-D specifications, which designates dimensions, hole spacings, rack openings and other physical requirements. Each cabinet accommodates modules which are 19 inches (480mm) wide and multiples of 1U (1.75 inches, 44.45 mm) high.

The challenge is to maximize the number of servers, storage units and network appliances that can be accommodated in the cabinet. Most racks are available in 42U form (42 x 1.75 = 73.5 inches high) so the space is limited. But the density can be augmented by increasing the proportion of 1U blades versus 2U and 3U rack-mountable components. Alternatively, server vendors such as HP and IBM offer enclosures (IBM BladeCenter, HP BladeSystem), which can host larger numbers of microblades than the U slots which they occupy.

These modules then need to be wired for power and connected to the network. Again, an advantage of the larger enclosures is the reduction in number of external wires that are necessary since much of the switching fabric is internalized to the system. This aggregation can lead to increased operational efficiency in that less manual labor is involved and the possibility of human error is reduced.

Figure 3-2: HP BladeSystem

For example, the HP BladeSystem (Figure 3-2) can consolidate cabling from 16 to typically 2 and run double density blades, thus fitting 32 server nodes into 10U of rack space.

Virtualization

One of the biggest advances in data center technology in the last decade has been the advent of virtualization. There are many forms of virtualization including:

Network virtualization includes concepts like virtual local area networks (VLANs) and virtual private networks (VPNs). Both of these notions are important in the data center. The VLANs help to segment traffic and provide a degree of isolation by compartmentalizing the network. VPNs can create a secure connection between cloud entities and enterprises, end-users or even other cloud providers. These allow applications to operate in a trusted mode whereby they can treat the cloud service as an extension of the private network.

There has also been extensive research into providing clusters of functionality, sometimes called cells that act as their own self-contained infrastructure.

These bundles of servers on dedicated networks contain their own management and security components to operate a fully functional, and often complex, system.

Software-Defined Networks (SDN) shows promise in accelerating these virtualization technologies by providing programmatic access to provision and configure them.

Storage virtualization involves redirecting I/O requests from logical, or virtual, units to physical storage devices. The abstraction of the physical infrastructure can facilitate higher utilization through pooling of units and thin provisioning. It also makes it much easier to migrate data without disrupting a service. The applications can continue to make the same logical requests even if the data is transferred to another device.

Memory virtualization can abstract volatile memory space and map it to a set of pooled memory resources among networked systems. Again, this offers flexibility, redundancy and better utilization.

Desktop virtualization is a term that embodies yet again a number of related concepts ranging from thin-client computing to application encapsulation, or streaming of the operating system and/or applications. These delivery models vary according to the degree of isolation they provide (applications, containers, operating systems) and the means by which they are delivered. They may be pre-loaded, loaded at boot time, streamed as needed or simply hosted remotely and presented on the desktop.

The main advantages of desktop virtualization (or virtual desktop infrastructure [VDI]) are standardization of the environment, ease of provisioning and the ability to manage the desktops while they are off-line. There is a significant opportunity to leverage cloud services to provide all of these functions in any of the delivery models.

Server virtualization: The virtualization techniques stated above all offer benefits to cloud-based services. But certainly the most prominent in the cloud context is server virtualization. Server virtualization abstracts the underlying physical resources and presents these as a set of virtual machines, each of which appears to its applications and users as though it were a physical system.

There are two kinds of management layers (or hypervisors) that facilitate the abstraction. Type 1 hypervisors (such as Microsoft Hyper-V, VMware ESX or Integrity VM) run on the bare hardware. Type 2 hypervisors (such as Microsoft Virtual Server or VMware Workstation) run on a host operating system.

Server virtualization provides a high degree of isolation between guest operating systems. This doesn't mean that it is immune to attack or vulnerabilities. There have been many kernel and hypervisor bugs and patches. Nonetheless, the hypervisor typically presents a smaller attack surface than a traditional operating system and is therefore usually considered superior to application isolation, which might be compromised through kernel exploits in the host operating system.

There are many reasons why virtualization has become so popular. The virtual machine can provide instruction set architectures that are independent of the physical machine thereby enabling platforms on hardware for which they were not necessarily designed. It improves the level of utilization of the underlying hardware since guest applications can be deployed with independent (and ideally complementary) resource demands.

Probably the most important driver is the fact that virtual machines can be launched from a virtual disk independent of the hardware on which they were configured. It is simply a matter of copying the virtual machine to a new machine that is running the same hypervisor. This encapsulation makes it very easy to load-balance and to redeploy applications as usage requires.

It also enforces a level of standardization in configuration between similar instances of the same application. And it makes it very easy to provision new instances instantly when they are needed.

One final feature of infrastructure services, which I have placed into the virtualization layer, is metering and billing. One of the reasons that cloud computing is becoming popular now is that capabilities have evolved to allow the service provider to recuperate its costs easily and effectively.

Fine-grained instrumentation provides the foundation by accounting for usage and delivering accurate information that can be used for internal cross-charging or fed into a billing and payment system for external collection.

Green Clouds

Environmentally sustainable computing is an important priority that IT managers need to consider as they develop their long-term infrastructure strategy. Energy efficiency and effective disposal and recycling of equipment are likely to become even more important in the future.

Cloud computing primarily shifts the location of processing and storage, which doesn't directly translate to a global ecological benefit. A study by Greenpeace picked up alarming trends on the growing carbon footprint of cloud data centers and cloud-based services (Greenpeace, 2010).

However, the economy of scale of the cloud service providers can also help to address environmental objectives more effectively. It is in the provider's interests to minimize energy expenditures and maximize reuse of equipment, which it can achieve through higher consolidation of infrastructure.

Its scale also increases the attractiveness of investments in sophisticated power and cooling technology, including dynamic smart cooling, elaborate systems of temperature sensors and air flow ducts as well as analytics based on temperature and energy logs.

However, it is important to consider that higher efficiency doesn't automatically equate to a superior carbon footprint. As the industry analyst GreenMonk (Raftery, 2012) frequently points out, non-renewable energy sources are often cheaper than the renewable equivalents. So providers may operate data centers with better power efficiency while simultaneously emitting more carbon compared to the traditional IT environment.

It is not easy for a consumer to identify the power sources that a provider uses. Fortunately, there is a trend to greater visibilty, particularly as some providers seek to highlight their differentiation in offering greener services.

Infrastructure Services

I like to divide IaaS services into three categories: Servers, Storage and Connectivity. Providers may offer virtual server instances on which the customer can install and run a custom image. Persistent storage is a separate service which the customer can purchase. And finally there are several offerings for extending connectivity options.

DEFINE

The de facto standard for infrastructure services is Amazon. While they are not unique in their offerings, virtually all IaaS services are either complements to Amazon Web Services or else considered competitors to them. I therefore find it useful to structure the analysis of IaaS along the lines of what Amazon's offerings.

Before diving in, I'd like to point out that there are open-source equivalents to Amazon Web Services that are roughly compatible to its interface. Eucalyptus ("Elastic Utility Computing Architecture for Linking Your Programs To Useful Systems") is available as a source package, RPM, and a Rocks disk image. It is also shipped with Ubuntu since version 9.04. Similarly, CloudStack offers a software suite that supports AWS along with other popular cloud interfaces.

Servers

Servers represent the allocation of computational resources along with minimal storage and input/output channels. Cloud computing can be seen as the evolution of managed hosting providers such as Navisite, Terremark or Savvis. They offer co-location capabilities as well as dedicated pools of rack-mounted servers. Their managed hosting capabilities often include virtualized resources on dedicated infrastructure with console-based provisioning.

The server outsourcing model can be divided into three allocation options: Physical, Dedicated Virtual and Shared Virtual. Physical allocation means that specific hardware is allocated to the customer as in the examples above. Dedicated Virtual servers offer dedicated hardware but provide a hypervisor on the physical machine so that the customer can run multiple operating systems and maximize server utilization. Shared Virtual servers are exposed to the customers as pools of virtual machines. It is not discernible on which physical equipment a particular instance is running or what other applications may be co-resident on the same machine.

Beyond these distinctions, the key differentiating options are the operating systems that are supported (usually confined to Windows and a set of Linux distributions) and the packages that are available off-the-shelf (e.g. application frameworks).

There are a variety of providers that offer multiple combinations of allocation options, operating systems and packages. Some of the best known include:

Amazon is perhaps best known and falls into the category of Shared Virtual machines, each based on an Amazon Machine Image (AMI). The customer can use pre-packaged AMIs from Amazon and 3rd parties, or they can build their own. They vary in resources (RAM, compute units, local disk size), operating systems (several Windows versions and many Linux distributions) and the application frameworks that are installed on them (e.g. JBoss, MySQL, Oracle).

DEFINE

AppNexus offers Dedicated Virtual servers based on Dell computers with Ipsilon storage. Their differentiation lies in the degree of visibility they provide on the location of the server with transparency of the data center as well as rack location and position.

LayeredTech provides co-location and Dedicated as well as Virtual Server offerings. They employ VMware and 3Tera Applogic for the virtualized solutions along with a proprietary technology called Virtuozzo Containers that differ from conventional hypervisors in isolating virtual machines while sharing the underlying operating system.

One challenge in using many virtual servers is that they do not maintain any local storage and may even lose their state between invocations. There are advantages to this approach. After all, any important configuration information or other data can be stored externally. But for some purposes, it may be easier, to maintain persistent local storage. Fortunately, some offerings do exactly that.

The Rackspace Cloud (formerly called Mosso) is another very well known IaaS provider with many managed hosting options, in addition to virtual server offerings covering a number of Linux distributions (such as Ubuntu, Fedora, Centos and RedHat Enterprise Linux). It has a large pool of dedicated IP addresses and offers persistent storage on all instances.

Joyent uses the term 'accelerators' to refer to its persistent virtual machines. They run OpenSolaris with Apache, Nginx, MySQL, PHP, Ruby on Rails and Java pre-installed and the ability to add other packages. A feature called "automatic CPU bursting" provides reactive elasticity. Joyent also offers a private version of their framework called CloudControl for enterprise data centers.

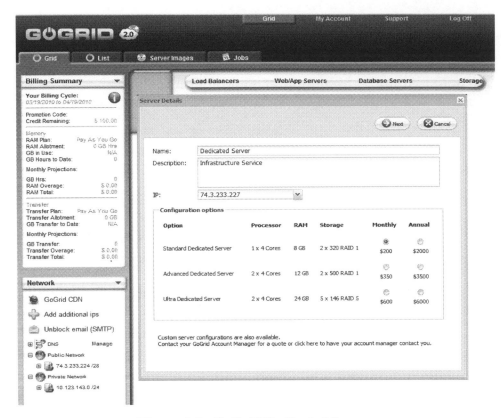

Figure 3-3: GoGrid Dedicated Server

GoGrid offers dedicated server configurations (Figure 3-3) as well as prein-stalled images of Windows and Linux with Apache, IIS, MySQL and several other applications. It also provides free hardware-based load balancing to op-timize the performance of customer instances.

ElasticHosts currently targets the British market with two data centers near London. Rather than using one of the more common hypervisors, they have selected LinuxKVM for their architecture and may appeal to organizations who have taken the same path. They also offer the ability to individually con-figure server specifications along a continuous spectrum of values (Figure 3-4).

Figure 3-4: ElasticHosts Server Specification

Storage

Storage services, such as StorageNetworks, have been around since the late 90s. Similar to the first application hosting providers, the initial offerings were not very profitable (Ruth, 2009). More recent on-demand offerings have changed the game, however, and made Storage as a Service one of the most promising areas of cloud computing.

The offerings are typically characterized by a location-agnostic, virtualized data store that promotes the illusion of infinite capacity in a resilient manner while their high level of automation makes them very easy to use. One of the most common applications is an online backup using SaaS delivery, such as Mozy or SugarSync. Storage services are also useful for archiving, content delivery, disaster recovery and web application development.

They still face some challenges such as outages, vendor lock-in, co-mingling of data and performance constraints. However, they also offer benefits of lower cost of storage infrastructure, maintenance and service, while reducing staffing challenges. At the same time, they provide increased agility and give the customer the benefits of the provider's expertise in compliance, security, privacy and advanced information management techniques, such as archiving, de-duplication and data classification.

In order to cater to the strict demands of cloud computing, many of the storage vendors, such as EMC with their Atmos product line, have begun to deliver hardware and software that is specifically designed for geographically dispersed content depots with replication, versioning, de-duplication, and compression capabilities. These appeal to both the storage service providers as well as many enterprises that are pursuing similar functionality in a private cloud.

In examining on-demand storage services, some of the factors to consider include persistence and replication options as well as the speed and latency with which they can be accessed. Note that due to the synchronization requirements of content delivery networks, you may observe very different speeds for reading and writing data. Also of relevance are the access protocols and mechanisms as well as the data structures allowed.

Amazon offers two persistent storage capabilities: The Simple Storage Service (S3) and Elastic Block Storage (EBS). As implied above, the Amazon AMIs do not have any persistent storage but locally mounted disks can be used for logs, results and interim data while the instance is active.

S3 is accessible through both REST and SOAP APIs. It offers distributed, redundant buckets that are replicated with Amazon's CloudFront content delivery network across Europe, Asia and the United States. S3 can accommodate data sizes from a single byte to 5GB and provides permissions for controlling access based on Amazon Web Services authentication.

Amazon S3 also facilitates versioning so that customers can recover accidentally deleted or overwritten objects. The feature lends itself to data retention and archiving requirements.

The Elastic Block Storage is intended as a high-performance virtual hard disk. It can be formatted as a file system and then mounted on any EC2 instance. The size can range from 1GB to 1TB. Amazon also provides a mechanism to store an EBS snapshot in S3 for long-term durability.

Other storage services include:

The Rackspace Cloud: Cloud Files is similar to S3 with access through a REST API. It provides containers for static content, which can be replicated via the Limelight content delivery network to over 50 edge data centers.

GoGrid: GoGrid Cloud Storage is less accessible through an API. But it supports other mechanisms such as Secure Copy (SCP), FTP, Samba and rsync.

Nirvanix: CloudNAS is a policy-based offering with an enterprise-focus. It works as a virtual mount point for Linux and Windows with dual/triple replication that allows zone specification (e.g. EU only for compliance or performance reasons).

Hadoop: The most important open-source contribution to cloud file systems comes from Apache Hadoop. It isn't a service, in and of itself, but rather an important component to many Big Data technologies. It is modeled on Google MapReduce and the Google File System.

The Hadoop Distributed File System (HDFS) partitions large files across several network hosts. It delivers blocks of data over the network using a HDFS-specific block protocol (or HTTP for browser access). Nodes can talk to each other to rebalance data, to move copies around, and to keep the replication of data high. By default, the replication value is 3, whereby data is stored on three nodes: two on the same rack, and one on a different rack.

There are also cloud database options for more structured data. Even though most of the information is tabular, it is typically not SQL-conformant and may not support joins, foreign keys, triggers or stored procedures. It is common for these services to also accommodate unstructured data (blobs).

The Amazon Simple DB (SDB), for example does not use a schema. Instead it defines "domains" with items that consist of up to 256 attributes and values. The values can contain anywhere from one byte to one kilobyte. It also supports simple operators such as: =, !=, <, >, <=, >=, STARTS-WITH, AND, OR, NOT, INTERSECTION, UNION. So most common queries are possible as long as they are confined to a single domain.

Some other interesting data services include:

Google BigTable is a fast and extremely large-scale DBMS designed to scale into the petabyte range across "hundreds or thousands of machines". Each table has multiple dimensions (one of which is a field for time, allowing versioning). It is used by a number of Google applications, such as MapReduce.

Hypertable is an open source database inspired by publications on the design of Google's BigTable and sponsored by Baidu, the leading Chinese language search engine. It runs on a distributed file system such as the Apache Hadoop DFS, GlusterFS, or the Kosmos File System (KFS).

Dynamo is Amazon's equivalent of the BigTable. It is a highly available keystore that distributes and replicates storage based on hashing rings. While Dynamo isn't directly available to consumers, it powers a large part of Amazon Web Services including S3.

Cassandra is Facebook's distributed storage system. It is developed as a functional hybrid that combines the Google Bigtable data model with Amazon's Dynamo.

Network

The notion of cloud computing would be very dull without connectivity. But merely having a network isn't sufficient. There are many variations in the kind of capabilities that the connections can have. For instance, by default Amazon EC2 instances will receive a single dynamic (DHCP) address. If they require additional addresses, static addresses, or persistent domains, then they need to request these separately.

There are two other network-related functions that cloud providers may offer. Firstly, there may be provisions for network segmentation and mechanisms to

DEFINE

bridge the segments. A second optional feature is performance-related functionality such as load balancing.

Many cloud server providers, such as Amazon EC2, allow the customer to define firewalls, which restrict the inbound and outbound traffic to specific IP ranges and port numbers. Additionally, the guest operating systems may apply further personal firewall settings.

AppNexus provides each customer with a private VLAN. Not only do these give you the advantage of static IP addresses and reduced exposure to broadcast traffic, but it is also possible to segregate traffic from that of other tenants through the use of Access Control Lists (ACLs).

CohesiveFT has a service called vns-cubed. It is based on OpenVPN (an open source SSL-VPN) and sets up an encrypted tunnel to the enterprise (and within the cloud if needed) by placing firewall servers that create inbound connections. They are able to persist the IP addresses by providing a virtual pool and can also deliver functionality around load balancing, failover and access controls.

In 2009, Amazon launched a service that enhances and secures connectivity between cloud services. The Amazon Virtual Private Cloud facilitates hybrid cloud implementations for enterprises by creating a secure virtual private network between the enterprise and the Amazon Web Services and extending the infrastructure, including firewalls, intrusion detection and network management to bridge both networks.

Once connectivity has been configured, the next task it to ensure that it performs satisfactorily. The network performance of cloud services is primarily defined by two factors. The latency is directly related to the geographical coverage (since it is bounded by the physical distance between the client and the server) and the throughput is defined by the amount of bandwidth available from the network provider.

However, there can also be internal bottlenecks that impact the performance. In particular, the servers themselves may become overloaded during periods of high activity and therefore not be able to service requests with sufficient speed. Assuming the application can be horizontally scaled to multiple servers, the solution to the bottleneck is to balance the load of incoming requests. This balance can be accomplished at a local level (internal to the data center) or a global level.

Many providers offer local load balancing capabilities. The simplest approach is to use a DNS Round Robin that involves adding multiple IP addresses to the same domain in DNS. Load Balancing may also be based on software such as the Zeus ZXTM LB used by Joyent, which offers high-performance SSL and content compression, content-aware traffic management rules and flexible health monitoring. Alternatively, many providers, such as AppNexus and GoGrid, use hardware load-balancing like the F5 BIG-IP Local Traffic Managers.

DEFINE

The focus of global load balancing is less on balancing the load over heavily utilized servers and more on distributing the load geographically so that users connect to the closest available services. This can be accomplished with special appliances such as the BIG-IP Global Traffic Manager. But it is also possible to partition DNS so that regional DNS servers point to a local load balancer for each domain. The DNS client will send a request for DNS resolution and will accept the first response, which should be from the closest server.

Finally, it is worth mentioning Software Defined Networks (SDN) as a very important emerging technology and an instrumental component in building a software-defined data center. SDN is a technology that abstracts the network while also providing programmatic control. As such, it not only lends itself the cloud objective of resource efficiency but also facilitates automation for operational benefits.

To achieve this objective, it fundamentally changes to the administrative perspective. The controller obtains a complete inventory of all components including switches, routers and firewalls. It then provides an abstracted flow-based view of all network connections and services that the applications require.

OpenFlow is the best-known effort to standardize software-defined networking. It is a generalized network tunneling protocol with programmatic interfaces to create control and management schemes based on the organization's application requirements. For example, OpenFlow can dynamically extend a private cloud into a hybrid model by masking the enterprise specific IP addresses from the cloud provider's infrastructure. The protocol can also assist service providers by dynamically provisioning WAN services, potentially across multi-provider/multi-vendor networks.

Integration

The next step after arranging network connectivity is to configure the applications to be able to exchange data and synchronize activity. There are differences in the level of support which IaaS providers offer. In theory, they do not need to facilitate the integration at all. The applications can interact directly and/or the customer can install dedicated middleware components. However, this is also an area where the infrastructure provider can demonstrate added value and many of them do.

Amazon offers a service called the Simple Queue Service (SQS), which is exactly what the name says. It provides an unlimited number of queues and messages with message sizes up to 8 KB. The customer can create queues and send messages. Any authorized applications can then receive and/or delete the messages. Since the messages remain in the system for up to four days they provide a good mechanism for asynchronous communications between applications.

As mentioned above, synchronous connections can be accomplished without any infrastructural support. Nonetheless providers such as OpSource provide additional web services that applications can leverage. The OpSource Services Bus exposes an API that allows applications running on the OpSource On-Demand platform to tap web services such as business analytics, on-boarding and billing. It facilitates reporting and visualization of key performance indicators (KPIs) based on data such as: Unit Metrics, Application Events, User Logins, Application Uptime, Bandwidth Utilization, Application Response Time, Monitoring Alerts and Billing Statistics.

The OpSource Connect services extend the Services Bus by providing the infrastructure for two-way web services interactions, allowing customers to consume and publish applications across a common web services infrastructure. This is of particular interest to infrastructure customers who intend to generate revenue from selling the application as a web service.

Apache Hadoop also provides a framework for much more tightly coordinated interaction of applications. The Job Tracker and Task Tracker were developed for Google's map/reduce engine, but have more general applicability for any data-intensive distributed applications. The client applications submit jobs to the Job Tracker which distributes any outstanding work to available Task Tracker nodes.

The technique assumes large amounts of data, which are distributed using the Hadoop File System. Since it is aware of the precise location (node, rack, data center) of all data, it allocates tasks as physically close to the data as possible, thereby minimizing the effects of latency.

Management

In the end, most infrastructure-layer components are managed through the facilities of the virtualization vendor. Depending on the hypervisor in use, there are third party and native components for Xen, VMware, Hyper-V, KVM and other virtualization solutions.

In addition to these, there may be requirements for umbrella management frameworks such as BMC Patrol, CA Unicenter, IBM's Tivoli product suite or HP's Business Technology Optimization solutions. For highly scalable private cloud solutions, software such as Moab Adaptive Computing can leverage HP's and IBM's tools to establish fully functional dynamic computing environments that automatically adapt and configure resources to fit the requirements of business processes.

In the public cloud, there are several services that help to manage established infrastructure providers. RightScale and enStratus, for example, offer front ends for managing Amazon EC2 as well as other IaaS offerings:

RightScale supports Amazon Web Services, Eucalyptus Systems, Flexiant, GoGrid and Rackspace. It provides cloud-ready server templates that come with packaged boot and operational scripts. The templates facilitate automatic deployments and portability between the service providers since the servers are able to perform functions such as obtaining an IP address, accessing storage and submitting monitoring data independent of the infrastructure being used.

RightScale also provides mechanisms for grouping servers with common input parameters (such as code repositories and databases) so that these can be managed and deployed collectively. This is a particular advantage when it is necessary to make systematic changes across very large implementations.

enStratus provides a console that displays real-time detail of both Amazon and The Rackspace Cloud infrastructure. It includes mechanisms to reserve IP addresses and to visualize the Amazon EC2 files through a file directory system. A cluster manager also offers the facility to define dependencies between servers, load balancers and databases as well as defining self-healing policies for the application.

CohesiveFT provides a central web-based console (which may reside in the cloud) that can be used to package application stacks onto virtual machine images. The customer defines the bundles of applications and configuration settings independent of the target provider. After assembling the image from its components, the factory creates a specific image based on the virtualization technology of the chosen cloud destination. Since bundles can be shared across the CohesiveFT community, there is a small, but growing, ecosystem leveraging the components of other customers.

Payment and Billing

Effective monetization of utility-based services relies on two capabilities: fine-grained metering and a simple, trustworthy payment system. Arguably, the leaders in these domains have been the telecommunications companies and, in particular, the mobile operators. It is therefore no surprise to see cloud offerings appearing from international communications giants such as BT, DT, NTT, Orange and SingTel.

However, eCommerce has also boomed in recent years based primarily on credit-card billing. Companies, such as PayPal, make themselves available as trusted intermediaries for smaller merchants that do not yet have the scale and visibility to establish public trust.

At the same time, many cloud service providers have developed their own instrumentation and billing systems, which they can use for their own business, but may also make available to their customers and partners for a fee.

To understand this multi-level business model, it is important to keep in mind that while there is a significant distinction between infrastructure services and software applications this doesn't mean they are unrelated. One of the most frequent uses of IaaS is as a SaaS enabler. In addition to providing the raw computing and storage power, some IaaS providers also help to facilitate SaaS with payment and billing services that the customer can leverage to monetize their SaaS services.

Amazon Flexible Payments Service (FPS) is a service, which Amazon has created for developers, that leverages Amazon's sophisticated retail billing system. The customers can use the same identities, shipping details and payment information as they would for ordering directly with Amazon.

The metering and billing includes dynamic usage tracking and reports as well as an extensive array of payment options including one-time payments, periodic charges, delayed payments and aggregation of micropayments. These can all be set and changed through the API.

For potential SaaS vendors using other platforms than Amazon, OpSource offers a Customer Lifecycle Management (CLM) solution which automates customer on-boarding and then manages the customer purchases with facilities to measure usage and to invoice the end customer.

IaaS Landscape

As mentioned above, Amazon is the de facto standard for infrastructure services today. However, they are seeing increased competition for this space as other vendors take aim at the market. For example, Microsoft and Google both initially focused on platform services, which we will see in the next chapter.

Although Microsoft Azure and Google App Engine offered storage services, the run-time environment was more restricted than would be expected of a typical infrastructure service. Microsoft Azure Virtual Machines and Google Compute Engine, released in 2012, have no such limitations, making them directly comparable to Amazon EC2.

There is also increased industry momentum for a standardization across the entire software stack used for cloud computing. The best-known initiatives to satisfy this requirement have concentrated on IaaS. At a high level, they have adopted two different approaches:

Eucalyptus and **CloudStack** provide compatibility with Amazon Web Services (AWS) and thereby facilitate hybrid clouds with Amazon. The choice of Amazon carries with it the both the benefit that the interfaces are well known and AWS has huge capacity to absorb temporary spikes in resource requirements. However, the fact that Amazon owns the APIs and can choose to develop them in any direction they choose implies that they are not completely open.

OpenStack is a collection of open-source technology projects co-sponsored by a broad consortium of industry leaders that provides an operating platform for orchestrating clouds on a massive scale. It is hypervisor-independent and includes software to provision virtual machines on standard hardware. It also provides a distributed object store. Other features include a scheduler, network controller and authentication manager.

DEFINE

Chapter 4

Platform as a Service

Platform as a Service has emerged from a confluence of two trends: the suboptimal nature of IaaS for cloud computing and the evolution of web applications.

Infrastructure service offers many benefits to customers who wish to extend or shift their applications into a cloud-based environment. However, infrastructure services tend to run on platforms that were designed for desktops and traditional client-server environments. They may now be virtualized, but they have not been optimized for the cloud.

To better address the specific needs and advantages of cloud delivery models, some vendors have crafted new platforms that enable faster time-to-market, a common user experience, and an easier development environment. You might see them as an evolution of conventional integrated development environments to support on-line collaboration and a cloud target platform. Ideally these platforms enable the creation of a new ecosystem that benefits both users and vendors.

Cloud platforms act as run-time environments that support a set of (compiled or interpreted) programming languages. They may offer additional services such as reusable components and libraries that are available as objects and application programming interfaces. Ideally, the platform will offer plug-ins into common development environments, such as Eclipse, to facilitate development, testing and deployment.

The second noteworthy trend is the evolution of web-hosting sites. GeoCities and others offered services as early as the mid-90s, whereby users could upload HTML pages to a server in order to establish an Internet presence. Simple hosting services still only allow HTML and, at most, client-side scripting capabilities, such as VBscript or JavaScript. Providing server interfaces such as the Common Gateway Interface (CGI) is more complex to implement and exposes the provider to significantly more security threats.

Nonetheless, there has been a marked increase in the number of web hosting services that support a variety of active server-side components, ranging from

Microsoft ASP.NET and Java to scripts such as PHP, Python and Ruby on Rails. Compared to infrastructure services, these platforms reduce the storage requirements of each application and simplify deployment. Rather than moving virtual machines with entire operating systems, the application only requires the code written by the developer. An additional benefit is the increased ease for the service provider to sandbox each application by only providing functions that cannot disrupt other tenants on the same system and network.

Platforms may also offer further functions to support the developers, for example:

Integrated Development Environment to develop, test, host and maintain applications

Integration services for marshalling, database integration, security, storage persistence and state management

Scalability services for concurrency management and failover

Instrumentation to track activity and value to the customer

Workflow facilities for application design, development, testing, deployment and hosting

User Interface support for HTML, JavaScript, Flex, Flash, AIR

Visualization tools that show patterns of end-user interactions

Collaboration services to support distributed development and facilitate developer community

Source code services for version control, dynamic multiple-user testing, rollback, auditing and change-tracking

From the provider perspective, PaaS is a mechanism for vendors to apply a specific set of constraints to achieve goals that they feel represent the value proposition for their end-users (developers directly, but indirectly also the enterprise IT organization). Those goals tie to the core attributes of cloud computing as follows.

- Elasticity
- Multi-tenancy
- Rapid provisioning and deployment
- Leverage of web technologies and open source
- Integrated monitoring, management and billing facilities

To achieve the above goals, the platform vendors usually must apply a set of constraints preventing functionality that might interfere with the required elasticity and security:

DEFINE

- Only specific languages and run-times are provided.
- Not all language/library features are enabled.
- Generic APIs typically replace some of the features or capabilities of traditional stacks.
- There may be size constraints on individual requests.
- Statelessness is encouraged to minimize the overhead of state management.

While these constraints are meant to allow vendors to achieve the cloud computing goals, some add additional value by providing the following to developers to sweeten the incentive of targeting applications to the platform:

- IDE plug-ins, SDKs and a local emulation environment
- Frameworks that provide the scaffolding and hooks to the platform
- Free developer accounts to accelerate or eliminate provisioning time

In summary, the value proposition for PaaS is that it shows some benefits over traditional web platforms in terms of geographically distributed collaboration, facilitation of web service aggregation through centralization of code, reduced costs of infrastructure through the pay-as-you-go model and cost reduction through higher-level programming abstractions. At the same time, PaaS is also simpler to manage than IaaS and represents a smaller platform to distribute while at the same time it can leverage more functionality and services from the provider.

So, PaaS can be useful. The rest of this chapter will examine some offerings in a little more detail and explore the distinctions we can expect to find between platforms. The support of optional services listed above is a starting point. They are not universally included in every service and depend on the layered services and object libraries included.

Some of the other key areas of differentiation in platforms include the programming languages (e.g. Python, Java, C#) supported and development environments (e.g. Eclipse, Visual Studio) for which there are plug-ins available.

Web Application Frameworks

Let's begin the description of application frameworks with a historic look at web hosting. While a simple web service only needs to serve HTML over HTTP, it is very cumbersome to build complex and dynamic web sites that do not utilize some level of server-side business logic built on the information contained in a data repository.

In order to facilitate the necessary functionality, a number of application frameworks have developed that alleviate the overhead of authentication, authorization, database access, page templating, server-side caching and session management.

These are often classified according to the programming languages that they support:

Visual Basic, C#: ASP.NET is based on Microsoft's Active Server Pages (ASP) technology, revised to leverage the Common Language Runtime (CLR), which is compatible with all Microsoft .NET languages such as Visual Basic and C#. It leverages .NET pages, which consist of HTML as well as dynamic code that is pre-processed when the page is rendered. In addition to in-line mark-up, it is possible to separate the .NET code into a separate file that is only referenced in the .NET page.

While ASP.NET is a component of Microsoft Internet Information Server (IIS) and is closely connected with Microsoft Visual Studio, it is also possible to extend it with other frameworks such as DotNetNuke, Castle Monorail or Spring.NET.

Ruby: Ruby on Rails is an open-source framework that supports Ruby, a dynamic and reflective object-oriented programming language that is based on Perl, Smalltalk, Eiffel, Ada and Lisp. Ruby on Rails received considerable attention as the original basis for Twitter. However, it suffered in equal measure when Twitter switched to Scala due to scalability issues.

Java: Java requires little introduction as it is a de facto standard for opensource software. However, not all Java environments are identical. There are several Java application frameworks. The best-known include Apache Struts and Spring Framework.

Perl: Perl is a general-purpose programming language that was originally developed for manipulating text but is now used for a variety of applications including system administration and web development. It is used in a variety of popular frameworks including Catalyst, Jifty and WebGUI.

PHP: PHP was originally developed for building dynamic web content, typically acting as a filter that processes input data and renders HTML. Application frameworks such as Drupal and Joomla have spawned popular ecosystems, which have delivered thousands of modules that enable developers to build extensive content management systems without any custom coding.

Python: Python is characterized by its support of multiple programming paradigms including object-oriented, structured, functional and aspect-oriented programming. One of its most popular application frameworks is Django, which is tailored toward complex, database-driven websites. Since Google App Engine was initially only released with Python support, Python (in conjunction with Django) is very popular for Google applications.

Web Hosting Services

DEFINE

The boundary is blurred between conventional web hosting services, such as 100Webspace, AwardSpace, X10Hosting or HelloHost, and Platform-as-a-Service providers.

The former offer hosting services using business models that range from placed advertisements to one-time setup fees or monthly subscriptions. In addition to simple web file services, they support a number of the application frameworks mentioned above. Most experts would not consider these sites to be PaaS providers simply because the provisioning support and value added services of the platforms are minimal.

On the other hand, Mosso, The Rackspace Cloud (primarily known for its infrastructure services) offers a service called Cloud Sites. These fully managed platforms can host Windows .NET or a complete LAMP (Linux, Apache, MySQL, Perl/Python/PHP) stack and would typically qualify as a PaaS offering.

Google App Engine

Google App Engine is one of the best known platform services. In addition to a basic run-time environment, it eliminates many of the system administration and development challenges involved in building applications that can scale to millions of users. It includes facilities to deploy code to a cluster as well as monitoring, failover, automatic scaling and load balancing.

App Engine originally supported runtime environments based only on Python. It has since added support for Java Virtual Machines (JVMs) thereby enabling applications written not only in Java but also other JVM languages such as Groovy, JRuby, Jython, Scala, or Clojure. The SDK includes a full local development environment that simulates Google App Engine on the developer's desktop.

There are some limitations to the programming languages. For example Python modules must be pure-Python since C and Pyrex modules are not supported. Likewise Java applications may only use a subset (The JRE Class White List) of the classes from the JRE standard edition, and they are prevented from creating new threads.

DEFINE

```
from google.appengine.ext import webapp
from google.appengine.ext.webapp.util import run_wsgi_app
class MainPage(webapp.RequestHandler):
  def get(self):
    self.response.headers['Content-Type'] = 'text/plain'
    self.response.out.write('Hello, World!')
application = webapp.WSGIApplication(
                                    [('/', MainPage)])
def main():
  run_wsgi_app(application)
if __name__ == "__main__":
  main()
```

Listing 4-1: Google App Engine "Hello World"

The actual code required will obviously vary according to the application. As shown with a Python example in Listing 4-1, the instructions can be very simple if there is little application logic. It is necessary to import a couple of modules that are included in the SDK and then define a request handler called MainPage, which processes all HTTP GET requests to the root URL. The method can write the HTTP response using the self.response object. The function run_wsgi_app() takes a WSGIApplication instance and runs it in App Engine's CGI environment. That's all there is to it if your needs are modest.

Unfortunately, even though the supported languages are quite standard, it isn't typically possible to take existing code and launch it by simply copying it to the Google AppSpot hosting environment. Nor is it always easy to port Google code to another web host running the same application framework.

There are two obstacles that tend to interfere. Most existing web applications use a relational database to store data. They may also leverage some of the rich functionality of their original platform. For instance, they may write to the local file system, interface with other installed software, or make a variety of network connections. The first challenge is that Google provides a non-relational datastore as the default option. And the second is its use of a sandbox approach to isolate instances in its multi-tenant environments. Let's look at these in more detail.

The App Engine datastore supports queries, sorting and transactions using optimistic concurrency control. It is a strongly consistent distributed database built on top of the lower-level BigTable with some added functionality. Unfortunately for legacy code, the App Engine datastore is not like a traditional relational database. In particular, the datastore entities are schemaless. Two entities of the same kind are not required to possess the same properties, nor do they need to use the same value types if they do share properties. Instead, the application is responsible for ensuring that entities conform to any schema required by the business logic. To assist, the Python SDK includes a data modeling library that helps enforce consistency.

Google App Engine's query language (called GQL) is similar to SQL in its SELECT statements however with some significant limitations. GQL intentionally does not support the Join statement and can therefore only accommodate single table queries. The rationale behind the restriction is the inefficiency that queries spanning more than one machine might introduce. However, Google does provide a workaround in the form of a ReferenceProperty class that can indicate one-to-many and many-to-many relationships.

The second issue for legacy applications is the sandbox, which isolates programs from other instances and tenants that may be running on the same web server. The application can only make outbound connections to other computers on the Internet through the provided URL fetch and email services. For its own protection, it can only receive inbound connections through HTTP and HTTPS on the standard ports.

In order to protect from malware, an application cannot write to the file system. It can read files, but only those files that have been uploaded with the application code. In order to persist data between requests, the application must use the App Engine datastore, Memcached or other services.

The only events that can trigger an application are a web request or a scheduled ("cron") job. Furthermore, a request handler cannot spawn a sub-process or execute code after the response has been sent.

Although the environment comes with some limitations, it also provides a rich set of APIs. We saw the datastore functionality above, but there are additional library functions:

Authentication: Applications can interface with Google Accounts for user authentication. It can direct the user to sign in with a Google account and then access the email address and display name once the user has authenticated.

URL Fetch: Applications can request resources on the Internet, such as web pages, services or other data with the URL fetch service. It leverages the same page retrieval mechanism that Google uses for its own services.

Mail: Applications can send electronic messages using App Engine's mail service. The service uses Google mail transport system to send email messages.

Memcache: The memcache service offers applications an in-memory key-value cache that is accessible by multiple instances of the application. It is useful for temporary data that does not need persistence and transactional features, such as a local cache of the datastore for high speed access.

Image Manipulation: The image manipulation allows the application to resize, crop, rotate and flip images in JPEG and PNG formats.

Scheduled Tasks: The cron service allows the user to schedule tasks that run at regular intervals, for example on a daily or hourly basis. The application can even execute tasks that it added to a queue itself. For example, it might submit a background task while handling a request.

Task Queues: While cron jobs are good for periodic tasks they are not always reliable and do not perform well for high-volume, high-frequency workloads. Task queues (currently only released as an experimental feature for the Python runtime environment) on the other hand are very scalable, low-latency, reliable services processed on a first-in-first-out (FIFO) basis.

Blobstore: GQL Data Store items are limited to a maximum of 1MB. However, the Google Blobstore provides an effective alternative for serving larger chunks of data, such as images, audio, video or executable files. Blobstore values, or blobs, can hold a maximum of 2GB. The store provides details about the object including its content type and upload time. Given the lack of structure, there is no facility to edit a blob. However, it is possible to delete and re-create it.

XMPP API: The Extensible Messaging and Presence Protocol (XMPP) is a standardized instant-messaging (IM) protocol based on Jabber. It provides instant messaging, presence information, and contact list maintenance and has also been extended for use in VoIP (Voice over Internet Protocol) and file transfer signaling. App Engine supports the API, which can be useful as an alternative to email for time-sensitive communications, such as alerts. In this scenario, the recipient must actively use an XMPP client, like Google Talk or Jabber, and must add the application to their buddy list.

OpenID Authentication: OpenID is a standard for federated authentication. OpenID users can create an identity (username and password or other credentials including one-time passwords and biometrics) at any OpenID provider and use that same identity to authenticate to an App Engine Application if the developers have chosen to support OpenID as an authentication mechanism.

MapReduce: Although Google has been a pioneer in developing the MapReduce processing model, the App Engine implementation is currently only experimental and not complete. Nonetheless, the mapper provides a fast and efficient way to iterate over datastore entities and blob files.

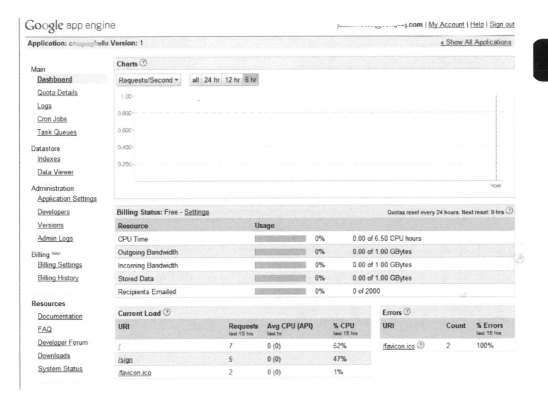

Figure 4-1: Google App Engine Console

Once development is complete and has been tested locally, the user can upload the file using tools from the SDK or the Google App Engine Launcher. The Administration Console (Figure 4-1) is a web-based interface that can then be used to create new applications, configure domain names, switch a version of the application to be live, examine access and error logs, and browse an application's datastore.

Microsoft Windows Azure

Windows Azure is Microsoft's Platform as a Service. Similar in concept to Google App Engine, it allows applications based on Microsoft technologies to be hosted and run from Microsoft data centers. Its fabric controller automatically manages resources, balances load, replicates for resilience and manages the application lifecycle.

Development Environment

To access the platform you typically use Visual Studio. Microsoft has made additional SDKs for Java and Ruby available to improve interoperability so there is no strict limitation to the .NET Framework. Eventually there should be some level of support for Java, Python, Ruby, PHP, OpenID and Eclipse. Nonetheless,

DEFINE

you will have much more information and community support available if you keep to a native Microsoft implementation, at least to get started.

What this means is that a Visual Studio[1] developer must download and install both:

- The Windows Azure Software Development Kit
- Windows Azure Tools for Microsoft Studio

After installing these components, a new set of solution templates appears in Visual Studio, called Cloud Service (Figure 4-2).

These are similar to the Web project types but are tailored to Azure. The developer can test applications locally (on port 81) until they are ready and then publish the solution to Azure.

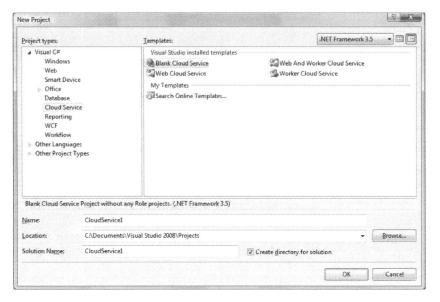

Figure 4-2: Visual Studio Cloud Service

---

[1] Supported on Visual Studio 2008 or higher

DEFINE

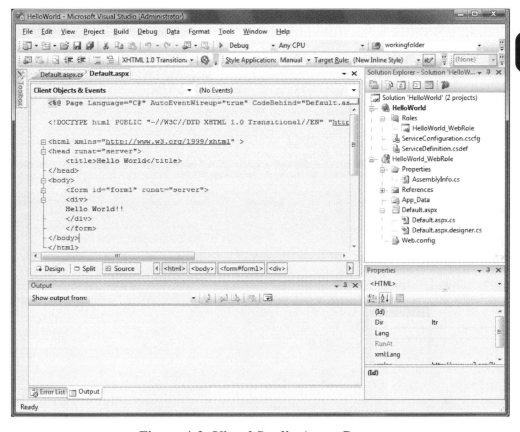

Figure 4-3: Visual Studio Azure Page

As shown in Figure 4-3, the simplest applications consist of a few lines of an .ASPX page along with a class structure in a .NET language such as C#.

Azure Platform

The Windows Azure platform is built as a distributed service hosted in Microsoft data centers and built on a special-purpose operating system called Windows Azure. It is implemented as three components: Compute, Storage and a Fabric to manage the platform.

The **Compute** instances are exposed to the customer as role types that specify tailored configurations for typical purposes. The Web Role instances generally interact with the end user. They may host web sites and other front-end code. On the other hand, Worker Role instances cater to background tasks similar to Google App Engine cron jobs.

While Web and Worker role types are the most popular, Windows Azure provides additional templates for specific needs. For example, the CGI web role supports the FastCGI protocol and thereby enables other programming languages including PHP, Ruby, Python and Java. The WCF (Windows Communications Foundation) service is a web role that facilitates support of WCF services. Azure now also provides an infrastructure service, in the form of a VM Role, which accepts the upload of a Windows Server 2008 R2 Virtual Machine Image.

For each service role, the developer can specify static configuration settings such as the end-point (URL), the number of instances and the size (indicated in number of cores and amount of memory and disk space). Load balancers will automatically distribute the incoming traffic to the full set of running instances. It is also possible to inspect and update the configuration using the Service Runtime and Service Management APIs, for example to implement auto-scaling based on computational load.

Azure *Storage* provides services that host three kinds of data:

- Blobs

- Tables

- Queues

A blob is simply a stream of unstructured (or at least opaque) data. It can be a picture, a file or anything else the application needs. There is a four-level hierarchy of blob storage. At the highest level is a storage account, which is the root of the namespace for the blobs. Each account can hold multiple containers, which provide groupings (e.g. similar permissions or metadata). Within a container can be many blobs. Each can be uniquely identified and may hold up to 50GB. In order to optimize uploads and downloads (especially for very large files) it is possible to break a blob into blocks. Each transfer request therefore refers to a smaller portion of data (e.g. 4MB) making the transaction less vulnerable to transient network errors.

Tables are used for structured data. As you might expect from the name, they typically hold a set of homogenous rows (called entities) that are defined by a set of columns (called properties). Each property is defined by a name and type (e.g. String, Binary, Int). Despite the conceptual similarity there are important distinctions to make between Windows Azure storage tables and relational tables. Azure does not enforce a schema nor does it support SQL as a query language. While this may lead to portability challenges for many legacy applications, Microsoft's strategy is similar to that of Google and reflects the importance of ensuring the new technology is optimized for the scalability requirements of cloud-based services.

Queues provide a mechanism for applications to communicate and coordinate asynchronously. This is an important requirement when applications are geographically distributed over high-latency links. Synchronous communication can severely degrade performance and introduces stability risks that must be minimized. Like Blobs and Tables, Queues are associated with a Storage Account.

They hold a linear set of XML messages. There is no limit to the number of messages per queue but they typically will be removed from the queue if they are not processed within seven days (or earlier if requested).

Similar to Amazon S3, it is possible to specify a region for any storage requirements in order to ensure compliance with local data privacy laws and minimize latency between applications and users. If performance is critical, the Azure CDN (Content Delivery Network) also provides distributed delivery of static content from Azure Storage from Microsoft's worldwide network of data centers.

The *Fabric*, in Azure terminology, refers to a set of machines running the Azure operating system that are collectively managed and generally co-located in the same region. The Fabric Controller is the layer of code that provisions all the user instances (web and worker roles) and performs any necessary upgrades. It also monitors the applications, re-provisioning and reallocating resources as needed to ensure that all services remain healthy.

Azure Services

Azure also provides a set of services that can be consumed both from the Internet (including the Azure platform itself) and on-premise applications.

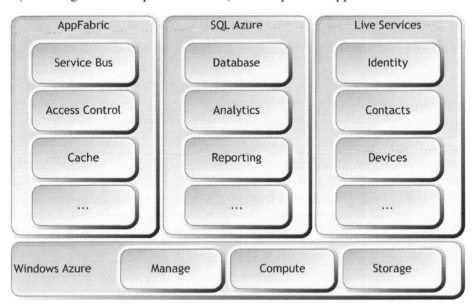

Figure 4-4: Azure Services

As shown in Figure 4-4, Azure services can be loosely categorized as:

- AppFabric
- SQL Azure

- Live Services

DEFINE

Azure applications can also access a set of Microsoft SharePoint and Microsoft Dynamics CRM services.

AppFabric provides a cloud-oriented service framework that is available through REST, SOAP, Atom/AtomPub and WS-*

- Microsoft .NET Service Bus

- Microsoft .NET Access Control Service

- Windows Azure AppFabric Cache

The purpose of the Service Bus is to relay connectivity between systems. When two applications share a Local Area Network, they can usually communicate directly. However, in a cloud environment physical adjacency cannot be guaranteed. Firewalls, NAT, Mobile IP, Dynamic DNS, and other advanced network components can make it difficult to maintain connectivity or even addressability. The Service Bus provides proxy connections where direct connectivity is difficult or impossible.

The Access Control Service authenticates and authorizes users, relying on Windows Live ID and other user account stores such as corporate Active Directories or federated identity management systems. An administration portal allows service owners to define the rules that grant access and authorization rights.

The AppFabric Cache delivers a distributed, in-memory, cache service for Windows Azure and SQL Azure applications. Similar to Memcached, it improves performance and scalability. It is also possible to enable a high availability option that ensures all data is replicated to multiple servers.

SQL Azure is relational storage that should not be confused with Azure Storage described above. It is essentially SQL Server offered as a cloud service. As such, it lacks the massive scalability potential of Azure Storage. (It can handle up to 10GB per database). However, it provides all the benefits of SQL including transactional integrity and powerful multi-table analysis. SQL Azure Reporting also extends the capabilities of SQL Server Reporting Services to SQL Azure with facilities to create reports with charts, maps, gauges and sparklines. But perhaps the most compelling argument in its favor is that it is easy to integrate with legacy (SQL) code.

Live Services provide a set of building blocks that can be used to handle user data and application resources including Identity and Contacts. These include Windows Live Messenger, Live Search and Maps.

At the foundation of the services is the Live Framework, or LiveMesh, which offers data synchronization across multiple devices using FeedSync (RSS extensions). They offer several benefits in terms of extending the reach of client devices accessible from the cloud and creating an integrated, comprehensive and consistent view of user data.

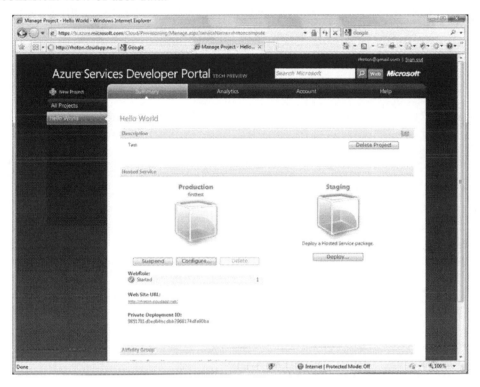

Figure 4-5: Azure Services Developer Portal

Once the application has been tested locally, it can be uploaded to Azure through Visual Studio and then managed through the Azure Services Developer Portal (Figure 4-5). It offers facilities to stage the application before deploying it publicly. Users can also suspend instances when they are not needed and restart them at a later time.

Force.com

Salesforce.com also delivers a Platform-as-a-Service which is called Force.com. It is very different from both Google's and Microsoft's offerings in this space. It does also offer hosting services based on its technology with the usual features of redundancy, security and scalability. But Force.com is much more data-oriented than code-oriented.

External Programmatic Access

Force.com exposes all customer specific configurations (forms, reports, work-flows, user privileges, customizations, business logic) as metadata which is programmatically accessible. A Web Services API (SOAP) allows access to all

DEFINE

Force.com application data from any environment. The platform also provides developer toolkits for .NET, Java, Facebook, Google and Amazon Web Services as well as pre-packaged connectors from:

- ERP: SAP R/3 and Oracle Financials
- Desktop software: Microsoft Office, Lotus Notes
- Middleware: Tibco, Pervasive, Cast Iron

In addition to conventional database access, Force.com employs an external search engine that provides full-indexing and allows searching for unstructured data.

Apex

Force.Com applications are built using Visualforce, a framework for creating graphical user interfaces, and Apex, a proprietary programming language that uses a Java-like syntax but acts much more like database stored procedures, (Listing 4-2).

```
// This class updates the Hello field on account records
that are
// passed to it.
public class MyHelloWorld {
    public static void addHelloWorld(Account[] accs){
        for (Account a:accs){
            if (a.Hello__c != 'World') {
                a.Hello__c = 'World';
            }
        }
    }
}
```

Listing 4-2: Apex Account Update

Force.com distinguishes between three kinds of program logic:

- Declarative logic: audit logging, workflow, approvals
- Formula-based logic: data validation, workflow rules
- Procedural logic: Apex triggers and classes (Listing 4-3)

```
trigger helloWorldAccountTrigger on Account (before insert)
{
    Account[] accs = Trigger.new;
    MyHelloWorld.addHelloWorld(accs);
}
```

Listing 4-3: Apex Trigger

Apex can run as a stand-alone script on demand or as a trigger on a data event (Listing 4-3). The language allows developers to add business logic to events, such as (user) button clicks or (data) record updates and Visualforce pages.

The workflow logic can trigger tasks, send electronic messages, update the database and interface with external applications through outbound SOAP messaging to any Internet destination.

There are three options for developing and creating the Apex code.

- The Salesforce.com user interface allows the user to include Apex code.
- Any text editor, such as Notepad, can be used to enter code which can subsequently be uploaded to the server.
- The preferred and most powerful mechanism is the Force.com IDE, which is a plug-in for Eclipse.

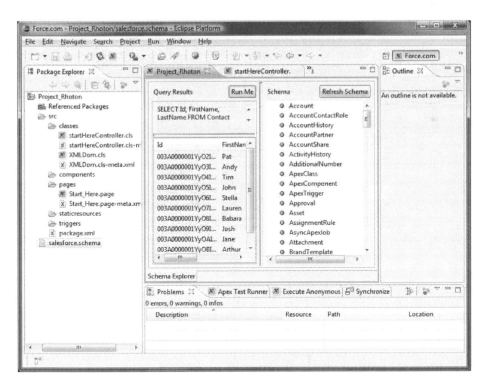

Figure 4-6: Force.com IDE

The Force.com Integrated Development Environment (IDE) is simply a plug-in to the Eclipse platform, which connects directly to the Force.com services in the cloud and acts on the test environment (Figure 4-6). It includes an embedded schema explorer for a live view of the application data base schema. The browser can also view and edit any metadata components.

DEFINE

Since Apex code is automatically sent to the server when saved, the developer is always working with server-based data in staging mode. In order to deploy the application into production, it must first pass a minimum threshold of unit tests.

Even though it is very convenient, there is no technical requirement to use the Force.com IDE. The full set of web services to deploy, compile and test the application are exposed and documented, so it is possible to call them directly and, indeed, even to develop another IDE that uses them.

User Interface

Two tools are available for building the user interface for on-demand applications: UI builder and Visualforce.

The UI Builder is the simpler approach. It generates a default user interface based on the data properties of the application. This includes data structures, internal composition and inter-relations. For example, the defined data types will influence input display components and options. The UI can be modified to change the layout and appearance or to add search functionality. However, it becomes difficult to make changes that involve the business logic.

Visualforce is much more powerful and can be used to create almost any user interface. It implements the MVC (Model: Data, View: User Interface, Controller: Business Logic) paradigm to enforce strict separation of logic from presentation and storage. The user interface can include callouts (e.g. to create mashups) and leverage dynamic, client-side display functionality, such as CSS, DHTML AJAX or Adobe Flex, in addition to ordinary HTML.

AppExchange

DEFINE

Figure 4-7: Force.com AppExchange

Force.com also provides a marketplace, called AppExchange (Figure 4-7), for buying and selling SaaS services. Once developers have completed and tested their applications, they can request publication on AppExchange providing a description of the services along with details of the pricing and support model. The process entails a security review by Force.com to check for exploits, such as cross-site request forgeries.

Customers can therefore avoid reinventing any functionality that has already been created. They can filter the application list by popularity, price or other criteria. And they have limited financial risk since they can sign up for a free trial before purchasing the service.

Additional Platforms

A large number of cloud applications are based on the services of Google, Microsoft and Amazon. As we have seen, they each have a rich set of offerings that span the spectrum from Infrastructure to Platform services. However, these three are not the only platform providers.

The landscape is very dynamic with vendors constantly redefining their offerings so that an extensive analysis, or even an exhaustive list, of the options would be pointless. To help give you a clearer picture and stimulate your imagination, I have briefly characterized a few vendors and delivery mechanisms.

Private Cloud: The choice to host your applications in a private data center gives you the most control and flexibility. After you install Apache or Microsoft IIS on the hardware of your choice with any web frameworks you need, you can upload applications developed in your own environment.

The biggest drawback is that you don't automatically gain any benefits related to cloud computing. You can replicate many of the advantages internally, but it requires significant effort as well as a level of investment that may only be realistic for large enterprises.

Engine Yard: Engine Yard Cloud provides a Ruby on Rails technology stack, including web, application and database servers, monitoring and process management. The Linux distribution is optimized for Rails and includes in-memory cache.

Heroku: Salesforce.com's Heroku is another cloud application platform for Ruby. It is a managed multi-tenant platform and hosting environment. Each service consists of one or more dynos, or web processes running code and responding to HTTP requests

Facebook: A key differentiator of Facebook applications is that they revolve around a "social graph", which connects people with other people and their interests. One way to conceptualize the potential of the Facebook Platform is by thinking of it in terms of a three-tier model: Presentation, Application Logic and Data.

Chapter 5

Software as a Service

Software as a Service (SaaS) differs from Infrastructure and Platform as a Service in that it provides a service that is directly consumable by the end-user. IaaS and PaaS offer infrastructure and platforms where system managers and developers can install their applications but they offer little immediate value to a non-technical user.

SaaS provides the full stack of cloud services, and ideally presents these to the end-user in a fashion that is not radically different from how users expect to use their applications. There may be some user interface changes that ripple through to the users, but the main difference is the deployment, licensing and billing model, which should be invisible to corporate end-users.

Consistent with the basic notion of cloud computing, SaaS is a model whereby the customer licenses applications and provisions them to users on demand. The services run on the provider's infrastructure and are accessed through a public network connection. Applications may be made available through the Internet as browser applications, or they may be downloaded and synchronized with user devices.

Some of the characteristics of SaaS services are that they are centrally managed and updated. Typically, they are highly standardized although they may vary in their configurability as well as their efficiency and scalability. The most common pricing model is based on the number of users, but there may be additional fees based on bandwidth, storage and usage.

There are many similarities between SaaS and the services offered a few years ago by application service providers (ASPs). However, there are also stark differences in the approaches to multi-tenancy, the pay-as-you-go model and the ability to provision on demand.

SaaS offers several compelling benefits. It simplifies licensing. In fact, the customer doesn't need to acquire (or directly pay for) a software license at all. This is a task of the provider. There is also no need to calculate maximum capacity. It outsources the tedious task of application maintenance and upgrades and ties customer costs to usage, which lowers fixed costs and capital investment.

However, it does so at the price of restricting customer flexibility in terms of configuration options and update schedule. It also entails a significant commitment to the provider since it isn't trivial to switch from one SaaS vendor to another (or back on-site). There may be APIs for extraction and loading but there are no standards on the semantics of these interfaces, so it requires significant effort to automate a migration process.

SaaS has both advantages and disadvantages compared to PaaS and IaaS. As long as the functionality offered by the vendor exactly matches the requirements of the customer, SaaS is a standardized and optimized solution that generally will result in the lowest costs to the customer. However, the flexibility to customize, or indeed to build additional applications, is much greater with PaaS or IaaS.

Again, I would emphasize that the three levels are not necessarily competitive and the higher levels tend to rely on the lower ones. In particular, SaaS providers are often customers of infrastructure vendors and leverage not only the base infrastructure but services, such as marketplaces, that help them in developing and selling software services.

It is challenging to provide any abstraction to SaaS services or to classify them according to the technology and approach that they use. They are incredibly diverse and can leverage any web-based tools to implement the application requirements. Rather than theorizing about their composition, it is more effective to provide an overview of the types of software they represent, the range of business sectors they span, and the functionality they can deliver and scale on demand.

Customer Relationship Management

One of the most popular and most publicized areas of Software as a Service is Customer Relationship Management (CRM) and in particular, sales-force automation. It includes functions such as account management, opportunity tracking and marketing campaign administration.

Salesforce.com

Arguably, the best known SaaS offering comes from Salesforce.com which provides a CRM solution consisting of several modules: Sales, Service & Support, Partner Relationship Management, Marketing, Content, Ideas and Analytics. It is available in over 20 languages and can be accessed from almost any Internet device including mobile platforms such as: Blackberry, iPhone and Windows Mobile.

Some of its modules include:

Accounts and Contacts manage all critical account data, including a company overview, key sales data, relevant documents and partners involved in the account.

Marketing and leads presents a hierarchical view of campaigns across all channels including leads and opportunities for each of the campaigns.

Opportunities can track information on owner, account, milestones, decision makers, customer communications, competitor tracking and product tracking.

Analytics and Forecasting include dashboards to show real-time status, broken down by department, role, account or individual and also highlight neglected leads.

Workflows can accommodate custom rules, triggers, approvals (discount requests), opportunity close, task assignment and help to manage territories.

Content Library facilitates sharing of documents, presentations and other common collateral.

Social networking includes a feature called Genius, which allows users to find similar opportunities and experts to help manage them.

Partners can be managed and tracked. It is also possible to share leads, opportunities, accounts, contacts and tasks.

Recruitment can help to qualify, on-board, train and track candidates for employment.

Users can also customize their CRM application. There are tabs such as "Contacts", "Reports", and "Accounts" which contain associated information including standard fields like First Name, Last Name, and Email, for Contacts.

The customer can add user-defined custom fields. But they can also customize the "platform" level by adding customized applications to a Salesforce.com instance. This means adding sets of customized tabs for specific vertical or function-level (Finance, Human Resources, etc) features.

Salesforce.com offers a Web Services API for data manipulation (E.g. SELECT, INSERT, UPDATE, DELETE). However it is restricted to client-side execution, resulting in suboptimal performance for large numbers of transactions. It therefore makes sense to leverage the Force.com platform for any completely new functionality.

NetSuite

DEFINE

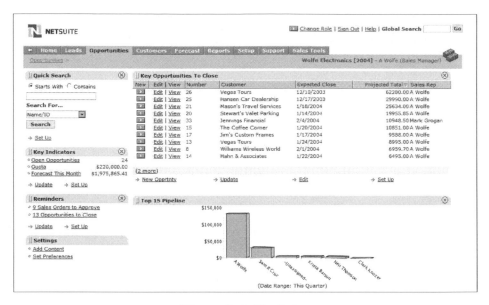

Figure 5-1: NetSuite

NetSuite is another popular CRM package (Figure 5-1). Its base service is called NetSuite 2007.0 while NetSuite and NetSuite CRM+ are the two primary product options. Other options and services include NetSuite Global CRM, Dedicated Server Options, OpenAir and Payroll.

Some of the primary features include:

Pipeline and opportunity management includes functionality to assign leads territories and examine all quotes, orders, and closed sales.

Order Management facilitates the action of turning quotes into orders.

Advanced forecasting includes capabilities, such as probability-based forecasting and weighted measurement of pending opportunities. It can offer more precision using forecast categories and deal ranges.

Incentive Management provides a multi-tiered commission structure (based on billing or payment), with roll-up reporting. It can consider target commission and provides flexible period assignment. If needed, it can also integrate directly with the payroll system to effect the changes.

Upsell manager offers insight into past purchases and makes recommendations of likely requirements.

Account management gives the account executive visibility into the history of sales, support, billing and shipping for a particular account.

DEFINE

NetSuite has also launched a global business management system called OneWorld, which offers on-demand international support to mid-market companies. Multi-national organizations can manage companies with multiple subsidiaries, business units and legal entities in their requirement for homogenous and integrated quotes, forecasts, campaigns and analytics. It can handle all local currencies, taxation rules, and compliance requirements.

As with Salesforce.com, the platform offers very rich support for developers and third parties in an effort to build an extensive ecosystem. The SuiteCloud developer network includes the NetSuite Business Operating System – a set of primarily two tools to build, integrate and deliver applications for the NetSuite platform:

SuiteFlex is an application development platform consisting of:

- SuiteBuilder rapid application development facilitates building user interfaces online.

- SuiteScript programming environment is a programming language modeled on JavaScript.

- SuiteTalk web services allow access to NetSuite data through a SOAP API.

- SuiteScript D-Bug interactive debugger facilitates live troubleshooting.

SuiteBundler is an application deployment tool that allows the developer to easily productize, package and deliver a solution.

SuiteApp.com is NetSuite's online solution directory, which acts as a marketplace for third party developers to sell their NetSuite extensions and layered functionality.

SugarCRM

SugarCRM itself is not an on-demand service. Rather it is an open-source software solution based on a "LAMP" stack of Linux, Apache, MySQL and PHP, that includes sales-force automation, marketing campaigns and customer support as well as collaboration and reporting functionality.

The fact that SugarCRM is open-source makes it very attractive for prospective SaaS providers who wish to reach out into the CRM space. It is very easy and cheap to build a SaaS solution on top of an IaaS by downloading the product and installing it on a virtual machine. In fact, there are already many pre-packaged machines that have SugarCRM with a base configuration ready for deployment.

SugarCRM has introduced a Sugar Data Center Edition (DCE) that further encourages SaaS with a set of tools for provisioning, monitoring and reporting as well as facilities to manage and deploy multiple instances from a central console.

Human Resources

Human Resources (HR), or Human Capital Management (HCM), includes administration processes to support personnel functions such as recruiting, developing, retaining and motivating employees. Due to the confidential nature of the data involved some organizations will be wary of placing the functionality outside the corporate firewall. However, there are an increasing number of organizations, especially smaller businesses that are willing to assume the risk in order to capitalize on the financial benefits.

Workday

Workday provides such features as:

Absence allows visibility of accrued vacation and facilities for registering planned leaves of absence.

Compensation includes salary, equity, benefits and allowances as well as bonuses based on both employee performance and business performance.

Benefits include health (medical, dental, vision), insurance: (long-term and short-term disability, life), spending accounts (healthcare and dependent care) and defined contribution (401k, 403b) with age validation. There are also options for new hire enrollment, open enrolment and changes based on life events such as marriage and birth.

Staffing entails functions such as position management, headcount management and job management.

Development helps to support business performance through talent management with a focus on technical skills, project roles, training and certification as well as tracking awards and accomplishments.

Performance management involves performance reviews and follow-up management that covers compensation, performance plans and disciplinary actions.

Workday Web Services (WWS) provide developers with access to Workday's business services via standards-based web services.

Taleo

Taleo is another well-known SaaS provider in the HR space. Some features include:

Recruitment: The module tracks and manages each job opening with clearly defined ownership. Users can post opportunities to internal career sites or expand to external free and paid job boards. It offers background checks, applicant pre-screen, as well as candidate ranking based on answers to online or phone questions. It also ensures the hiring system is compliant with federal, state and local regulations and processes.

Performance Management: Users can establish quantitative and qualitative employee goals, define expectations, and align employee goals to broader company objectives. They can use configurable templates and business processes to define and monitor the employee review cycle. The module includes a behavioral competencies library and facilities to monitor employee self assessments and manager appraisals.

Employee Lifecycle: Taleo OnBoard automates the new hire process by enabling electronic signatures and by supporting the assignment and tracking of key tasks to bring employees up to speed quickly. It can package forms into bundles and then create new-hire packets for various job types and locations. A consistent onboarding process also ensures legal and policy compliance.

Career Management: Career scenarios motivate and empower top performers to generate career tracks and identify steps for success. The system encourages employees to further their professional development and help them stay on track. It increases inter-departmental cooperation through expanded mentoring and networking opportunities and automatically informs the workforce when new employment, networking, mentoring, education, training or certification opportunities arise.

Succession Planning: Scenario planning increases the visibility into a team's capabilities and supports executive decision-making. Succession Plans couple individual career plans with data captured in the performance review processes to create backfill strategies. The notion of Succession Pools represents candidates in the succession short list who are not necessarily officially included in the plan. The system tracks candidate readiness based on skills, competencies and performance and makes it easier to promote top candidates based on relative ranking and composite feedback scores.

Taleo also exposes a SOAP-based Web Services API that developers can leverage to integrate HR functions and data in other applications or to build data extracts for backup purposes.

Financial

There are a variety of financial applications that are available on-demand, ranging from accounting to procurement and inventory management.

Workday

DEFINE

In addition to its human capital management modules described earlier, Workday also offers some functionality related to financial tasks such as:

Payroll: pay groups, reporting, tax updates, earnings/deductions, accumulations and balances

Worker spend management: reporting, expenses, reimbursements; onboard contingents

Financial accounting: for investors and creditors as well as internal validation of Sarbanes-Oxley compliance

Customer accounts: invoicing, accounts receivable

Supplier accounts: all information for vendor management and accounts payable

Cash management: bank statement reconciliation

Procurement: information policies for acquiring goods, services and contract labor

It can provide reporting functionality for all of the modules and includes logic to enforce all legal and company-specific accounting rules.

Netsuite

NetSuite Financials supports similar back-office operations and business processes which are classified as:

Financial Management: Financial controls and processes include general ledger, accounts receivable, accounts payable, budget management, multi-currency transactions and reporting, revenue recognition, recurring revenue management, allocations, and financial reporting.

Financial Planning: Planning and "what-if" financial modeling capabilities provide a real-time, end-to-end business management solution for strategy, planning and execution.

Inventory and Supply Chain: A set of inventory management, manufacturing, and procure-to-pay process management features control supply chain activities within the organization as well as with partners, vendors and customers.

Order Management: Order Management is the link between the sales organization, financial management and order fulfillment.

Services Resource Planning (SRP): A single workflow integrates the services project lifecycle from marketing and sales to project management, services delivery, billing, revenue management and driving repeat business.

Human Capital Management (HCM): Employee resource management tools for streamline payroll operations and employee compensation.

Business Intelligence and Analytics (SuiteAnalytics): Embedded role-based dashboards include pre-built key performance indicators, trend graphs, scorecards and graphical report snapshots.

Intuit

Intuit Inc. is a software company that develops financial and tax preparation software, such as Quicken and TurboTax, for consumers, small businesses and financial institutions (Figure 5-2). Its online services include web-hosting, accounting, payroll and payment solutions.

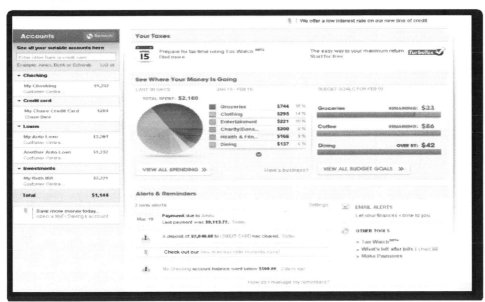

Figure 5-2: Intuit FinanceWorks

Collaboration

Since collaboration involves establishing connectivity between people it is natural to also use a technology that is built on networking and utilizes a common infrastructure. There are a growing number of Web 2.0 services that are almost exclusively delivered over the Internet. But even some of the more traditional applications such as desktop productivity and conferencing can benefit from cloud computing.

Chapter 5: Software as a Service

Google Apps

Google offers a set of applications under the banner of Google Apps both as a free service to individuals and a competitively priced service for companies or individuals who may require higher storage limits. These include: Gmail, Google Calendar, Talk, Docs, and Sites:

Gmail (also called **Google Mail** in some countries) is a webmail service provided with a thread-structured, search-oriented interface. At the back end, Gmail runs on Google Servlet Engine and Linux-based Google GFE/1.3. In addition to browser access, it also supports POP3, and IMAPv4.

The user experience is characterized by the extensive use of Asynchronus Javascript and XML (AJAX) to pre-fetch and pre-send information without the user needing to refresh thereby dramatically reducing response time and improving the user experience.

Gmail is noted for its spam filtering which leverages a community-driven system: when any user marks an email as spam, the system leverages the information to identify similar future messages for all Gmail users. Commercial customers can also use Postini as an alternative to Google's own malware detection.

Google Calendar is a time-management web application. In addition to viewing, adding and modifying entries, the Ajax-driven interface allows users to drag-and-drop events from one date to another without reloading the page. It supports view modes such as weekly, monthly, and agenda. Users can add calendar events by typing informal English phrases, such as "Team call at noon next Sunday". They can set the number of days to show in their custom view mode and can add descriptions to all events in the Google Calendar.

Other features of Google Calendar include offline support and to-do lists. Multiple calendars can be created and shown in the same view. They can be shared either with read-only permission or full control and either with only a specified list of people or made public to everyone.

Google Talk (GTalk) is a Windows and web-based application for instant messaging and internet telephony. Instant messaging between clients and the Google Talk servers uses the standard Extensible Messaging and Presence Protocol (XMPP), which provides real-time extensible messaging and presence events, including offline messaging and voice mailing. VoIP (Voice over IP) is based on the Jingle protocol, an extension to XMPP proposed by Google, which accommodates peer-to-peer signaling for multimedia (voice and video) interactions.

Google Docs is a web-based desktop application suite. It allows users to create and edit documents online while collaborating in real-time with other users. Documents, spreadsheets, forms and presentations can be created within the application itself, imported through the web interface, or sent via email. They can also be saved to the user's computer in a variety of formats (the ISO standard OpenDocument format as well as OpenOffice, HTML, PDF, RTF, Text, Microsoft Word). By default, they are saved to the Google servers.

Google Docs serves as a collaborative tool for editing amongst users and non-users in real time. Shared documents can be opened and edited by multiple users at the same time. In the case of spreadsheets, users can be notified of changes to any specified regions via e-mail.

For Microsoft Office users who may find uploading changed documents via a browser interface to be tedious, Google offers a free plug-in (Google Cloud Connect for Microsoft Office) that automatically synchronizes edits in the Word, Excel and PowerPoint with Google Docs. It supports multi-user concurrent editing, synchronization of both online and offline modifications as well as conflict resolution and a revision history for rollback capability.

Google Sites is a structured wiki offering the following features:

- A web address of the form "http://sites.google.com/site/sitename/"
- A limited number of themes
- Limited use of HTML coding
- Ability to insert: Videos from Google Video/YouTube, Google Docs document, Google Calendar, Google Maps, AdWords and AdSense

Microsoft Online Services

Microsoft Online provides distinct sets of services for consumers, and enterprises. Windows Live covers the former while Office 365 targets the latter.

Windows Live includes a number of consumer-oriented modules that cater to some of the most common requirements of home users and small businesses:

- Windows Live Family Safety (parental control system providing website blocking, content filtering and web activity monitoring)
- Windows Live Mail (Email client for Windows Live Hotmail, Gmail, Yahoo! Mail and any POP accounts)
- Windows Live Messenger (Instant Messaging client)
- Windows Live Movie Maker (Video editing software)
- Windows Live Photo Gallery (photo management and sharing)
- Windows Live Writer (Desktop blog publishing application)

Windows Live SkyDrive is an online file storage and sharing service that allows users to upload files to cloud storage and then access them from a Web

DEFINE

browser. The authentication system uses Windows Live ID to control file access, allowing users to keep data private, share it with contacts, or make content public. A downloadable plug-in allows drag-and-drop uploading from Silverlight enabled browsers, such as Windows Explorer.

Office Web Apps is a web-based edition of Microsoft Office. It includes versions of Word, Excel, PowerPoint and OneNote. Office Web Apps can integrate with SkyDrive to simplify uploading Microsoft Office documents to the cloud and sharing them with others. Users can then also edit Microsoft Office Word, Excel, PowerPoint and OneNote documents from a web browser.

Office 365 caters to enterprises and comes in two editions, called Professional and Enterprise subscriptions. The standard offering operates using a multi-tenant model and comes at a very attractive price point for smaller organizations. A dedicated option involves a higher degree of isolation, which is often required by larger enterprises.

The main components of the Office 365 suite include:

Exchange Online with Forefront anti-virus checking and spam-filtering. Support to client devices through Outlook Web Access, Outlook Anywhere (RPC/HTTP) and ActiveSync enables access to Outlook from any network allowing outbound HTTP access as well as any browser and many mobile platforms such as Windows Mobile, BlackBerry, iPhone and some Nokia devices.

SharePoint Online offers content management with version control and support for wikis, blogs, surveys and RSS feeds. It also supports Forefront anti-virus.

Lync Online provides presence capability and instant messaging. It also can facilitate person-to-person audio and video on LAN. Its meeting capabilities include both live and recorded whiteboard and presentation sharing with audio and video.

Microsoft Office Professional Plus in Office 365 is the rough equivalent of the same product available through Microsoft Volume Licensing. It is licensed month-to-month on a per-user basis and can be installed by users from Microsoft Online Services or from a customer-managed server.

Office Web Apps are browser-based versions of Microsoft Excel, Word, and PowerPoint similar to the same service offered as part of Windows Live.

Cisco Webex

There are several other web presentation tools on the market including Citrix GoToMeeting, Dimdim and Cisco Webex, each with their own strengths and weaknesses.

For example, CiscoWebex combines real-time collaboration with phone conferencing. It is effective for showing demo applications and conducting web tours.

Users can share documents, presentations, and applications, passing control to anyone in the meeting. They can also include video from multiple webcams and use integrated VoIP, audio broadcast or dial-in conferencing as well as hybrid combinations.

It is possible to record, edit, and play back meetings after the event for review and compliance purposes. The meeting history facilitates billing and can provide information on attendance and test results.

Backup and Recovery

Cloud-based backup has an intrinsic benefit over on-site alternatives that the physical storage is generally very far removed from the users and their source data. As such, it is resilient to many of the risks of natural disasters and other localized outages.

These solutions could equally well fall into the category of Storage as a Service since most of the computation takes place in an on-premise client stub. On the other hand, the end-user interaction is more typical of Software as a Service. Regardless of how you categorize them, they are an important emerging area that needs to be considered.

Some of the offerings on the market include Box.Net, which doubles as a collaboration tool, and SugarSync, which leverages the online backup and storage to provide a vehicle for synchronizing multiple user devices. Mozy is more typical of a personal backup solution.

Mozy

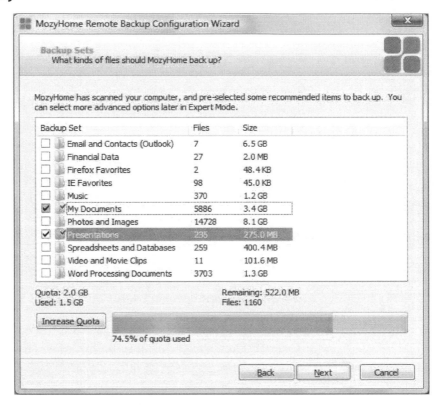

Figure 5-3: Mozy Backup

Mozy allows users to specify folders and files that should be backed up to the cloud on a regular basis (Figure 5-3). The service automatically detects and backs up new and changed files while the computer is not in use. Scheduled backups can be performed daily or weekly at a specified time of day. At the beginning of the backup process, all files are locally encrypted with 448-bit Blowfish encryption. The encrypted files are then sent via 128–bit SSL to a managed data center where they remain in their encrypted state.

The tool backs up common business applications such as SQL and Exchange. It includes support for open and locked files, such as Outlook PST files. Mozy only backs up new or changed portions of files in order to optimize network traffic. Users can also specify how much bandwidth they want to dedicate to their backups so other high-priority services can run unimpeded.

Users and administrators can restore data via the Mozy software client, through the web, or by ordering a DVD restore. Windows users can also restore data via right-click or through the Mozy Virtual Drive.

The professional version of Mozy adds the role of administrators who can view individual and aggregate account history, reset account password and distribute license keys. They can also create customized email alerts regarding the backup health of their account.

Zmanda

Zmanda is a backup solution that takes a very different approach. It is based on the Amanda open-source backup software and provides a central console where administrators can specify hosts, paths and backup destination. Zmanda does not run in a cloud. It is a centrally administered solution that can backup data to disk and tape. However it also provides an option to back the data up to Amazon S3.

It is of interest for enterprises that may need to run in a hybrid environment. The central management server can interact with application agents that cover Microsoft Exchange, Active Directory and SQL Server as well as Oracle 10g and Oracle 11g.

It does not use any proprietary data formats so it is relatively easy to integrate the solution with other storage solutions. In particular, its ZCloud API is publicly documented and can be leveraged by other storage services to become potential destinations of the ever-growing eco-system of backup-to-cloud applications.

Industry Solutions

One of the most intriguing areas for cloud services will be in delivering vertical solutions that help to automate processes in particular industries.

Healthcare

Pharmacy OneSource offers several services in the healthcare sector, such as:

Sentri7 is a real-time patient surveillance system that can provide a list of hospital patients who are most at risk from medication-related falls so that appropriate precautions can be put in place.

Schedule OneSource is an online pharmacy staff scheduling solution that streamlines creating, changing and communicating staff schedules. Each customer subscribes to a license of Schedule OneSource that is unique to that department, its employees, shifts and other requirements. It aids compliance and provides visibility into time off, labor cost, and other reports generated for individuals, shifts and departments. The built-in rotations and templates include set shifts and cycles, taking into account needs such as double shifts, preferred consecutive scheduling patterns, training, night/day shifts and weekend rotations.

Quantifi is a customizable clinical documentation and reporting tool for hospital pharmacies and health systems. Pharmacists document and monitor their clinical interventions, medication errors, and adverse drug reactions via the web or handheld computer. Pharmacy managers can run detailed reports.

DEFINE

trends in intervention acceptance, time spent doing clinical activities, and costs avoided.

Transportation

Active On-Demand's APT is an Internet-based transportation management system (TMS) that connects commercial shippers with hand-delivered couriers, ground express truckers and dedicated air charters, matching requests to quotes. It also manages the end-to-end shipment process with functionality to administer the shipment, track cargo location, and provide complete, detailed logistical visibility to shippers, consignees, and carriers.

The Carrier Dashboard provides a view into carrier activity over a date range and shows shipment volumes, transportation expense, and carrier quality ratings. The user can drill down for data mining, including cargo records, carrier notes and a complete audit trail for a specific shipment.

Logistics

One Network offers solutions in the retail and consumer products sector and supplies technology for logistics service providers. Some of its functionality includes:

Data Management brings together the supply chain community of retailers, suppliers and carriers by providing them with a data sharing framework.

Order Management delivers an automated order process that can be viewed and collaborated between sales representatives, customers, suppliers and distribution.

Procurement integrates demand signals across each node to facilitate control over the complete purchasing process.

Manufacturing is an end-to-end process flow for manufacturers from production to purchasing to inventory. It caters to manufacturing processes ranging from make-to-order to custom and mixed mode.

Inventory Management offers inventory visibility and management across multi-party users. It works with the underlying replenishment engines to maintain optimal inventory levels throughout the value network across stores and plants.

Deployment coordinates activities of deployment planning and execution to meet customer's service levels with the lowest total landing cost. It includes decisions on where to stock, how much to stock and where to source.

Demand Driven Logistics is a multi-tenant, multi-party, sense and respond solution for transportation and appointment scheduling that integrates into a company's overall supply chain process.

Demand Management integrates a retailer and its suppliers in processes focused around actual shelf consumption with a collaborative architecture.

Replenishment defines replenishment policies ranging from static to completely dynamic as well as postponement techniques to generate the most accurate orders.

Store Operations aligns all the processes around store shelf, continuously adjusting forecasts according to the latest demand patterns, using analytics that not only provide visibility into historical issues but also project future problems.

Spare Parts is a module to manage and replenish spare parts.

Assess

Chapter 6

Benefits and Challenges

There are three primary benefits that cloud computing promises to enterprise customers: cost, agility and focus. They can reduce and simplify their cost structure. They can leverage the elasticity of cloud computing to make their business more agile. And they can take advantage of the fact that they have outsourced some of their IT focus by dedicating their freed resources to activities that improve their core competencies.

There are also some drawbacks and challenges surrounding cloud computing. The opacity of location and internal operation makes it difficult to track information and processing. This can lead to a loss of control over vital operations. And it can expose the company to risks without recourse to address them.

Before embarking on a cloud strategy it is imperative to weigh the pros and cons of all IT delivery models that are available. We need to make a sound assessment of what makes sense for each application and business process and then determine the timeline for transitioning current services.

Benefits

Some of the primary benefits of cloud computing derive from improvements in cost, risk, security, flexibility, quality and focus. Let's look at each of them.

Cost

The most apparent benefits of cloud computing are around cost. In order to quantify the benefit, you will need to perform a complete financial analysis of both a cloud model and any alternative options. We will pursue this track in more detail in Chapter 9. At this stage, we will focus on the main cost differentiators.

There can be a significant reduction in up-front investment since there is no need to purchase extensive hardware infrastructure or software licenses. Instead you

Chapter 6: Benefits and Challenges

can align your costs to actual usage. This means that you can allocate costs to the contributing revenue much more easily and accurately.

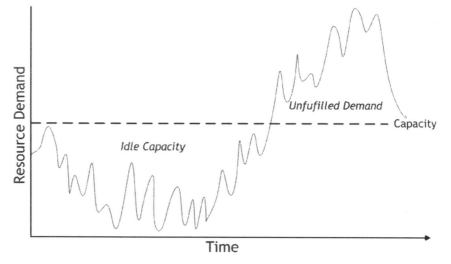

Figure 6-1: Fixed Capacity Utilization Curve

You also no longer need to over-provision resources in order to meet spikes in demand (Figure 6-1). High-end industry server utilization rates currently run at 15-20%. In the cloud, you do not pay for idle capacity which further reduces costs.

And finally, some benefits that the providers have acquired in terms of economies of scale and their place on the experience curve will translate into cost savings for the customer. Certainly, the providers will try to retain most of their advantage as profit; but, in a competitive environment with other efficient providers, you can also expect some savings to be passed on to customers.

Risk

Cloud computing can offload some risks from the customer to the service provider. By contractually stipulating data protection and disaster recovery provisions, and attaching them to indemnities in the case of failures, the company can mitigate its own risks.

It also reduces the likelihood of under-provisioning. Since it is not possible to accurately predict customer demand, there is always the possibility that there will be sudden unanticipated spikes of resource utilization. If the company owns its own resources, then there are limits to the amount of idle capacity that they will procure on the off-chance of a sudden increase in activity. On the other hand, the elastic capacity of a cloud provider should not often be exceeded.

It would be hard to over-emphasize this point. Scalability disasters can cause both direct and indirect costs. Lost revenues through unplanned downtime cost

ASSESS

enterprises an average of over a hundred thousand dollars an hour and can exceed a million dollars an hour[1] (Forrester 2004). In addition, there are numerous other consequences. The company may lose potential customers who are irked by the unpleasant experience of losing a transaction. Employees cannot work which increases their hourly costs. There may be compensatory payments. The brand damage can hurt relations with customers, suppliers, financial markets, banks, business partners and investors.

There may even be an impact on financial performance through interruptions in billing or investment activities. Revenue and cash flow recognition may be delayed and distort the financial picture and there are risks of lost discounts from accounts payable, which can also damage the credit rating. If that isn't enough, then consider the contractual payment obligations to temporary employees, schedules for equipment renewal, overtime costs, shipping costs and travel expenses, which can all be adversely impacted.

Rogue clouds represent another potential risk that an authorized cloud service can mitigate. Historically, when a technology is not deployed in an organization the likelihood of an unauthorized deployment increases. A stark example was that of wireless LANs, which can easily be added to most corporate networks with twenty-dollar appliances to create a huge attack surface. By implementing authorized WLANs, many organizations removed the incentive for unauthorized WLANs.

Similarly, there is an incentive for many users or departments to leverage cloud-based services for personal and group use. It is extremely easy for them to access these on their own since many of the providers offer free functionality or credit-card-based payment. Their rogue use may jeopardize sensitive company information or expose the business to severe sanctions for non-compliance with industry regulations.

It is impossible to completely remove the threat of departmental cloud use. However, if the functionality is available on an authorized and supported basis then the incentive for unauthorized and unmonitored usage declines.

Security

Security is usually portrayed as a challenge for cloud computing, and rightfully so. Nonetheless there are several benefits that cloud computing may offer with respect to security. That is not to say that these benefits are necessarily exclusive to cloud computing, merely that they align very well with cloud computing.

Cloud providers typically undergo very strict security audits. An enterprise may also institute the same audits but, on average, many businesses do not enforce the same level of rigor as a cloud provider. On a similar line, the cloud providers

---

[1] Estimates in U.S. dollars.

ASSESS

have access to the best-of-breed security solutions and procedures. They have also been forced to inculcate a deep sense of security concern in their administrative staff. Again, this is not typically matched by smaller organizations.

The cloud also offers a platform for many security functions ranging from disaster recovery to monitoring, forensic readiness and password assurance or security testing. Its location makes it ideal for centralized monitoring.

It is easier to isolate customer and employee data if they are managed in different environments. It might therefore increase security to segregate the data such that customer information is housed in the cloud while employee information is processed on the internal network.

Virtualization carries with it the inherent advantage that it is much easier to deploy preconfigured builds. It is possible to pre-harden these by locking down all traffic, eliminating unnecessary applications and features and applying the latest security patches.

There is some arguable advantage to the fact that the cloud obfuscates the physical infrastructure. Since virtual images may be brought up anywhere in the cloud and tend to move frequently, it makes it much more difficult for a hacker to launch a topology-based attack.

Finally, there is some arguable advantage to the fact that the cloud obfuscates the physical infrastructure. Since virtual images may be brought up anywhere in the cloud and tend to move frequently, it makes it much more difficult for a hacker to launch a topology-based attack.

Flexibility

A cloud infrastructure adds considerable flexibility and agility to an enterprise architecture. It makes it much easier to roll out new services as they become necessary and to retire old applications when they are no longer needed. There is no need to procure hardware for the former or to cost-effectively dispose of the equipment in the case of the latter.

Similarly, a particular service can scale up and down as needed. There are cases where resource demand has spiked ten-fold overnight only to fall back to its original level shortly afterward[1]. The elasticity of a cloud allows the enterprise to exactly match the resources to the demand without overpaying for excess capacity or losing an opportunity to address market demand.

The flexibility also facilitates a faster time to market. The usual lead time for procuring necessary equipment can be compressed to a few minutes when re-

---

[1] Animoto is a popular example: They scaled from 50 Amazon Servers to 3500 Servers in three days (16-19 April 2008)

sources can be provisioned on demand. Ultimately, the speed and reduced commitment also lower barriers to innovation, which can encourage a more agile organizational culture.

A globally replicated cloud facilitates access from any place using any device at any time and therefore contributes to user flexibility and productivity. This advantage becomes even more visible when there is a need to integrate with business processes with suppliers, partners and customers. The absence of a firewall makes it easier to authorize fine-grained access to services and data without compromising or exposing other organizational assets.

ASSESS

Quality

Quality of service in all dimensions is a major concern around cloud computing. But in many cases it is actually a benefit. Cloud service providers have great economy of scale and specialization. They have developed rigorous processes and procedures to maximize uptime and optimize performance. They run best-in-breed software to monitor and manage the infrastructure and they employ some of the most skilled practitioners to oversee the management tools.

An on-demand model also differentiates itself from purchased and installed-software in that the service provider can distribute new functionality transparently without an IT intervention. As a result users can benefit from more frequent updates and newer functionality.

Focus

The fact that some of the IT services are outsourced to a cloud provider reduces the effort and administration that is required by the corporate IT department. These responsibilities extend from user provisioning and support to application management and troubleshooting. Once service evolution is automated, experts can refocus on activities and opportunities that help to solidify the core competencies of the firm.

Challenges

Although there are some very compelling benefits to cloud computing, a BT survey in November 2009 found that the majority of CIOs do not see value in cloud computing (BT Global Services, 2009). Some of their concerns can be dismissed as over-generalization of bad experiences from previous hype cycles and lack of familiarity with the essence and benefits of cloud computing.

But, in fairness, there are also legitimate drawbacks and challenges that new technologies bring with them. A realistic assessment must consider both sides of the equation.

Financial Structure

The absence of capital investment and reduced fixed costs may seem very attractive, but it is important to realize that there will probably also be significant implementation and migration costs associated with the move to a cloud platform.

ASSESS

Sunk costs in existing infrastructure may also act as a deterrent toward migration. Keep in mind that the historic costs, regardless how recent, are irrelevant from a financial point of view. They may represent an emotional barrier but it is much more important to examine the future costs.

Another challenge can be the existence of current contracts with service providers. These may preclude (or heavily penalize) early exits. That doesn't necessarily mean the service cannot be moved to a cloud, but double-payment to multiple providers is certainly a significant financial barrier.

Security and Risk

The security and risk concerns are probably the best known and most challenging to address. That is the reason several chapters in this book address these topics.

A common obstacle to the adoptions of cloud computing is the fact that the service provider hosts sensitive data – potentially in a multi-tenant environment. The customer must consider the host to be trustworthy enough not to intentionally, or inadvertently, compromise the information.

The fact that there is only limited standardization of cloud functionality leads to interoperability barriers, which lock the customer into a given vendor's service. This presents a risk if the vendor faces insolvency or if the customer subsequently chooses to switch vendors.

A general governance problem can give many customers cause for concern. They have only limited recourse if the system performs unreliably or doesn't scale to their required capacity.

Integration and Transition

There are numerous technical challenges that an enterprise needs to address if it is considering adopting a cloud model. It is not trivial to integrate the networks in a reliable, scalable and secure fashion. There may be uncontrollable sources of latency or data transfer bottlenecks. It can be difficult to manage the encryption keys needed to protect all channels of communication.

It is also a challenge to integrate applications, which may need to connect between organizational boundaries. Again, there are security precautions to consider, but there are also more general problems of interoperability and standardization of interfaces. It can be difficult to maintain data integrity when critical parts of typically synchronous activities need to be handled asynchronously.

And across these, there are many questions about support in a multi-vendor, multi-provider environment, which can complicate operational processes such as incident management.

Organization

Shifting functionality to the cloud essentially means outsourcing that service. And outsourcing usually has personnel implications. It doesn't necessarily mean that the groups who were performing that service are no longer needed. However, it does mean that there will be a need to reassess their responsibilities and ensure that they can continue to add net value to the business. This evaluation is an additional burden, which can slow down the adoption of a new technology.

Recommendations

Every enterprise will follow a unique course of action as it makes its way toward the cloud. The specific tasks will follow from a more diligent analysis as you read the coming chapters. However, even at this stage, you can make some general observations that apply to most organizations.

Preparation is Critical

It's never too early to begin planning for the cloud. Many activities have extended duration or are restricted to infrequent intervals. It can be difficult to terminate a contract but much easier to negotiate favorable exit provisions from a contract renewal. It may be challenging to effectively dispose of newly purchased hardware but it's not hard to refrain from a future purchase.

The earlier a cloud transition is planned the easier and cheaper it becomes to execute. Cloud computing is about more than just a technology, it is a frame of mind that maximizes agility and flexibility. Adopting that mindset early makes it easier when the actual time comes to implement the technology.

Validate the Corporate Strategy

Most (successful) organizations already have a process in place to continually reassess and refine the corporate strategy. It is important to monitor the competitive landscape and compare company performance with industry benchmarks on a regular basis.

This process will uncover certain areas where improvement is needed, or at least desired. Depending on who is performing the exercise, the strategists may or may not consider how cloud computing can play a role in revamping the company strategy.

Chapter 6: Benefits and Challenges

Since cloud computing does have the potential of profound impact at many levels, it is important to ensure that the strategic analysis includes its consideration, ideally by including participants with a sound knowledge of the technology and its implications.

Evaluate the Components

ASSESS

A critical part of the early-planning process is to take an inventory of the existing applications, requirements, user groups and infrastructure and perform a survey of the potential service providers on the market. Equipped with this information, you can begin to investigate which services are most likely to be relevant to your business in the short term and which providers might best be able to deliver these services.

Keep in mind that you don't need to completely overhaul your architecture in one big bang. Many enterprises will adopt a hybrid and flexible sourcing model for some time to come.

Modernize the Existing Infrastructure

One of the best ways to prepare for tomorrow is to optimize what you are doing today. As you assess your existing applications, determine whether any of them are legacy applications that might benefit from a redesign for service orientation. Look at your infrastructure and operational procedures, and determine whether you have any opportunities to virtualize, standardize, optimize and automate.

It is also helpful to ensure that a systematic and structured approach to service management is in place. ITSM provides the elements for a solid management design that facilitates a flexible and extensible operating model, which will also make it easier to embrace new forms of service delivery.

Determine the Business Case

Finally, take a stab at the business case. Even if it isn't compelling yet, you will want to gauge how close you are and what likely changes will make it compelling in the future. Keep in mind that the business case is more than a simple ROI calculation. There are many financial metrics to consider as well as the implications for risk and the ramifications of cloud computing on the competitive environment of your business.

Chapter 7

Strategic Impact

In some ways, cloud computing is only a small part of a much larger trend that is taking over the business world. The transition to a services-based economy began several decades ago in most of the industrialized world. However, it has long been constrained by inter-organizational barriers and lack of technical infrastructure.

In the past decades a great deal of corporate strategy has focused on even though their chance of success is usually slim (Knowledge@Wharton, 2005). Whether companies pursue an effort of vertical integration along the value chain from raw materials to finished product, or horizontal integration across products and markets, most acquisitions fail to add value to the organization.

The alternative of partnerships and strategic alliances promises much more flexibility. However, it has been difficult to break services down into basic components that are assembled from a range of optimal sources in an efficient manner. The transaction costs associated with selection, negotiation, billing, collection and monitoring have simply been too high to justify a wide range of business partners.

As we progress toward an economy where everything is available as a service, we need to consider much more than IT. Business processes from manufacturing and logistics to sales and marketing, or finance and human resources, can potentially be handled by a strategic partner. And, by providing the necessary information and technology framework, cloud computing can be a critical component in this transformation.

A classic assessment of technology strategy would begin with the observation that the overall corporate strategy will shape how cloud computing is adopted in an enterprise. However, in that way cloud computing is no different from any other technology, process or procedure. What I find much more interesting is that cloud computing has the potential to fundamentally impact many company strategies.

ASSESS

It can do so at two levels: internal (strategic) and external (competitive). If a company decides to embrace cloud computing then it may dramatically change some of the strategic assumptions around organizational structure, IT responsibilities and cost allocation mechanisms.

Regardless of whether a company seeks to adopt cloud computing, the technology may have a significant impact on the competitive landscape of many industries. Some companies may be forced to look at cloud computing simply to keep up with external efficiencies. And others may find that their core business is being eroded by the arrival of newer, more agile competitors.

What is Strategy?

Strategy is an interesting term. It is a word that most adults use at some point but struggle to define. Some suggest, facetiously, that if you ask ten executives for their interpretation of corporate strategy you will receive eleven different answers.

That said, in a business context most people equate it with a notion that involves setting long-term objectives according to stakeholder priorities and then selecting the best options in order to execute according to the plan.

ITIL recommends that a Service Strategy be derived from business and customer requirements and that it map to Strategies, Policies, Resources, Constraints and Objectives from Requirements (Figure 7-1).

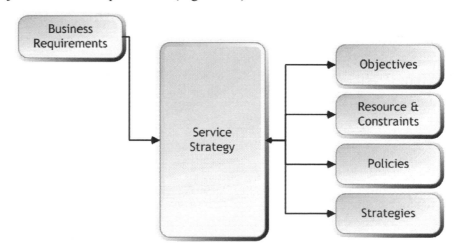

Figure 7-1: Strategy Formulation

More practically, the strategy proceeds in four phases: Define, Analyze, Approve and Charter (Figure 7-2).

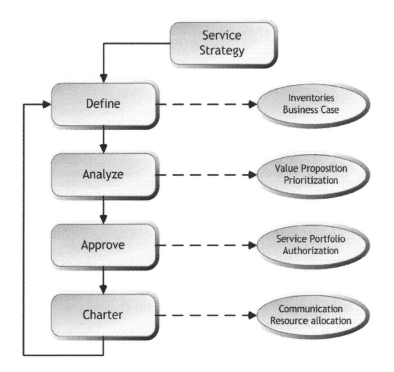

Figure 7-2: Service Strategy Phases

Bear in mind that not all businesses follow a structured top-down approach for identifying the strategy and mapping it to policies, resource allocation and objectives. Some adopt an emergent bottom-up strategy based on the decisions of managers who are in close contact with customers and, collectively, presumably have a more accurate picture of the market and competition than individual strategists. Nonetheless, those businesses that succeed generally perform some degree of strategic analysis whether it is explicit or implicit.

Strategic Analysis

The starting point of any analysis, strategic or otherwise, involves setting the objectives. For most publicly held corporations these will include profitability, sales growth, market share, relative costs and competitive position as well as possibly customer and employee satisfaction. The priorities vary but, where shareholder value is the highest priority, these are some of the main contributors.

There are certainly other forms of companies including governments and religious and social charities, which seek to maximize their impact in other ways, while usually also keeping an eye on costs. This does not prevent them from defining a strategy in their own terms and aligning their resources to the strategy.

Once the objectives have been set it is useful to perform both an external analysis of the environment and an internal analysis of the organization. Then management can match internal strengths with external opportunities and realign the focus for the company to optimize its chances of success.

External Analysis

The external analysis begins with an environmental threat and opportunity profile. Many would subdivide this according to Political, Economic, Socio-cultural and Technological (PEST) dimensions. In addition to the general environment, it is worth taking a closer look at the competitive pressures in the industry, for example using Michael Porter's Five Forces framework.

PEST

As described in Chapter 1, cloud computing stands to exert a powerful influence across political, economic, socio-cultural and technological lines. The impact of these changes can shape the business environment of many organizations.

Political: There are many increasing regulations and compliance requirements surrounding data privacy and audit requirements that apply across information technology. To date the laws largely ignore the complexity that cloud computing introduces in terms of segregating the responsibilities of data owners and controllers. As the business model matures and becomes more commonplace there may be additional legislative changes that impact the political environment of corporations.

Economic: The IT financing model introduced by cloud computing tends to shift fixed and capital expenditures to variable and operational costs. As this approach takes hold across a given industry, it has the potential to reduce the average cost curves and accelerate break-even points for companies across the board, which can lead to increased price competition. Similarly, the refocus on core competencies may lead to increased product and process differentiation.

The outsourcing of IT infrastructure reduces the responsibilities and focus in the area of IT. This can be leveraged to realign the internal IT resources with the core competencies of the organization. Rather than investing energy and managerial commitment to industry standard technologies these can be redirected toward potential sources of sustainable competitive differentiation.

Socio-cultural: The social impact of cloud computing affects large organizations on two primary levels: customers and employees. Customers are beginning to see IT has an integrated fabric that combines both their physical and virtual worlds. Cloud computing promotes this notion by enabling large-scale interconnection of functional primitives through a publicly available service-oriented architecture.

The analytics that derive from the exponentially increasing information repositories enable new financial models at the expense of privacy and lowered privacy expectations. We are also witnessing a cognitive blending of human intelligence with system and network intelligence.

Technology: Cloud computing will directly impact all the technologies that are directly related to it, including IT services, software and hardware ranging from networking equipment to processors and memory. It may also spawn new technologies or interactions between technologies, such as mobile and print devices. But the most pervasive impact to monitor is how increased agility, risk-reduced experimentation and modular service-orientation can lead to a faster pace of launching new technologies.

ASSESS

A general theme, which cuts across all aspects of the environment, is the increased agility that cloud computing promotes. There are several operational imperatives that follow from living in an agile world. First-mover advantage becomes paramount. It therefore is critical to act early, potentially at the expense of deferring systematic planning. If the initiative does succeed, it needs to have the support in place to build on it, globalize it and scale it up, before the competition can catch up.

Disruptive changes in the environment can also lead to dramatic market shifts in seemingly unrelated areas. Carr (2009) describes how the advent of distributed electricity enabled distributed refrigeration which, in turn, led to the demise of the ice distribution and storage business.

Cloud computing may facilitate significant growth in social collaboration technologies, which need little more than a software platform, some creative ideas and an excited user base. But it is also putting severe pressure on traditional content and media industries. Carr (2009, p. 152) elaborates on the decline of print media which is hard-pressed to compete with electronic distribution and print-on-demand business models.

Porter's Five Forces

The impact of cloud computing will vary by industry. We would expect the information technology business to be profoundly affected, for example. But they are not the only ones. Any segment that commands a highly visible customer Internet presence or requires tight integration with suppliers and partners may also experience significant changes. Generally, the larger the proportion of the information technology budget is, compared to total spend, the higher the potential to leverage improved analytics and connectivity, which cloud computing may facilitate.

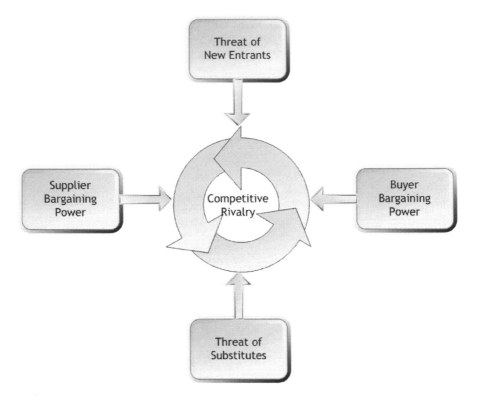

Figure 7-3: Porter's Five Forces

In order to assess a given industry, it is helpful to use a tool such as the Five Forces framework developed by Michael Porter(1979). He identified five areas that tend to influence the level of industry competition and therefore the profitability of businesses in the industry (Figure 7-3).

Threat of new entrants considers the likelihood that additional competitors will enter the industry. It is primarily influenced by various forms of entry barriers, such as economies of scale and switching costs of customers.

The main thrust of cloud computing is to lower entry barriers. Utility-priced computing reduces the up-front capital investment, which is an important entry barrier. But the significance of this reduction will vary by sector according to the proportion of IT spend from the overall budget. Increased outsourcing may also minimize learning curve effects since customers can rely on external competencies.

At the same time, a lack of interoperability may inflate switching costs since customers cannot easily replace one product with another. This obstacle represents an increased entry barrier, which may be addressed over time with future standardization efforts.

While these considerations apply most prominently to computing resources, they are not limited to them. As we evolve toward everything as a service, we can expect to also see a trend of information, processes and physical operations (e.g. printing) offered as services. If they are available on-demand they may also represent historic barriers that no longer effectively inhibit market entry.

ASSESS

Buyer Bargaining Power refers to the ability of customers to dictate business terms. If they are easily able to switch to other providers or products, they can demand lower prices for increased functionality and quality. Some trends that cloud computing might accelerate include improved information, facilitated backward integration and the collective power to impose service orientation.

Since the web model increases the availability of information regarding substitutes and competitive products, buyers find it increasingly easy to determine which products suit their needs at the best price. Rather than relying on historic relationships with the suppliers they can leverage online auctions and marketplaces. These facilities, in turn, represent pure services that can benefit enormously from utility models as well as the functionality incorporated into many of the cloud platforms.

Backward integration potential toward service providers is another factor that influences customer power. It is very closely related to the threat of new entry. Since services should be modular to facilitate universal consumption, it is much easier for a potential buyer to assimilate its supplier (or supplier's competitor).

Another factor in a flat global market is that the sheer number of potential customers can allow them to impose collective conditions if the requirements are common to all buyers. The fact that increased service orientation and standardization allow the customers greater flexibility can mean that they will come to expect and demand it from all providers.

Supplier Bargaining Power is the other side of the coin from buyer bargaining power. The comments above could be inverted for this section. However, it is important to consider that for any given organization the suppliers are probably in a different market than the buyers. The same conditions will therefore not necessarily apply, only the same principles.

Certainly the perspective will change and the focus will be on increasing your own information, investigating substitutes, and averting lock-in from your suppliers. But, in abstract terms, the same factors require consideration.

Threat of Substitutes refers to the availability of products that are not identical to yours but share common usage characteristics. Whether there are any and whether they represent a threat will depend very much on the industry. The key changes you can expect going forward are the increased agility that customers will have to experiment and compare relative price-performance information.

The current trends might not directly affect the availability of substitutes, but can have a significant impact on the speed with which they take hold if they are attractive to your customers. It is therefore critical to be more vigilant of market developments.

ASSESS

Competitive Rivalry is a measure of the competitiveness of the industry in dimensions of price as well as quality, innovation and marketing. As illustrated in Figure 7-3, it is a direct outcome of the other forces as well as factors such as the number of competitors and the rate of industry growth. If the environment becomes very hostile then it is questionable how profitable the industry will be in the long term.

Porter's Diamond

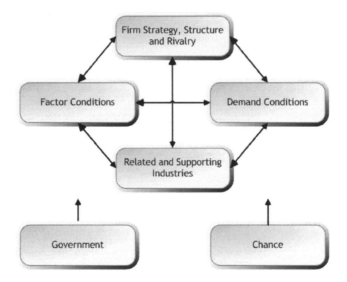

Figure 7-4: Porter's Diamond

Another contribution from Michael Porter is an economic model (called the "diamond model", Figure 7-4) that investigates the sources of international competitive advantage and postulates that six factors drive the regional success of a particular industry (Porter, 1998):

- Factor conditions such as human, physical and capital resources
- Demand conditions such as sophisticated customers
- Related supporting industries
- Firm strategy, structure and rivalry
- Government influences

- Chance

It is no coincidence that Japan leads the automotive industry while Italy excels in textiles and the U.S. in software. Porter makes the case that conditions which appear unfavorable, such as strict government regulations, demanding buyers and intense local rivalry, can increase the efficiency and innovation of the industry in a given region and make it easier for the companies domiciled there to compete internationally.

An interesting effect of cloud computing is that it all but eliminates the physical barriers required for service delivery. The global nature of the Internet means that consumers and producers need no longer be part of the same territory or jurisdiction. Credit-cards and other online payment services are virtually agnostic to the location of their users. Processes, information, computation and storage can easily cross regional boundaries.

However, there still are physical resources that underpin the services and they will dictate the competitiveness of the providers who leverage them. Internet-based service delivery facilitates increased flexibility of organizations to source their services internationally and to market their products to other geographies. It may be worth considering other options than those that have been successful in the past.

Internal Analysis

In addition to understanding the external environment, a corporate strategy also needs to consider its internal position. Some of the main topics to consider are the overall strategy used to achieve differentiation, the core competencies that help to establish this differentiation and the portfolio of products that the company will take to market.

Generic Strategy

Many business strategists use Michael Porter's classification of three general approaches to strategy (Porter, 1998):

- Segmentation
- Differentiation
- Cost Leadership

While no strategy is necessarily better than the other, each carries implications for the rest of the strategic process.

ASSESS

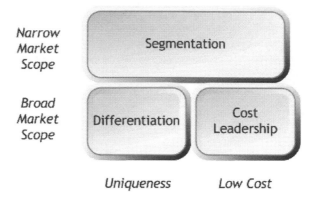

Figure 7-5: Generic Strategy

The two dimensions to this strategy are its market scope and the source of its differentiation (Figure 7-5). The scope refers to whether the company is targeting all segments of a particular market or instead is pursuing a niche. For those that are addressing the broad market, Porter distinguishes between those who are competing on cost and those that compete on unique competencies and qualities.

Agility

Conventional wisdom would suggest that cost leadership is generally less lucrative than differentiation and, obviously, only permits one clear winner while there may be several successful differentiated offerings. However sustainable differentiation, whether on cost or quality, is becoming increasingly difficult in a transparent world with widely published information that travels at the speed of light.

A consequence of these changes is a need for agility on two levels. Since first-mover advantage may be short-lived if the competition is able to successfully copy it, there is a requirement for an accelerated time to market. On-demand computing and services can add value by expediting the process of launching new market offerings. The sooner any advantage is implemented the longer the opportunity to skim high profits.

A more general means of attaining agility is by refocusing as much of the business as possible on core competencies. As Carr (2004) describes, IT is a critical corporate asset but often does not add any competitive value since most organizations have little unique competence in the area. If the resources can be redirected into areas of strategic specialization, they can more easily provide regular innovation that forms the basis of a sustainable advantage.

Core Competencies

Regardless of the generic strategy, the source of differentiation must be rooted in unique capabilities or it will not be possible to gain and maintain market share. If the advantage is to be sustained, it also needs to be an integral part of the organization.

We refer to these advantages as core competencies when they cannot be easily emulated and are able to contribute toward added value either in terms of product capabilities and quality or else in terms of more efficient production processes.

Product Focus

Once the sources of differentiation have been distilled into a set of core competencies, the challenge will be to determine how to leverage the advantages by developing and promoting the right products. This might mean investment in research and development, but it will also imply a vehicle for allocating resources amongst product lines and businesses.

Figure 7-6: Growth-share Matrix

A common model for resource allocation is called the growth-share matrix, which was originally developed by the Boston Consulting Group (Figure 7-6). The basic idea is to take the existing product portfolio and classify each according to its relative market share (compared to the largest competitor) and the overall market growth rate. A 2x2 matrix yields four quadrants:

Stars have a high share of a growing overall market. These are often targets of high investment since it is likely they will be quite profitable.

Question Marks currently have low market share but are placed in markets with high growth. It is possible that with some additional investment they may be able to become "Stars".

Cash Cows, on the other hand, have high market share but in a declining market. It may be possible to harvest the profits from this product line and redirect them toward "Question Marks" or "Stars" where higher returns on investment are possible.

Dogs have low share of a market that is not expected to grow. In most cases, the best course of action is to divest, or reduce investment in, these products.

There are three key questions to consider with respect to cloud computing:

- Will there be any market shifts that drastically change the anticipated market growth of any of the products?
- Can market shifts change the relative market share of any of the products?
- Does the advent of a utility model change the financing requirements for pursuing any of the products?

Strategic Realignment

After you have looked at both the developing environment and the internal structure of the company in light of cloud computing, the next step is to match the two and draw your own conclusions as to how you can best meet and exceed your strategic objectives.

In order to maximize chances of success, it is vital to perform a multi-tier analysis. It may be worthwhile to begin with a high-level workshop and follow up with interviews of all key players. The mechanics will vary from organization to organization, but cloud computing will impact the business across the hierarchy, so it is necessary to solicit input from all businesses at both executive and operational levels.

A gap analysis can be a good starting point. If you can identify the pain points in current operations, and the obstacles that inhibit performance, there may well be areas where aspects of cloud computing, service orientation and outsourcing can contribute to realignment with the strategy.

Similarly, industry benchmarks, often expressed as ratios that can be used as baselines for costs, performance and quality, can uncover areas where improvement is necessary in order to address competitive disadvantages or leverage advantages to their maximum.

	Internal	External
	Strengths	Opportunities
	Weaknesses	Threats

Figure 7-7: SWOT Analysis

A full SWOT analysis (Figure 7-7) can be instrumental in carrying forward the exercise. There is no reason to restrict it to the effect of cloud computing but it is worthwhile to reconsider every aspect of strategic choice from the perspective of the cloud. In particular, two questions should challenge every decision:

- How will cloud computing change the market landscape, including customers, partners, suppliers and competitors? How will the company react to those changes and leverage them to its benefit?
- How can the business leverage new service-based resources to its competitive advantage?

Let's go through a few topics that might merit consideration.

Minimize Costs

Improvements in cost structure are vital to companies pursuing a cost-leadership strategy. But even for those that focus on other forms of differentiation, additional cost relief will improve profitability and give more flexibility for other investments.

Cloud computing can help to pursue this strategy but there is no guarantee that it will always save costs. And even if it does, there may be other means to achieve the same results through standardization and outsourcing.

Maximize Agility

Similarly, flexibility is very important to companies in a rapidly changing environment. An agile infrastructure makes it much easier to accommodate innovation and experimentation. It also facilitates a quick path to market if pilots and prototypes prove successful.

Improve Integration

A global service-oriented architecture presents many opportunities for improved integration between partners, suppliers and customers. External resources can be easily shared and Web services can facilitate extensive collaboration.

Thomas Friedman (2007, p. 457) makes the case that value creation is becoming so complex that no single firm can master it without closely collaborating with a wide set of partners. From an infrastructural perspective, externalization of data and processes, for example through cloud computing, can create a secure foundation for collaboration that will eventually be indispensible.

The ease of provisioning extranets makes the organization more agile as it establishes lightweight, short-term partnerships and outsources granular services to external providers. By reducing the transaction costs of contractual collaboration, the company can effectively leverage external resources without engaging in full-scale mergers and acquisitions or setting up joint ventures.

At a lower level, an increasing number of data sources are becoming available in the form of web services. Companies that are able to leverage these effectively have an advantage over their competition, especially if they are able to extract business intelligence by combining the data with their internal information and that of their partners.

By the same token, there can be significant benefit in exposing connection points to internal services. While some caution is necessary, maximizing the integration surface can facilitate additional channels of transporting value to the market. Simply put, an ecosystem can have more impact and generate more collective capability than any one organization.

Whether the interfaces are inbound or outbound, they are safer and easier to federate if the content and services reside outside of the enterprise. There is still a need to diligently define connectivity and access controls. However, this effort does not need to be fully replicated for each partner who comes on board.

Focus on Core Competencies

The increased service orientation of cloud computing elevates the importance of identifying and analyzing competitive differentiation. After establishing core competencies and determining whether they lead to a business benefit, the key question is whether they are indeed unique and the uniqueness is sustainable.

For example, it is worth asking how much of IT should be delivered by internal sources. If similar commoditized services are available on the market for a much cheaper price, then it is certainly legitimate to investigate whether it would be possible to leverage them.

There may also be alternate forms of delivering the services. Again using IT as an example, self-service portals can reduce human involvement and lower the costs of the same basic service. The resources released would then also be free to focus on other areas in which they can increase shareholder value.

In some cases, elements of a competency may be truly unique and valuable but they are intertwined with other tasks and responsibilities that are undifferentiated. A general purpose IT application with customized enhancements for key business processes might fall in this category. The question is whether it will be possible to extricate the generic function and source it from another provider. There is no universal answer but it is a point that deserves consideration where it applies.

A related question is whether it is possible to monetize the core competencies in other ways than they were originally intended. The competitive advantages may be intended for streamlining production processes or developing higher quality products. But that doesn't mean that they cannot also be leveraged for other purposes.

In the same way that intellectual property can be used internally and/or licensed, you may decide that you can have your cake and eat it too. Particularly if you have software-based solutions, you may want to consider the business model for packaging the functionality and selling it as a service to other customers.

Note that there may be far-reaching ramifications to a refocus of competencies. If the product portfolio is overhauled there may be cause for reshuffling the resources and responsibilities between divisions. There could even be further implications. For example, if central functions (e.g. IT) become less horizontal in focus it might make more sense to allocate them to the business units or to move the entire organization to a divisional rather than functional structure.

Shift to Maintain Competitive Advantage

Market shift is nothing new. It is a continuous process that every company should be monitoring. The corporate strategy should always reflect changes in the industry landscape not only of competitors but also of suppliers and customers. The markets may also be in flux as new segments gain, and others lose, in importance or as some geographical barriers dissolve while others are erected.

The impact of cloud computing on these shifts can come in two variants. There may be a direct effect of on-demand services in some industries. Even where the effects are not as obvious, it may accelerate changes in the landscape so that vigilance becomes much more critical.

The direct impact of utility models is not limited to technology. Information, consulting and business processes may also be made available on demand. Almost all industries consume these and most of them also provide them – or at least have the potential to provide them.

Chapter 7: Strategic Impact

The indirect impact is even more extensive. Even those organizations that do not offer any form of service will undoubtedly engage in transactions with others that do. If cloud computing is truly disruptive and impacts this ecosystem, it will accelerate the changes in the partner landscape.

ASSESS

On a practical level, it may be necessary to review and revise strategies more frequently in the future than in the past, regardless of industry. For those companies that see changes on the horizon, it may be wise to begin considering alternatives. If entry barriers are disappearing, is there any way to erect new barriers by focusing developments in a direction that is less accessible? If some product lines are under threat, are there others that were previously dismissed due to prohibitive investment requirements but are now viable? If some market segments are approaching saturation, is it possible to pursue others, for example through micro-segmentation or focus on the "long tail" of low-volume merchandise?

Chapter 8

ASSESS

Risk Impact

One of the most important aspects of strategy is risk. It is impossible to predict with any degree of accuracy what will happen when an organization begins to execute on its plans. Humans define strategy, so there is also some room for error in the original plan. It's quite possible that executives misinterpreted some of the environmental pressures or are misguided in their view of the internal competencies. Even if the plan is optimal, there is always the chance it will go off course because the environment or the organizational change.

Emerging technologies and novel service delivery models introduce new technical challenges and business risks. Of the millions of companies that eventually adopt outsourced utility services, some will be successful while others will become less profitable and competitive. A few will barely survive, and the least fortunate may not even manage to stay solvent.

Notion of Risk

The worst-case scenario serves as a deterrent for any change in the organization. However, risks are not all bad. In fact risks can be used to establish and maintain competitive advantage. As such, risk avoidance may actually put a company in a worse position than it would be in by taking some chances – failing in some and succeeding in others. The challenge is to select which risks to accept and how best to cope with them.

Risk Management

ASSESS

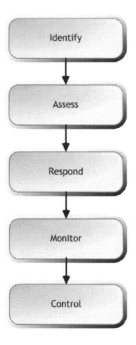

Figure 8-1: Risk Management Steps

There are many ways to break down a risk analysis. I have divided it into five phases which flow sequentially from one to the next (Figure 8-1).

Identify

Risk identification often starts with informal collection processes, such as brainstorming. A more systematic approach would consider all physical and logical assets (such as payment and personal information, intellectual property or even business processes) and attempt to enumerate all the threats they could undergo. Even though it may be an unattainable goal to come up with an exhaustive list, there is some value in going through a rigorous process to uncover as many risks as possible.

An alternate, or preferably parallel, approach is to keep abreast of industry information (such as analyst recommendations and publicized vulnerabilities). Although there are no guarantees that you will stumble across all pertinent analyses, this does provide a good way to tap into the collective experience of the rest of the industry. And typically, forums and newsgroups that focus on risks and security are very quick to report any recent interesting developments.

You can get a good start by leveraging some of the published and ongoing risk assessments that relate to cloud computing including:

- Cloud Computing Risk Assessment (ENISA, 2009)
- CSA Guidance (Cloud Security Alliance, 2011)
- ISACA Cloud Computing White Paper (ISACA, 2009)
- Cloud Security and Privacy, a book that takes a focused look at potential risks of cloud computing (Mather, Kumaraswamy, & Latif, 2009)

To develop a full threat and risk model, you need to consider all the interrelationships between events. Some risks (called cascade risks) may trigger other events that have further side-effects; and you may find that some events can be caused by other sources than the initial threat model exposed.

The collection of interrelated effects may be analyzed in an integrated fashion through the use of a Risk Interdependency Field. Roberts, Wallace and McClure (2007, p. 8/3) define a three-dimensional field for structuring all the risks experienced by an organization. It is possible to categorize risks into a two-dimensional matrix based on their level (Strategic, Change/Project, Operational and Unforeseeable) as well as the functional divisions affected (e.g. Process/Production, People/HR, Finance, Support/Administration/IT and Interface/Sales/Marketing).

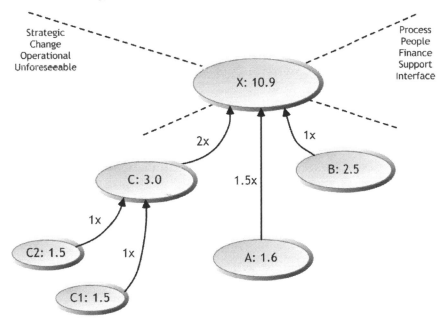

Figure 8-2: Risk Interdependency Sub-nodes and Link Multipliers[1]

[1] Reproduced by permission of Alex Roberts, William Wallace and Neil McClure.

Chapter 8: Risk Impact

Within the intersections of risk level and function, there are often hierarchically structured risks. For example, component failures in an IT system can lead to server failure, which may subsequently lead to service and system failure. A visual depiction of a risk breakdown structure can be helpful in clarifying the interdependencies between risks (Figure 8-2).

One last consideration that is very important in identifying security risks is that the environment is highly dynamic. Regulations are constantly updated and enforced with varying levels of rigor. New technology exploits and patches are released regularly. The cloud service provider landscape is still volatile with many new entrants, and some failures, every year.

It is important to look not only at current issues but also attempt to contain possible future risks. Predicting the future is never easy. However, there are techniques that can help. For example, the ENISA Emergent and Future Risk Framework is an approach that uses trend analyses and scenario planning (ENISA, 2009).

Assess

	Static	Speculative
Internal	System Failure	Availability, Performance
External	Terrorist Attack	Market Shift

Table 8-1: Examples of Risk Types

The next step is to classify and evaluate all the risks that we've identified. There are several dimensions of classification (Table 8-1). It may be useful to distinguish between risks where there is a potential benefit (speculative risk) or only a potential loss (static risk). For instance, the risk of a reduction in availability is speculative since there is also the possibility that availability will increase. On the other hand, the risks of data leakage or natural disasters are static risks. The best case is that they do not happen.

It is common to differentiate between internal and external risks. Internal risks are often easier to contain since the organization exercises some degree of control over them. External risks are largely random or a function of the environment that is difficult to predict or influence.

This distinction is very relevant to cloud computing. Public cloud services are, by definition, external. The release of control that cloudsourcing implies is one of the biggest obstacles in the adoption of cloud computing. By itself, externalization of control increases risk. However, it is possible to compensate the effect with supplementary controls and governance mechanisms.

Another factor is the scope of the risk, which measures the amount of the organization that is exposed to it. A risk that jeopardizes the whole organization is obviously much more serious than one that affects only a single business or project. Most importantly, it is critical to estimate the potential impact that the risk can have and the likelihood of it becoming real.

A mathematical calculation is very convenient since it can help to aggregate multiple risks together and present the combination with a single number. Unfortunately, precise quantification can also be misleading since it masks much of the complexity and hides the assumptions used to make the estimate. Furthermore, it tends to neglect some of the unforeseen risks that do not lend themselves to quantification at all.

Respond, Monitor and Control

At this stage we are looking at risk primarily from the vantage point of whether cloud computing is a viable solution at all. We will return to the question again in Chapter 27, where we will consider how to respond to specific risks that arise in the course of implementing and operating outsourced services.

For the sake of completeness, however, I'll finish off the overview of the process here by stating that after we have established the risks and their importance we must decide what to do about them. We have several options including transferring the risk to other parties, accepting the risks or walking away from the opportunity.

Regardless of the option we choose to address the risk, we need to establish procedures to continuously monitor the risk profile. This means we must detect and prevent any threats that have been identified.

Cloud Impact

The impact of cloud computing on enterprise risk can be both positive and negative.

Reduced Risk

Every case of outsourcing changes the risk profile of the customer since it shifts some responsibilities (and therefore risks) from the company to the provider. Although the same problems may still present themselves, the contractual transfer mitigates the customer risks by providing some form of indemnity that should compensate for any loss.

There may also be reason to expect fewer incidents to occur given the cloud providers' advanced position on the experience curve. With best-of-breed processes and personnel, they can afford specialized staff and are in a position to

Chapter 8: Risk Impact

rapidly provision and scale security resources both proactively and reactively (after an incident breaks out).

The economy of scale of the provider also reduces the risk of exceeding capacity when demand surges. Cloud services can draw on a larger pool of resources, so they can absorb localized spikes much more easily.

The wide geographical presence of many cloud service providers allows them to replicate remotely much more effectively thereby reducing the likelihood of a complete loss in the face of a natural or man-made disaster.

Cloud providers may also improve content delivery through extensive geographical representation. Decreased latency and dependency on fewer network hops reduces the number and magnitude of service delivery failures to end customers.

Considered from a very different perspective, officially authorized cloud service solutions may reduce the number and usage of rogue clouds. Without an official cost-effective solution to trial new services in a timely manner, the businesses, some departments, or even individual users, may subscribe to their own external services. The result can range from suboptimal resource allocation, to non-compliance with legal restrictions and a compromise of information security policies.

Finally, cloud computing provides a company with a means to reduce strategic risk. In a highly dynamic environment with regular market and industry shifts, the organization may need a way to react quickly and scale faster than it has been able to do in the past. On-demand activation and elasticity of resources give the company this flexibility.

Increased Risk

Unfortunately, there are also some areas where cloud computing can increase the risk of a company.

The aforementioned shift of some responsibilities from the company to the provider may reduce some risk through contractual transfer. However, it may also increase risk by diminishing the control of the company over business-critical services. This means that customers cannot dictate the amount of effort that should be directed at solving a particular problem nor can they shape the direction of that effort.

Service-level agreements can cover broad performance indicators, but they only serve as an approximation of the enterprise needs. Outages, downtime and poor user experiences can have direct financial consequences in terms of failed transactions. Furthermore, they can diminish user acceptance and tarnish the image of the company. It is difficult to accurately quantify these effects and convince the service provider to compensate them fully.

Storing data outside the corporate firewall will be seen by many security practitioners as a potential vulnerability. If the information is exposed to hackers or competitors, there is potential damage in terms of exposed intellectual property and competitive information, a loss of confidence from customers, suppliers and partners and, in some cases, potentially also legal liability for the damages that result.

In the past few years, there has been an increase in the number and scope of regulatory provisions that govern information processing across the world. Violation of these articles can carry heavy financial penalties to companies as well as to board members and senior management. Cloud computing obfuscates the location as well as the security provisions that protect it. While this lack of visibility may inhibit targeted attacks, it makes it very difficult for an enterprise to validate compliance with all relevant laws.

The problems are only partially mitigated by standards and third-party auditing mechanisms, which are not yet fully refined for cloud computing and typically do not cover all components involved in the service delivery. Furthermore, problems of control and accountability are complicated by the fact that the architecture caters to openness and heterogeneity with the consequence that there are often many different service providers and subcontractors involved in any solution.

Lastly, there is an inherent risk in adopting any new technology. By definition less is known about it and it is less mature than conventional mechanisms. Intuitively, it will almost always be easier and less risky to stay stationary with the existing products and processes than to embark on an unknown experiment. However, in a dynamic business environment staying stationary may no longer be an option.

Risk Assessment

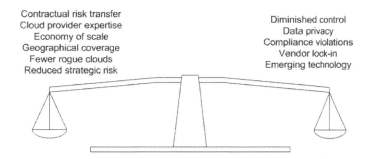

Figure 8-3: Risk Balance

After putting together the list of risk-related arguments in favor of cloud computing and against it, we need to determine how they weigh up (Figure 8-3). The most primitive test would be a simple count. It would be easy. However, it

ASSESS

would add little value since it depends very heavily on how the issues are dissected and classified. Anyone could manipulate the balance by simply decomposing an issue into multiple parts.

Some organizations use ranking and prioritization mechanisms to differentiate between the issues. A better option is to assign a weight to each of the concerns. Even better is to also estimate both the impact of a threat and the probability that the risk will become active.

Table 8-2 and Table 8-3 offer simple examples of what such a prioritization might look like, both for the case that the enterprise pursues cloud computing and the scenario that it chooses to defer or avoid cloud services.

The estimates are ultimately subjective at this stage. Nevertheless, the numeric values provide a systematic framework for analyzing the risks and helps to focus discussions. It is also noteworthy that neither the probability nor the impact of the risk is necessarily a static value. In Chapter 27 we will look at options that the enterprise may pursue to reduce some of the risk.

	Impact	Probability	Product
Data Leakage	10	2	20
Service Failure	9	4	36
Resource Exhaustion	5	2	10
Non-compliance	8	2	16
Data Loss	7	3	21
Technology Shift	1	5	5
			108

Table 8-2: Sample Risk Prioritization of Cloud Adoption

	Impact	Probability	Product
Idle Resources	2	10	20
Resource Exhaustion	8	4	32
Hardware Obsolescence	3	7	21
Technology Shift	7	6	42
Inability to react to market change	8	6	48
			163

Table 8-3: Sample Risk Prioritization of Cloud Avoidance

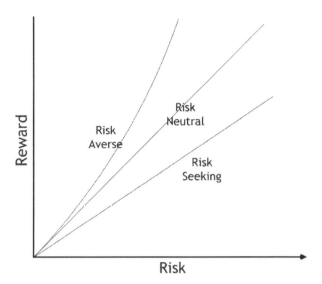

Figure 8-4: Risk Attitude

Another dimension to consider is the risk appetite of the decision makers (Figure 8-4). This is traditionally done by classifying them as risk seeking or risk averse depending on the value that they demand from a given risk. While both personalities would prefer maximum value for minimum risk they differ in the thresholds they require. A risk seeker is willing to accept considerable risk for relatively little value in return. On the other hand, a risk-averse strategist would only undertake significant risk for very high potential returns.

Enterprise Wide Risk Management

A simple classification of risk tolerance has advantages. The organization can quantify the risk and then make a simple calculation to determine what the necessary return would be to justify the risk. However, a growing awareness of the importance of risk in corporate business has spawned the development of more sophisticated tools to deal with it.

The trend today is to look at risk management across the organization in an integrated manner (Meier, 2000), not unlike the approach generally taken for financial planning. No enterprise would allow completely unconstrained and uncoordinated budgeting across its line management.

ASSESS

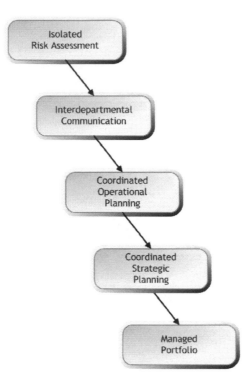

Figure 8-5: Risk Management Maturity Level

From a perspective of Risk Management there has been an evolution that began with each department assessing each project on its own. The first step of integration was simple cross-functional communication followed by a common risk management strategy (Figure 8-5).

The second phase includes considering risk management in general planning decisions, first at the operational and then at the strategic level. A fully integrated system is one where the risks are not only considered collectively in aligning with objectives but are treated as a single risk portfolio.

Portfolio Risk

Financial institutions exhibit the greatest variety of portfolio risk. It is no surprise, therefore, that the model originated in their sector. The Basel II accords are intended for banks, funds and insurance companies and help to calculate minimum deposit requirements for these institutions, but the model is being increasingly adopted for firms in other industries too.

Basel II classifies risk into three categories and recommends a valuation model for each:

Market Risk (Value at Risk approach preferred)

- Equity risk (stock prices will change)
- Interest rate risk (interest rates will change)
- Currency risk (exchange rates will change)
- Commodity risk (commodity prices will change)

Credit risk

- Risk of loss due to debtor's non-payment
- Standardized approach: (risk is weighted according to external credit rating agency) * percentage of portfolio

Operational risks (e.g. information, personnel)

- Risks resulting from failed internal processes, people and systems
  - E.g. internal/external fraud, employment practices, workplace safety, damage to physical assets
- Basic Indicator Approach (annual revenue of institution)
- Standardized approach (revenue of business lines)
- Advanced measurement approaches including IMA, LDA, Scenario based,) – own empirical model with regulatory approval

Collective consideration of all risks of an organization is useful because it provides insight into the overall exposure of the company. An organization is limited in how many concurrent problems it can withstand and what level of management can be dedicated to monitoring and mitigating risks to avoid these problems.

A unified architecture can set portfolio targets and risk limits. It can then draw information across all organizational activities to present a transparent and complete picture to all stakeholders including the board of directors, regulators and equity analysts. As an added benefit, it also facilitates the development of advanced risk analytics to monitor risk-adjusted profitability and optimize the portfolio composition.

Chapter 9

ASSESS

Financial Impact

In Chapter 1, we looked at financial benefits and drawbacks in conceptual terms. In order to argue a business case, we need to look at several financial indicators. The most important consideration will usually be the return on investment (ROI), which can be quantified with metrics such as net present value (NPV) or internal rate of return (IRR). But there are several other points to consider including cash flow, financial visibility and return on assets.

Resource Costs

Before looking at the structure of an investment proposal, let's begin with an assessment of variable and fixed resource costs. The tradeoff between these two underpins the value proposition of usage-based pricing over a capital investment.

It would be challenging to cover every single scenario, but I have chosen four different workload patterns to illustrate the main factors of volatility and predictability.

Static Workload

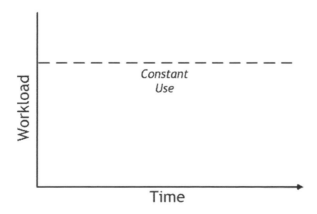

Figure 9-1: Static Workload

The simplest scenario is a static workload, where the application requires a constant amount of resources (Figure 9-1). Imagine a public service that is priced at $2000/month for the combination of compute instance and storage required.

To determine the private equivalent, we can start with hardware depreciation and software license costs. For example, $18'000 in hardware and software depreciated over three years (36 months) would yield a rate of $500/month. Your initial impression may therefore be that the public service is unattractive.

However, the picture tends to change as you add an allocation for the infrastructure, including facilities, networking and power/cooling. Combined, these often exceed the hardware costs and might put you at $1000/month.

Finally, you would add the fully loaded cost of all operational personnel. If the cost of an administrator is $10'000/month and your average administrator manages 100 servers, then the operational cost for each server would be $100/month. If we assume the workload requires the administrative equivalent of ten servers, we would arrive at an operational cost of $1000/month.

In this simple calculation, the monthly cost of the private implementation is $500 (hardware/software) + $500 (infrastructure) + $1000 (operations), which is equal to the public cost of $2000, and there is no strong case for or against cloud computing.

However, the numbers will vary radically between organizations and applications. It is not uncommon to find support and administrative costs in the region of ten times the hardware costs, for example. It is also important to consider the governance costs, which may be higher for a public than a private service.

Finally, when faced with static workloads, some large organizations can match and beat the costs of cloud services since they can achieve similar efficiencies through their own economy of scale. In these cases, the financial analysis requires a deeper study. For the remaining discussion, let us assume the internal cost of the workload is only $1000/month. Does that mean the cloud service priced at $2000/month is out of the question? It depends!

Periodic Workload

The calculation is fundamentally different for periodic workloads (Figure 9-2). If the resources are only used part of the time, then we bear the full cost with a fixed investment but only pay a fraction for a variably priced service.

For example, if we assume usage of 25%, then the internal monthly cost would still be $1000 while the cloud cost would drop to $500 ($2000 x .25) and suddenly look much more attractive.

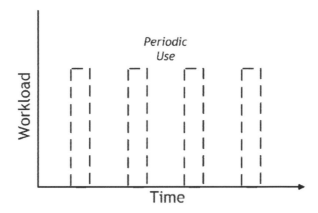

Figure 9-2: Periodic Workload

Before we let the pendulum swing too far in the other direction, however, we need to consider the case of a private cloud. The fact that a particular service has an irregular usage pattern doesn't immediately lead to the need for a public service. If workloads are complementary, many organizations can achieve similar benefits through virtualization.

Periodic Incremental Workload

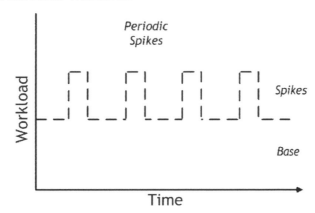

Figure 9-3: Periodic Incremental Workload

The picture in Figure 9-3 is typical for some workloads. Furthermore, when application consumption is aggregated through virtualization, almost all private clouds will manifest an uneven usage pattern over time. For organizations that are able to run a static workload more efficiently internally, the combined pattern presents a new opportunity.

Conventional wisdom would recommend to "own the 'base' and rent the 'spikes'" (Weinman & Lapinski, 2009). For example, if the workload represents the sum of the two previous examples, then we would invest in an internal im-

ASSESS

plementation of the minimum workload and source the additional periodic requirements from the public cloud.

	Private	Public	Hybrid
Fixed Workload	$1000	$2000	$1000
Variable Workload	$1000	$ 500	$ 500
Total	$2000	$2500	$1500

Table 9-1: Hybrid Cost

As shown in Table 9-1, this allows the organization to combine the lower cost of the fixed workload in the private cloud with the utility-priced variable workload and thereby achieve a financial advantage over the basic private and public options. The numbers certainly look compelling!

However, unfortunately the implementation is not always trivial. It means that there must be a mechanism to connect applications and transfer parts of the workload from one service provider (e.g. the internal private cloud) to another (e.g. the external public cloud). As discussed in Cloud Computing Architected (Rhoton & Haukioja, 2011), workload mobility is a highly desirable feature that is still rare.

Unpredictable Workload

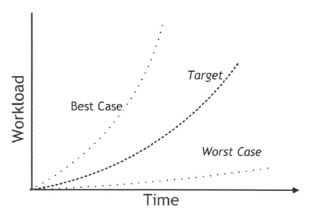

Figure 9-4: Unpredictable Workload

One last factor to consider is the predictability of workloads. Many applications may grow and shrink in many unforeseeable ways. The launch of a new application is probably the most typical case of unpredictable demand. Since the projections for usage and associated resource requirements may diverge widely depending on the success of the service, it is often very difficult to allocate fixed infrastructure that is cost-effective for both a best and worst case scenario (Figure 9-4).

To top it off, it may be almost impossible to determine a reliable range of outcomes at all. The projections may be widely off-base. We may calculate optimistic and pessimistic cases and arrive at the conclusion that a private implementation is the most cost-effective; but reality may turn out better or worse than we expected.

Since the risk of both under-provisioning (and not being able to fulfill the service) or over-provisioning (and wasting idle resources) can be costly, there is a case to be made for paying a premium to preserve agility.

ASSESS

Return on Investment

The value proposition of usage-based costing sets the scene but doesn't complete the business case. In simple terms, the profit equals the revenue less the costs.

$$Profit = Revenue - Cost$$

So, you must quantify the relevant impact on revenue and cost of a given proposal and take the difference in order to determine if it is profitable.

In a typical scenario, you make a one-time investment (such as the transition to a cloud service), which temporarily increases your costs above the current baseline (shown as a dashed line in Figure 9-5). However, after the initial investment, the ongoing costs reduce to below the baseline. Your financial budgeting task is to determine whether the total is better or worse than if you don't undertake the investment.

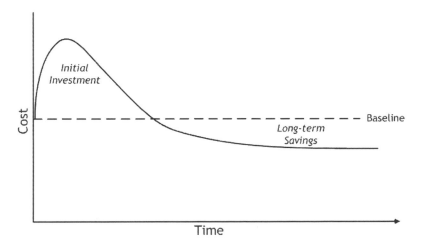

Figure 9-5: Cost of investment

An alternate visualization would be to look at the cumulative cost of the investment over time (Figure 9-6). Assuming an initial increase and subsequent reduction in costs, the curves should intersect when the "payback period" is complete. After this point the investment can be considered profitable.

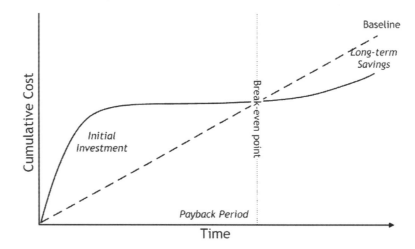

Figure 9-6: Cumulative Cost of Investment

Unfortunately, financial analyses are seldom quite this simple. There are two complicating factors. Firstly, you must identify and measure the relevant costs. Secondly, it is not sufficient to make a profit. You need to make a profit in excess of what could be achieved from alternate investments. Let's look at both of these in more detail.

Relevant Costs

You can consider a number of different cost categories that may be relevant to the adoption of cloud computing:

Capital costs: The expected implication of utility computing is that you should see a curtailment in capital costs. These can include data center property and equipment costs as well as computer and networking infrastructure costs. Over the long run, there should definitely be a reduction in some of these areas. However, the biggest challenge is that a great portion of these costs have already been incurred and are therefore not relevant for near-term future considerations.

You can only justify inclusion of optional future costs in the equation. If the data centers are nearing capacity, and additional space would be needed in order to pursue internally sourced computing solutions, then these represent a significant capital cost. Shortage of energy in metropolitan areas makes building "local" data centers very difficult today, which has led to an escalation in costs.

Similarly, you may have existing equipment that is still operational. These historic costs are not relevant for current financial evaluations. However, once the technology has reached the end of its expected refresh cycle, it is valid to include the replacement costs in the investment decision.

Both property and equipment leases are common as an alternative to purchase. This only superficially changes the question, however, since relevance is directly related to the duration and renewal terms of the lease. If it can be terminated, the costs become relevant. Until then, they should be ignored.

Transition costs: The transition costs would include migration of data and applications to the selected cloud platforms and any necessary retraining of employees. It may also entail penalties for early termination of existing contracts and/or double-charges that must be sustained in order to avoid violating the contracts.

The costs of migrating to a cloud platform bear some similarity to the capital costs. Very often the main financial drivers are the reduction of capital costs versus the transition costs of moving to a new platform. It may be tempting to pit the two against each other.

However, there is one important distinction between them. Capital expenditures carry a recurring component. Property purchases from cash reserves may be an exception, but most other equipment, both in terms of buildings and information and communications technology, need to be renewed periodically. Accounting processes use a depreciation schedule based on the useful life of the assets to highlight this link.

On the other hand, transition costs, are truly one-time expenditures. It may be necessary to migrate other users or applications in the future, or in rare cases, to roll back and re-apply a migration. But for financial planning purposes these are independent, non-recurring costs.

Operational costs: The operational costs are an interesting area to examine. There will be some benefits that the cloud service provider can pass on to the customer in terms of economies of scale and advanced position on the experience curve. On the other hand, the operational expenditures now include not only the administrative tasks but the software licensing and equipment lease.

Small organizations that have little economy of scale of their own may still come out ahead, but large corporations often find the operational costs, examined in isolation, unattractive. The picture changes dramatically when you also include the amortized costs of equipment and property and the benefits of increased efficiency and reduced over-provisioning.

Personnel costs: If the transition to the cloud impacts employee roles and responsibilities, and particularly if it involves significant outsourcing, then it is necessary to look at the financial impact incurred. If there are directly at-

ASSESS

tributable redundancies, then the cost of the severance packages is a relevant cost.

Similarly, there may be costs associated with redeployment and retraining employees for other functions and responsibilities. It does not immediately follow that these will be net costs. Retraining can lead to improved efficiency and refocus may allow the workforce to add more value. However, unless it is possible to estimate the benefits with any degree of confidence, the convention of conservatism will mandate that the costs be allocated to the transition.

Support costs: These may change if, as a result of a transition of service, we see an increase or decrease in the number of calls/user/month or the average resolution time.

Soft costs: There are many internal metrics that do not directly equate to financial gain or loss. Reductions in user productivity and satisfaction have direct cost implications, but there is no standard way to measure them or to value them.

User productivity can be affected by the up-time of systems, the reliability of applications and connections, quality and efficiency of support. Customer satisfaction levels are tightly correlated to customer retention (which is generally considered to be vastly cheaper than targeting new customers). Employee satisfaction leads to reduced turnover as well as retention of company, customer, product knowledge and lower recruitment costs.

Under-provisioning costs can have huge impact as described in Chapter 6. However, they are also difficult to estimate both in terms of magnitude and frequency.

While these soft costs are all valid, they typically meet with significant skepticism from financial and executive officers. The premises of the calculations are easy to challenge and the estimates cannot be empirically substantiated. It is therefore usually better to add these arguments to the business case as "icing on the cake" rather than to base the case on them.

In order to make a viable proposal for cloud computing, it is necessary to consider all relevant costs of the baseline system and compare those with the costs of a cloud-based option. Some of the line items to consider include:

- Server hardware
- Storage hardware
- Client hardware (desktops and mobile devices)
- Network infrastructure (routers, switches, load balancers)
- Security infrastructure (firewalls, VPN concentrators, intrusion detection)

- Network connectivity (corporate bandwidth, employee remote access, cloud transfer charges)
- Software licences (clients and servers)
- Operations (backup, restore, upgrades)
- Support (troubleshooting, helpdesk)
- Service management (definition, negotiation, governance)
- Contract management (suppliers, service providers)

As alluded to above, the costs of each of these items may not easily be accessible and the comparison between historical costs and cloud-based estimates may not be straightforward. In some cases, there will be no reason to expect a change in costs. For example, it is possible that client hardware will be unaffected. However, it is also feasible that new applications will imply new end-user access devices.

The cost-basis could also differ. Cloud services will very often be billed according to usage rather than footprint, so it is critical to devise a means of calculating equivalence.

It would be legitimate to ask why we do not also consider relevant revenues in addition to relevant costs. There are certainly some opportunities that increased agility promises to provide. The challenge is similar to that of soft costs. It is difficult to project the potential benefits with any degree of accuracy. Nonetheless, it is certainly worth taking note of any specific ideas that appear probable and adding them to the business case even if they remain unquantified.

You may, for example, want to estimate productivity differences, whether they are in manufacturing, sales or administration. It can also be helpful to calculate the benefit of a faster time to market with new products and services or the advantages of accelerated partner on-boarding.

The most likely tangible revenue benefit is typically associated with any online services that the organization offers of its own. The elasticity of resources allows the company to react more quickly to surging demand, which directly equates to increased profitability.

Capital Budgeting

I hate to reflect on how many business cases I have seen put forward by expert technologists that have met with overwhelming skepticism from business leaders. All of the proposals forecast profitability and most were founded on compelling arguments.

Unfortunately, merely projecting higher revenue and lower costs, while necessary, is not sufficient cause for justifying an investment. I have observed two problems that tend to burden proposals, particularly around emerging technologies. The first is that anything new is inherently riskier than something that is known. Higher risk requires a higher rate of return. The second challenge is that most proposals compete with alternate investments for funds. As such, they must demonstrate that they are superior to the alternatives. These two obstacles are closely related.

Capital budgeting is a set of tools that can be used to measure the opportunity cost of an investment or to compare multiple alternate investments. At its simplest, it reflects the time value of money. If you don't invest the money in the project, you could earn interest at the bank or through other financial investments. We call this the opportunity cost of capital. In order to factor in this cost you need to discount all future cash flows (positive and negative) by the rate of interest you can expect.

$$NPV = \sum_{t=1}^{T} \frac{CF_t}{(1+i)^t}$$

To keep it simple, you assume each cash flow is at the end of a fixed period and that each period has the same anticipated rate of return (i). If the sum of the cash flows is greater than zero, then you have a positive net present value (NPV). You can also compare to alternate investments and select the one that promises the greatest NPV.

Another common approach for comparing investments is to calculate the internal rate of return (IRR). The IRR is the rate that would need to be selected in order for the investment to break even (with NPV=0). You can then determine whether your IRR is greater than the "hurdle rate" expected by the organization for this class of investment.

There are several technical drawbacks and restrictions to the use of IRR, particularly for comparing investments. NPV provides more reliable results and is universally applicable. However, IRR is still attractive to many managers, perhaps because it is a little easier to informally gauge the level of risk that the investment can sustain.

The biggest challenge in using these formulas is that the expected return, or hurdle rate, should be dependent on the risk of an investment. If you are able to quantify that risk then you can use the Capital Asset Pricing Model (CAPM) to determine the expected return with the following formula:

$$E(r_j) = rf + [E(r_m) - rf] \times \beta_j$$

where:

$E(r_j)$ is the expected return on the capital asset

rf is the risk-free rate of interest

$E(r_m)$ is the expected return of the market. $[E(r_m) - rf]$ is also called the market price of risk or market premium.

β_j is the beta coefficient of the asset returns to market returns (the covariance of j with the market divided by the standard deviation of the market)

Don't panic if you find some of the terms in the above equation daunting. Unless you are a financial analyst, you shouldn't need to work these formulas. The point is that you quantify the risk of an investment by examining the standard deviation of possible returns (simply put, whether there is a significant amount of variation between good and bad expectations). We call this value the beta coefficient, which is directly correlated to the required return on a capital asset.

However, we skipped the biggest challenge which is how to determine the risk. It is difficult to obtain empirical data on the possible returns for cloud computing, and without historical data you cannot calculate a standard deviation. This lack of insight may convince some business leaders to imply a high rate of risk and therefore demand an exorbitant rate of return.

Quite frankly, they may be right. It may be advisable to be conservative in estimating cloud computing until the services mature. However, it is always in your best interests to determine the risks and variability as precisely as you can so that you can address and monitor areas of uncertainty.

Assessing the financial risk of an emerging technology is challenging. You do have some options but they have their limitations:

Poll experts: You can ask subject matter experts for their estimate of the risk of the project and average those estimates.

Identify similar projects: If you can find sufficient similar projects that involve migrations using disruptive technologies and you can gather empirical data on those, then you could use it as a baseline.

Observe market: Over time there will be analyst data and published accounts of cloud-based implementations and migrations.

You may want to consider each of these to some degree. The bluntest instrument, but probably also the most common, is not to use any: just apply a standard companywide hurdle rate, optionally padded with a very subjective safety buffer. This is certainly easiest, but if you do have some additional insight you can bring to the table, it is well worth considering. If all indications converge, you can move forward with increased confidence; and if they diverge, then you may want to investigate the reasons.

ASSESS

Cash Flow

Profit and cash flow are two distinct financial indicators. The profit measures the amount of money accrued during a specific period, including discounts and deductions less the costs associated with producing the goods and services sold. The cash flow represents the amount of cash received less the cash outlays from financing, operations and investments.

While the two are closely related in the long term, they may differ significantly in the short term. For example, if the value of goods sold does not match the amount collected from customers, or the value of capital expenditures differs from the total depreciation, these will both lead to a divergence in the two metrics. There is no need for the two to be tightly correlated as long as the differences are understood. Company officers and financial analysts are generally much more concerned that both demonstrate a very healthy and profitable financial state even in the short term.

The same benefits of cloud computing typically apply for cash flow as for profit. For example, if it is possible to reduce capital expenditures, it will positively affect both the depreciation schedule and debt financing. However, the same challenge of an initial expenditure for implementation and migration also impacts the cash flow.

Even though a project may have a compelling long-term benefit, the fact that it requires an investment can be a deterrent, particularly in a very conservative economic climate. It is possible to circumvent the obstacle with "financial engineering", which is a fancy name for borrowing money. Some IT vendors have access to financing, which can be made available to customers who run into these obstacles. The benefit to the customer is that it is possible to accelerate the payback period by deferring some of the costs. The total amount will still be the same, or actually larger due to the financing charges, but the shape of the curve will change.

Other means of improving cash flow include reduction in inventory levels, faster billing and collection as well as deferred vendor payments. Cloud computing doesn't directly impact any of these. However, they all require very tight integration and flexible terms with partners along the supply chain, which is much more attainable when data and processes are standardized and securely externalized – features that are very closely associated with cloud services.

Financial Visibility

A utility pricing model greatly enhances financial visibility. Since costs are directly correlated to the revenue-generating products, and services that incur them, there is less need for assigning overhead costs and differentiating between direct and indirect costs.

If the resources are allocated to product lines during the subscription process, then it is possible to apply an activity-based costing model, which assigns the cost directly to the product lines that consume them. Even if the resources are shared within the organization, it may be possible to leverage the fine-grained instrumentation of the provider in order to apportion and assign the costs to the appropriate owners.

Return on Assets

One last financial metric that is worth mentioning is Return on Assets (ROA), computed as the net income divided by the average total assets. The ROA measures how well a company can leverage its assets and is often used to gauge efficiency. A high ROA can lead to better analyst and shareholder valuations and can even improve the cost of financing debt as it may impact the credit rating.

Since it varies inversely according to the asset valuation, it is in the company's best interest to keep the assets to a minimum, in order to be compared favorably to other companies in the same industry. Public cloud services can help in this regard. As they are not owned by the customer, they do not appear in the balance sheet and therefore imply lower asset values than privately run services.

Note that the ratio becomes dubious if taken to extremes. If you imagine a hypothetical example of 90% of your assets being in IT, you can multiple your ROA tenfold simply by outsourcing all services. It is unlikely that your efficiency will truly improve that dramatically. For this reason, ROA is not generally used to compare companies in different industries and should never be considered in isolation.

Design

DESIGN

Chapter 10

Requirements Analysis

DESIGN

Even the best strategy will fail unless a solid implementation process ensures a line of sight between the overarching mission of the organization and the execution of each element that supports it. It is impossible to overemphasize this point. Most projects fail because they are disconnected from the strategic thrust of the business, either because they are not aligned to the requirements, or because they have lost the executive commitment to see them through.

This need becomes even more obvious in the case of cloud computing, which is itself disruptive at many levels throughout the business. This chapter will examine several processes, or methodologies, to ensure alignment between the strategy and the implementation. There is some overlap to them. However, each has a slightly different focus and perspective, making them all useful at successive stages in the analysis.

The *Making Strategies Work* process caters to strategists, providing them with a means to validate that their plans and objectives are preserved in the organizational designs, processes and systems.

TOGAF provides a generic architectural framework, defining standard building blocks that can be used in conjunction with a variety of specific methodologies.

HPGM for ITSA, based on the Zachman framework, defines a succinct architectural process for ensuring that IT designs are aligned with business requirements.

Strategic Alignment

Most change in IT is driven bottom-up. Upper management does not typically monitor technology for opportunities that may impact strategy. However, they may dictate new requirements, in support of the business, that compel significant changes in IT.

Regardless of the catalyst for change, it is important that stakeholders retain involvement in the execution if it is to be successful. Particularly, if the changes are likely to disrupt business and impose changes, there is a good chance they will meet with some resistance.

DESIGN

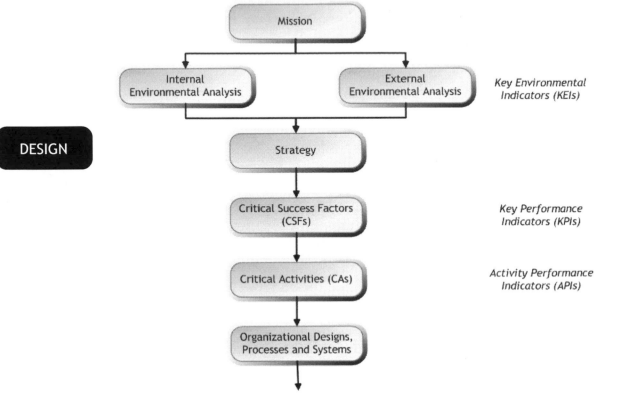

Figure 10-1: Making Strategies Work Framework[1]

Roberts and MacLennan (2006) have defined a framework (Figure 10-1) illustrating a chain of activities and deliverables that can help to maintain alignment between the strategy and implementation. The mission must be analyzed in terms of both the internal and external environment to obtain a strategy. From this strategy, it is critical to isolate the factors that are necessary to ensure its success and the activities that will guarantee those factors. The result may lead to implications for the organizational design as well as processes and systems.

From the perspective of the strategists, or executive sponsors, the decision to implement cloud computing is not a simple handoff to IT. It implies ramifications that may restructure the business. So it is imperative that there be ongoing executive commitment, oversight and, above all, a continuous reassessment of how, and where, to leverage cloud computing throughout the organization.

---

[1] Adapted with permission from Roberts and MacLennan

Architecture Development Cycle

When any new technology is introduced into an enterprise, it is important for the system architects to use a systematic methodology that aligns business requirements with design and implementation decisions. In the case of cloud computing, given its potential impact on corporate strategy, it is worthwhile to reassess the business drivers and enterprise architecture as comprehensively as possible.

DESIGN

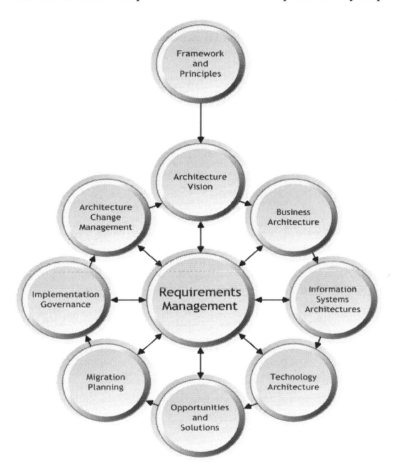

Figure 10-2: Architecture Development Cycle

As long as you follow a rigorous process there are many good methodologies you can use to build your architecture. TOGAF is rapidly becoming one of the most popular reference architectures, but there are others that accomplish the same objectives. The TOGAF Architecture Development Cycle involves a set of phases that all interact with the Requirements Management (Figure 10-2):

Preliminary Phase defines the roles and responsibilities of all involved in developing the architecture and ensures their collective commitment. It sets the foundation of the architecture by defining architectural principles, scope, assumptions and any component frameworks.

A: Architecture Vision defines the architecture scope. It also obtains the necessary approvals including endorsement from corporate management as well as validation of the business principles and goals from the respective business leaders. It is a concise sales pitch that articulates the key benefits of the proposal and a high-level description of the target environment.

B: Business Architecture defines a baseline business architecture that describes the product and service strategy as well as any relevant organizational, functional, process, information and geographic aspects of the business environment. It may involve significant modeling using activity models, use-case models, logical data models, node connectivity diagrams and information exchange matrices.

C: Information Systems Architecture includes the *Data* and *Applications Architectures*. The *Data Architecture* may encompass business data models (defining entities, attributes and relationships), entity-relationship diagrams, logical data models and data management processes including data dissemination, data lifecycles, and data security. The *Application Architecture* leans on views and models such as those from the TeleManagement Forum and the Object Management Group.

D: Technology Architecture defines a process that begins with a baseline description of the existing architecture. It considers alternative reference models, viewpoints and tools and uses these to create an architectural model of building blocks. After selecting the services portfolio per building block it confirms that the business goals and objectives are met. It then determines the criteria for specification selection, completes the architecture definition and conducts a gap analysis.

E: Opportunities and Solutions acts as a checkpoint to verify suitability for implementation by selecting among the primary options identified and assessing the dependencies, costs and benefits of each alternative. With these it generates an overall implementation and migration strategy accompanied by a detailed implementation plan.

F: Migration Planning includes work prioritization and the selection of major work packages. After assessing the dependencies, costs and benefits of various migration options, it specifies a detailed migration plan and further refines the implementation plan.

G: Implementation Governance provides architectural oversight of the implementation. This involves an architecture contract which governs the overall implementation and deployment process.

H: Architecture Change Management establishes processes and procedures for managing any subsequent changes to the architecture. They include continual monitoring for new technological developments and changes to the market and competitive environment. A change classification differentiates between simplification requests, incremental functionality and re-architecting changes.

Requirements Management defines a process to identify and store all enterprise architecture requirements so that they can feed into, and out of, all development phases.

Stakeholder alignment

DESIGN

The fact that Requirements Management is placed in a central position of the TOGAF Architecture Development Cycle illustrates its importance. A key consideration of TOGAF is the continuous alignment of all phases with the requirements and this process begins in the preliminary phase with the collective commitment of all stakeholders.

View	Primary stakeholders
Business	Business managers
	System acquirer
	Business analyst
Functional	System users
	Business process designers
	Information modelers
Technical	System developers
	Technology consultants
	Subsystem suppliers
Implementation	Project manager
	System developers
	System testers
	System deployers and operators/managers

Table 10-1: HP ITSA Stakeholders

To dig a little deeper into this notion, it is helpful to classify the stakeholders. I borrow from the HPGM for IT Strategy and Architecture (HP ITSA) – HP's structured approach to architecting Information Solutions. It is organized as a set of four fundamental views that address key stakeholder concerns: Business, Functional, Technical, and Implementation (Table 10-1).

Chapter 10: Requirements Analysis

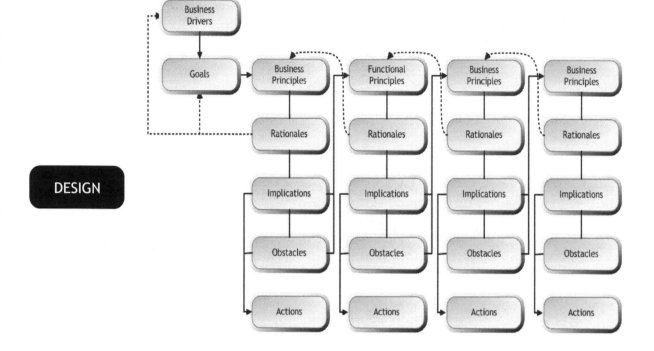

Figure 10-3: HP ITSA Stakeholder Alignment

All solutions are motivated by business drivers, goals, and metrics and expressed as a set of principles, models, and standards. These, in turn, are supported by an extensible framework of methods, tools, and techniques and linked to actions that ensure timely progress (Figure 10-3).

Since the process is not associated with any particular technology or service delivery model, cloud computing does not directly impact the approach itself. However, given the disruptive nature of cloud computing across many aspects of business and technology, it is likely to have a profound influence on the actual execution of a design based on ITSA. This impact can be visible in any of the four views (Table 10-2):

DESIGN

View	Content
Business	Business context for the solution. Why is the engagement being done–the motivations? • What are the internal and external business drivers? • What are the business models and processes? • Who participates in the business processes? • What are the project goals? • How will the success of the solution be measured?
Functional	What will the completed solution do? How will it be used? What information will it provide and to whom? What qualities must the system have? How will it be controlled? • Overall view of system operation, capabilities, services, attributes, … • Independent of technologies, products, and implementation
Technical	How, in general, will the system be structured and constructed with IT components? What standards will be used? • View of the applications, data, interfaces, component relationships, infrastructure • Focus on how the system attributes (such as performance, availability, scalability, security, evolvability, management, and others) will be achieved
Implementation	How, specifically, will the system be realized with IT components? • With which specific products and other components, from which vendors? • In what organization? • Using which processes? • How will it be validated, managed, and funded? • According to what plan (focus on staging/roll-out)? • View of the existing and/or known future technical and organizational constraints

Table 10-2: HP ITSA Views

The *Business* view targets business managers and analysts. It defines the business context for the solution by confirming the motivation for the engagement.

The view details the internal and external business drivers, business models, processes and key stakeholders and ensures they are aligned to project goals and success criteria. Cloud computing may trigger a shift in many markets due to the elasticity it introduces and many of the high capital expenditures it eliminates. It is critical to investigate whether this shift may disrupt the competitive landscape and also whether existing revenue streams may be jeopardized and/or alternate revenue streams may be created.

The *Functional* view is oriented toward business process designers and information modelers. It describes what the completed solution will provide and how it will be used. It provides an overall view of system operation, capabilities, services and attributes. The impact of cloud computing at this level is significant but indirect. It is important to analyze the new business models introduced in the business view and align these with the availability of new functional capabilities and services through a changing service provider landscape.

The *Technical* view addresses system developers and technology consultants. It offers technical insight into how the system will be structured and constructed with IT components and specifically which standards and interfaces will be used. The focus is on how the system attributes (such as performance, availability, scalability, security, evolvability, management, and others) will be achieved. For cloud computing it is important to consider the availability of new service delivery models, which offer public, private and hybrid cloud services and the complexity of multi-sourcing services from multiple providers. This may be partially achieved, or at least facilitated, through a strong service-oriented architecture. Standardization is a critical weakness in today's cloud offerings which makes it imperative that the technical view address options for avoiding vendor lock-in.

The *Implementation* view caters to project managers, system deployers and operators / managers. It describes in detail how the system is to be realized with IT components. This includes complete specifications of vendors, products, processes and configurations. In light of the trend toward Everything as a Service, it is worth considering cloud-based offerings for an increasing proportion of all the identified components of the system. These might be available at a high user and functional level through Software-as-a-Service offerings. It may be worthwhile developing parts of the system on a new cloud platform (e.g. Google App Engine, Microsoft Azure). Or it may be sufficient to leverage Infrastructure as a Service (e.g. Amazon EC2) merely to avoid capital expenditures and low-level system management. There are also cloud offerings covering a variety of other functions such as Identity Management, Governance and Testing. On the other hand, there will be situations where there is no need to use any cloud offering at all.

Chapter 11

Draft Architecture

DESIGN

The business strategy generates requirements, or critical success factors, that translate into activities with associated outcomes. Our next step is to chart out these processes and create an architectural design that supports them.

Business Process Modeling

Virtually all enterprise computing services support business processes. The best way to capture the required functionality in business terms is to model these processes and then map them to the technologies required to implement them.

Business Process Discovery

There are several ways you can go about identifying the business processes. There may already be a catalogue available if the organization has undergone a systematic Business Process Analysis exercise. Business leaders and other key stakeholders will typically have a good idea of the most important processes needed for their operations and may be able to provide a good overview through informal interviews. You may also be able to leverage a business analytics solution (such as Fujitsu's Automated Business Process Discovery service) to crawl your network in search of business processes.

Business Process Analysis

Once you have a set of processes to work on, the next step is to break them down into components. The human interface represents the primary set of constraints within which the systems will need to perform. In order to define the workflow, it is vital to identify authority boundaries, required expertise/experience and workload limitations. The analysis will also dictate who is able to execute each process as well as when, where and how they will perform their activities.

No process exists in isolation. There are inter-process relationships along the lines of shared information, technology and users. It is also important to highlight any external constraints, such as interfaces with partners, information from public sources, or government regulations.

A thorough analysis has the potential to highlight business process activities that may be optimized. In particular, procedures that can be defined deterministically often cover tasks that are suitable for automation. It may also be possible to identify synergies across processes or areas where processes can be consolidated.

DESIGN

The final result should give some assurance that the process will efficiently and reliably deliver the outcome expected. Checks and balances, combined with solid lines of governance and accountability should validate alignment with the corporate strategy.

One key aspect of this analysis is that it should clarify the parameters and specifications of all its interfaces. In the event that the process is chosen for outsourcing, or cloud-based delivery, these descriptions can form the basis of the contractual agreement.

Business Process Design

A comprehensive design involves a description of relevant processes at three layers.

- User Interface
- Business Logic
- Data model

You can build your designs with a tool to model data and control flows. The Unified Modeling Language (UML) from the Object Management Group (OMG) is an extensible and standardized general-purpose modeling language that offers a way to write system blueprints with conceptual components such as actors (users), business processes, system components and activities. These can be extended into the technical specifics of programming languages and database schemas.

The UML model is often depicted with a variety of graphical representations that have come to be closely associated with the language. These include Structure diagrams (illustrating the composition and behavior of system entities in terms of Class, Component, Composite structure, Deployment, Object structure, Package dependencies), Behavior diagrams (describing Use cases, Activity and State machines) and Interaction diagrams (portraying Communications, Interaction, Sequence and Timing).

Very similar diagrams are also possible using the Business Process Modeling Notation (BPMN) from the Business Process Management Initiative (BPMI). As is very often the case, the challenge is not in finding and selecting a good tool but in systematically applying the tool to achieve its objectives.

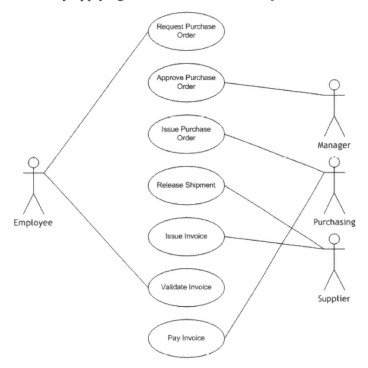

DESIGN

Figure 11-1: UML Use-Case

The starting point is to identify the relevant stakeholders and business partners and derive (e.g. by asking or inferring) from them the users of the application. A UML Use Case diagram may help to give a simple overview of who is involved in a given process (Figure 11-1). These individuals can provide you with further information on the business requirements, how the application should look, what data needs to be stored, reported, processed and what access controls you need to enforce on the information.

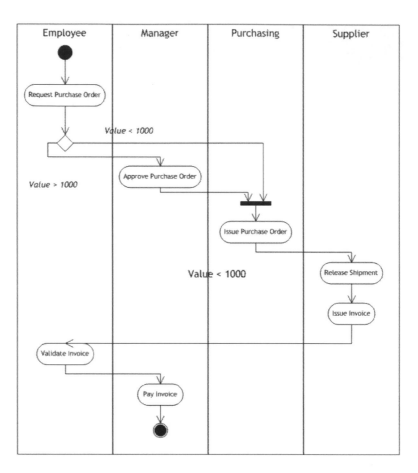

Figure 11-2: UML Activity Diagram

As you interact with the stakeholders you can progressively add elements of business logic such as sequencing and workflow (Figure 11-2). From these you can derive the supporting data models based on the requirements to store, report, process and secure information.

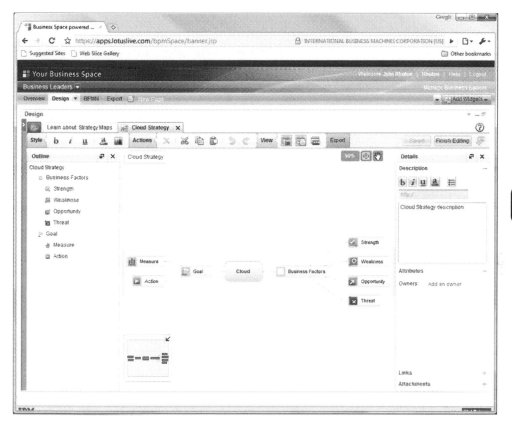

Figure 11-3: IBM BPM

You can use Business Process Management tools to assemble components and orchestrate them into a solution that achieves strategic outcomes. There are several business process design, monitoring and optimization tools available, including IBM BlueWorks, which is available as a cloud-based service (Figure 11-3).

You might also take advantage of the overhaul of your business processes to re-engineer them in other dimensions too. For example, you might want to include additional self-service provisioning, investigate whether you can use a general purpose BP framework such as a BPEL engine or consider opportunities for analytics of business process data.

Alternatively, you may want to look at a tool such as Appian, which provides both on-premise and SaaS-based management software to design, deploy and manage business processes. It is a modeling tool that includes a portal with form creation tools enabling users to build their own web-based processes (Figure 11-4).

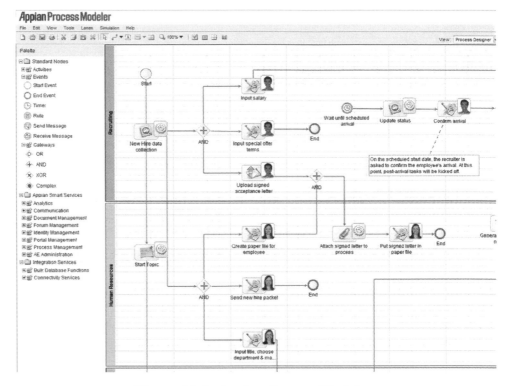

Figure 11-4: Appian Process Modeler

While moving business processes to a utility model can increase efficiency, it is not mutually exclusive with business process outsourcing (BPO). BPO providers have access to cheaper labor pools, reusable frameworks and architectures as well as experience in transformation that allow them to operate very cost-effectively. You may run hybrid operations or you may contract with an out-sourcer that utilizes public cloud services in its operations.

Architecture Modeling

The business processes provide a description of the activities that are ongoing in the organization and need technical support. Before proceeding with what HP ITSA calls the Implementation View, and actually selecting the components, it is helpful to have an architecture blueprint that maps the relevant business process-es against the high-level technical architecture.

Architectural views

	Data	Function	Network	People	Time	Motivation
	What	How	Where	Who	When	Why
Planner: Scope	Business Priorities	Business Processes	Business Locations	Important Departments	Business Events	Business Strategy
Owner: Enterprise Model	Conceptual Object Model	Business Process Model	Business Logistics System	Work Flow Model	Master Schedule	Business Pan
Designer: Information Systems Model	Logical Data Model	System Architecture Model	Distributed Systems Architecture	Human Interface Architecture	Processing Structure	Business Rule Model
Builder: Technology Model	Physical Data Model	Technology Design Model	Technology Architecture	Presentation Architecture	Control Structure	Rule Design
Subcontractor Detailed Specification	Data Definition	Program	Network Architecture	Security Architecture	Timing Definition	Rule Speculation
User: Actual System View	Usable Data	Working Function	Usable Network	Functioning Organization	Implemented Schedule	Working Strategy

Table 11-1: Extended Zachman Framework

DESIGN

As shown in Table 11-1, the Zachman Framework illustrates the role of business processes ("Function") in the context of the larger enterprise architecture. It defines a number of different models, schedules and architectural documents, which may be relevant depending on the view, or role of the team member and the various components of the solution.

Planner's View (Scope): The first architectural sketch corresponds to an executive summary and takes the shape of a Venn diagram, depicting the size, shape, partial relationships, and basic purpose of the final structure.

Owner's View (Enterprise or Business Model): The architect's drawings that depict the final solution from the perspective of the owner correspond to the enterprise (business) models, which constitute the design of the business.

Designer's View (Information Systems Model): The translation of the drawings into detailed requirements involves a model designed by a systems analyst who determines the data elements, logical process flows, and functions that represent business entities and processes.

Builder's View (Technology Model): The builder's perspective describing the constraints of tools, technology, and materials corresponds to the technology models, which must adapt the information systems model to the details of the programming languages, as well as hardware and software interfaces.

Subcontractor View (Detailed Specifications): Detailed specifications that are given to programmers and hardware designers who develop individual modules. Alternatively, they may represent detailed requirements for various commercial-off-the-shelf (COTS) software modules or hardware appliances.

Actual System View or the Functioning Enterprise

DESIGN

Enterprise Architecture and Cloud Computing

Ross, Weill and Robertson (2006, p. 27) classify enterprise architectures along two dimensions: standardization and integration. Standardization refers to consistency in process execution across the business. High standardization implies efficiency and predictability at the cost of innovation.

Integration links organizational tasks through shared processes and data. Its benefits include transparency, efficiency and agility. However, it is not trivial to implement since it involves common definitions and formats across the business.

The choice of architecture along these two axes sets the foundation for an operating model. No option is necessarily better than the others. However, it is critical that the decision align with the corporate strategy. A cost-leader may be more concerned with efficiency, while a differentiation strategy requires a high degree of innovation. Similarly, the resources that can be allocated toward higher integration depend on the long-term priorities of the organization.

Cloud computing can support very different strategies but the underlying rationale will influence many of the design decisions. For example, if the objective is to minimize costs then efficiency becomes paramount. On the other hand, if differentiation and agility are required then investments in long-term flexibility through architectural redesign may take a leading role.

Service-oriented Architecture

For any organization pursuing a strategy of agility, a service-oriented architecture (SOA) lends itself as a flexible and extensible foundation. Application modernization also carries with it several benefits that make services suitable for cloud deployment.

Linthicum (2009, p. 5) identifies the primary advantages of SOA as:

- Reuse of services without recoding or integration
- Agility to change business processes easily
- Real-time information on service health
- Ability to expose enterprise processes to external entities

Pursuit of a service-oriented architecture means breaking all the functionality into loosely coupled atomic primitives and implementing a governance/orchestration layer that binds the elements together to deliver business value.

Historically, the notions of loose coupling and tight cohesion related to the arguments that were passed between components. Narrowly defined data structures reduce dependencies between modules making it easier to replace or enhance them.

The geographic dispersion and technical diversity that are inherent in cloud computing add additional considerations to the notion of loose coupling (Linthicum, 2009, p. 120). Location independence has implications for discoverability and latency. Communications independence describes the interoperability requirements of services in a multi-protocol environment. Security independence relies on federated identity and access management systems.

Asynchronous, stateless interactions between elements provide a versatile foundation. However, integration of the elements is still necessary in order to add value. The benefit of SOA is the abstraction it provides. The business logic can easily and flexibly recompose the architecture and leverage an orchestration layer for governance functions such as discovery, delivery, monitoring, validation, audit and logging.

Preliminary Design

Once you've determined what you need to do, the next step is to decide how to accomplish it and, in the context of this analysis, how you might leverage cloud computing to achieve your objectives. The rest of the book is dedicated to this task.

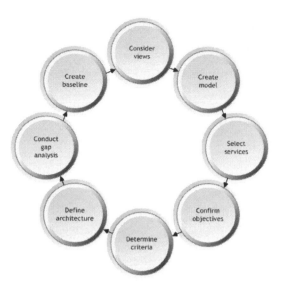

Figure 11-5: Technical Architecture

But before we dive into the details I think it is worth putting the architecture in context. TOGAF represents the technical architecture as an endless cycle (Figure 11-5). This book is sequential because that is the traditional way to write a book. However, it is very unlikely that any design will be completely linear. For example, you may go through the process of an extensive connectivity and security design, only to determine toward the end of your analysis that your solution cannot comply with all government regulations, so you need to select a different application or provider.

There is always the risk that you will need to start from scratch. Some cycles of refinement are inevitable in large projects. Nonetheless, you can reduce the chances of last-minute failure by making a first pass of your design that covers all the important points at least superficially.

The bases to cover are the same as are required for the full-scale design. They are described in more detail in the following chapters.

Selection: The applications and user groups that are initially considered for cloud services need to be prioritized by the key stakeholders and assessed for security, resilience and costs considerations. It is also critical to consider a full list of potential providers and delivery models (SaaS, PaaS, IaaS) before deciding how to move forward.

Integration: There can be many different components to a service-oriented solution. In addition to each of the potential applications, which may rely on other services, there are devices and physical infrastructure that need to be included in the solution. These parts need to be connected at all layers from the network to the applications, and all elements must be verified to determine if they meet minimum resilience and security thresholds.

Implementation: It isn't sufficient for the end-state to be viable. There needs to be a clear path that takes data, applications and users from the status quo to the full service-based implementation. In addition, to a set of project management responsibilities this means a plan to migrate the applications and data and to refocus and retrain the users in order to transition them to the new operating model.

Operation: Cloud computing will have a profound impact on the operating model. It can impact all service management functions from provisioning and administration to monitoring, troubleshooting and support. It is important to have clear plans for request fulfillment and change management as well as mechanisms to adjust capacity and ensure availability. There must be explicit escalation paths across all providers for problem and event management. And there needs to be a defined process for handling end-user and IT support including a central help desk with hand-off mechanisms between the service providers.

Control: There will be new challenges in an opaque, globally dispersed and outsourced delivery model. You will need to consider questions of legal compliance on topics such as data privacy and electronic discovery. There will be new sets of threats that arise from hosting your computational and storage resources on a public network. And you will need to think about governance controls, such as service-level agreements, to ensure that your providers do not compromise your objectives.

If your planned approach appears viable when you consider these factors, then you are ready to proceed to the next steps, which should lead you to a more extensive design.

Select

SELECT

Chapter 12

Application Inventory

The essence of cloud computing is services. So, it is a good place to start in selecting the components for an initial cloud-based solution. Not all applications
lend themselves to an Internet-based service delivery. Some may work but don't
deliver any benefit. Yet others may appear very compelling but face opposition
from key stakeholders.

SELECT

Options

As you examine potential applications to move to a service-based delivery you
should first differentiate between the applications that you already have running
in your data centers and new potential applications that might run in the cloud.

You have several options that you can pursue with existing applications, in addition to transitioning them to a public service. You might replace them with an
entirely new cloud service that provides similar functionality or helps to solve
the same business problem. Alternatively, you might want to look at modernizing the application according to service-oriented principles so that you have a
high degree of flexibility in transitioning to other providers in the future.

You might retire the application because you have determined that it is no longer
necessary or doesn't add sufficient business value to justify the investment in
licensing and support regardless of the delivery model. Or, you might decide that
the best course of action is simply to leave the application running exactly where
it is without any changes.

New applications/opportunities are a little simpler since they have no legacy
considerations. You still need to ensure that they fit a business case. However,
from a technical perspective, your primary decision will be whether to host the
application internally, in a partner or public cloud, or in a hybrid constellation
that involves multiple providers.

Stakeholders

There are several stakeholders in the application selection that may have varying degrees of interest and influence over any decisions relating to applications that affect them. While it would be risky to try to make the application strategy contingent on universal consensus, it will certainly reduce resistance if all stakeholders have a general understanding of the plan and have had the opportunity to voice their concerns.

The most obvious stakeholder group is the application users and their management who have an interest in the business outcomes that the application helps to secure. Additionally, you need to consider the application developers who maintain the source code and the application managers who ensure that the software keeps running.

SELECT

In a multi-tier architecture, the data is stored separately from the application. It is advisable to also check with the database administrators and designers to ensure that there are no reasons why data cannot easily be moved if necessary.

The infrastructure managers, while not directly concerned with any particular application, will also be able to provide valuable input on the ramifications for networking and security.

Business Criteria

In line with our general top-down approach to architecture, you begin by assessing the business criteria for moving an application to a public service as opposed to any of the internal options you might have for retaining or refining the software.

There are several areas that are worth examining:

Cloud Benefit

Applications will vary in their ability to leverage the benefits that the cloud provides. If the workloads are constant, there will be little performance advantage to virtualization. On the other hand, if demand is volatile and processing is highly dynamic then there is a high potential to flatten the utilization.

But, even if virtualization is attractive, there is still the question of whether the benefit can be achieved internally rather than requiring movement to a public cloud. This will depend on several factors. If the load demands are countercyclical to the resource requirements of other internal applications, a private cloud may be sufficient. In other words, if the application tends to peak when other software is running idle then there is a good opportunity to share resources.

It also depends on what share of the total load this application represents. If it is a small proportion, then it is much more likely that the total capacity of the virtual environment can absorb its spikes. On the other hand, if over half the data center is dedicated to a particular application and that application doubles its requirements temporarily there will be no room for accommodating the load.

Another long-term consideration is the degree of virtualization in the internal data centers. If they are only minimally virtualized or have small compartmentalized resource pools, then it is much more difficult to plan these so that they can accommodate irregular bursts in activity. It is not necessarily a given that every organization will strive toward maximal virtualization. The implications on application isolation are not always trivial and many companies will not have the necessary competence to manage the complexity reliably.

Administration Costs

Another financial consideration is the cost of managing the application. The administration costs may decrease as a result of the outsourcing, but the benefit could be diluted if the challenge of integrating the application with internal systems offsets some of the reduced responsibilities.

SELECT

Support costs may also be affected if the cloud service provider takes over the back-end support of the application. On the other hand, users will probably still call the same central helpdesk, which may find it more difficult, or perhaps in some cases easier, to triage and refer incidents.

Obviously, you need to make sure that the amounts being measured reflect actual changes in total cost to the company. If overhead costs for support and administration are simply reallocated from one application to others, they do not reflect a net gain to the organization.

Cloud Risk

Risk is an additional consideration in prioritizing the applications for cloud suitability. Mission critical applications may not be the best choice for piloting new technologies. Similarly, customer-facing services will have a more pronounced negative impact on your business than employee or partner services if they provide a poor user experience during a transition phase.

There are several categories of risk that need to be assessed for each application:

Data loss: There is the possibility that data may be dropped or corrupted leading to a loss of data integrity. Important information entered by the user may not be registered in the database, which can lead to an inconsistency between the data view of the user and the internal systems. Finally, data may be leaked if the transaction channels or internal storage suffer from any vulnerability. The extent of this risk depends on the criticality and sensitivity of the data as well as the extent to which it is exposed.

Incomplete transactions: In some cases, transactions may be aborted without data loss. Even though the user is aware that the processing did not complete, this still presents several problems. If the error persists, the user cannot achieve the intended outcome. Even if it eventually does work, the user is likely to be frustrated by the experience.

Poor user experience: There may also be other factors that irk the user such as a confusing interface or slow response time. If user acceptance is important to the operation and the operation is vital to the company (for example, if it represents a customer purchase), then moving the functionality to a different environment will impact the risk.

Finally, there are a number of technical considerations that may influence the riskiness of the application in a public environment. We will look at them next.

SELECT

Technical Criteria

The architectural design and technical implementation of an application can have an impact on the ability to move it seamlessly into a public and highly distributed environment.

Service-Oriented Architecture: If the application already implements a high degree of service abstraction, reusability and composition, it is much easier to migrate it to a service-oriented environment and to leverage the benefits that existing services can provide.

Customization: Public services are notable for the high dependency on standardization in order to achieve operational efficiency. Clearly some degree of customization will be needed in order to accommodate the diverse requirements of different organizations. However, ensuring that code and configuration are maintained separately will reduce maintenance burdens and maximize the agility of the developers as they add and change functionality.

Application independence: A high degree of interconnectivity between applications makes it difficult to transfer them individually to different service providers. On the other hand, isolating the interactions and ensuring that all requests use standardized interfaces makes the applications much more versatile. In every case, you should consider all interfaces (Web APIs) that may be needed or can be leveraged and verify whether, and how, they will work when the application is moved and/or transformed.

Loose coupling: Loose coupling and tight cohesion are important architectural principles that carry many benefits. But in addition to the number of connections and interfaces, it is necessary to look at the context and implications of each. What will be the impact if they experience high and unpredictable latency? How will they perform if network bandwidth suffers a bottleneck? If network conditions translate directly to user-visible response times or the reliability of transactions, then geographically distributing the application may not be wise.

Horizontal Scalability: The trend in the industry is toward scaling out rather than scaling up. Computational requirements continue to increase while we seem to have met some obstacles in increasing the CPU clock speed (see sidebar). The effect is that you need to look at how you can parallelize your workloads so that multiple cores, processors, or systems can work together to increase your speed.

There are some challenges in scaling horizontally. Concurrency means that you need to lock and unlock shared resources for every method. Memory locks have been effective in the past, but are no longer viable when systems are only connected via high-latency links.

If you are able to decompose the system into stateless transactions, you can maintain integrity. This means that all state information (e.g. shopping cart) must be preserved in persistent/durable storage, such as a network file system, or a cloud storage service.

SELECT

Redundancy: A tenet of cloud computing is increased reliability through high levels of replication. The code can take responsibility for handling redundancy, for which it has multiple options. It can rely on the platform and infrastructure services of the provider, who may guarantee replication.

Alternatively, it may call replication services or it may explicitly duplicate data by storing it in multiple repositories. It may also utilize the user device as a redundant data store. Client-side caching and synchronization services have the added benefit of improving the user experience during periods of disconnectivity.

Tolerance: A cloud environment is uncontrolled and chaotic compared to a single system or private network. As mentioned above, network connections can be unstable. Furthermore, underlying datasets may not be fully synchronized and component services may also be unreliable or return incomplete, inaccurate or obsolete results.

Some applications are more tolerant to imprecision than others. An inventory management system will quickly lose its value if there is no two-phase commit that guarantees system integrity. On the other hand, analytics and search can accommodate reasonable amounts of invalid content and still deliver immensely valuable results.

SELECT

Need for Parallelization

Parallelization was on the increase long before cloud computing became fashionable. Until recently, it was possible to satisfy the increasing appetite of software applications for processing power, memory and storage through advances in transistor density and clock-frequencies, which improved single-threaded performance in an almost linear manner (Kaufmann & Gayliard, 2009).

This approach has run into physical limits that prevent further advances without dramatically increasing power consumption and heat dissipation and are therefore not cost effective or ecologically responsible.

By increasing the number of processor cores per socket, it is possible to reduce per-socket power consumption. However, the job for the software developer becomes more difficult in exchange. An application cannot run faster than the aggregate of its sequential components. If an application does not parallelize, performance will not improve (and may degrade) with additional cores.

There are several approaches to parallelize code. It is possible to explicitly separate and designate independent threads. JIT compilers (e.g. Rapidmind) may assign threads to the appropriate processor. Also, tools such as Acumen SlowSpotter sample execution of the live application to optimize execution.

Some prominent examples of parallelism include Google MapReduce library, Apache Hadoop and most High Performance Computing applications (often developed using the Message Passing Interface [MPI] or OpenMP models).

Cloud Opportunities

The preceding guidelines were an attempt at some general observations on what constitutes an optimal cloud computing application. Theoretical advice can be useful for understanding the background as to why particular software works well, or not so well, in a distributed and public environment.

Yet it is hard to apply conceptual advice to thousands of applications, which many enterprises have in their inventory. A faster, albeit somewhat rough, categorization process is to look at which classes of software may typically lend themselves best to cloud computing.

Suitable workloads might include:

- Storage as a service
- Backup/Restore as a Service
- Single virtual appliances
- Test and pre-production systems
- Software development tools
- Batch processing with limited security
- Mature packaged SaaS offerings (collaboration, CRM, HR)
- Isolated workloads without latency sensitivity and well-defined APIs

On the other hand, the following are not typically suitable:

- Sensitive data (e.g. primary LDAP server, healthcare records)
- Multiple co-dependent services (high throughput online transaction processing)
- Applications with stringent audit and accountability requirements
- 3rd party products without virtualization or cloud-aware licensing
- Applications that require detailed utilization measurement and charge-back
- Applications that require a high degree of flexibility and customization
- Systems that rely on specialized infrastructure, physical location or custom hardware

SELECT

This is only a rough list, intended as a starting point for finding some suitable applications. Unfortunately, it doesn't remove the need to diligently assess any candidate application before even beginning to plan for its transition to the cloud.

An alternate approach for preselecting candidate applications is to consider systems that currently represent pain points, whether they be in financial, operational or functional terms. Capacity problems and user dissatisfaction can be an opportunity for change. Even major upgrades may signal that there are deficiencies with the current system that need to be addressed. Quite often, funds have already been allocated for these changes.

Analysis

Assuming that you have identified some candidates for a transition to cloud computing, how do you determine the extent to which the applications meet the selection criteria, both on a business as well as technical level? There are at least three options:

User/developer survey: Users and administrators will usually have some insight into the business dimensions of the tools they are using. Code developers and maintainers as well as database administrators will have some idea of the technical details.

It may be sufficient, at least as a first pass, to interview some of the stakeholders and get their input on the current details along with their preferences for the future delivery of the software.

Manual expert analysis: You may feel a higher degree of confidence if you are able to validate survey data with independent analysis. Someone with cloud computing expertise may need to observe the application in operation, measure network activity, assess the technical design documentation and perhaps even scrutinize some of the source code.

SELECT

Tool analysis: Needless to say, an exhaustive code analysis could be a very resource-intensive activity. There are tools available that can assist in the process. For example, EvolveWare, Relativity, Trinity Millennium and TSRI offer services to catalog legacy applications and migrate them to a service-oriented architecture. There are also numerous network monitoring tools that can offer insight into some of the inter-process communications that are taking place.

Unfortunately, at this point there is no singular solution to magically recommend the best applications. However, a clever combination of surveys, manual and automated analyses can provide very good results.

Net Benefit and Risk

Once you have analyzed a set of applications for their suitability as cloud-based services, you need to make a decision which, if any, of them will benefit from the new delivery model.

The primary dimensions of evaluation are usually financial (benefit) and risk. Figure 12-1 is purely conceptual since there is no universally accepted formula for translating between risk and benefit. However, it is important to clarify that there will always be both benefit and risk associated with cloud computing.

If we compare the net change that a cloud transition would imply, we can assess whether the switch is worth it or not. In the long term, the tradeoff is quite straightforward. However, if we are looking at initial pilots of cloud computing then it is important to take special care (Figure 12-2).

An application-specific analysis of a pilot system will typically understate both the benefits and risks of a transition to an emerging technology. By laying the foundation for future services it facilitates future migrations and therefore adds value that is not directly measurable in a narrow analysis.

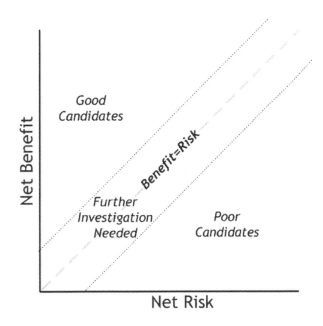

Figure 12-1: Net Benefit and Net Risk

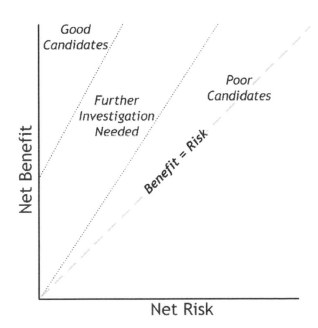

Figure 12-2: Risk-averse Bias for Cloud Pilots

At the same time, the first application is also exposed to many first-time risks that may be fully addressed by the time future services undergo a transition. Unfortunately, these risks tend to receive more attention than the benefits and there-fore establish a risk-averse tendency. There is some merit to the bias since the risk exposure takes place immediately and is not dependent on future applications. On the other hand, there is the possibility that there will be no further transitions that reap incremental benefits.

On a more practical level, it is also much easier to obtain executive support for projects that do not jeopardize important operations, at least until the new technology has proven itself to be viable and trustworthy.

New Opportunities

SELECT

At no point in the process should you lose sight of the fact that cloud computing has a disruptive impact across multiple layers of business activity. It's critical to look at the existing applications for potential transformation, replacement or retirement. But, it is just as important to determine if there are any new strategic opportunities that might lend themselves to a cloud service delivery model.

The cloud lends itself particularly well for new applications, which do not have some of the transitional drawbacks of legacy tools and can immediately incorporate design considerations that leverage its benefits, such as persistency, pervasiveness and increased context.

Persistency: The cloud is equipped with a highly reliable backing store. The network traffic and bottlenecks may pose a short-term problem for latency-sensitive thin clients and battery-powered mobile devices. However, it simplifies the job of the application developer.

Pervasiveness: Synchronization addresses the problem of multiple devices, which may not always be connected. All personally relevant information can be retrieved through a variety of channels.

Increased context: Network-centric services are able to build an increasingly complete picture of the user's behavioral patterns and immediate context based on timing, locations and activity. This information can be leveraged through analytics to improve the user experience and target user-specific business operations.

There may be new applications that are able to exploit salient characteristics of the cloud to create additional revenue streams and optimize current business processes.

Chapter 13

Service Components

After determining the potential new and legacy applications that might benefit from an Internet-based service delivery, the next step is to figure out what cloud components are needed.

Service Delivery Model

There are several dimensions to this task, including the decision of whether to build or buy, which service delivery level to use and the diverse requirements of application and management components.

Build or Buy

At a high level, this means first determining whether the application should be internally developed or acquired (Table 13-1). The driving factor is likely to be the availability of the required functionality that fully meets the needs of the corporation. If the gaps are small, and can be ignored or addressed with a workaround, then the economics will usually be in favor of using what has already been developed and deployed.

Chapter 13: Service Components

	Internal expertise with functionality		No Internal expertise with functionality	
	Internal Software Competence	No Internal Software Competence	Internal Software Competence	No Internal Software Competence
OTS Available	Buy OTS	Buy OTS	Buy OTS	Buy OTS
No OTS Available	Develop internally	Contract externally	Contract externally	Contract externally

Table 13-1: Service sourcing matrix

SELECT

On the other hand, if there isn't any equivalent off-the-shelf (OTS) offering, and something must be developed from scratch, then the key question changes. A match between the core competency of the firm and the technical requirements of the application would strengthen the case that it should be developed in house where the coders would also have some appreciation for the requirements.

However, if the organization doesn't have any experience in programming with cloud platforms, the case becomes much less attractive. By the same token, if the firm has little knowledge of the technology involved in implementing the needed functionality, then there is little reason to develop the code internally. In both of these cases, an external contract is the only viable solution.

Service Delivery Level

At the same time, you need to consider another dimension to the same problem in a cloud-based architecture. Should the service run as SaaS, PaaS or IaaS? The question is somewhat correlated to the preceding discussion.

If there is a SaaS service available that meets the requirements in its standard offering, is priced appropriately and doesn't expose any security concerns, then it may be a compelling proposition. However, there may also be other off-the-shelf offerings that the organization could purchase or license. These might run either on a cloud platform or infrastructure.

The key question regarding a SaaS offering is whether the customer will require significant customization (Figure 13-1). There is a clear trade-off between customization requirements and the cost involved to develop, maintain and support the application.

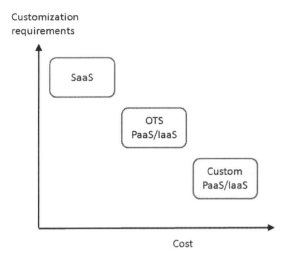

Figure 13-1: Customization versus Cost

If there is no suitable SaaS offering available, there may still be a commercial off-the-shelf offering that runs either on a cloud platform or can be virtualized and run on cloud infrastructure. The configuration and customization options are significantly greater in an environment that is owned and controlled by the customer, a responsibility that carries with it also some additional costs.

Nevertheless, there are limits to the functionality that can be changed when the source code is owned by another party. The most flexible option is to develop a complete custom application. It can still be cloud-based if it runs on a cloud platform or infrastructure. The costs are the greatest with this option since the code must be developed and maintained in addition to the responsibilities of application management and user support.

So far, the analysis has focused on the distinction of SaaS compared to PaaS and IaaS collectively. There are also some considerations when selecting between these latter two delivery models.

IaaS is the most flexible of options. It can accommodate almost any applications that can run on a physical computer. Some legacy applications can be made cloud-capable with relative ease, particularly if they already expose the user interface through a web server and have few external dependencies. However, IaaS also leverages few of the benefits of an Internet-based, virtualized, utility-priced delivery model.

PaaS is tuned for the cloud. It provides a run-time environment that offers a rich set of cloud services and makes it easy to deploy streamlined cloud-tuned code. Unfortunately, the functionality and efficiency also comes at the price of flexibility. Cloud platforms offer a restricted set of programming languages and programming interfaces. They deliberately do not expose functions that would be damaging to other tenants in the environment, which may also limit some productive operations. Another consideration may be the higher risk of vendor lock-in, which is associated with current cloud platforms. This will be explored in more detail in Chapter 27.

All three delivery models will have their place in enterprise architectures for some time to come. It is likely that IaaS will be more common in the short term but as the platforms mature and more applications become available on PaaS the increased benefits will begin to outweigh the disadvantages. Similarly, as SaaS offerings begin to accommodate more flexibility, they will become even more attractive to enterprises. The bottom line for a customer is that they will be able to extract the most cloud-based benefits by adopting the highest level of the SPI stack that meets their requirements for flexibility and interoperability.

Integration with Management Components

Keep in mind that while it is imperative to understand the appropriate service delivery model for each business application, there is additional infrastructure that you must also consider. Management software for monitoring networks, applications and systems needs to be integrated into the proposed architecture as do security components ranging from intrusion detection and firewalls to antivirus policy enforcement and spam filtering. There may be requirements for developers to simplify testing, staging and deployment. The master directory needs to support federated authentication.

All of these functions could also be delivered from the cloud itself and should be considered as part of a comprehensive analysis. Even if there is no current offering that would be acceptable, it is important to identify a flexible future path and to ensure that, in the near term, all the pieces will be able to fit together.

Strategic Options

For the sake of completeness, it is worth stating that there are many more strategic options than building or buying components and internally or externally hosting them. In addition to the possibility of outsourcing services to a partner cloud, there may also be possibilities of vertical integration by acquiring suppliers or customers. A wide variety of partnership and licensing options may also be relevant.

Potential Providers

It would be impossible to fully evaluate the target service delivery model without at least some understanding of the provider landscape since you would want to make sure there is at least one offering that meets your requirements.

Trying to get an exhaustive view of other providers is not easy. The market is in constant flux with new vendors entering the scene regularly and, unfortunately, some also being forced away. There is no central registry or even universally accepted taxonomy of providers that would facilitate a search.

Nonetheless, you can find lists of prominent cloud offerings provided by reputable analysts or groups such as the OpenCrowd. You can probably also find more than you would like with a Google search. Should you miss a recent entry, you may just have saved yourself considerable due diligence in investigating an option that has yet to prove itself reliable.

Evaluation Criteria and Weight

I use four main categories of evaluation criteria for selecting a cloud provider: Environmental, Technical, Contractual and Financial.

Environmental

At the highest level, the key environmental factor is the location. If the data center is positioned on an earthquake fault line, or above a dormant volcano, that would be an unnecessary risk. Your cloud provider will also have conducted a risk analysis, so don't expect anything quite so obvious. Nonetheless, given the potential effects of a natural disaster, you will want to investigate any cause for concern. For instance, even a higher concentration of electrical storms might increase the chances of a power outage that mandates additional safeguards and precautions.

SELECT

Power is an absolute requirement for a data center. An ideal location is able to tap into more than one power grid. Even so, it should also have considerable redundancy in alternate sources from batteries to diesel generators. Similarly the heating, ventilation and air conditioning should be able to sustain any single point of failure. Furthermore, given the dependency on connectivity, network resilience should be guaranteed from multiple internet service providers.

Physical access controls are also an environmental consideration. Does the facility have solid security procedures that prevent unauthorized access to the building and computer equipment? These controls might include everything from biometric and multi-factor authentication systems to electrical fences and state-of-the-art surveillance systems.

Technical

From a technical viewpoint, the most important considerations are around security, interoperability, and the ability of the provider to fulfill the service requirements.

Security: Security criteria might include PCI compliance, which includes security provisions that range from physical to operations. Thereby, not all regulations are applicable for the lower-level (PaaS, IaaS) service providers.

Generally, it is worthwhile investigating all of the security and audit precautions that are in place – to the extent that the providers describe them.

In a multi-tenant environment, the degree of tenant isolation and mechanisms used to enforce it are critical. Since attacks on co-tenants can conceivably impact your services you may be curious as to who they are. In some cases, their identities may be publicly known, but you can expect the providers to be reluctant to breach confidentiality where it is not. On the positive side, this confidentiality can also be to your advantage since it makes it slightly more difficult to target you for an attack.

If you are relying on your provider for encryption, then a very important consideration is how they implement key management. In particular, you should feel more comfortable if they do not use the same keys to encrypt the storage of all their customers. You may even want multiple encryption keys for your organization. For PaaS and IaaS, you have the option to encrypt the data yourself so that the key management is not necessarily relegated to the provider.

SELECT

Interoperability: It is worth determining at an early stage what connectivity options you would have between your internal data center and the cloud provider. Depending on the nature of your required interconnection, you might investigate co-location options so that you can place bridge servers at a low-latency, low-cost connection point to the cloud provider.

In any case, you will need to understand all the interfaces, for example, for backups, archiving and data extraction as well as staging, deployment and system management. Where there are (de facto or de jure) standards in these areas, you will reduce your lock-in if you can leverage the standards.

Service availability: Service availability is largely a contractual issue. However, if the service provider cannot physically provide the service, then a contract can only compensate you for the loss. It cannot prevent it. You may want to have some insight into the existing capacity and utilization of the provider's data centers in terms of floor space, power and bandwidth. If you are not comfortable with the expected trend, you can investigate whether there are alternate sources available or if the provider has already engaged in building out new data centers.

The provider will also put some effort into ensuring that it doesn't run out of capacity. However, keep in mind that it is in the provider's interest to maximize utilization. It is in the enterprise's interest for the provider to maximize spare capacity. It never hurts to ensure the incentives are aligned.

Additionally you may have criteria that relate to specific service delivery models:

SaaS: For a software service, it is vital to understand the functional roadmap and release process. In order to reduce vendor lock-in, you may also want to understand all data extraction options.

PaaS: A platform provider should offer backward compatibility guarantees so that applications developed on the current platform version will not suddenly fail in the course of future upgrades. You also need to evaluate the available programming languages and all the services and programming interfaces available in the framework.

Developers will also be interested in which integrated development environments (IDEs), such as Eclipse or Visual Studio, interoperate with the platform and what mechanisms there are to automate deployment and manage instances.

IaaS: Infrastructure services rely very heavily on the virtualization platform of choice, be it VMware, Hyper-V, KVM, XenServer or any other virtualization technology. Again, the important point is to know which vendor options are supported and what management interfaces are available to deploy, load balance and relocate instances.

SELECT

Contractual

In December 2010, Amazon Web Services discontinued service to WikiLeaks without notice in response to a violation of the published terms of service (Amazon Web Serivces, 2010). Few readers are likely to generate the same level of controversy as this particular customer. Nonetheless, Amazon's action is noteworthy since it highlights the importance of carefully examining any agreement for a hosted service. The contract may involve a number of legal subtleties. Some of the most important considerations include:

Metering: How is the service measured? How granular is the metering (e.g. do you pay by the second or by the day)? Do you have access to up-to-date reporting? Can you put a cap or alert on your default quota so that you don't inadvertently incur a huge liability?

Billing: The most obvious billing consideration is the price of the services. These will involve multiple components, such as storage, CPU and I/O in a typical IaaS offering. If you have unique requirements, you may want flexible billing and bundling options that meet your needs better than the standard list prices.

Terms of Service (TOS): The required terms of service vary greatly from business to business. A 60 day notification on termination of service may be sufficient for a small business using a non-critical application. It might not be acceptable for an enterprise running a very important customer application.

SELECT

The TOS are often negotiable. Even Amazon will provide different terms to an enterprise if the potential contract value is attractive enough. But the potential to gain from negotiating will depend very much on the clout of the customer. After all, a customer's excessive demands make it onerous for providers to pursue the contract, so the incentive needs to be clear.

One of the most important components of the terms of service is the service level agreement (SLA). Although the negotiation typically focuses on legal and financial obstacles, the basis of the agreement is technical.

Incident handling: A critical aspect of the terms of service is the process for dealing with incidents. It might include attacks on the customer platforms as well as technical faults with the services. There need to be bi-directional communication flows that inform both parties of what is happening in a timely manner. The triggers for these, and the amount and type of information to pass, are all part of what needs to be defined.

For instance, a customer may wish to be alerted immediately if there is a denial-of-service attack on its platform (or another neighboring tenant). Even if the attack is not successful, the customer may wish to take some action to reduce its future exposure. The provider, on the other hand, may wish to minimize any visibility into attacks on its services. Unless these processes are clearly defined and monitored, it is unlikely that the customer will receive the information it expects.

Visibility: Service providers publish limited amounts of information on their operational procedures. Revealing too much can erode their competitive differentiation, expose them to attackers who suspect weaknesses, and open them up to ongoing negotiations with their customers.

On the other hand, customers have a legitimate need to understand what operational procedures are in place to protect their data and ensure availability of their services. Before selecting a service provider it is good to understand how much they are willing to reveal about their internal processes.

Audits/Certifications: Typically service providers undergo very rigorous internal audits. Many also have certifications that should convey a higher degree of confidence to customers. Unfortunately, there are no thorough cloud-specific certifications that would address all possible concerns. Nonetheless, weak certifications are better than no certification at all.

Some of the most popular include:

SAS 70 Type 2 certifications are the most common. They are very flexible and, in particular, allow exclusion of critical systems from scrutiny. They are much better than no certification at all, but it is important to carefully examine their scope. Fortunately, there is now growing momentum to replace SAS 70 with SOC 1 / SSAE 16 as we shall see below.

ISO 27001/2 is more prescriptive although it is not tailored to cloud. It is probably the most common certification, particularly in the financial and health care industries, where privacy is an important requirement.

NIST 800-53 Revision 3 describes the security controls that are recommended for US Federal information systems and organizations. It defines an effective, and increasingly popular, framework using a security control structure including management, operational and technical classes.

SAS 70 (Statement on Auditing Standards No. 70) was released by the AICPA (Auditing Standards Board of the American Institute of Certified Public Accountants) in 1992, and became the predominant standard for data center users to assure customers that their data center is secure. A SAS 70 audit verifies that the controls and processes that the data center operator has in place are followed. However, the fact that there are no mandatory controls or processes makes a systematic enforcement almost meaningless.

SELECT

Recognizing some of the weaknesses in SAS 709, the AICPA replaced its guidance with three Service Organization Control (SOC) Reports.

SOC 1 Report verifies controls that are likely to be relevant to user entities and is focused primarily on particularly financial statements. It relies on Statement on Standards for Attestation Engagements (SSAE) No. 16, which requires the auditor to obtain a written confirmation from management regarding the design and operating effectiveness of the controls being reviewed. SSAE 16 is closely aligned with the international audit standard ISAE 3402.

SOC 2 Reports are more technical in nature. They are modeled around Policies, Communications, Procedures, and Monitoring and address five system attributes:

- Security - The system is protected against unauthorized access.
- Availability - The system is available for operation and use.
- Processing integrity - System processing is complete, accurate, timely and authorized.
- Confidentiality - Information designated as confidential is protected.
- Privacy - Personal information is collected, used, retained, disclosed and disposed of in conformity with the entity's privacy notice and generally accepted accounting principles.

SOC 3 Reports are similar in focus to SOC 2 Reports. The main difference is that a SOC 2 report contains a detailed description of the service auditor's tests and results along with auditor opinions on the effectiveness of the controls. This information is generally not intended for broad distribution since it would expose many implementation details. A SOC 3 report provides only the auditor's report on whether the system achieved the trust services criteria. It can therefore be shared with customers or published on a website.

Financial

Lastly, one of the most important considerations of a service provider is that it will continue to be in a position to provide its services in the long term. The cloud provider landscape is very dynamic. There are new entries every month. And there are also occasional exits.

If your cloud service provider goes bankrupt, you can be in deep trouble. Certainly there are technical precautions you can take by maximizing interoperability, maintaining a secondary provider, and backing up all information locally. Nonetheless, it's a good idea to also keep an eye on the financial condition of the vendor.

This may be difficult if the company is privately held. That might also be a reason for preferring an established, publicly traded partner where more data is easily accessible. Alternatively, you may insist on information about the financing and communicate directly with owners and investors.

In any case, you will want to obtain as much information as you can about the financial health of the company. You might look at superficial indicators, such as its size and the number of years the company has been in business. You might also be interested in profitability, growth and cash flow. You could even undertake an in-depth financial analysis poring through the balance sheet to determine gearing and debt ratios, financing structure, return on assets and a host of other metrics.

One of the most revealing indicators would be the credit rating assigned by an agency such as Moody's. One value captures the results of a diligent credit risk analysis performed by experts in the area. The subprime crisis may have damaged the trust you put into credit ratings. But unless you have a background in finance, or are able to subscribe to a service such as Hoover's or Bureau van Dijk, it may be the best summary you will get.

Chapter 14

User Profiles

Once you've decided on the applications, the next step is to identify the impacted user groups, so you can assess the impact your cloud strategy will have on them. This will range from training and support requirements to ensuring that they have the appropriate devices and necessary connectivity options.

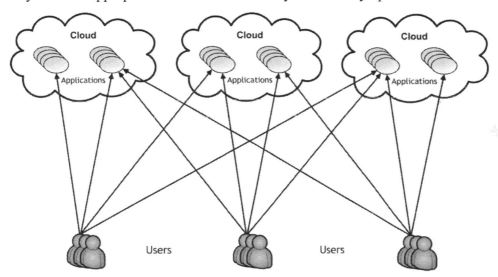

Figure 14-1: User-Application Combinations

There is a many-to-many relationship between applications and users, with a large number of combinations possible (Figure 14-1), so this step isn't completely sequential. It is also necessary to have a general idea of who the user groups will be during application selection. For example, you may also want to use your knowledge of user communities to help prioritize and select which applications to migrate.

The two steps run in parallel and are tightly interrelated. You can consider user and application selection different dimensions of the same process. If, at the end of the analysis, the two perspectives yield different results, then there will be a need to resolve them.

Options

Before delving into the segmentation too deeply, it's worth having a good idea of what the potential impact of the segmentation might be. Certainly, you might decide that some users should not use cloud-based resources. You might come to this conclusion for any or many reasons including their support requirements and the sensitivity of their data.

If the user group is to take advantage of the cloud, you also need to decide which cloud. There may be several cloud services and/or cloud providers that offer functionality relevant to them. For instance, you may decide to subscribe to two different email services. One low-cost service available through SaaS might be acceptable for the bulk of your users. On the other hand, your executives might continue to use an internal email-server or a partner-based outsourcing solution.

SELECT

Segmentation Criteria

You can choose the lines along which to segment your users. One very coarse approach is to begin with employees, contractors and visitors. If you take that division a step further you might come up with several user groups such as employees, contractors, partners, customers, auditors, government, all of which might have very different application access and authorization levels.

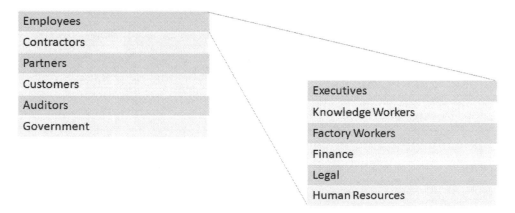

Figure 14-2: User Segments

Typically, there are also large variations in the user groups among employees. You might distinguish between executives, knowledge workers, factory workers, as well as having special confidentiality requirements for finance, legal and human resources employees (Figure 14-2).

User clustering

In addition to classifying users according to roles and organizational function, it can be helpful to understand their actual interaction patterns. Typically a large proportion of time, particularly for knowledge workers, is spent in cross-functional teams that may span geographical and organizational boundaries. This includes peer communities and project teams.

If it is possible to identify user clusters, it can be beneficial in terms of allocating users to storage and server groups and planning migration schedules so that network activity is minimized and data can be more easily de-duplicated.

Performing an exhaustive analysis is not necessary. There are many social networking and social mining tools available, but it is unlikely you'd implement them for this exclusive purpose. If you have good information, you should make use of it. Otherwise, even a rough estimate of departments and divisions most likely to interact will be better than random placement.

Partner integration

One of the benefits of externalized data and processes is the ease of integrating external users. Improved access to suppliers, customers and partners can improve supply chain efficiency. It is also less complicated to provide limited visibility to governmental regulators, auditors and contractors.

That is not to say that external extensions are trivial. However, once the services have been relocated outside the corporate perimeter, and a refined access control system governs roles, responsibilities and authorization levels, then it is a much easier step to grant limited access without risking other assets and services.

It is therefore worthwhile for the segmentation process to consider all stakeholders that might have an interest in some of the cloud-based services. They may not have had direct access to the legacy systems, so it is easy to ignore them. Unfortunately, doing so misses an opportunity to leverage the cloud transition to dramatically overhaul, and improve, business processes.

Profile Classification

	Executive	Knowledge Worker	Factory Worker
Investment level	High	Medium	Low
Flexibility	High	High	Low
Access Mode	Remote, Mobile, Office	Remote, Office	Factory
Devices	Desktop, Laptop, Mobile	Laptop	Terminal
Applications	Data Warehouse, Office	Office Suite	Email
Authorization	Approval	User	User
Support	High	Medium	Medium

Table 14-1: Profile Classification

After identifying user groups, you can evaluate each of the user profiles along several dimensions (Table 14-1):

Investment level: How much are you willing to invest in infrastructure and services to support this profile? You don't necessarily need to put down a monetary amount. Instead, it is important to differentiate between WIT users, such as executives, where you will do "whatever it takes" and BYO ("Bring your own") users benefiting from recent consumerization policies. Between these extremes, you can accommodate several levels of granularity.

Flexibility: To what extent can you mandate that users install certain applications and refrain from adding others? If the device is consumer-purchased, do you have any say in the make, model and platform? There are benefits and drawbacks to standardization. Nevertheless, it is important to establish the parameters.

Access modes: The modes of access may differ between users who need remote access over low-bandwidth and high-latency networks versus dedicated office users. These differences may, in turn, lead to different synchronization requirements.

Devices: User devices can range from desktops and laptops to thin clients and mobile devices, with many variants in these classes. In some cases, users will have multiple devices that they use to access corporate services.

Applications: The set of applications to which each group needs access is bound to be different. In fact, there may even be significant variations within user groups.

Authorization: For each of the applications, the users will have a given authorization level. They could be simple users or have elevated user privileges for approvals. A few will have restricted administration or full management rights.

Support: Some user groups tend to be very tech-savvy. In contrast, others have very high support requirements. The priority of support is often derived from the users' downtime costs, which varies by role. Furthermore, the complexity of the desktop environment may be vastly different between users who run a single application in a standard setting and those who use many applications on a non-standard device connecting to multiple networks.

SELECT

Application Map

The analysis of user requirements is mainly conducted to prepare for user and employee impact in terms of training and support. However, it can also have an influence on the design.

Application	Devices	Connectivity
Email	Mobile, Laptop, Desktop	Remote, Mobile, Office, Factory
Analytics	Mobile, Laptop, Desktop	Remote, Mobile, Office
Human Resources	Laptop, Desktop	Remote, Office
Sales Force Automation	Laptop, Desktop	Remote, Office
Calendar, Contacts	Mobile, Laptop, Desktop	Remote, Mobile, Office

Table 14-2: Application Classification

To circle back to the applications, if you can reconcile the end-user requirements, in terms of devices and connectivity, with the applications that they use, then you can generate an applications map (Table 14-2). You can use this classification to determine the back-end connectivity, manageability and security requirements that you will need to consider for each application that you implement.

Identity Management

From a technical perspective, one of the biggest implications of user selection will be the requirement to manage their identities in a federated system. Particularly where external users are involved, there will be a need to synchronize user stores in order to provide access. Even if the applications are only rolled out to employees, there will still be a requirement to share user account information, provision new users, de-provision employees who leave the organization and, potentially, facilitate a single sign-on to simplify user access and reduce help-desk costs.

We will return to the topic of identity management in Chapter 18. For now, it is important to identify the user groups, internally and externally, and realize that their selection will carry some infrastructural ramifications.

Compliance

Another potential implication of user selection can be compliance with national laws, particularly around data privacy. Depending on the location of the users, there may be regulations that restrict what kinds of personal data can be recorded and where the information can be physically stored. EU directives, for example, place some stipulations on where personally identifiable information can reside and what safeguards must be in place to protect it. If a company does business in the EU, this is an area that will require further investigation.

Chapter 26 will discuss compliance in more detail. As with identity management, above, the objective in this chapter is to identify the user groups and salient characteristics of those users (such as location). We will cover the implications later, but it is important to realize at an early stage that user selection is not necessarily trivial and may need to be revisited after further analysis.

Integrate

INTEGRATE

Chapter 15

End-to-end Design

Once you have identified the components that you will use in your solution, the next challenge is to determine how to put them all together. Established businesses usually have a complex legacy infrastructure that needs to interoperate with the new services. Except in a greenfield scenario, most of the local and end-user infrastructure will already be in place and fulfill current needs. However, you cannot afford to ignore it since it will impact your design. You can also investigate if it is optimal or needs to change.

INTEGRATE

There will be challenges in connecting all the components and making sure they are reliable and scalable. It will be necessary to look at each component and connection from many security perspectives to make sure you aren't introducing any vulnerabilities that could compromise your network and resources.

In addition to the complexity of making multiple heterogeneous parts interoperate, you also have two time dimensions to consider. At a high level, you need to determine the sequence for rolling out new cloud functionality since you are unlikely to conduct a wholesale overhaul of your entire IT landscape at once. Secondly, for each rollout, you need to consider interoperability throughout the entire transition process.

Technical Design

In its simplest form, the end-to-end design will include the end-user device, user connectivity, Internet, cloud connectivity, and the cloud itself (Figure 15-1).

At a minimum, most organizations will have users who connect to the cloud services remotely (e.g. from home or while traveling) and through the internal network. In addition to connectivity at the network level, the interfaces at the application layer need to be compatible, and it will be necessary to ensure this connectivity is reliable and secure.

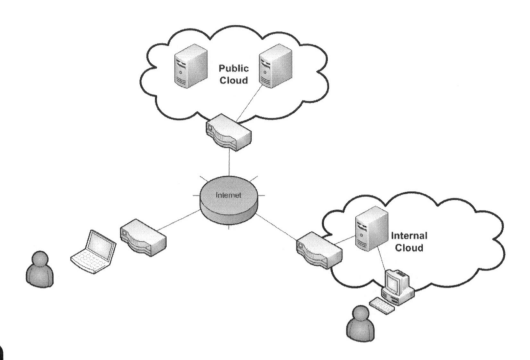

INTEGRATE

Figure 15-1: Simple end-to-end design

In a real enterprise environment, the topology is likely to be much more complex. The connectivity combinations will grow exponentially if you are using multiple cloud providers, particularly if the cloud applications are interconnected or connect to third parties and partners. There may also be some need to interconnect with the local physical infrastructure and to ensure that the whole system is manageable and supportable.

Devices

Cloud services should be device agnostic. They should work with traditional desktops, mobile devices and thin clients. Unfortunately this is much easier said than done. Regression testing on five or ten client platforms can be challenging. Moreover, if you consider every single end-user operating system, device manufacturer and even model then exhaustive interoperability testing becomes unmanageable. And still, there are additional levels of granularity if you consider all the operating system languages and application bundles that may be installed on the systems.

At the same time, it is critically important to have some idea of the end-user systems because they can have a significant impact on the machine interfaces and form factors that the applications must consider. The synchronization capabilities, which are important in a partially connected scenario, will vary from platform to platform. You need to ensure that you have some device-compatible mechanisms for remote access and secure connectivity and that you are able to manage the devices and enforce any corporate policies on them.

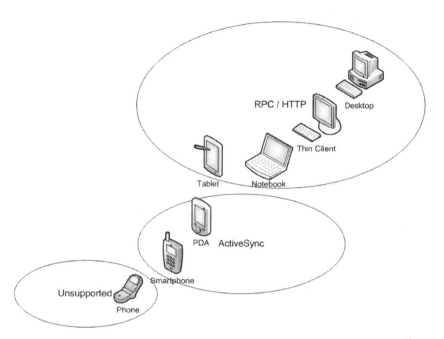

Figure 15-2: Supported Device Configurations

A good start is to bundle the sets of supported devices into separate services. Figure 15-2 illustrates one scenario. With Microsoft Exchange 2007 you have the option of supporting Windows platforms through HTTP (Outlook Web Access) and using RPC over HTTP. You might select the latter option. You can also support Windows Mobile (as well as some Symbian, iPhone and Blackberry devices using ActiveSync). There are means of connecting other phones using IMAP; however, in the case of the example above you may decide this is not a service you want to provide.

The platform is just the beginning. You would also want to take an inventory of existing systems to determine the actual operating platforms, which might range from Mac OS X and Linux to Google Chrome, Android, Symbian, RIM Blackberry and iPhones. Within these there will be multiple operating languages and versions. If you have an inventory tool running on your network, you may also be able to determine patch levels and applications running on these systems. However, even then you still need to make sure the devices actually connect to the inventory tools.

Consumerization

Device standardization is made more difficult by another common trend in enterprise IT. Many organizations have looked for ways to leverage the fact that their employees utilize a number of technological tools at home. This has several implications. From a cost perspective, users may already have hardware and software the corporation can exploit rather than duplicating it. At a minimum, the users will have a set of preferences for certain technologies and products. By allowing them to blend home and office use of their devices and tools, it can be possible to maximize user productivity and minimize duplicated costs. It's an apparent win-win situation.

Unfortunately there is also a drawback. Allowing users to bring in their own applications carries with it a host of security concerns and drastically increases the management task due to the reduction of standardization. Simply put, the number of devices, operating systems, configuration preferences and installed applications tends to grow exponentially if there is no standard operating environment. Untested applications may introduce malware onto the corporate network and can destabilize installed applications making them more difficult to troubleshoot.

INTEGRATE

In a distributed scenario, the combination of public web services and diversity of client applications creates an overwhelming challenge for support. It becomes very difficult to diagnose any problems when neither the client nor the server is within the control or direct visibility of the helpdesk.

Desktop virtualization

Another trend in the device world can serve as a partial solution to consumerization challenges – at least in some cases. Desktop virtualization provides a means to standardize parts of the technical environment while still giving the user some flexibility on the platform and other applications.

There are many different variants of desktop virtualization, which tend to address different requirements.

- *Full desktop virtualization:* Thin clients connected to dedicated blade PCs

- *Virtual desktop infrastructure:* Desktop operating system hosted on the network

- *Presentation virtualization:* Terminal services

- *Application virtualization:* Application streaming and application isolation

The primary distinctions relate to the scope of virtualization (OS, application or other container) and the timing of delivery. In some cases, the desktop component is provisioned to the thin client before the user accesses the device and is only refreshed as needed. It could also be transmitted, on demand, when the user boots the system or accesses the application. A streaming mechanism also involves transmission of the image on demand but allows the user to begin use before the delivery is complete, similar in concept to media streaming.

In addition to user response time differences, there are also implications in total bandwidth consumption and support for offline access. The latter is important in the case of lost network connectivity, which could manifest itself through complete session loss, a stalled application or, if caching is in place, normal user operation and subsequent reconciliation of changes.

Without dwelling on these distinctions, it is worth mentioning that collectively they provide three capabilities that can be helpful in addressing the twin objectives of standardization and user flexibility.

Static base images: Whether they are in the form of virtual hard disks, streamed applications or any other mechanism, the source image can be read-only so that it is not vulnerable to compromise through malware.

INTEGRATE

Automatic deployment: If a desktop is corrupted, it is easier to provision a new image to the user than it would be to rebuild the physical device

Compartmentalization: If the device is used for multiple purposes, it is easier to isolate usage so that threats and exploits do not pass from one compartment to another.

In the context of cloud computing, desktop virtualization can have some implications for the design. In particular, it influences the user device selection since the terminal systems must have the necessary client stubs to be able to connect to the back-end virtualization servers. It is possible to configure compartments on traditional desktops, but typically the greatest benefits are achieved when there are a large number of thin clients in use.

Desktop-as-a-Service also usually implies a different set of protocols. Most cloud services are browser-based and run over HTTP. On the other hand, Terminal services, and other desktop virtualization mechanisms, typically use other protocols. This can have implications on firewall settings as well as other network infrastructure components, such as proxies and load balancers.

Connectivity

In order to assess connectivity demands, you need to identify all required connections. If you wanted to approach the task systematically, you would list all applications (services being consumed) and all consumers (both users and applications) and create a map between them. You should be able to abstract some of the providers and consumers into groups to simplify the task but only if you can do so without losing any important differentiation within the group.

At a high level, the connections will include categories such as:

- Remote to cloud
- Enterprise to cloud
- Remote to enterprise
- Cloud to cloud
- Cloud to enterprise

Once you put these together into a high-level connectivity diagram (Figure 15-3), you can proceed to the next step of identifying and selecting connectivity options. We will look at this process in more detail in Chapter 16 but there are some questions that you may already want to consider at this stage.

INTEGRATE

How do you discover services? Will there be a directory with interface definitions or do you need to configure each one individually? How will data be passed between applications? For example, will you use files, asynchronous messages or synchronous web services? Do the applications have compatible services, or will you need some middleware to broker the requests?

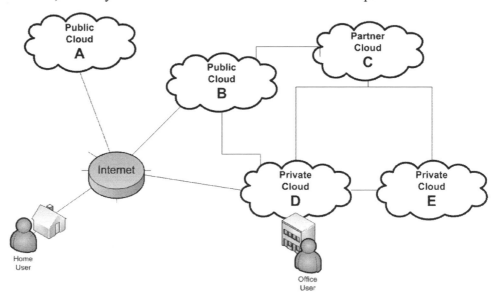

Figure 15-3: High-level connectivity diagram

How will you address remote services? How do you establish connectivity across security boundaries and address spaces? What impact is there on the corporate LAN and/or legacy remote access? Will interactions of VPNs and WLANs have any impact on the network performance of remote requests and, if so, will it influence the user experience?

Physical Infrastructure

Some infrastructure will necessarily be located outside the cloud because it involves a physical interface that must be located in proximity of the user. For example, most offices maintain printers as well as possibly scanners and fax machines. These devices need to be physically accessible to the users.

In addition to common purpose equipment there may also be line-of-business infrastructure such as point-of-sales terminals, barcode or RFID readers, surveillance cameras or even manufacturing and robotics equipment that interacts with cloud-based applications.

Challenges include the ability to create compatible connections and securing the transactions between the services and the devices. On the other hand, there are also many opportunities for cloud services in the intersection between physical and electronic print media ranging from scanning to storage, sharing and printing services.

Photo-sharing sites such as Kodak Gallery and Snapfish offer services for consumers to print high-quality pictures, which they can pick up in a store or have posted to them for convenience. In addition to traditional paper prints there are also services for cards, photo cubes (Tabblo), mugs and T-shirts.

INTEGRATE

For customers who like to produce albums of memorable events and topics that they would like to share with their friends, there are similar services such as MyPublisher, which offers photobooks and calendars, and Blurb which offers a range of book options.

For higher volume books that are intended for sale, Amazon provides a service called Createspace that competes with Blurb, Wordclay and Lulu. In addition to printing, these offer distribution and marketing services to help prospective authors who are interested in publishing their work.

Tabbloid provides a magazine publishing service that involves aggregating RSS feeds and composing a PDF file, which is mailed to subscribers. MagCloud also targets magazines but very differently. It offers a printing and publication service similar to the book publication above. Editors can upload a digital magazine, which MagCloud offers for resale, passing on a portion of the profits to the editor.

Figure 15-4: HP ePrint

HP ePrint is yet another printing service, which addresses an entirely different use case. It provides a secure way for users to print their private documents from public kiosks using any SMS-enabled mobile phone. It assumes the user has previously uploaded the file to the ePrint service using a special printer driver. A document ID is sent via SMS to the user's mobile phone and, with that ID, the user can print the document from any web browser.

ePrint also has facilities for printing from a laptop or BlackBerry PDA. In the case of the latter, a new Print button uses GPS data, coupled with an online catalogue of enterprise (and public) printers, to suggest nearby print options (Figure 15-4).

These are just the tip of the iceberg. There has been a lot of publicity over Google's efforts to digitize all printed books. HP's BookPrep also enables publishers to digitize any existing book and turn it into a virtual asset that can be sold over the Internet and printed on demand, which is attractive for older works that do not warrant being kept in stock but may nonetheless be of interest to some readers.

Management

Generally, for each component in the design we need to investigate how we will manage it. This includes all the end-user devices, the connectivity, any legacy infrastructure and all the applications involved.

You might consider pushing some of the management system into the cloud. But regardless, you need to investigate the management interfaces that are available and ensure that you can establish any necessary connectivity to access all managed entities (Figure 15-5).

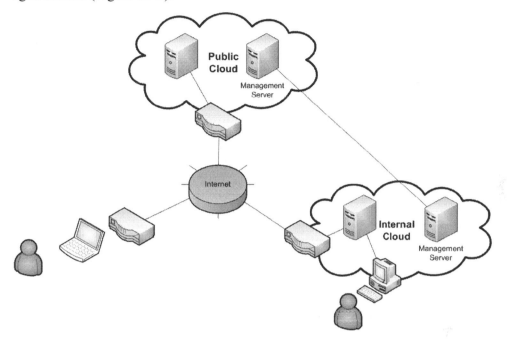

Figure 15-5: Management Servers

One challenge of splitting management components will be that you may have policies that need to be kept synchronized. Imagine for example, that you have a minimum password length of 8 characters which is increased to 10. If you have only two management servers and this is not a frequent type of occurrence, you can easily apply the change manually. However, if you are dealing with hundreds of management servers and you receive minor policy changes on a weekly basis, you can imagine how cumbersome and error-prone the task will become.

Support

Support is a potential nightmare in an organizationally distributed multi-provider outsourcing solution. It becomes very difficult to assign ownership to incidents before it is clear what is causing them. Diagnosing problems manually, without access to most of the components in the solution, complicates the task of isolating a root cause.

Nonetheless, the user should be shielded from the problems that the new architecture provides. Ideally, the user should not experience any problems at all. Self-healing infrastructure should identify issues before they are visible to the

INTEGRATE

user and should initiate a problem response to address them. When users require additional functionality or resources, they should be able to request them through a self-service portal rather than waiting in line at a call center for a service representative to validate and provision the request.

But, when there are problems, it is imperative for an integrated helpdesk to be able to escalate the problems to the correct responsible teams and for those teams to be able to access all valid components of the solution. This may include remote desktop assistance in order to observe the user's actual problem first hand and to help the user through the solution efficiently.

Metering and Billing

It is almost always useful to be able to meter the usage of cloud services. Even if the customer is internal and pays a flat cross-charge for the delivery, it is easier to demonstrate the value to the organization when you can quantify how much it is used. If you do want to attach utility pricing to the service, then it becomes even more critical to offer fine-grained metering based on a number of different usage parameters including disk space allocation, CPU cores and utilization, as well as reserved and utilized network bandwidth.

INTEGRATE

Most instrumentation is now compatible with the Web-Based Enterprise Management (WBEM) and Common Information Model (CIM) standards from the Distributed Management Task Force (DMTF). However, depending on the platform you are using to develop and host the applications, the implementation options will vary.

You may also want to bill based on less technical metrics such as subscribers, concurrent users, user-hours or transactions. External payment options include modalities ranging from credit cards to payment on invoice.

There are various cloud services that you can use to facilitate financial transactions, such as Amazon Payment Services. These are particularly attractive if you are selling to consumers and small companies and cannot afford to invest a large effort in setting up and enforcing contractual obligations.

Hybrid Cloud Design

Once an organization decides to embark on the journey of hybrid cloud, the task is not only to selectively source an increasing number of services from public providers. The bigger challenge is to integrate them dynamically with other services running internally and externally.

Figure 15-6: Hybrid Silos

To illustrate, consider some of the integration options for hybrid cloud computing. The first step of a hybrid cloud is for the services to run in independent silos without any interaction (Figure 15-6). For example, an organization might run Microsoft Exchange internally and use Salesforce.com as their publicly procured CRM service. If the two do not interact, this is not a difficult achievement.

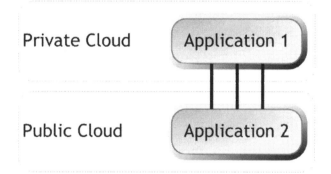

Figure 15-7: Static Hybrid Integration

INTEGRATE

The next step would then be to integrate them where it makes sense (Figure 15-7). There might be a connection from Salesforce.com to the internal Active Directory for single sign-on or the service might leverage Microsoft Exchange to deliver email notifications and schedule tasks. This integration needs careful planning to ensure compatibility and safeguard any sensitive data.

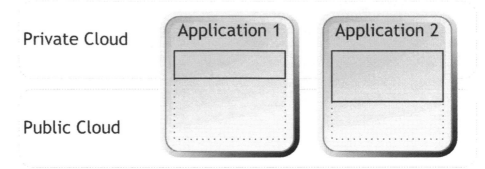

Figure 15-8: Dynamic Hybrid Integration

The last step is support for dynamic workload distribution (Figure 15-8). This means that there must be equivalent internal and external services and they need interface compatibility. One reason for this approach would be to establish a disaster recovery facility. In the event of catastrophic failure of the internal data center, the company could shift the workload to the cloud and restart the service there.

INTEGRATE

An even more ambitious goal is cloudbursting, which can be used to optimize costs and flexibility. If the organization is able to shift workloads in real-time, then it is possible to run services internally as a standard practice. However, if there are spikes in activity or the service grows faster than anticipated, the company can off-load any processing that exceeds its internal capacity.

Chapter 16

Connectivity

An essential ingredient of any network-based solution is connectivity. Unless the systems are connected, they cannot operate, at least for any extended period of time. In the case of cloud computing, data and processing are both highly distributed making reliable, efficient and secure connectivity all the more critical.

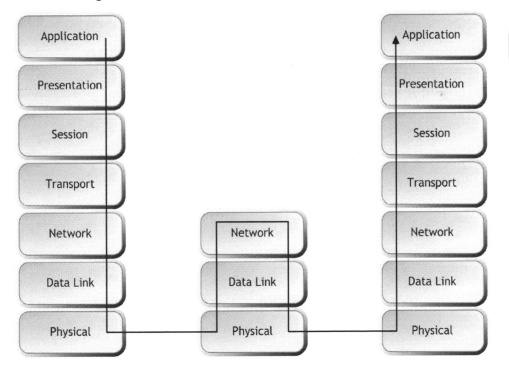

Figure 16-1: OSI Network Model

The International Organization for Standardization (ISO) defines seven different levels of connectivity in its reference stack as part of its Open Systems Interconnection (OSI) initiative (Figure 16-1). While networking appliances may only include the bottom layers, all end-nodes running networked applications will need connectivity of the whole stack:

Physical Layer defines the electrical and physical specifications of devices and connection media including pin layouts, voltages and cable specifications.

Data Link Layer provides physical addressing, flow control, media access control, and optional error detection and correction over a single link of physical media.

Network Layer routes data packets from a source to its destination over one or more hops, in some cases also fragmenting and reassembling the packets.

Transport Layer provides additional error control as well as controlling the reliability of a given link through flow control, segmentation and retransmissions.

Session Layer manages and terminates connections between hosts providing synchronization, checkpoints, termination and restart procedures.

Presentation Layer provides an application independent data format for network transmission as well as serialization, encryption and compression facilities.

Application Layer provides an interface to applications that identifies hosts and represents the network services to the applications.

INTEGRATE

Since cloud services are almost entirely Internet-based, your primary concern is the Network Layer (IP) and Application Layer, but it is good to understand how they all interact together. Frequently problems in Network Layer connectivity are due to Physical Layer faults or misconfiguration at the Data Link Layer.

The Network Layer is typically implemented with the Internet Protocol version 4 (IPv4) but, increasingly you may also encounter requirements for IPv6. We will return to this topic in Chapter 30.

The most common Transport Layer protocol on the Internet is the Transmission Control Protocol (TCP), for reliable connections, followed by the User Datagram Protocol (UDP) for stateless transmissions such as packet broadcasting and multicasting. A more recent protocol designed for streaming media is the Stream Control Transmission Protocol (SCTP), which combines some of the advantages of both TCP and UDP.

Tunneling protocols (such as IPsec[1]) are also often placed in the Transport Layer. This can be confusing since the tunnels then typically enable a virtual Network Layer protocol (such as IPv4). The OSI model was designed before virtual private networks became so popular so it doesn't deal with the problem elegantly.

The Session layer is largely absent in the Internet Protocol stack, whereby some of its functions are included in other layers. For example, TCP includes capabilities to gracefully close sessions.

The Presentation Layer is also not an explicit part of Internet applications. Many use various forms of XML encodings, which would be a responsibility of this layer. However, the packaging and interpretation is performed by the applications at both end-points and is not considered a network task.

Internet Applications very often encapsulate all traffic in HTTP – at the Application Layer. The user-oriented traffic may actually include HTML that is to be presented in visual form. But HTTP is also very popular for application-to-application traffic because it is one of the few protocols that can pass through most firewalls.

Network Connectivity

INTEGRATE

Required Connections

The first challenge to address is how to provide network and transport connectivity between each of the end-user and back-end systems. You can begin by determining which end-points need to interact with each other.

---

[1] Note that tunneling is not restricted to traditional VPN protocols. It has become very popular to wrap many traditional protocols in HTTP in order to facilitate firewall traversals. Some applications also build on the Web 2.0 protocols, such as Twitter, to leverage some of their rich sets of features.

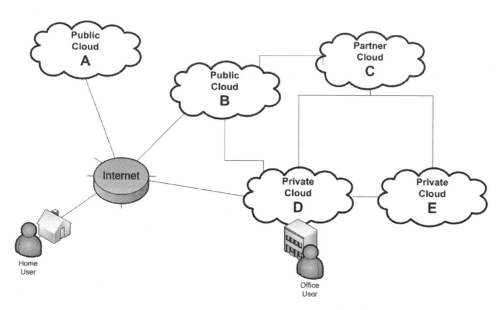

Figure 16-2: Basic Cloud Connectivity

INTEGRATE

It may not be necessary to create a full-mesh network architecture. For example, in Figure 16-2 the network design shows that services from Public Cloud A are accessed via the Internet regardless of where the users connect. Public Cloud B, on the other hand, is accessible from the Internet for remote users. But there is also a private connection to the internal network Private Cloud D. Partner Cloud C does not offer any Internet access at all. Users and services from Private Cloud D and E can access C, and C can interact with services on Public Cloud B. There are also two private networks, which might be used for disaster recovery and/or load-balancing. Office users can connect to these directly, whereas a Home user would connect via the Internet over a secure channel.

An actual enterprise implementation will vary significantly from the example. A real deployment may be considerably more complex, but the basic principles are the same. The first step is to identify and classify all the required connections. Some of these may already be in place, but they should still be included in the design since there may be potential impact on them from the shifting of services and network traffic.

It is also important to consider internal connectivity within cloud providers. If a given cloud is geographically dispersed, it may be useful to break it apart as in the example above with Private Cloud D and E.

Even if the cloud is confined to one data center, it is critical to understand the routing topologies and bandwidth utilization on each of the links. If the data center is approaching capacity constraints, it may be necessary to re-architect the network or upgrade some of the links.

Connection Requirements

The next step will be to describe the requirements for each connection.

- What applications and traffic will run over it?
- How critical is the connection to the business?
- Are there any bandwidth/latency constraints?
- Who can access the connection? Is it secured?
- How reliable is it?
- Can you implement any fail-over or redundancy?

Link	Bandwidth	Latency	QoS	Security
I-A	10 Gbps	10 msec	No	SSL
I-B	1 Gpbs	10 msec	No	SSL
I-D	100 Mbps	10 msec	No	SSL
B-C	50 Mbps	20 msec	Yes	SSL
B-D	30 Mbps	10 msec	Yes	SSL
C-D	1 Gbps	20 msec	Yes	IPsec
C-E	1 Gbps	20 msec	Yes	IPsec
D-E	10 Gbps	10 msec	Yes	IPsec

Table 16-1: Connection Requirements

INTEGRATE

Some of the main categories are bandwidth and latency. You may also have specific requirements related to Quality of Service (QoS) and security (Table 16-1).

The bandwidth requirement you specify will range from your average bandwidth to your peak load depending on the criticality of the data that goes across it. Anything less than your average requirements will create a bottleneck that isn't sustainable. Allocating above your expected peak load (including some margin for error and growth) will not present a technical problem but is probably not economical.

Within that range, it is important to consider the impact of some amount of data loss during peak usage. If you are likely to lose major transactions, or even violate some laws, then you will want to err on the side of caution and overcapacity. On the other hand, if the loss can be easily sustained and the traffic resent at a later time, then you may be able to save costs by allocating resources more stringently.

Latency is largely independent of bandwidth and represents the delays that occur between sending a packet from the source and receiving it at the destination. It is one of the most critical factors affecting the user experience and speed of transactions. A brokerage can lose up to $4 million per millisecond of latency(Reporter, 2008). Google estimates that an additional 500 milliseconds of latency result in a reduction of 20% of traffic to its sites. And Amazon is calculated to lose 1% of sales for every 100 milliseconds of latency (James & Stolz, 2009). Given such drastic financial implications, it is wise to consider the geographical placement of any key distribution points.

QoS includes considerations of latency but also the percentage of dropped packets and jitter (or variance in latency). Browser-based HTTP access is largely resilient to minor transmission problems. The upper layers in the protocol stack can recover errors without the user noticing a difference. However, interactive streaming media, such as Internet Telephony and Video over IP, tend to expose network glitches and variability much more awkwardly to the user.

If the connections carry any sensitive traffic, it is also necessary for them to be secured. This doesn't necessarily mean they must be encrypted at the Network or Transport Layer. The applications may use the Secure Socket Layer (SSL) which will provide a similar level of protection. Nonetheless, the requirement should be documented so that it isn't inadvertently lost if the application provider assumes network-layer security.

Connection Options

INTEGRATE

After considering the requirements for each of the connections, comes the task of examining the possible options that meet the needs. There may be multiple telecommunications providers that offer network links between two end-points. In some cases, it may just come down to a financial decision on the costs (fixed and variable) that both demand. However, it is also worth looking at the service-level agreements, ability to expand and redundancy capabilities.

You may have additional options. For example, if you discover that one application is responsible for a high proportion of network activity, or cannot cope with the link latency the providers can offer, then you could look at restructuring the topology. One possibility would be to choose an alternate cloud provider, but you may be able to displace some of your internal infrastructure to improve the network performance, instead.

Imagine that you have a latency or bandwidth problem with link BD above. You might be able to move a server that interacted heavily with cloud services in Public Cloud B from Private Cloud D into a co-location with Public Cloud B. Obviously, this would have ramifications for connections that the server initiates with other internal systems; but if they are not as network-intensive or network-sensitive, it may be the better option.

You may not have control or responsibility over all the links that are critical to your business operation. Link BC, above, would be administered between your partner and cloud service provider. You may also depend on links between cloud service providers that are not contractually your responsibility. Nonetheless, it is in your best interests to verify that these links exist, meet your requirements and are governed by service-level agreements.

Finally, you need to look at which mechanisms you will use to secure the connections. It may depend on how you are connecting to the cloud service provider. If you have a dedicated connection (e.g. through an MPLS network), you may not feel the need to further protect it even though it is not encrypted. On the other hand, if you are leveraging a shared Internet connection or are not comfortable with the security precautions of your ISP then you may want to protect the connection with IPsec or an SSL VPN.

Connectivity Configuration

Every network configuration involves some largely manual tasks to ensure that all configuration settings match at each end. Presumably all your cloud providers, including your own business, have experts who can make these happen.

At a network design level, however, there are some considerations that are good to verify early.

INTEGRATE

Addressability: How will the connection end-points locate their communications partners? You may choose to request static IP addresses, which will simplify connectivity issues. You may also want to register the servers in the global Domain Name System so that the address space can change at a later point in time without disruption to the applications.

Firewall configuration: All clouds will probably have one or more firewalls that separate them from the Internet and other security domains. If your applications need to connect through firewalls, you need to ensure that the protocols and host IP addresses are registered in the firewalls. Your connections may also pass through HTTP proxies which rewrite headers and/or present their own IP addresses to the firewalls. There are many possibilities. The bottom line is that you need to test your application through the firewall to ensure that it works.

Routing: IP traffic needs to be routed from each end-point to the other. In a globally routable address space this is not ordinarily a challenge. Your network administrators will have ensured that all external traffic is funneled in the right direction. However, if the service provider uses Network Address Translation to create address space, then you may need to update your routing tables in order to be able to communicate with the correspondent.

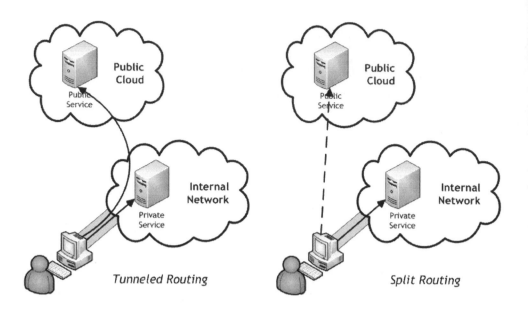

Figure 16-3: Tunneled versus Split Routing

INTEGRATE

Split Routing is another potential area for consideration (Figure 16-3). The most common use-case is a remote client connecting through a VPN to access corporate resources. If the tunnel is exclusive, then all the traffic from the user's PC goes through the corporate network - even the traffic that is destined for the Internet. This routing is inefficient but it also allows the enterprise to more closely monitor traffic and enforce policies. The tendency today is to split the tunnels so that traffic is directed along its most efficient path. However, it is not necessarily the best solution for enterprises with tightly enforced network filtering.

Unfortunately, it's impossible to enumerate all the configuration pitfalls you may encounter. Each case is unique in its requirements. The key consideration is not to underestimate the complexity which new delivery models entail. Let me illustrate with a non-intuitive example of a problem we encountered:

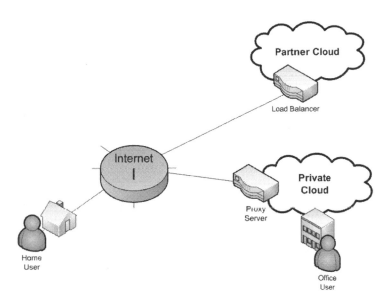

Figure 16-4: Proxy-channeled Traffic

Figure 16-4 is a simplified version of our previous topology. In this case, the private cloud (internal LAN) connects with the partner's cloud via the Internet. Users can also access the partner resources remotely, which presents an elegant and versatile solution. The challenge is that all outgoing traffic is routed through the internal firewall via a proxy server. Thus, all outgoing traffic presents itself with the same IP address, which is not ordinarily a problem. However, if the Load Balancer receiving the connections is only expecting one IP address per connection and one connection per user, then it may diagnose the incoming traffic as a denial-of-service attack and reject further connections leading to unavailability of the service.

Virtual Private Cloud

As alluded to above, establishing secure connectivity between an enterprise data center and components is not trivial. When you compound the complexity of discovering network resources, addressing them and ensuring all traffic is protected as it passes through public networks, the result is a challenge some organizations choose to forego.

One means of facilitating the task, and thereby seamlessly extending legacy applications into the cloud is through the use of a so-called Virtual Private Cloud (Figure 16-5).

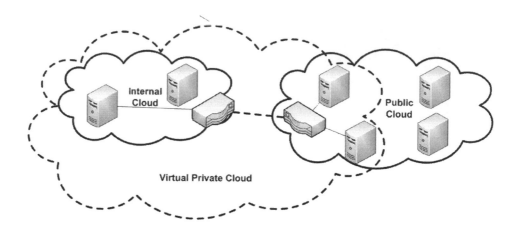

Figure 16-5: Virtual Private Cloud

Amazon runs a service by the same name, which essentially provides secure connectivity into a segment of Amazon's EC2 cloud. Other solutions, such as CohesiveFT's vns-cubed, provide similar functionality across cloud service providers. CloudSwitch also offers facilities to migrate virtual machines from the enterprise data center into the cloud. Layer-two bridging ensures that the network environment, including host names, IP and MAC addresses, remains intact thereby making it relatively easy to migrate legacy applications into a secure hybrid environment.

Content Delivery Networks

In some cases, content delivery (or distribution) networks (CDNs) can also help to improve performance and scalability when there are bottlenecks in backbone capacity or if there is excessive latency between two end-points. CDNs are networks of computers that collaborate to distribute content. They replicate content (media files, software, documents, and real-time media streams) to so-called edge servers that are as close as possible to end-users.

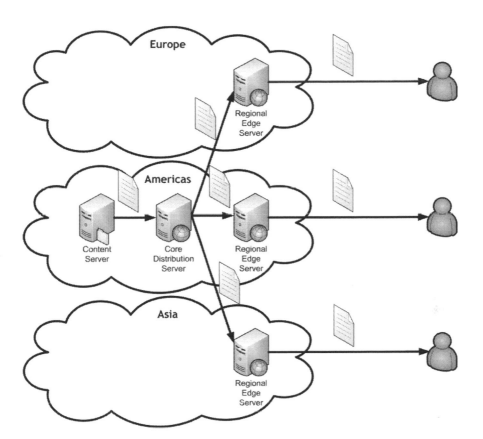

Figure 16-6: Simple Content Distribution Network

Figure 16-6 illustrates a simple content distribution network. Content is created on the Content Server and replicated into the CDN initially through synchronization with a core distribution server. The data is then propagated to multiple edge servers and the user can retrieve the content from the closest distribution point.

To understand the value proposition, imagine that the initial content is created in the United States. It is copied first to a core CDN server and then once each across transoceanic links to Europe and Asia as well as to one edge server in the Americas. The benefit in the Americas is not pronounced. But if thousands of users retrieve the content in Europe and Asia, they will only be loading the regional links and the intercontinental traffic is minimized.

Content delivery networks are not simple to build. In order to work effectively they must determine user proximity, for example based on reactive or proactive probing. They may even monitor the connection and redirect users in-session. In addition, they typically employ advanced systems for web caching, server-load balancing and request routing (HTML rewriting, DNS-based). In some cases, they also provide real-time statistics and usage logs to their customers.

INTEGRATE

They help off-load the traffic on the Internet backbone and along the entire routing path which equates to decreased bandwidth bottlenecks and end-user latency. They also reduce jitter, packet loss and minimize peak/surge performance degradation. Finally, the additional redundancy of the CDN can ensure higher availability in the face of local outages that might affect individual edge servers.

In summary, organizations that deliver significant volume of content that is sensitive to delivery times and patterns may want to investigate both the content-delivery capabilities of their cloud provider (e.g. Amazon CloudFront) as well as some of the leading CDN offerings, including Akamai and Limelight.

Application Connectivity

Once the network infrastructure is in place, it is time to move on to the applications, which also need to be connected. In order to determine if the components can interoperate, you need to establish which interfaces/protocols are used between them and whether they are standard, or at least common, between the endpoints.

Common integration styles to couple applications include:

INTEGRATE

- Data-scraping
- File Transfer
- Shared Database
- Message Passing
- Remote Procedure Call

Data-scraping is one of the oldest, and most primitive, forms of application integration. It refers to a mechanism of parsing the output user interface for application information. Screen-scraping was a popular technique used to upgrade and interface with terminal-based applications. Web-scraping is still often used to extract information from browser applications when no other interface exists.

The challenge of this approach is that the applications are designed for human, rather than programmatic, access. It can be difficult to navigate the user interface without a thorough understanding of the application logic. The data may not always be positioned consistently on screen and may not correspond directly to the stored data. These problems lead to scalability and stability problems and make the approach a case of last resort.

Nonetheless, there may still be instances in a cloud-based implementation where it presents the only connectivity option. In this case, there will be a need to install a client stub (which might be a standard browser in the case of web scraping) on the system running the consuming application. It will also be necessary to deliver application-level connectivity between the client and any servers or databases that it requires. In some cases, it may be possible (and simpler) to relocate the whole application stack onto the same subnet as the consuming application instead of arranging for complex connectivity requirements.

File Transfer is the next option. It is suitable when applications don't expose any programmatic interfaces but do offer capabilities to import and export data, for example through reporting functions. Typical formats might include comma-delimited text files, fixed-field-size reports and, more recently, XML or JSON. If the two end-points don't share a common format, an additional transformation step may also be required.

In the cloud environment, file transfer is one of the simplest mechanisms to accommodate as it only requires a means of copying files from one system to another. This can be accomplished through FTP, HTTP or SMTP, and other protocols. The key requirement is therefore only to enable the relevant protocol between the two end-points, or at least from the cloud application to the drop and pickup point.

Shared Database allows for tighter integration between applications. They can share data while also leveraging the transactional capabilities of the database management system. The main application requirements will be the use of a common schema by both applications as well as database connectivity between the cloud application and the database repository. Don't forget the operational responsibilities this may imply if the database ownership and management cross organizational boundaries.

A related approach would be to synchronize independent data repositories leveraging the replication capabilities of most relational database systems. This is a simple, low-cost solution. A more sophisticated mechanism would be the use of a transaction processing monitoring such as BEA Tuxedo, Microsoft MTS or IBM CICS, which can guarantee integrity of transactions, while also providing queuing, routing, and load balancing capabilities.

Message Passing is currently the most popular of the asynchronous communications mechanisms (such as File Transfer and Shared Database). It passes information in the form of messages, which have a predefined structure (schema) and embed the information as content (data). Very often these messages are queued with a message-oriented middleware (MOM) component. MOM, usually visualized as a bus or hub with spokes, can also structure the information flows in channels, pipes and filters and can transform or route the messages according to business logic rules.

The key considerations with MOM mirror those of database-oriented integration. It is essential that the end-points share a common schema; and all applications need to have connectivity to the central MOM component, often called the Enterprise Service Bus.

Remote Procedure Calls offer a synchronous alternative to message passing. This means that the calling application is blocked until the call completes. The logic of the application is therefore simpler since it is much easier to guarantee data integrity. However, the blocking nature may also introduce delays in processing, particularly if the calls involve large amounts of computation or run over high-latency links.

Some of the most common synchronous communications mechanisms in the past have included OSF DCE and distributed objects such as CORBA, JCA and Microsoft COM. Current web-services architectures more frequently use SOAP (formerly XML-RPC) and REST.

In addition to ensuring connectivity of the transport protocol (typically HTTP for SOAP and REST), it is necessary for the calling application to issue requests that align with the published interfaces of the providing application. It may be possible to derive these from a WSDL definition or look them up in a UDDI repository. But most commonly, the developer is familiar with the interface definition and codes the client accordingly.

INTEGRATE

As noted in the preceding discussion, application connectivity intersects with network connectivity at the application protocol level. In other words, the application must use a transfer protocol such as HTTP, FTP, SMTP or a database-oriented connection protocol such as JDBC or ODBC. It will be the task of the network and perimeter security managers to establish this connectivity through all relevant firewalls and middleware.

Beyond establishing protocol connectivity, it is important to verify that business processes will be viable across all the applications that are involved. This means that service levels, reliability and performance expectations of each of the applications must be determined, as well as their impact on other applications that might interact with them.

Application Integration Services

An interesting area that is currently developing is the emergence of vendors, such as Dell Boomi, IBM Cast Iron, Informatica and Pervasive that provide integration services to connect on-premise, as well as cloud-based, applications at the data level.

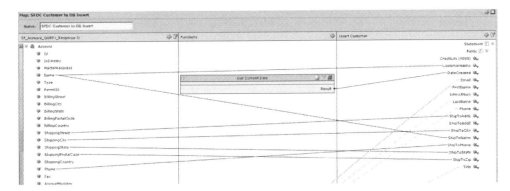

Figure 16-7: Boomi Data Mapping

These integration services allow customers to define data mappings (Figure 16-7) and transformations between a wide range of application sources using web-based portals. Some offer rich sets of templates and packaged integration processes as well as graphic workflow and business logic development capabilities (Figure 16-8).

INTEGRATE

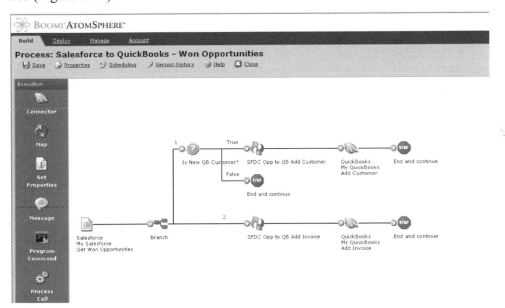

Figure 16-8: Boomi AtomSphere Workflow

Information Connectivity

There is another conceptual level of connectivity that is located above the application and business process layer. All Information Technology has an ultimate purpose of gathering and providing information to its users. It is important for this information to be accessible as an integrated whole even if it is dispersed among multiple providers and distributed across geographical boundaries.

Therefore, content repositories including portals, collaboration tools, messaging systems and data warehouses need to be aggregated, classified and connected. An advanced archiving system can help to provide enterprise search functionality to company users and can also facilitate compliance for legal electronic discovery requests.

In order to provide these securely and efficiently, it is necessary to consolidate and de-duplicate all the information sources, maintain and enforce authorization and access controls, and ensure that no data is inadvertently leaked. This means enforcing encryption and data destruction policies – both locally on user devices as well as centrally in the data repositories.

Archiving in the cloud is not trivial since large amounts of data are involved. While cloud storage is convenient in that it is elastically scalable and implies a certain amount of data redundancy, it is not typically viable to constantly replicate all data from an enterprise into a cloud service provider for archival.

INTEGRATE

This leads to the question of where to position the archival system, co-located with the storage, or alternatively closer to the data source. Since the archivable information is already de-duplicated and compressed it would usually be efficient to place the archiving system closer to the information source. However, the situation may not be quite as simple in a real scenario, which includes multiple distributed information systems and a geographically distributed cloud storage provider.

Chapter 17

Resilience

Cloud computing introduces new topologies, architectures and infrastructural components that an organization needs to consider as it strives to ensure that its services will be able to continue reliably in the face of subsystem failures, major disasters as well as the natural growth and evolution of the system. To address these I have collected the topics of Availability, Business Continuity and Capacity Planning under the header of Resilience.

INTEGRATE

Uptime

Availability measures the percentage of time a particular resource or service is in a usable state over a measured time interval. Ideally, all resources would be available 100% of the time. In practice, there is always some downtime due to technical problems or planned maintenance.

Nines	Availability	Downtime per year (d hh:mm:ss)
2	99%	3 15:39:29
3	99.9%	8:45:56
4	99.99%	0:52:35
5	99.999%	0:05:15

Table 17-1: Availability / Downtime matrix

It is common to describe approximate uptime in terms of the number of "nines" of availability. As illustrated in Table 17-1, five nines is a very ambitious objective indeed, one that can typically only be achieved in a Tier-4 data center under tightly enforced conditions. Cloud providers may technically also be able to offer these service levels but the associated costs would usually make the packages financially unattractive. So, it is much more common to see availability on the order of three nines, or 99.9%.

Service levels are not transitive. In other words, if you use Amazon Web Services and they promise 99.95%, this doesn't automatically imply that your services will have the same availability. Your services may fail while your AWS infrastructure remains intact. In other cases, your services may be resilient to underlying AWS failures.

By the same token, you may be able to increase uptime beyond that of your infrastructure providers if you can successfully leverage multiple providers and create a redundancy layer that spans them.

Before becoming too obsessed with a high level of availability, consider the price. The cost of each additional 'nine' increases exponentially. Yes, there is less than one hour per year difference between four 'nines' and ten 'nines', which is not significant for most services. It is important to match the costs of downtime with the costs of increasing uptime.

INTEGRATE

What constitutes a reasonable level of availability will also depend very much on the resource in question. Hardware resources have physical limitations that make them prone to failure over time. However, if sufficient redundancy and transparent failover is incorporated into the system, then these failures may not be noticeable by the service consumers.

Cloud Availability

In spite of potential fault tolerance at the virtualization layer, current cloud implementations typically present a higher number of failures on virtual platforms than you might expect on a physical machine (Reese, 2009, pp. 54, 56). Furthermore, due to their non-persistent nature, all changes are lost when the VM is powered down.

However, they also have a significant benefit in that they are much easier and faster to repair. Rather than isolating and replacing a faulty component, it is sufficient to re-launch a virtual instance on another physical machine. Thus, you need to design redundancy into a solution at an application and management layer. If you are able to fail-over between virtual instances without data loss, and if your user transactions are stateless, then you may well be able to hide any downtime from your users.

For each connection and component you should determine who is responsible and how critical it is. You can then assess the controls that are in place to establish whether there is any redundancy or if it represents a single-point-of failure.

Redundancy

The most common way to achieve high uptime is through redundancy, whereby there are multiple approaches you can use to configure it. The simplest is to replicate all components. This means that you have two or more of every system, storage device and network appliance. When one unit fails then you can designate the backup as the primary device. This may be a highly available solution, but it is not particularly efficient since you have idle hardware waiting only for a failure.

An alternative is to configure one original system and replicate it into multiple zones but not start the system until it is needed. This may involve some switchover time but at least the standby costs are minimal.

A third option is to implement load balancing (through round-robin DNS or dynamic DNS) with some excess capacity to accommodate an outage of one or more components. This also has the drawback that the systems will not be fully utilized possibly even during peak loads. However, it has the benefit of improving performance and providing seamless failover.

Over the past few decades, a large amount of the focus on distributed, load-balanced systems has been centered around clustering. The idea of a cluster is a set of computers that work together so closely they can be viewed as a single system. High-availability clusters (also known as HA clusters or failover clusters) are groups of computers supporting server applications that cannot afford down-time. They are well suited for critical databases, business applications and electronic commerce websites.

INTEGRATE

Reliability

Clusters can be very effective, but they are also quite expensive. There are several strategies to achieve high uptime with commodity components. Traditionally the focus has been on ensuring high reliability of all components. Where this is not possible, or insufficient, there is an option of pursuing fault tolerance through redundancy and fast failover capability. At the same time, it is worth looking at the overall architecture to ensure that components are loosely coupled and complexity is kept to a minimum. A more recent approach is to accept occasional failures and instead concentrate on expediting the restoration of the service.

Component Reliability

The first approach tries to select the highest grade parts for each component of the solution. In the past, disciplines such as Total Quality Management and Six Sigma have demonstrated that a lot can be achieved through diligence and a commitment to quality throughout the whole system.

There is much to be said for a focus on quality. However, it is not trivial to pursue this avenue in a cloud-oriented solution due to the complexity of the system and the lack of control over all the elements.

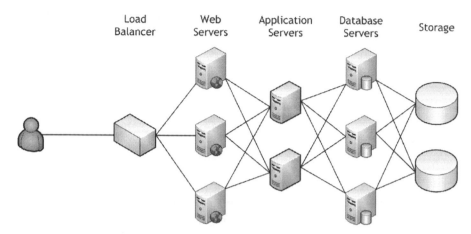

Figure 17-1: Application Components

On the one hand, there are a number of components to consider (Figure 17-1). The applications may run over many different physical and virtual systems with data distributed even more widely. In addition to the three tiers of most web applications, you need to look at load balancers and the entire network infrastructure including the physical links, the routing tables and DNS.

Simply validating the hardware configuration will not be sufficient. The biggest threat to availability is typically software bugs, which are notoriously difficult to pinpoint. You need to ensure that all services perform as expected both in terms of functionality and performance. This guarantee doesn't automatically follow from a collection of error-free components. As the system scales, the number of linkages and dependencies tends to grow exponentially. A second problem is that many of the components are likely to be outsourced. Even in a pure private cloud implementation, there are network links and infrastructure that may be outside the control of the organization.

In addition to these technical obstacles, there are financial considerations. Adoption of premium components and systems runs counter to the principle of cloud computing to minimize costs by relying on standardized and commoditized parts. Even if systematic quality processes are achievable, they may not represent the most cost-effective avenue to reliability.

Fault Tolerance

In the world of Internet, services fail. Servers fail, networks fail, connections get stuck and responses are not sent back to requests in a timely manner. When dealing with massive volumes of compute capacity and complex network connections, it is a statistical fact that some elements will fail.

Given the challenges of ensuring that no part in the system fails, the next logical step is to accept that there may be local failures but strive for the system to be able to hide them. In other words: build the system assuming that things will fail, but ensure users never see outages and data is never lost.

You need to provide fault tolerance for all components at all layers of the architecture including: applications, file systems, CPU, I/O ports, network links, etc. In practice, tolerating faults involves making provisions for common failures or bottlenecks. A cloud-aware application must be able to cope with failures in services and infrastructure that lead to both planned and unplanned downtime.

Immunity to failures means never expecting the system to be stable. Instead, the application must assume nodes are continuously leaving, joining and failing. The most common technique in achieving fault tolerance is to provide some amount of redundancy along the same principles of Redundant Array of Interchangeable Disks (RAID), which has achieved great success in the area of storage.

Reduced Complexity / Loose Coupling

Unfortunately, true fault tolerance is a very difficult objective to achieve. A less ambitious approach to solving the problem in a scalable manner is to reduce the interlinked complexity of the system. By enforcing strong functional cohesion internally, and decreasing external dependencies through loose coupling, you can minimize the impact of local failures and thereby allow the system to continue even when a component encounters major problems.

Werner Vogels, Amazon CTO, has provided copious advice in his blog[1] on how Amazon has been able to maintain high availability of one of the largest Internet storefronts using techniques that follow this methodology. Some points to consider include autonomy, loose coupling and acceptance of failure. It's hard to argue with success so we've drawn on his wisdom.

An autonomous system is able to make decisions based on local state using inferential and probabilistic techniques. It should be able to configure and manage itself as well as diagnose and repair any faults. Full autonomy removes the dependency on other components so that failures remain isolated. This can be partially achieved through effective hierarchical and functional decomposition of workloads into well-understood building blocks.

In most cases, however, some interconnections are inevitable. The objective then becomes asynchrony. By minimizing concurrency, it is possible to reduce the

---

[1] www.allthingsdistributed.com

propagation of failures from one module to another. Locking, in particular, is the most dangerous form of concurrency since anything that requires agreement will eventually become a bottleneck.

Where possible it may be sensible to define internal SLAs between web services (from client to services), so that consuming applications can determine the degree of reliance on other services. However, rather than aspiring to an almost perfect availability rate and passing that expectation on to clients, it is safer to consider failure a common occurrence and pass the burden of redundancy and tolerance on to the application, which can manage it most effectively. If nodes are symmetric (homogeneous), then it is relatively easy for client nodes to fail over when needed and a single failure should not interrupt the service.

At the heart of this guidance lies a trend to weaker consistency where possible. Historically, online transactions processing has used the ACID (atomicity, consistency, isolation, durability) test to ensure that database transactions are processed reliably. This test enforces strong consistency. However, in accordance with the CAP model, it also fails easily, especially in a distributed environment.

INTEGRATE

An alternate approach called BASE (Basically Available; Soft-state/Scalable; Eventually-consistent) emphasizes availability and offers only weak consistency on a best-effort basis. ACID guarantees are useful, but become costly with scale. BASE, on the other hand, is simple and fast.

In spite of its advantages, weak consistency is not necessarily easier to implement. In fact, it is more difficult to program as it needs to explicitly consider technical details such as quorum, information lifetime, leases, cache and optimistic updating with posterior conflict resolution.

The choice begins at the data design and modeling stage and derives from the basic question of why you need transactions. A two-phase commit will eventually fail in a distributed environment due to locking problems. But you may be able to address it by denormalizing the tables, running the transactions on a single physical node or splitting the transactions with compensating actions for recovery.

Fast Recovery

One final approach to cloud-related failures again assumes there will be problems, but deals with them by trying to minimize the impact through a fast recovery. In its extreme form, this means avoiding all troubleshooting (hence it is often called "lazy") and simply reinitializing the system when there is an incident.

The most important activity in this space is called "recovery-oriented computing". It focuses on synchronously redundant and heavily monitored data that is seamlessly partitioned. The underlying premise is that availability is not only determined by the mean-time-between-failures (MTBF) but also the mean-time-to-repair (MTTR). In a highly virtualized system it can be at least as effective to pursue MTTR which involves a focus on (Berkeley/Stanford, 2008):

- Isolation and redundancy

- System-wide undo support

- Integrated diagnostic support

- Online verification and recovery mechanisms

- Modularity, measurability and restartability

Business Continuity

There are many kinds of disaster. Some are part of nature, such as earthquakes, tornados, floods and hurricanes. Others are caused by human intervention, including wars, terrorism, sabotage as well as accidents or errors.

A business continuity plan should make no assumptions on the cause of the disaster. It needs to plan for a complete failure and be in a position to rebuild anything and everything.

INTEGRATE

Business Impact Analysis

That said, not everything is worth saving at any cost. It is important to determine the valuation of all important assets, whether they be tangible, such as hardware or intangible, such as data.

IT systems are typically most concerned with the recovery of information. It is possible to quantify the requirements with two important metrics:

The *Recovery Time Objective* (RTO) measures the amount of time until the system is operational again.

The *Recovery Point Objective* (RPO) measures how recent the information must be. Stated differently, how much data can you afford to lose (e.g. most recent day, minutes, seconds)?

It's important to note that the RTO and RPO are both financial, rather than technical, calculations. It might seem attractive to aim for an RPO of no data loss and a near-instantaneous RTO. Technically, it is possible to achieve these objectives but they come at a cost, which is likely to increase exponentially as the metrics approach zero.

There are customers, such as banks, who cannot afford to lose a single transaction. Each customer is also likely to have some applications that are more sensitive to failures than other. The key is to ensure that your approach captures your business objectives but does so without spending more on the solution than the underlying data or service availability is worth.

Business Continuity Plan

The business continuity plan entails three phases: Prevent, Detect, Correct.

Prevent: There is only limited recourse against natural disasters. They cannot be prevented; however, the damage can be controlled. The selection criteria for the location for a data center should include statistical information on the occurrence of earthquakes, floods, tropical storms and other localized phenomena.

The mission-critical buildings (not only the data center) must also be built to specifications that can sustain earthquakes, fires and tornados and be equipped with safety systems to deal with fire and possibly flooding. Electrical problems can be reduced with a redundant UPS and diesel generators as well as surge protectors.

Not to be neglected are systematic procedures that prevent accidents, intrusions and sabotage.

INTEGRATE

Detect: If a disaster does occur, it is vital to trigger emergency precautions as soon as possible. An active disaster monitoring system may predict a disaster before its full impact is felt giving sufficient time for a graceful shutdown of applications and potentially even additional backups and data replication.

Correct: The two primary mechanisms to deal with IT loss in the case of a disaster are redundancy and backup. We will look at both of these in more detail below. An important part of the plan is that these precautions must be fully and frequently tested from the backup to the restore phase.

Redundancy

The physical infrastructure should be replicated in a geographically removed location so that it is unlikely to be affected by the same disaster. The more distant the two locations are the better the chances that the second will survive a disaster of the first. A different continent is therefore ideal, but that level of precaution may not be necessary in every case.

An additional level of independence can be achieved if a backup is hosted by a second provider. In this case, an incident (e.g. large-scale intrusion or malware attack) cannot easily affect both the backup and the primary system.

Backups

Multiple levels of backups can help to achieve different RPOs. The most secure and reliable are off-site since they are not affected by regional outages and losses. These might be off-site tape backups, disk backups or simply off-site replication (to an auxiliary data center).

While off-site backups may be more reliable, there are obvious performance implications related to the additional physical distance and network latency. This may impact the cost and therefore the frequency with which backups are feasible. Given increasingly demanding business requirements for more frequent backups and faster restores, off-line backups may not be sufficient. In order to improve both the RPO and RTO, it makes sense to complement them with more frequent on-site tape or disk backups.

A common scheme would foresee weekly off-site backups in addition to daily on-site backups. It is possible to maintain much more current backups by clustering servers and storage, implementing continuous replication or by taking frequent snapshots and maintaining differential transaction logs.

Keep in mind that backup requirements are changing. Virtualization can help to automate disaster recovery by packaging images and making them easier to deploy. However, it also minimizes scheduled downtime, which might sound attractive but complicates the backup process at the same time that the information load to be backed up continues to increase. The task is further complicated by the need to encrypt the media and ensure its long-term readability.

INTEGRATE

A complete backup/restore plan is likely to include a range of components, ranging from virtual tape libraries to disk appliances, and incorporate a variety of techniques such as disk-based data protection, continuous replications, snapshots and transaction logging. As mentioned above, the tradeoff between better, more accurate information and the higher cost of maintenance need to be evaluated to determine the best mix of backup for any given application and organization.

Archival

One of the reasons that backup has become a monumental task in many organizations is that it attempts to simultaneously address a number of requirements. In addition to facilitating both short-term data restoration and disaster recovery it can be used to ensure compliance with local laws. However, it is a very blunt instrument for achieving these objectives.

Archival provides a streamlined mechanism to comply with e-discovery laws. It also facilitates classification and enterprise search across de-duplicated and compressed repositories of critical information. It doesn't remove the need for backups but it ensures that on-line and off-line data is reduced to its minimum and becomes as accessible and usable as possible.

Some examples of cloud-based archiving vendors include (Staimer, 2010):

- Sonian – email, messaging, and e-discovery

- Iron Mountain – general archiving, content distribution, email archive and e-discovery
- i365 (Seagate) – archive and e-discovery
- Nirvanix – rich media archive
- Clearspace – structured data

Disaster Recovery

The Disaster Recovery Plan (DRP) defines the criteria that constitute a disaster. It specifies who should be notified when a disaster hits and which communication channels should be used. It also indicates who conducts a damage assessment and then decides which back-up resources to utilize. This includes where any backup sites are located and how they are maintained as well as what service level agreement the service provider offers its customers. Finally, it must specify when and under what conditions the plan should be updated

The DRP also encapsulates a number of other plans. Some that need to be included are an Emergency Response Plan including Emergency Evacuation Plan and Procedures. It is critical to define Physical and Environmental Security Policy and add a Contingency Plan including test procedures.

Some of the Documentation/Plans/Instructions include the Facility Layout (emergency exits, positioning of CCTV cameras, secure entry points, Fire Exit Route Map) and Fire Order Instructions and Crisis Communication Procedures. There is also a need to carefully maintain Technical Documents (electrical wiring diagrams, BMS, UPS, AHU details, Maintenance Schedules) and make sure they are accessible in the event of a disaster.

Since there is a significant human element to addressing a disaster, it is important to clearly determine and communicate the member of various teams including Emergency Response Team (ERT), Crisis Management Team and Incident response team. There should be a list of Authorized Personnel allowed into the facility along with their emergency contact details, including pager, home, office and mobile numbers and instant messaging names.

An organizational chart should detail job functions and responsibilities and identify which employees have been trained for which roles. These teams should receive continuously updated Security Awareness Training documentation and ideally employees should be cross trained in multiple roles allowing for more flexible operation during a crisis.

Data center employees should regularly practice telecommuting. If the data center is damaged or the ability to reach the data center is diminished then work can still be performed remotely. If the organization has multiple data centers, then personnel performing duplicate functions should be placed in disparate centers.

This allows for job consciousness to remain if personnel at one center are incapacitated.

Capacity Planning

One of the great advantages of cloud computing is its elasticity. It can scale seamlessly up and down as resources are required. However, this doesn't automatically mean that no capacity planning is required. It is much easier and faster to change capacity, but you may still need to intervene to ensure your applications have the resources they need.

There are monitoring systems, such as RightScale and Morph, which observe load usage patterns and perform advanced analytics to project future resource requirements. If you do choose to use these tools, you should still have a good understanding of what your applications are using so that you can double-check the results and be aware of the costs you are incurring.

A solid capacity plan is based on extensive knowledge of current usage patterns. This includes a trend analysis and examination of any unanticipated spikes and drops to determine cause. Based on these, it is possible to project potential future bottlenecks, which could be along dimensions of CPU, RAM, I/O read or writes, disk space and network bandwidth. These metrics need to be investigated not only for the application servers but for the database servers, proxies, firewalls, load-balancers and any other nodes that may be part of the overall solution.

INTEGRATE

An impending bottleneck doesn't necessarily mean that you need to increase capacity. It is important to perform a marginal analysis on the additional resources to determine your anticipated costs and revenue both in the case that you expand and the case that you don't. If the resources are required for mission-critical or customer-facing operations, the equation is probably compelling. In other cases it may not be.

Vertical Scaling

The tendency in cloud environments is to scale horizontally when additional capacity is needed. This means that the application is installed in parallel on additional servers. However, this is not the only possible approach. It may be that selecting larger, more powerful virtual servers will be more cost effective.

The main criteria in selecting the approach are the relative costs of different server instances and the degree to which they address the performance bottleneck. However, there may also be instances where a legacy application is not able to scale horizontally at all. In this case, vertical scaling is the only option.

Unfortunately, most public infrastructure service providers are specialized in low-end server instances and offer only limited high-performance virtual machines. Nevertheless, it may be possible to arrange for high-end system through special terms.

Another approach is to aggregate low-end systems into consolidated virtual machines. ScaleMP, for example, offers a hypervisor that aggregates x86 nodes into larger systems of over 255 virtual processors. There would be latency challenges in implementing this technique in an opaque cloud but it is possible in a private data center or a dedicated segment of a public cloud.

Private Cloud Planning

The notions in the paragraphs above refer primarily to public cloud computing. The challenges are different for private cloud. Capacity planning is more critical given the hard barriers of fixed resources and the lead time in provisioning additional hardware. In some ways, the additional importance is offset by the fact that it is a known art – enterprises have been monitoring performance and using it to project future requirements for decades.

INTEGRATE

However, it should not be so easily dismissed. Increased virtualization and service orientation have the effect that the internal constitution of services running on hardware becomes opaque to the infrastructure managers. As a result, it is difficult to manually identify patterns and plan accordingly. It therefore increases the need for analytics that can mine aggregated performance information and correlate it to processes and activities.

Chapter 18

Security

The impact of cloud computing on security is profound. There are some benefits and unfortunately also some hurdles to overcome. One challenge in trying to evaluate security is that it tends to relate to all aspects of IT; and since cloud computing's impact is similarly pervasive, the analysis can be very lengthy.

This chapter will provide some insight into the subject. If you are interested in more detail, you can find a more extensive treatment of the topic in my book *Cloud Computing Protected*.

INTEGRATE

Trust Shift

The most pronounced impact of cloud on security is that it accentuates an ongoing shift in the trust model from direct personal observation to indirect reliance on third parties. The movement is not new. Outsourcing services also require customers to rely on contractual terms rather than allowing them direct control over their operations.

This trend is an inevitable consequence of increased specialization. Unless an individual or organization is completely self-sufficient, there is always a need to rely on other entities to fulfill important parts of an activity. As a first step, it may be possible to monitor them rigorously to ensure that they follow the correct process and perform to the expected level. However, time constraints and lack of specialized knowledge will eventually lead to the point where this is no longer practical.

There is a parallel to the development of early civilization. There was a time when most families farmed, hunted, built their own dwellings and made their own clothing – all by themselves. But it was only when some decided to specialize as farmers, bakers, tailors and other professions that the cultures were able to flourish and the economies to thrive.

Indirect visibility

A focus on core competency is one of the driving factors for cloud computing. It allows organizations to exploit one of the benefits of specialization. However, it does mean that the customer is no longer directly engaged in the operation of its information technology services. The users do not see the hardware where the applications are running and they do not know the people who are running the systems (Figure 18-1).

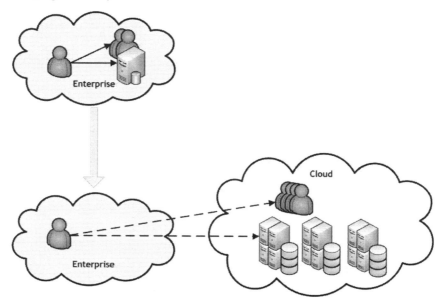

INTEGRATE

Figure 18-1: Transition to Indirect Trust

This can be quite a change when the services are critical to the business and contain sensitive information. In fact, for many it represents an unnecessary and unacceptable risk. Before coming to this conclusion, however, it is necessary to look at the whole picture.

On the one hand, cloud computing increases risk by introducing a third party whose employees and physical resources are outside the direct control and visibility of the customer. On the other hand, there are provisions in place to mitigate and compensate these risks:

- Contracts can specify in detail what services should be provided as well as the precise characteristics of these services
- Penalties will compensate the customer in cases where the agreed services levels are not achieved
- The customer can actively monitor key performance indicators to ensure that the provider delivers on all objectives

These techniques can even serve to reduce the overall risk of customer. While some organizations may use internal service level agreements that appear similar to the above, they only represent an internal redistribution of risk. External contracts can actually shift the risk outside the organization.

Indirect verification

The next level of specialization involves not only the delivery of the services but also the operational verification operation itself. Cloud infrastructure and services can be very complex and ascertaining their security level is no trivial task. Even expert security practitioners will have difficulty conducting an exhaustive analysis unless they operate as part of a large, well-structured team. To compound the issue, cloud providers are unlikely to offer indiscriminate access to their operations. Providing access would increase their exposure and make their customers more vulnerable.

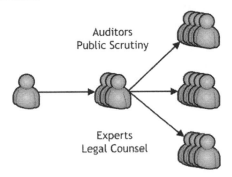

Figure 18-2: Indirect Verification

INTEGRATE

Instead, customers need to rely on third parties to validate the cloud services and ensure that they are secure (Figure 18-2). These experts may include:

- Recognized auditors who receive unfettered access to the data center and issue a periodic report
- Standards organizations who certify aspects of the operations
- Legal counsel who verifies the contract and confirms that the conditions are fair
- Experts from the general public who share their experience with the services provided

This last point may not be intuitive. One advantage of cloud's popularity is that there is intense public scrutiny of its offerings. Since cloud providers are typically very large and their infrastructure is accessible through the Internet, it is technically possible for anyone test for security vulnerabilities and broadcast the results. This can be a disturbing thought for customers who are uncertain whether their data is secure. But it also has the benefit that cloud providers invest heavily in security and are diligent in reacting to any incidents. If they are not, the fact becomes public knowledge very quickly.

Direct	Indirect
Physical observation	Public verification
Personal experience	Legal contracts
Human insight	Penalties and compensation

Table 18-1: Direct and Indirect Trust

In summary, we are used to making decisions based on what we have seen with our own eyes and touched with our own hands (Table 18-1). We trust processes and technologies that we have experienced firsthand. We may also feel comfortable with people we know directly if we feel that we have enough insight into their competence and professionalism.

Trust in an outsourced environment is very different. We need to rely on contractual frameworks with defined service levels and clauses that specify the consequences of any deviation from the agreements. And we need to consider an organization's reputation as well as the reviews that it receives from experts and other customers.

10 Security Domains

As a next step, let's try to look at security in a structured way. One challenge in trying to evaluate security is that it tends to relate to all aspects of IT; and since cloud computing's impact is similarly pervasive, the analysis can be complex.

The International Information Systems Security Certification Consortium, (ISC²) has defined ten security domains. It is not the only taxonomy for IT security that is possible, or that is available, but it is widely used and recognized. I find it helpful in performing a security analysis simply because it is quite comprehensive and therefore can be easily applied to a systematic assessment of any new technology, including cloud computing.

I will briefly step through the domains and then focus on a few areas where there are specific concerns relating to cloud computing.

> *Access Control* provides mechanisms to protect critical resources from unauthorized access and modification while facilitating access to authorized users. This domain intersects with cloud computing at multiple levels. Physical Data Center access may be based on advanced multi-factor authentication mechanisms such as biometrics and smart cards. Logical access to resources managed by the providers should also be strictly segmented and controlled.

Furthermore, end-users access can be an authentication nightmare without some mechanism for identity management and federation as we shall see later in this chapter.

Application Security covers the Software Development Lifecycle and Principles as well as multilevel security for in-house applications.

Business Continuity and Disaster Recovery Planning includes planning for catastrophic system failures and natural disasters. It also includes a comprehensive backup schedule and contingency plans for restoring the backups when they are necessary. This task is greatly complicated through the interaction of multiple providers, so it is mandatory that all responsibilities be clearly defined.

Cryptography is at the heart a large portion of data security techniques today. It would lend itself exceptionally well to many of the privacy concerns around cloud computing except for one problem: key management is very difficult to orchestrate effectively. Homomorphic encryption may provide a solution one day; but for now, in order to use or manipulate the data, it is necessary to have the encryption keys.

Information Security and Risk Management discusses policies, standards, guidelines and procedures for risk management. As discussed in Chapter 8 the risk profile may change significantly when an enterprise implements cloud computing since the organization loses control of critical activities, on the one hand, and on the other hand, is able to transfer some risk to its partners through contracts and service level agreements.

Legal, Regulations, Compliance and Investigations cover regulations and laws governing information security, which may also be very relevant in a cloud scenario. Due to the multi-jurisdictional nature of cloud computing and the decoupling of data owner and data controller, legal questions become much more complex.

Operations Security includes procedures for backups and change control management. These tasks become more complicated in a multi-provider environment. However, there is also the opportunity to outsource some of the responsibilities to third-parties.

Physical (Environmental) Security is extremely important for the data center and potentially for any network links that lie outside the corporate perimeter. This domain looks at layered physical defense mechanisms and site location principles.

Security Architecture and Design includes security policies covering a range of areas from data center backups to user desktops and antivirus planning. It also includes trusted computing and virtualization. All of these areas also intersect with cloud computing.

INTEGRATE

Telecommunications and Network Security covers perimeter and communications security. Since cloud computing is closely related to the notion of de-perimeterization and involves a significant amount of networked communications, the impact of this security domain is obvious.

In practice it is difficult to dissect security neatly along taxonomic lines. I have found it more logical to cover some of these topics in other sections in this book.

- Business Continuity and Disaster Recovery Planning (Chapter 17)
- Information Security and Risk Management (Chapter 27)
- Legal, Regulations, Compliance and Investigations (Chapter 26)
- Operations Security (Chapter 17)

Let us look at the remaining six topics in more detail.

Access Control

The two key areas of access control as it relates to cloud computing are physical access controls and Identity Management.

Identity Management

The trend toward multiple service providers has the potential for creating an identity nightmare unless it is coordinated across all platforms. Each service will need to identify the user and may carry a number of user attributes including preferences and history.

It is cumbersome to the end-users if they need to re-authenticate with each service, possibly using different credentials, and then provide the same basic information to each. A silo approach also misses the opportunity to share certain acquired information (e.g. browsing history and analytics) as authorized by the user.

In order to optimize the user experience, it is necessary for service providers to standardize on mechanisms for sharing authentication, authorization and access (AAA) information with each other and releasing other personal information upon request.

Federated identity solutions also benefit enterprises in allowing them to perform better logging and audit functions, reduce their costs associated with password reset and secure access to existing heterogeneous applications (PingIdentity, 2009). Similarly, they reduce the risk of orphan accounts, thereby preventing application access by former employees who have left the company. They replace spreadsheet-based reporting with a comprehensive view of access rights that provides a clear understanding of security posture and helps in implementing centralized, enterprise-wide controls.

Single sign-on (SSO) is the term used for facilitating user identification, authentication and authorization. It is typically based on a primary identity store such as Microsoft Active Directory or Sun Identity Manager. In a cloud-based world, it has become increasingly desirable to also use application-based user-stores such as Salesforce.com or Google Apps as the primary directory.

These can be linked to other identity stores through standards such as Liberty Alliance Identity Federation Framework (ID-FF), Web Services Federation (WS-Federation) or the Organization for the Advancement of Structured Information Standards (OASIS) Security Assertions Mark-up Language (SAML). In some cases, OAuth, OpenID and information cards are also being used to authenticate users for off-premise applications.

While granular application authorization is still relatively immature, the federation standards themselves are robust enough to be deployed in many enterprise scenarios, including those with SaaS requirements, assuming that the SaaS providers do implement a mechanism for federated SSO.

The current trend in preferences appears to be toward SAML-based SSO complemented with eXtensible Access Control Markup Language (XACML), which describes both an access control policy language and a request/response language for the policies ('who can do what when'), accommodating queries for specific authorization.

INTEGRATE

Although there are exceptions, such as Google, most SaaS providers do not yet offer full SAML support. So there is a need for Identity Management services, such as PingIdentity, TriCipher or Symplified, that can bridge multiple different standards and proprietary interfaces.

OAuth is also gaining popularity due to its simplicity. It provides a means for one application to access data (e.g. images, documents, contacts) stored with another service provider without revealing the credentials to the consuming application. Typically, a new browser window appears that allows the user to supply credentials directly to the data source. For example, if these were Google Contacts then a secure Google URL would display in the address. After successful authentication, the storage provider would release the requested data to the consuming application.

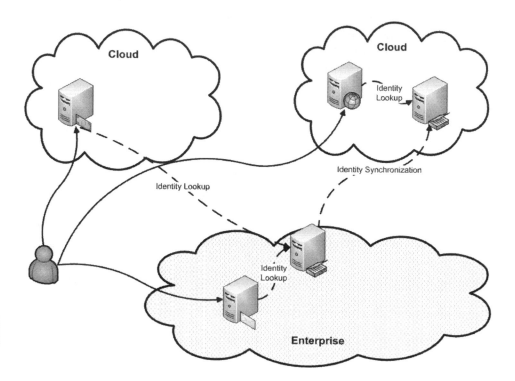

Figure 18-3: Identity Management

As mentioned above, cloud-based Identity-as-a-Service providers may also be helpful in federating identity management (Figure 18-3). For example, they may help to abstract and manage complexity between versions (e.g. SAML 1.1 vs. SAML 2.0) and frameworks. However, in including them in the solution, it should be clear that they become critical cloud providers with all the drawbacks of vendor lock-in, service level negotiation and single point of failure.

While interoperability and standards are a critical part of the identity management challenge, there are other considerations as well, such as supported authentication mechanisms, provisioning and precautions for identity theft.

Where security is a concern, it is vital that, in addition to robust password policies, cloud providers support strong authentication either natively or via delegation and support. Even strong passwords can be compromised and, in the case of a breach, a hacker can automate attacks involving compromised credentials with relative ease.

It is much more difficult to circumvent biometric and token-based authentication or secure combinations of multiple factors. Identity solutions, such as TriCipher myOneLogin, provide a variety of authentication mechanisms such as SMS delivered one-time-passwords, browser certificates, smart cards, security questions,

INTEGRATE

biometric scans and secure tokens. An organization can combine these to achieve its preferred balance of usability and strong security.

Another operational consideration is provider support for provisioning/de-provisioning. Provisioning should be rapid to expedite on-boarding new employees and changes in roles and responsibilities. De-provisioning is even more critical. In cases of identity theft there must be a facility for immediate de-provisioning.

The primary standard for provisioning is the OASIS Service Provisioning Markup Language (SPML). SPML is not yet widely implemented across cloud services. However, it is still possible to achieve a certain degree of centralized provisioning. For example SinglePoint Sync, coupled with a set of SPML gateways, can automate user account management and integration across many services in the cloud.

Application Security

The cloud offers very little protection against application-level attacks. Applications must therefore be much more secure in a potentially hostile environment than they would need to be on a private network.

INTEGRATE

One level of protection is to harden the platform itself and ensure that no unnecessary services are running, traffic is only accepted from trusted IP addresses, all patches are applied, antivirus software is running and all organizational security policies are active and enforced.

In an IaaS model this is quite straightforward to implement. However, if you are using PaaS and SaaS, then it becomes the responsibility of the service provider to ensure the platform is secure. This may, or may not, be the case, so it is important to be vigilant of any reported attacks and ask for as many details as possible on the hardening procedures.

The application developers should have a good knowledge of common coding pitfalls that lead to security breaches. As we shall see below, multi-tenancy in traduces a set of new attack vectors, including cross-site scripting, cross-site request forgery and hypervisor escape.

But those aren't the only vulnerabilities that developers need to consider. There is nothing cloud-specific about buffer overflows or injection attacks based on SQL, HTML or PHP. On the other hand, cloud applications are not immune to them either. It is just as important to check all code against known attacks and exploits as it would be for other applications placed on the public Internet.

All network-based communications should be encrypted. This means that synchronous communication should use channel-based security such as SSL or IPsec, while asynchronous communications must encrypt all messages in transit.

Ideally each application should use a dedicated set of keys to minimize the impact of a successful attack on one application.

Given the exposure of the system, it is also vital to log all intrusion attempts, exceptions and other suspicious events and to monitor the patterns for any irregular activity.

The software development process can change significantly in a cloud delivery model since the trust relationship between development and deployment environment are not always given. Internal developers may operate on assumptions that are not valid for an external deployment and need to revisit their approach.

Cryptography

There are many reasons to encrypt data that is outsourced and delivered through a public network. All the communications between applications and system within a particular cloud are exposed to the possibility of interception if another tenant installs a sniffer on the same network.

Furthermore, the data storage may not be compartmentalized as well as anticipated. So another tenant (or a malicious provider employee) could copy and analyze sensitive information. Similarly, if the data destruction policies are not enforced completely, there may be possibilities of data leakage.

Encrypting all data, whether it is in motion or at rest, is the only secure solution for sensitive information. Unfortunately, the task is more difficult than simply deciding to encrypt. The customer should indicate, or at least approve, the algorithm, key length, and key management procedures.

The biggest practical cryptographic challenge is determining how to manage the keys. If the provider takes responsibility for key management, it may use a single key for all customers, one key per customer or multiple keys per customer. It is in the interests of the customer to isolate encryption realms as much as possible and not to share them with any other tenants. However, this also increases the management burden for the provider and is a potential item of negotiation. Regardless of the number of keys, it is critical to ensure data and keys are kept separate and that the chain of custody for the keys is well documented.

An alternate approach is for the enterprise to implement its own encryption to protect any sensitive data. This is advisable even if the provider offers basic encryption of the platform as described above. Nonetheless, it also comes with two drawbacks. The first is that the customer must implement its own key management, which is an additional burden and may require key management software. The second is that the data becomes opaque to the provider who cannot offer any value-added services on top of it.

There has been some recent work to address this problem through a technique called homomorphic encryption, which is a cryptosystem with the property that algebraic operations on the ciphertext result in the same identical operation on the plaintext after decryption. In 2009, IBM developed a system of lattice-based cryptography that was able to fulfill these conditions. Unfortunately, the enormous computational overhead associated with lattice-based encryption limits its practical viability. Nonetheless, this is an important breakthrough that may be able to facilitate functions such as archiving, classification and analytics on opaque data in the future.

It is worth noting that although encryption is a vital component for securing data in a public environment it doesn't guarantee that the information is safe. Its efficacy depends on the attack vector. For example, it is a sound recommendation to encrypt SQL databases that are stored in the cloud. If someone is able to copy the repository to another system, the data will still be protected. However, if a hacker is able to launch an attack using a SQL injection then the application engine will decrypt the data and serve it back to the hacker in plain text.

Physical (Environmental) Security

Physical security is a consideration wherever sensitive information, intellectual property or business processes may be exposed. The scope includes all offices and, potentially, even user's homes and hotel rooms. Fortunately, there are also other mechanisms to safeguard security without creating an onerous, and perhaps unrealistic, burden on every user. Nonetheless, it is a message that needs to be clearly articulated to all users of corporate assets.

INTEGRATE

The locations with the highest concentration of valuable information assets are typically the data centers. In order to protect them, very stringent physical security may be necessary. All data centers are not equal in their approach to security, but enterprises also differ in their requirements for safeguarding their data. It is important to match the two well in order to protect the information without paying for unnecessary services.

Some of the aspects of physical security at a data center might include:

External Perimeter: The simplest form of protection is to keep unauthorized persons at a sufficient distance from the assets to prevent any interaction. Horizontal protection may include high (for example, over 2 meters) walls and fences with barbed wire and outward-facing top guard. Additional vertical safeguards might involve heavy steel mesh in the roofs and under raised floors.

The minimum number of entry and exit points will be dictated by safety requirements. However, since they also represent points of vulnerability, it is best not to exceed the number by far and to ensure the passages are adequately protected, for example by armed guards. Vehicular access can be further restricted with wedge barriers and reinforced gates. In some cases, the control points may resemble strict border patrol stations with mirrors to monitor the underside of vehicles and regular manual searches.

Structural internal barriers: Inside the perimeter there may be additional barriers to segment the facility, including interior fences and walls. Roadblocks and turnstiles may control vehicular and pedestrian traffic flow, facilitate identity checking, and define a buffer zone for more highly classified areas. Opaque barriers can prevent visual compromise and reconnaissance. Particularly sensitive areas may be further excluded with cribs, cages, lockers, containers and vaults.

Access control: Access to the site, and to restricted areas, may require multifactor authentication including tokens and biometric access controls such as retinal scan, voiceprints, palm and fingerprints.

Surveillance: Surveillance may include closed-circuit television (CCTV), which may also be recorded and streamed off-site for further and later analysis. Additionally, manual patrols of varying frequencies and schedules can ensure a more comprehensive view of any anomalies.

INTEGRATE

Power backup: Uninterruptible power supply is mandatory in a data center. Short-term outages may be bridged by batteries and flywheels (high-mass metal discs spinning at many thousands of rotations per minute). Additionally, diesel-powered generators can kick in on a few seconds notice.

Fire: Protection against fire involves a comprehensive smoke alarm and sprinkler system. Ideally, it is able to segment the facility into granular compartments and isolate incidents to the smallest possible area. It needs to be integrated into the internal access control and lock-down systems (so that firefighters are not delayed but the fire cannot spread). It is also critical that the entire detection and sprinkler system be regularly checked and tested.

The challenge with all these controls in an outsourced scenario is that they are outside the control of the customer. Nonetheless, although it may be the responsibility of your service provider, it is your data that is at stake; so it behooves you to verify that adequate protection is in place. You may want to specify certain precautions in your service contract or request the right to inspect the facilities. At a minimum, you should ensure that you are aware of what procedures are in place so that you can actively gauge how secure your information and processes are.

Security Architecture and Design

This domain considers the enterprise architecture, policies and platforms, which each may be affected by cloud computing.

Data Architecture and Topology

The data architecture needs a systematic assessment of potential security concerns. If the abstraction layers of the storage architecture cross trust boundaries, it may be much more vulnerable than its owners expect.

Multiple layers of network abstraction can potentially hide ingress and egress points making it unclear where data and processing are located. In particular in a hybrid private and public cloud scenario there is a significant incremental risk if applications pass sensitive private cloud data to the public cloud for processing, either regularly or only through sporadic cloudbursting to accommodate spikes in demand.

The obfuscation of infrastructure makes it all the more important to segment the network into access-controlled zones, for example through VLANs or ACLs, that help to compartmentalize sensitive data and restrict the impact of vulnerabilities in any given point.

In addition to limiting data traffic, appliances at zone junctions can enforce intrusion detection/prevention, perform deep-packet inspection, and limit the impact of distributed denial-of-service (DDoS), or economic denial-of-sustainability (EDoS) attacks.

INTEGRATE

Policy Enforcement

The complexity and opacity of cloud computing make it difficult to enforce corporate policies. As the same time, the threat of data leakage and malware infection increase through the use of a public network. In some cases, such as the pharmaceutical industry, outbound computer viruses can have very severe financial implications. In almost all cases, they represent an annoyance and lost productivity.

User education is an important component of an overall plan to ensure internal compliance. However, it has its limitations and needs to be complemented with automated policy enforcement. Since it is difficult to ascertain where data may be directed, it becomes imperative that the data be protected at all points, including client devices, cloud egress/ingress points and, potentially, application gateways or proxies.

One of the key compliance requirements will be to ensure that clients are running up-to-date antivirus signatures as well as fully patched applications, browsers and operating systems. Providing a means to enforce end-point protection prior to granting access to resources is only one part of the problem. The other is to ensure that clients can access remediation services in order to restore compliance. Cloud-based services are well suited for remediation since they run outside the firewall, so infected or exposes clients will not jeopardize other resources in accessing them. The services can also scale elastically if there is a major attack that compromises a high proportion of clients at the same time.

Platform

In order to ensure policy compliance, you need the applications to be running on trustworthy platforms. When you operate your own infrastructure, it is much easier to gain visibility into the details of the platform.

In the long term, Trusted Platform Modules (TPM) may be able to establish trust paths that validate the integrity of all layers of software from the BIOS and hypervisor to the applications and configurations. This is not trivial today. It is certainly possible to harden all VM images, but a secure platform doesn't necessarily remove all the risks around virtualization and multi-tenancy.

Virtualization

Virtualization offers inherent security advantages through isolation. It has the capacity to prevent cross-over interference from other applications with better defined memory space. This minimizes application instability and facilitates fault isolation and system recovery. Cleaner images contribute to application longevity. And automated deployment can increase redundancy and facilitate failover.

INTEGRATE

On the other hand, as complexity goes up security goes down. Even though virtualization simplifies the application context it adds more components to the overall stack which introduces additional points of potential vulnerability. These include the hypervisor, the virtualization control layer and the internal virtual network.

To date there have been few breaches against the virtualization layer. The management control plane usually offers a very small attack surface making it difficult for attackers to target it. This reduces the threat considerably, but it doesn't completely eliminate it as buffer overflows and other vulnerabilities are still possible.

For example, at Black Hat 2009, Kostya Kirtchinsky described an exploit called "Cloudburst[1]" that allowed a VMware guest to escape to the host. VMware had already issued a patch, so it is unlikely that this particular problem will lead to a breach. Nonetheless, it highlights the importance for enterprises to constantly monitor for any suspicious activity.

At earlier Black Hat conferences, Joanna Rutkowska, Alexander Tereshkin and Rafal Wojtczuk presented several hypervisor attacks, often specifically targeted against Xen, including a rootkit, called the "Blue Pill Project", and in-place replacement of the hypervisor.

---

[1] Note that "Cloudburst", in this context, is unrelated to the idea of "cloudbursting", used to designate elastic provisioning of public cloud resources in a hybrid cloud environment.

A more immediate concern in the short term is the network activity that the virtualization layer hides from the physical network links. It is critical that virtual network appliances monitor traffic crossing virtualization backplanes and make it accessible through hypervisor APIs since the virtual interfaces will be opaque to traditional network security controls.

Unless a rigorous authorization process oversees provisioning, there is a risk that default, or poorly hardened, images may be released onto the network. Virtualized operating systems should be augmented by 3rd party security technology (e.g. layered security controls) to reduce dependency.

Strong authentication should be integrated with the enterprise identity management for access to the virtual operating system (especially the administrator interface). This would include tamper-proof logging and integrity monitoring tools.

It is also critical to have a comprehensive procedure for patching virtual machines with security and reliability updates. This process is much more challenging in a virtual environment where some machines may not be active when updates are released.

Multi-tenancy

INTEGRATE

Multi-tenancy provides great financial benefits by allowing customers to benefit from the economies of scale of the cloud service providers. However, it also carries with it a certain risk of data co-mingling and crossover. In particular, there is always the potential that malicious co-tenants will exploit shared infrastructure (LAN, hypervisors, storage) to stage attacks. Threats such as Cloudburst, mentioned above, or cross-site scripting, cross-site request forgery, SQL injection and authentication weaknesses are all real and must be evaluated.

Before categorizing and mitigating the risk, it is useful to differentiate between the multiple different levels of multi-tenancy, since they do not carry the same exposure (Table 18-2).

Isolation	Sharing
Data center	None
Physical server	DC infrastructure
Virtual machine	Physical servers, Hypervisor
Application	Virtual machine and connectivity
Data base	Application instances
Data tables	Database
Data	Data tables

Table 18-2: Multi-tenancy levels

The most isolated environment would prevent any co-location and ensure that all servers in a particular data center were owned and operated by the same organization. A somewhat less stringent requirement might be to fully isolate the business with separate physical servers in a shared data center.

INTEGRATE

The next step would be to take advantage of shared physical servers and networks but maintain separate virtual servers. This would correspond to the offering that most IaaS vendors provide. Another level would be to run separate application instances in the same virtual machine. In this case, the business logic must separate sessions or threads.

A common approach in the SaaS space is to run a single application and segregate the customers' data. The separation can be in the form of different databases, different tables or simply tagged data.

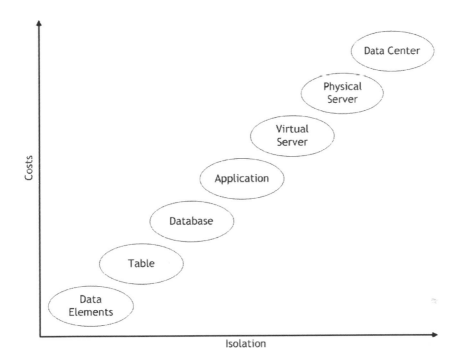

Figure 18-4: Multi-tenancy Cost and Isolation

One of main factors driving the decision will be cost (Figure 18-4). Typically the higher the data isolation the less benefit of synergy and therefore the higher the cost. The second consideration will be the degree of isolation required, which will derive from several other factors:

Regulatory stipulations may mandate a certain minimum level of data isolation for information such as health records and credit-card information. Even where there is no absolute legal requirement, there may be a major risk in liability for security breaches if insufficient precautions have been taken to safeguard the data.

Maintenance costs and business continuity processes may be impacted by the sharing of data and other assets with co-tenants. If an electronic discovery action is initiated against someone sharing the same database, it could compromise your data and/or degrade your performance.

Sharing a database with another stakeholder decreases your flexibility to make changes to it. If you are hoping for rapid growth, you may want an extensible schema that could involve customized fields or tables. You may be able to achieve these with predefined fields and tables or dynamic fields but only if they are included in the initial deployment.

Note that even if data is deployed into a multi-tenant environment this doesn't mean that it is necessarily vulnerable to misuse. There are several ways to enforce data protection including:

Proxy filters: Proxies or web traffic managers control access to cloud resources according to client source, target and access credentials.

ACLs: Access Control Lists may restrict resource access based on a central authorization mechanism such as Kerberos or an Identity Provider.

Cryptology: If data is encrypted securely, it can only be used by others who have the encryption key. Cryptology only enforces privacy and internal integrity. It cannot reduce the risk of data loss through malicious modification so it must be complemented with other security precautions.

Telecommunications and Network Security

The trend to de-perimeterization began long before cloud computing became popular. However, it has now reached a point where it is necessary to assume everything is a threat rather than (or at least in addition to) trying to lock down specific infrastructure.

INTEGRATE

Consequently, all platforms must be hardened and all inter-host communications must be secured. There can no longer be an assumption of a secure channel between hosts in a common data center. In the cloud, for instance, a competitor or attacker may have placed a sniffer on a co-located virtual machine.

Another increasing concern is that the cloud may be used as an attack platform. Since it is accessible with few network restrictions and often poor user identification/authentication it can lend itself to password cracks, distributed denial-of-services (DDoS) attacks or Captcha[1] breaking.

There are two perspectives to consider. On the one hand, you may be more exposed to attacks if you are using cloud services. The homogeneity of cloud systems makes them an attractive target. Any vulnerabilities identified may be leveraged and propagated at a breathtaking speed. Botnets orchestrating distributed denial-of-service attacks against a major cloud service provider may also catch your systems in the cross-fire.

The opposite point of view is no less alarming. If you are deemed, legitimately or not, to be the source of an attack there will be serious consequences impacting the delivery of your services. Firstly, you need to ensure that your own applica-

---

[1] "Completely Automated Public Turing test to tell Computers and Humans Apart." – the jumbled letters and characters some web-sites require at registration in order to prevent automated sign-on and ensure human entry

tions are not compromised as you could be liable for some of the damages that are caused from your platforms.

Secondly, in a multi-tenant environment you also need to consider that if another customer sharing some of your infrastructure and/or address space is compromised and leveraged as an attack platform there could be consequences for you, too.

This problem can be particularly devastating if the cloud service provider reuses IP addresses between tenants. If you try to operate using an address that was previous assigned to a malicious co-tenant, you may face obstructions in your service delivery. Not only might your performance degrade but you could be the target of email-domain blacklisting or IP-range blocking.

INTEGRATE

Implement

IMPLEMENT

Chapter 19

Transition Management

Unfortunately, many projects fail. My experience, at least with emerging technologies, is that most initiatives never make it to implementation due to lack of executive commitment. In some cases, strategic alignment has been neglected. In others, the business case is simply not compelling enough. The result is the same. Small obstacles obstruct, and eventually stall, any project without sufficient thrust.

Those that make it to the execution phase encounter a new set of challenges. The most formidable is simply a lack of qualified personnel. New technologies engender a great deal of enthusiasm among the individual contributors. Many see them as a potential stepping stone in their career aspirations. So, they tend to overstate their qualifications and experience or oversimplify the task at hand. Enthusiastic sponsors also try to squeeze the business case by minimizing all but the most vital staffing costs. Without the right people, projects often go off-course in the design phase, but the results only become visible during the implementation.

IMPLEMENT

Recurring problems, such as these, are not inevitable. A small amount of awareness can go a long way in addressing them. In some cases, a closer look will foretell that the project is unlikely to succeed and even its initiation is an unnecessary expense. In other cases, it may be possible to correct the problems with a little project discipline.

Transition Success Factors

This chapter covers the task of managing the transition. It would be difficult to come up with a failsafe recipe for success in implementing cloud computing. However, there are a set of factors I would like to highlight since they can very easily lead to failure when they are neglected.

- Clear and compelling objectives
- Strong executive backing

- Access to appropriate resources
- Regular multidirectional communications

Objectives

A cloud implementation is just like many other projects. It involves setting objectives and success criteria, staffing a team, monitoring time, cost and quality constraints, and ensuring a communication flow between stakeholders.

The move from a legacy environment to a cloud-based solution can be a very disruptive exercise. It has potential impact on data, applications, users, managers, developers and business processes.

Except in a greenfield scenario, most of the local and end-user infrastructure will already be in place but may benefit from optimization. You may want to leverage the transition to fine-tune the existing architecture. Even more importantly, there may be a significant impact of cloud computing on the local environment. Either way, you can only optimize the complete solution if you look at all the components of the end-to-end design.

As you put together your architecture, it will become obvious that some changes are necessary. You will be able to create, modify and retire components. There may also be a need to move resources, establish new connections or enable new functionality in existing systems.

IMPLEMENT

As you examine what needs to change, you can ask four questions for every task:

- What needs to be done?
- Who will do it?
- When will they do it?
- How will they do it?

For each of these, it is critical to identify the end-point and objectives. Someone must be assigned responsibility for making it happen. There should be a schedule describing the sequence of tasks and their dependencies. Finally, there should be a plan for how to orchestrate the changes so that the transition doesn't compromise availability, connectivity, resilience or security.

Executive support

In order to achieve this, it will have been necessary to present a compelling business case to senior management. Before beginning the implementation, it is necessary to have strategic commitment, sufficient resources and an individual to coordinate the effort.

A good starting point is visible executive backing. The project will not get off the ground unless there is a heavyweight sponsor who has the clout to break through any organizational obstacles that delay the changes. Even better is a cross-organizational endorsement that is backed by a steering committee from multiple business units.

This commitment needs to be communicated clearly as well as the buy-in of all key stakeholders. It is valuable to have additional champions in each of the key businesses who can help work through any challenges in their organizations.

Appropriate Resources

Another pre-requisite is sufficient resources. A budget will define the financial constraints on the project, and it must be large enough to realistically cover all project costs. Human resources may also need release from their functional roles or other projects. These must include qualified specialists in all relevant domains – from business analysis and legal to technical experts in networking, applications and security.

Above all, it is necessary to find a skilled and experienced program manager who will assemble a team, create a project plan, ensure its execution and report regularly to all stakeholders. Ideally, this individual will have a proven track record of implementing new technologies across large and complex organizations.

Systematic Communications

IMPLEMENT

One of the key tasks of the program manager will be to ensure that all interested parties, from the executive sponsors and implementation team to the end-users, are kept abreast of key developments that may have an impact on them.

Project Plan

The project plan should take the high-level objectives given by the steering committee and break them down into a structure of tasks and deliverables.

Objectives

All objectives must be realistic, yet also specific and measureable. This includes defining the time-frame and scope of migration in terms of users, functionality and data to be migrated. It may be desirable to also include cost constraints, user satisfaction levels and performance measures as part of the objectives.

Within any environment, there will be barriers that make it difficult to achieve the objectives, and enablers that facilitate the objectives. For example, you might consider standardization of some of your services an enabler. On the other hand, a lack of skilled resources, data center saturation or major platform changes might introduce additional obstacles.

After identifying these environmental indicators, the team can determine the amount of control that can be exercised over them. If you can identify measures over these indicators, it helps in monitoring them and assessing whether they pose a threat or an unrealized opportunity over time.

If it is possible to crystallize a set of necessary and sufficient conditions for meeting the objectives, these can be consolidated into a list of Critical Success Factors (CSFs) and matched with supporting Critical Activities that will support the factors. These activities might include contracts with service providers, data and application migrations, employee management and communications.

On this basis, the team can craft a Statement of Work (SOW) that defines the overall content and limits of the project and then proceed to derive the Work Breakdown Structure (WBS) by decomposing each task until it is possible to easily assign ownership and estimate accurately.

Overall Approach

At the highest level, the approach taken will impact a number of stakeholders. Questions of whether to migrate in a "big bang" or split all the users and applications will have significant impact on the amount of downtime, the duration of the transition and the level of interoperability during the migration.

IMPLEMENT

After defining the overall approach, it important to verify that it is acceptable to all stakeholders and to communicate the impact and implications widely to all who may be affected.

Timeline

In addition to the complexity of making multiple heterogeneous parts interoperate, you also have two time dimensions to consider.

At a high level you need to determine the sequence for rolling out new cloud functionality as you are unlikely to conduct a wholesale overhaul of your entire IT landscape at once. For each roll out, you also need to consider the actual transition process.

Obviously critical applications are not the best trial candidates. It makes sense to begin the process with short-term projects and pilots that can scale. It is also valid to prioritize applications with volatile resource needs or other factors making them particularly suitable for cloud computing. Alternatively, you may want to begin with infrastructural services that you can implement redundantly, such as Disaster Recovery.

In orchestrating the individual migrations, it is important to look at the total migration effort and resources available as well as any dependencies. Especially for the first deployments, there is value in planning for extended staging, testing and pilot stages in order to absorb any delays that may surface.

Task Allocation

Once all the critical activities have been broken down into individual tasks, it is necessary to make sure that ownership and milestones are clearly communicated.

Project Team

The project manager must put together a team that has sufficient resources and is able to cover all the internal and external interfaces that the project needs to maintain. Given the complexity and number of interactions, clear roles and responsibilities become vital.

Staffing

One of the first project tasks is to assemble a virtual team. The program manager must ensure that all required skills are represented, from contract negotiation to technical design and implementation. In order to cover all bases, it is critical to have cross-functional representation from the relevant departments. In addition to the businesses that are affected and the technical implementation teams, this includes legal counsel, professional negotiators and human resources representatives.

IMPLEMENT

It is not necessary for all of the team members to be available to the project full time. Depending on the workload and project patterns, some of them may only be required for a few hours. However, especially if it is difficult to predict when they will be needed, and the urgency with which their input and services are required, it is vital to identify the relevant individuals early and clarify what will be required to engage them when the time comes.

Given the immaturity of cloud computing it is very likely that additional training and development may be required for some of the new platforms and services. Not only is it important that team members have a broad understanding of cloud computing, the extent of its impact and its ramifications on the project deliverables, but it is important that some subject matter experts also participate in the design to validate the feasibility, raise any important risks or obstacles and highlight any opportunities for optimization.

It is also vital to clarify whether these team members will be dedicated to the project or, if not, what part of their time may be allocated to it. As in every project, it is absolutely essential to ensure that the members are motivated and have some incentive in seeing the successful implementation of the project.

External Interfaces

Part of the complexity of a cloud-based solution derives from the fact that it necessarily involves additional partners in the form of service providers. There may also be system integrators, additional outsourcing partners, consultants and software developers who all play a key role in building the complete solution.

The project manager must clarify and communicate the contractual and authority linkages as well as the contact points with all providers and the escalation paths for disputes and incidents.

If the external agreements are not yet concluded, the program manager must oversee the negotiation and ensure that the terms are consistent with the overall project objectives.

Additionally there are mundane issues to resolve such as logistics, venue reservations and meeting schedules, which are not necessarily cloud-specific.

Roles and Responsibilities

Finally, it is important for the manager to obtain agreement and commitment on the roles and responsibilities of all team members and stakeholders. Internally, this means all the members assigned to the team, including technical, networking, security, legal and financial personnel must have a clear definition of what is expected of them. Externally, all parties will need a similar definition that should be backed up by clauses in the contract.

IMPLEMENT

Communications and Knowledge Transfer

As in every project, it is important to monitor the milestones and report the progress regularly to all concerned stakeholders. If the project starts to stray in terms of functionality, cost or schedule, this needs to be signaled early and corrective action taken.

Figure 19-1 illustrates the multidirectional nature of project communications. While there are often standard reporting mechanisms directed upward to the executive sponsors, it is also critical to ensure that the end-users are informed of any changes that may impact them. There may also be a number of external resources and stakeholders such as outsourcing partners, cloud service providers and other organizational departments such as human resources, finance and legal counsel, who all need to be aware of the progress of the project as well as any hurdles that it encounters.

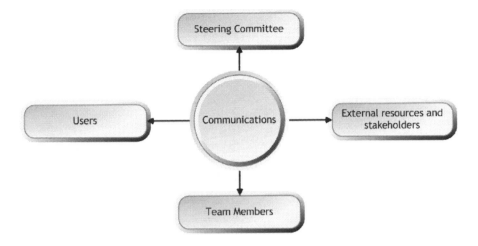

Figure 19-1: Multidirectional Communications

The team members represent a specific case with particularly high needs for effective communications. On the one hand, there is a need for immediate access to current specifications and status information as well as ad hoc queries. It is worth taking some time to ensure that appropriate collaboration tools are in place to facilitate all necessary interaction. Some of the SaaS-based tools for conferencing, communications and information sharing may lend themselves well given the ad-hoc nature of project activities and the potential for collaborating across organizational boundaries.

On the other hand, there is a need for retaining project history and lessons learned on a more permanent basis in order to benefit from the project experience during subsequent cloud implementations. Again, there are archival systems and SaaS-based knowledge management portals that can prove themselves useful for these purposes.

IMPLEMENT

Chapter 20

Migration

The implementation of a cloud computing solution will involve a number of technical and infrastructural changes as well as movement of data repositories, applications and network infrastructure. The term 'migration' implies that an organization already runs an IT environment. This covers most large and medium-size companies other than, potentially, newly formed joint ventures. In any case, even if there is no legacy system, it may still be necessary to pre-load template data and configurations. The task is simpler and less risky, but elements of the process are still necessary.

Code Migration

There are three basic options for migrating application code from an internal-physical to an external-virtual environment:

IMPLEMENT

- Redeploy
- Re-architect
- Replace

The choices are correlated to the distinction between IaaS/PaaS/SaaS but the alignment is not absolute and must be considered individually.

Redeploy

A redeployment of existing code is often called a Physical-to-Virtual (P2V) migration. It involves five steps:

- Create the virtual machines
- Configure all connectivity and system settings
- Copy all applications and data to the new virtual machine
- Deploy the virtual machine(s) in the cloud
- Redirect users to the new service locations (URLs)

The process is often manual but there are some tools that can help. Virtualization vendors often offer some P2V tools. For example, Microsoft Virtual Server Migration Toolkit and VMware Converter provide at least partial automation. There are also a set of third party tools that offer a higher degree of automation, such as:

- AutoVirt
- Leostream
- PlateSpin PowerConvert
- Virtuozzo
- Visioncore vConverter

IaaS providers also often build a catalog of template virtual machines, which can be used to avoid creating all settings. Amazon EC2 provides some basic machines for free while others can be acquired for often very reasonable prices. 3Tera AppLogic also offers several dozen templates and facilitates the minimal configuration that is needed through a graphic user interface.

Nonetheless, the question of whether code can be migrated automatically depends largely on its internal logic. If it has few external connections and only a simple or web-based user interface, it should be very straightforward. On the other hand, if the application was developed for a client-server model using proprietary protocols and exchanges complex traffic with many internal systems, then it could be a difficult chore to make it cloud-ready.

IMPLEMENT

One interesting variant of a redeployment option is to use a virtual private cloud to extend the legacy environment into a public IaaS cloud. For example, CohesiveFT vns-cubed or CloudSwitch, provide facilities to bridge or route network traffic between a cloud-based network container and the private data center. In such a scenario, the amount of reconfiguration of the servers and applications can be minimal, or even none.

For all practical purposes, the redeployment option is now currently confined to applications built on IaaS. There may be some exceptions where .NET applications can move fairly simply to Azure, and Java or Python applications to Google App Engine, but some degree of analysis will almost always be needed.

This doesn't mean that the application cannot offer a higher-level service to its users. You may build an IaaS application, which you offer to your customers on a SaaS basis. The Etelos Application Platform could help you meet this need by moving a legacy application into its marketplace. It provides a plug-and-play graphical user interface and offers fast time-to-market, application cataloging and syndication capabilities, so you can resell partner software with or without value added services.

The benefit of an approach like that of Etelos is that it can provide billing and licensing based on a variety of metrics (CPU, disk space, memory, users, accounts), purchasing mechanisms (credit cards, promotions) as well as bundling and upselling options. This allows you, as the application provider, to focus on the actual functionality rather than the mechanics of online sales.

Re-architect

The next option is to re-architect the application. An analysis of the strategic impact of cloud computing may have revealed that this application can, and should, now serve other markets and that these markets have different requirements. It may be possible to harvest analytics from the transactions to derive additional value. Or social networking options may extend the ability to penetrate some new market segments. The entire value-chain may even have changed, creating new opportunities (such as the aforementioned SaaS option to customers).

There are also a number of technical developments that you may be able to leverage for better efficiency, reliability and easier maintenance of the applications. This could include a more service-oriented architecture, a richer user interface (e.g. using Adobe Flex or Microsoft Silverlight). You may even want to re-architect an existing application to be able to run on one of the cloud platforms such as Force.Com or Google App Engine.

Finally, if you are expecting to exploit the maximum benefit from cloud computing then you need to look at how to parallelize workloads to ensure the highest degree of horizontal scalability. At a high level this means:

IMPLEMENT

- Break into the smallest services possible
- Allocate to workloads as network- based services
- Orchestrate workloads with maximal parallel threads

The biggest challenge will be in the latter since it is not trivial to synchronize independent threads when they are not co-resident. You can only use network mechanisms such as message queues, databases, network files, and non-blocking web services. More explicitly, you cannot take advantage of some of the simpler and certainly faster local techniques such as memory locks, mutexes and other semaphores.

Agile Development

When some functionality is developed (or at least owned) in-house, the question of development methodologies may arise. The traditional enterprise approach to development is very process-oriented, geared toward the highest Capability Maturity Model Integration (CMMI) levels.

Frequently, it employs a strict sequential Waterfall methodology, which is suitable for projects where the requirements are clearly articulated and static. However, in a dynamic environment, such as cloud computing, the driving force is agility. So a rigid approach may not be appropriate, no matter how well optimized it is.

Emerging approaches often focus, instead, on high levels of parallelisation in development phases, which can speed the time to completion. Lighter methodologies are useful in an unknown territory where requirements cannot always be foreseen. It therefore also makes sense to look into some of the more agile approaches such as Extreme Programming, Scrum, Crystal, Dynamic Systems Development Methodology, and Rapid Applications Development.

IMPLEMENT

Replace

If you are looking at subscribing to SaaS-based delivery, the option will always be to replace the current solution. You do not have control of the underlying infrastructure so you cannot redeploy or re-architect it. Your only choice is which SaaS you wish to use.

You may also be considering installing new software for IaaS (or even PaaS). If commercial-off-the-shelf software is available and meets your requirements, then typically the licensing costs are much lower than the costs of maintaining and supporting an application in-house.

The drawback of externally sourced software, regardless of the delivery model, is the control you sacrifice in using code that is owned by others. In order to minimize the risk, it is critical to test the software extensively for reliability, availability, integrity, and functionality. You should document all gaps from the current functionality and ensure that no stakeholders require these capabilities. You will also want to identify any major changes in the user interface so that these can be communicated to the users.

During testing, you can determine the optimal configuration settings and investigate customization options that may permit you to add new or missing functionality. Even if these options exist, it doesn't necessarily mean you should avail of them. Every customization needs to be supported and verified with new releases in the base system. Ensure that you have a valid business case in terms of the perceived value for the functionality before making a commitment that is costly to keep.

Data Migration

Applications use a combination of data that can be both structured (e.g. tabular) or unstructured (e.g. text, audio, video). When an application is migrated, it is necessary to also consider what will happen with the data it is using.

There are at least five options:

- Don't migrate (Connector access)
- Don't migrate (Start new)
- Migrate with code
- Copy databases
- Transform data

Any given application will probably have multiple sources of information, so it could use a combination of these options.

Connector Access

It may be possible to move the application to a public platform while maintaining the data repository internally (Figure 20-1). In this scenario, the application would connect to the database through a web services or database interface, such as ODBC or JDBC.

IMPLEMENT

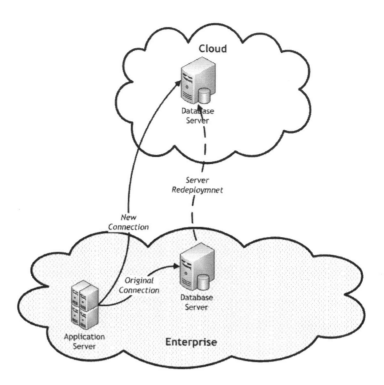

Figure 20-1: Connector Access to Remote Database

From an application perspective, this is fairly straightforward and is also a very useful option if the data is used by other internal applications. However, the connectivity can only be established by permitting inbound connections through the internal firewall or by placing a proxy server in the DMZ. Both of these requests tend to meet with some resistance from corporate security departments.

Start New

If data is relatively static and needs to be renewed due to changes in functionality anyhow (e.g. configuration settings, help pages), then it may possible to discard the old data and rewrite it from new. When very little data is involved, this can be attractive since it is simplest. However, as the amount of content increases, it becomes less likely that there is no overlap at all.

It may, however, be possible for someone to manually download all the old content, process and refine it offline, and then upload the new content again as a manual action.

Some organizations, take this approach for email and other collaboration software. It is not particularly user-friendly, but it is the cheapest way to migrate to a new platform. Users can either start from scratch or retain and reload their application information manually through their desktops.

Migrate with Code

In some cases, the content may actually be very closely related to the code. Web servers, for example, may store some data in the same folder structure where they keep the HTML pages along with Perl, Python and PHP scripts. If that is the case, the code migration is likely to include the data migration as a single action.

Copy Databases

When the databases are exclusively used by the application(s) being moved to the cloud and don't synchronize, or otherwise interconnect, with internal systems, you may have the option of simply copying the database files into the cloud.

This could involve setting up a database server and copying the databases. Or, if your database server is already virtualized, you may be able to just copy the virtual hard disk of the instance. In either case you can use whichever transfer protocols the service provider supports (e.g. FTP, SFTP, HTTP, WebDAV) to copy the data into the cloud.

You will probably still need to update the configuration of your applications since the naming conventions and address space in the target cloud are likely to be different from the source environment. You may also need to consider how you will continue to manage and support the databases in the cloud. Compared to the alternatives, these may be relatively easy obstacles to overcome.

Transform Data

The most complex option is to extract the current data, transform it into a format suitable for the target platform, and then load it into the cloud. The nature of the Extract, Transform, Load (ETL) will depend very much on the type of data involved.

Structured information such as relational databases have standard tools that can facilitate the extraction and load. So, you only need to determine what kind of transformation is required between the source and target formats.

Unstructured information such as electronic messages and collaboration portals are more difficult, but there are some automation options there too. For example, BinaryTree offers facilities for migrating from Microsoft Exchange, Microsoft SharePoint and Lotus Domino into cloud platforms from Google, IBM and Microsoft (Figure 20-2).

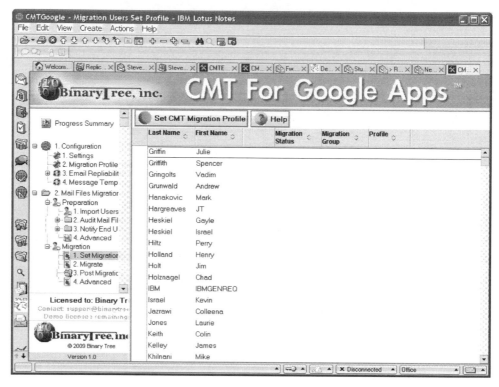

Figure 20-2: BinaryTree migration of Lotus users to Google Apps

IMPLEMENT

Desktop Migration

One of the most difficult parts of any migration is the end-user device. Whether it is an on-premise desktop, a notebook at home or a handheld being used on the road, it can be very difficult to make changes since they can impact the user in a very direct way.

User devices also tend to be unpredictable in terms of installed software and configuration settings. Connectivity cannot always be assured to the device. Furthermore, it can be a challenge to coordinate the timing so as not to impact the user experience or risk an interruption in the middle of an update.

Management systems such as CA Unicenter, IBM Tivoli, BMC Patrol, HP OpenView and Microsoft System Center can help to address the challenge, but it is still one of the largest risks in any deployment and should be carefully planned. This means identifying all the new software and configuration settings, automating silent updates to the extent possible and informing users of any user-visible implications from the update.

Infrastructure

In addition to the management system, there may be other infrastructure that is necessary for the transition. Electronic messaging and portals may be required for communications particularly to the affected users. There may also be a need for external access to the corporate directory in order to load and verify user information.

An area that is easily overlooked is that the connectivity and security links between the cloud and the enterprise may also have special requirements during the migration in order to facilitate the transfer of some of the data. It probably wouldn't be that difficult to open up the ports in the firewall that you need in order to get through the migration. However, if this wasn't part of the plan and you only become aware of the need shortly before you need the connections, then it may be difficult to perform a diligent security assessment of the process.

Transition Interoperability

The general approach taken for the transition in terms of sequencing and duration will have a direct impact on the interoperability requirements. If any application is migrated over the weekend, and all users are able to do without the tool while it is being moved, then there is no requirement for transitional interoperability.

On the other hand, if the application is migrated in stages with certain user groups preceding others then a complex mechanism of synchronization may be needed in order to ensure the integrity of all shared information. Ideally only one source should be considered authoritative with read-only replicas made available to other users. Otherwise, the locking requirements can quickly become unmanageable.

IMPLEMENT

Another dimension of the migration is the transition that a user may experience during the move. Ideally, the user will not require the software for the duration of the move or will be able to work from a read-only cache on the personal device. If it is necessary for the user to make changes, these may be collected and queued for later replay, whereby this will require additional work.

If it is mandatory that the user be able to work seamlessly on the application for the course of the migration, it becomes necessary to run two parallel systems and continuously replicate the changes between them. This is clearly a complex undertaking.

Chapter 21

Employee Changes

In a project with a focus on technology that is executed by technologists, it is easy to forget the most important elements of a successful IT project. The project will succeed or fail depending on how well it meets the end-user requirements and allows them to succeed in the jobs they are supposed to perform.

Cloud computing can have a very disruptive impact on the user community. The specter of large-scale outsourcing will certainly frighten many employees. On the other hand, there are also tremendous opportunities to enrich their work experience without necessarily jeopardizing anyone's professional career.

Note that while the largest impact will be felt by the IT department, cloud computing is a technology that can also be very disruptive to end-users and employees across all businesses since many departments provide – and even more consume – services.

IMPLEMENT

Impact

The impact on IT usage will be felt across all areas of the organizational structure as business processes change to accommodate self-service, leverage different tools, and facilitate remote access. There may be changes in functionality as well as reliability and performance.

During the transition, there will be an increased workload for many who are facilitating it including legal, human resources, IT, business contacts and even executive management.

Once the service is underway and the legacy system has been retired, there may be a shift in responsibilities with some tasks no longer required while others take their place. There may also be a general shift in requirement for certain skills, such as on-premise IT support and management, while new requirements associated with business strategy increase in demand.

Refocus

In order to help the employee population accommodate this shift and align with the strategic requirements of the firm, it is first necessary to identify what the requirements will be. The release of day-to-day management requirements and other capital expenditures should allow the company to pursue its core business interest with additional resources although some of the cost savings may also need to be dedicated to addressing the increasing complexity of the service consumption model.

On the core business side, there may be an opportunity for better market analysis and pursuit of new ventures. These will require business analysis skills. But they may also need support from data mining tools and optimized line-of-business developments. These new opportunities imply an increasing demand for architects who understand both the underlying technologies and the unique business requirements of the organization.

It becomes critical to keep abreast of the changing business models of suppliers, customers, competitors and partners where there is potential for increased interaction. Even complete ecosystems built on Web 2.0 interactions can be facilitated by cloud computing.

IMPLEMENT

At the same time, cloud computing also introduces a certain complexity into the IT landscape that wasn't present before, with implications across the organization. There is a need to negotiate and monitor a new set of service providers. The security practitioners have a whole new set of vulnerabilities to consider and the legal department needs to assess regulatory compliance over an opaque and geographically dispersed infrastructure.

Retraining

There are different ways to approach the variance in skills. A simplistic way would be to let go all those who are in functions that are no longer needed and hire in new talent for the new focus areas.

However, there are some drawbacks with simply replacing the workforce.

- There may be legal scrutiny and barriers in some countries to widespread redundancies in a profitable company.
- It can lower morale of the employees who remain if they see their colleagues treated in a way they perceive to be unfair.
- The departing employees would be taking with them their knowledge of the internal operation and culture of the firm.
- It can take many months for new employees to acquire the same level of familiarity with the internal business processes and years to establish the same internal social network.

- Advanced skills and experience in cloud computing are still rare. It can also be very difficult to locate, attract and retain experts in the required areas.

There are dedicated skill-management applications, which will help to identify the gaps between current and required skills so that they can be addressed systematically. If they are in use it is advisable to include some of the cloud-related dimensions in the definition of the jobs to be executed. Otherwise, the same dimensions must be evaluated manually. Either way, it is important not to miss the fact that there will be a cloud aspect to many roles that are not specifically dedicated to the technology.

- IT architects must become familiar with cloud platforms, infrastructure and software.
- Security practitioners need to investigate cloud vulnerabilities.
- Network administrators will analyze cloud-based connectivity.
- IT support will need to interact with the support of the other service providers.
- Super-users need an early introduction into the service-based tools and products.
- End-users may require retraining if the applications change dramatically. In every case, they should receive extensive communications, documentation and support.

IMPLEMENT

Communications

Communicating is critical during any disruptive process. When change goes as planned, early knowledge can help people cope with the new technology and working model much better. When change fails, it is even more important to communicate. Users can often adapt if they can understand or deduce what is happening. When they are taken by surprise, without the ability to adjust or take precautions, they tend to become frustrated and resistant to change.

Regular communications are therefore mandatory to all those who will be potentially affected. This includes all the stakeholders who should receive regular progress updates identifying the schedule and alerting them to any obstacles or risks.

Everyone on the project team should have an understanding of all aspects of the project and how they are progressing. This includes a definition of the roles and responsibilities and a comprehensive schedule of remaining tasks. It is useful to encourage regular interaction between all team members and informal information sharing to complement the formal reports. Collaboration tools, such as

Microsoft SharePoint, or even just messaging distribution lists, can be helpful in fostering this level of communications.

Most end-users will not be interested in the details of the project or the underlying technologies. However, it is important to give them as much advance notice as possible on the changes they will encounter so that they can take any necessary precautions (e.g. completing certain transactions before the transition), prepare for any changes they will have to make and ask any questions they have.

Documentation

One form of communication and training is documentation. By providing all stakeholders with the information they are most likely to require ahead of time, it is possible to reduce unnecessary confusion and reduce the support burden.

The type of documentation will vary by stakeholder. Executives and business contacts may be interested in project reports. Technical contributors will want specifications. End-users are likely to be best served with simple guides such as FAQs and quick start guides.

Motivation and Incentives

One of the key success factors is to engage all the users and stakeholders throughout the change process. This entails several stages:

IMPLEMENT

Inform

The first challenge is to ensure that all employees understand not only the change impact but also its purpose. Their first impression is often difficult to dispel, so it is important to create a clear case to the employees that describes the benefits of cloud computing, not only to the organization, but also to them individually.

Empower

The more influence employees perceive that they have over a process the more likely that they will identify with it and support it. It helps to take every opportunity to engage them and solicit their feedback. They should also feel as though their input is taken seriously and merits a response.

It may be worthwhile to set up discussion forums, mailing lists or interactive portals to engage the user community. However, it only makes sense to set up the tools if someone actually monitors them regularly and interacts with the participants on an ongoing basis.

Sell

Throughout the process it is critical to demonstrate and reiterate the benefits that the new change, cloud computing in this case, will have on the users. They should also see a direct linkage between their support and contribution and the benefit they will receive.

One dimension may include providing extrinsic (compensation) rewards, which tie the transition (and their roles in it) into the performance appraisal system. If there is any form of profit-sharing, the simple fact that cloud computing can save costs and increase profitability may increase its support.

But it is even more important to focus on intrinsic factors such as level of challenge, clarity of job description, variety of skills and opportunity to learn/grow. Cloud computing entails a number of new technologies and has the capacity to facilitate a growing number of new services based on collaboration and sharing. If growth-seeking employees can tap into this potential, they can learn a number of new skills.

These can have a dual benefit in job satisfaction by increasing the intrinsic motivation through job enrichment and enhancing the opportunity for extrinsic rewards, whereby the instrumentality of achieving the latter through the former needs to be clearly articulated.

Enable

IMPLEMENT

Motivating the employees to support the change is not helpful unless they have the capacity to contribute. This includes putting together all necessary training, or allocating time for self-training, and providing any other resources that they may require.

Reinforce

It is necessary to continuously communicate with the employees to reinforce past messages and update them on any new developments. Short lapses in communications are fertile breeding grounds for concern and discontent.

Support

As the transition takes place, there will inevitably be incidents and questions that crop up. Users should be able to call the helpdesk at any time and be directed to someone who is tied into the transition process and can give them user assistance as well as updates on the status of the migration.

Operate

OPERATE

Chapter 22

Service Management

As radical as the impact of cloud computing may be during design and implementation, it is the ongoing operations where the disruption is most pronounced. Outsourcing shifts the primary responsibility from direct control to the governance of external services. The layering of applications, platforms and infrastructure makes it difficult to isolate problems and tune performance. Usage-based cost poses a risk of unlimited liability unless carefully monitored and managed. The fragmentation of providers increases the challenge of multi-party coordination. And an agile architecture accelerates the pace of change, both internally and externally initiated.

There is a clear need for a systematic framework to address these challenges. Unfortunately, ITIL, the most common service management methodology in use today, was largely designed before the impact of cloud on operations was well known. It doesn't specifically address all cloud-specific concerns. Nonetheless, it is a helpful backdrop against which to describe service management in the cloud. So I reference it to provide some context for cloud operations.

OPERATE

Conceptually, operation is the next phase after the transition. The implementation is complete as soon as the solution is used in production. It is a project with a defined end-point that winds down once a set of acceptance criteria are met. However, the system still needs to be monitored and updated in order for it to keep functioning.

This requires a hand-over from the implementation project manager to a service manager who can ensure that the system meets a given set of service levels on an ongoing basis. This is not to say that the service manager is inactive until this point. Indeed, it is vital that the service manager run the service strategy and design in parallel with the overall solution strategy and design, and ensure that the two processes are closely linked. This section is merely a different perspective and dimension of the implementation process.

In an ITIL model (Figure 22-1), services derive from a Service Strategy which implies a Service Design, Service Transition and Service Operation. These three ongoing phases feed into each other and are refined with Continual Service Improvement.

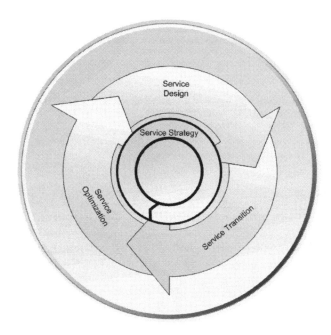

Figure 22-1: ITIL Service Lifecycle

Service Strategy

The Service Strategy relates very closely to the Strategic Impact discussed in Chapter 7. Service providers (whether they cater to an internal or external customer base) only have limited resources and usually have more requests for services and functionality than they can provide within their budget. In order to maximize their impact, they must therefore prioritize these services.

To manage the portfolio effectively, the provider must conduct a market analysis to ensure what value these services present to the users. Based on the results, the provider can quantify the service value and construct a business case for the investment of resources that is likely to offer the best return.

In a cloud solution this means that the IT organization must determine the value of potential internal and external services. In order to assess the external value it may be necessary to survey potential users and customers. In the simplest case this would mean quantifying their anticipated spend on the services and multiplying it by the projected number of customers to derive the value.

For an internal service, the simplest case would be to estimate the direct cross-charge that a business is willing to accept in order to obtain the service. There are additional considerations as discussed in Chapter 9, but the key point is that the service manager must determine which services bring the most benefit to the organization.

Service Design

The Service Design is covered in large part in the preceding chapters. In addition to the technology, this phase covers all elements relevant to the service delivery including service catalogue management, service level management, capacity management, availability management, IT service continuity management, information security management and supplier management.

It also defines multiple delivery model options including insourcing, outsourcing, co-sourcing (as a cooperative arrangement), multi-sourcing and using specific functions such as business process outsourcing or knowledge process outsourcing. These options translate very well into the cloud environment where all variations are on the table.

A key aspect of this design is the definition of service levels in terms of key performance indicators (KPIs). The key challenge is not to derive a large number of KPIs, but to select a few that are critical to the overall strategy. They should enable staff to limit their focus to the areas that have most impact by delivering the most value to the overall objective, e.g. cost savings, service improvement.

ITIL Service Design cost components include (2007, p. 38):

- Hardware acquisition costs
- Software license costs
- Hardware and software maintenance fees
- Administrative support costs
- Utilities, data center or facilities costs
- Taxes, capital, interest charges
- Compliance costs

OPERATE

Each approach can be assessed in terms of estimated costs, risks, management overhead and functional flexibility. As described in Chapter 13, it is critical to determine which factors will drive the selection and to evaluate all the alternatives.

Service Transition

Service Transition represents the intersection between project and service management. While the ITIL focus is on the ongoing operations, there are individual transitions, such as the initial implementation or major upgrades in functionality that need to be handled as projects. The Implement chapters in this book (Chapter 19 through Chapter 21) are one example of such a transition.

In a cloud-based solution, this not only covers the initial implementation of cloud services but also any updates to them, launches of new services or retirement and migration of existing services. Some ITIL considerations also include service asset and configuration management, transition planning and support, release and deployment management, change management and knowledge management. Most of these topics are covered in the coming chapters.

Service Operation

Service Operation is the core of the ITIL model. Its focus is on the day-to-day operations that are required in order to deliver the service to its users at the agreed levels of availability, reliability and performance. It includes concepts such as event management, incident management, problem management, request fulfillment, access management and service desk.

The cloud-related aspects to these topics will be covered in the next three chapters.

Continual Service Improvement

Continual Service Improvement attempts to maintain the alignment between IT services and the corporate strategy by constantly reassessing the IT capabilities and investigating opportunities to refine business processes. This includes up-front planning but also ongoing training and awareness with roles and responsibilities assigned for measurement, analysis and reporting activities.

OPERATE

This is a particularly important task in the area of cloud computing given the immature state of the delivery model and the rapid changes afoot in the underlying technologies. It will be covered in more detail in Chapter 29.

Chapter 23

Administration

As IT administration evolves in sophistication, system managers are spending less time on day-to-day repetitive tasks and instead must focus more on the strategic requirements and plans for IT. An increasing number of monitoring and diagnostic tools can automate some basic operational procedures.

Self-service portals are now common for end-user functions such as password reset, account unlock and employee updates. These reduce the IT burden. At the same time, they improve security and reduce user frustration at raising a ticket and waiting on hold for a call center to take and process support requests.

Nonetheless, there is still a need for IT technical support as well as service managers to have full visibility and traceability of all processes and transactions in order to identify root causes of problems and to ensure that the system is functioning as anticipated. There may also be additional requirements for obtaining logging and accounting information in bulk and mining this data for improved planning of functionality and capacity.

OPERATE

Administration Portal

Since cloud computing is primarily web-based, the logical interface for administering it is a portal with facilities such as:

- Billing
- Analytics
- Account management
- Service management
- Package install, update
- Configuration
- Instance flexing
- Tracing problems and incidents

A challenge arises when several different cloud providers each offer their own portal. As long as administrators are specialized on given services, they will not see this as a problem. However, it becomes tedious for an overall administrator to obtain a synoptic view when the information is dispersed across many different pages.

If the capabilities all have public interfaces and are accessible, for example through RESTful web services or SOAP requests, then it may be possible to aggregate the most important functions and indicators into a dashboard, which can serve as an entry point that directs the user to the appropriate service portal for further action. This is an approach that is facilitated by cloud management solutions such as RightScale and enStratus.

IT Service Management as a Service

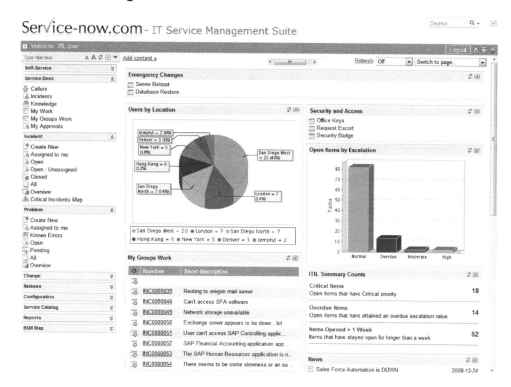

Figure 23-1: Service-now.com IT Service Management as a Service

While this chapter is primarily about running Service Management *for* the cloud, it is interesting to note that there are also SaaS-based offerings, such as Service-now, that facilitate running Service Management *in* the cloud (Figure 23-1). They are a logical choice for organizations that have no in-house service management platform and wish to minimize any further on-premise installations.

Service Request Fulfillment

Most cases of user-based service requests are very simple. They might include password assistance, software installation and configuration, or provisioning access to services for themselves and others.

In some cases, these requests will be the outcome of a call, or ticket, that the user has logged with the helpdesk. In other cases, the user will be able to trigger the request through a web-based portal. In order for the process to work in a scalable fashion, there must be some agreement on standard services. They should be published as part of a service catalogue so that users can easily understand the request process and eligibility.

For requests that carry significant risk or financial consequences, an authorization and approval process may also be required, which should be included in the functionality of the service desk. What is important from a cloud perspective is to ensure that the workflow can be validated by the organization fulfilling the request.

If the service desks of the cloud providers do not have visibility into the organizational structure of the customer, it is difficult for them to verify and ensure managerial approval. This implies a need for Identity Management federation or at least replication of organizational attributes as part of a directory-synchronization with the provider.

A request that is likely to become much more common in the future is the deployment of new services. In the past, this would hardly be considered a user request as it would have entailed procuring additional hardware and software and would need a series of approvals. However, in a utility computing model it is now possible to dispatch new services at very low risk and cost. It therefore becomes possible to reduce the overhead needed to manage the request.

OPERATE

Nonetheless, there are still some risks and concerns that need to be addressed before dispatching additional services, including reservations, scheduling and compliance checking. If these, and the necessary authorization, can be accommodated in a workflow, it can be possible to automate the entire provisioning with a self-service portal that allows a user to choose a virtual machine, configure it and launch it as needed.

Change Management

The area between user-based service requests and more extensive change management is not always obvious and depends to a large extent on the organization involved. However, in all companies there are likely to be services that are too critical for automated change requests.

It isn't a question of the type of operation on the service. These can include adding and removing server instances, changing system and networking configuration settings, deploying or removing software, deploying patches and upgrading versions, or changing memory and storage allocation. The issue is much more related to the criticality of the service and the impact that any changes can have on it.

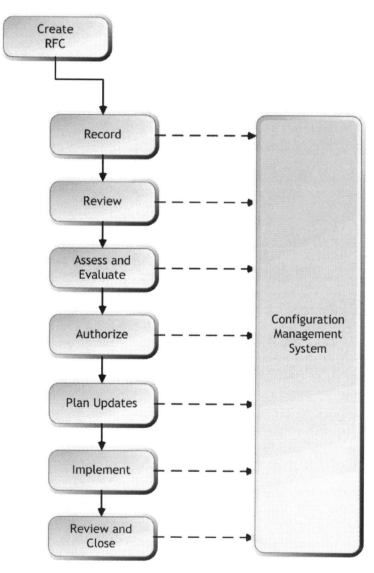

OPERATE

Figure 23-2: Change Management Process

If a service is important to the business, it is necessary to have a process in place to record, assess, authorize and monitor the change (Figure 23-2).

In order to analyze the potential impact, ITIL offers a set of nine questions (called the 9 Rs) that should be addressed for any of these changes:

- Who Raised the change?
- What is the Reason for the change?
- What is the Return required for the change?
- What are the Risks involved in the change?
- What resources are Required for the change?
- Who is Responsible for the change?
- What is the Relationship between this change and other changes?

Evaluating these questions and recording the responses can help to identify potential impact as soon as possible. Furthermore, it facilitates problem analysis and correction if it does ultimately contribute to subsequent failures directly or indirectly.

Change management can become very complex when many parties are involved. As the number of service providers increases, the combinations of potential intersections grow exponentially. It is therefore vital to receive as much information as possible in a structured manner.

The processes for requesting and approving changes also need to be co-ordinated with internal mechanisms regulating network connectivity, directory and remote access.

New Release Management

One major recurring change is the need to perform upgrades to increase functionality, solve problems and sometimes improve performance. New versions can disrupt services because they may drop functions, implement them differently or contain undiscovered bugs.

It is therefore important to understand whether they will have any adverse impact on business processes before rolling them out live. One approach is to stage all services locally and test them with on-premise equipment before overwriting the production services.

The opposite approach is to leverage the cloud as a test platform. Vendors such as SOASTA provide an on-demand infrastructure that is well suited to highly scalable beta and load testing. The absence of need for acquiring any equipment is attractive in itself, but it is also helpful to have a cloud-based reference case to test against.

The types of test and release processes will depend on the service delivery model in use. In the case of IaaS or PaaS, the new releases refer to the platforms and should largely go unnoticed by the users. However, it is vital to ensure that the service provider makes new versions available in advance so that application compatibility can be assured. If the provider doesn't have a mechanism for pre-release and testing, it is critical to validate the platform at the earliest possible time after release.

In addition to the platforms, there will also be new releases of the software. Whether it is commercially acquired or developed in-house, it needs to be carefully regression tested against all known use cases before it is made live.

There is some flexibility in the granularity of release units. Due to the complexity of interfaces in a service-oriented architecture, there may be a case for infrequent major releases that are rolled out in bundles in order to minimize the total testing effort. On the other hand, an automated testing process may be able to handle frequent minor releases, which will provide user benefits more quickly. The question is ultimately a business decision that pits the value of accelerated functionality against the incremental costs of additional testing.

SaaS release management is much more difficult for the enterprise to dictate. The service provider has a cost incentive to keep all customers on a common release. They may offer previews or even some discretion over the timing of the upgrades, but generally the customer has much less flexibility and control than over their own software.

Again, the key is that whenever new versions are made available they need to be tested before the users begin to encounter problems. The shorter the time frame the more intensive the testing needs to be. If there are problems, there should be a defined escalation path with the SaaS provider to isolate the issue and find a work-around.

Capacity Management

As mentioned in Chapter 17, long-term capacity management is less critical for on-demand services. Elasticity of resources means that enterprises can scale up and down as demand dictates without the need for extensive planning. You can even employ reactive monitoring tools such as RightScale and Morph to automate the requests for more resources.

Nonetheless, there is some value in proactively estimating requirements. Even though the costs of increasing demand may be absorbed by corresponding additional revenues, this doesn't mean that your financial officers don't want to see an estimate and budget for how these costs may develop. In addition to ensuring profitability, they also need to plan for cash flow, taxes and capital budgeting, which may be impacted by the numbers.

You may also uncover idle capacity that is limited due to unforeseen resource bottlenecks when you have scaled too much in one direction and not enough in another. For example, you may be adding network bandwidth to solve a problem that is actually based on contention for disk I/O or even server utilization.

It's also a good idea to verify that your service provider will actually be in a position to deliver all the resource requirements that you anticipate. If you will be requiring more vertically scaled capacity for single-threaded processes and your provider has specialized in low-clock-speed multi-core chipsets, then you may need to look at other alternatives that match your requirements for that service.

There are several aspects of capacity planning that need to be evaluated in parallel. You can monitor existing performance and extrapolate future patterns based on anticipated demand. You can model current and future applications based on specified performance parameters. You may also have the possibility to influence the demand and usage in terms of timing and volume so that you can optimize your resource reservations for the best value.

Availability Management

Chapter 17 covered several dimensions of availability as part of the integration phase. Just like capacity management, this is not a one-time action. In addition to reactive management, such as monitoring, measuring and analyzing incidents, you also need to proactively plan and design availability improvements.

There are many dimensions to availability. If there have been outages, it is important to identify frequency, duration and timing (night, week-end, peak time). A deeper look at the components of the incident response (detection, diagnosis, repair, recovery) is also helpful since each phase has different implications in terms of the amount of information the helpdesk can communicate to users about expected uptime.

Other metrics that may be relevant are:

OPERATE

- Mean time between failures
- Mean time to restore service
- Mean time between system incidents

The service-level calculation implies an in-depth understanding of user requirements, which are monitored against SLAs. The question is not only whether the service-levels are being met but whether they adequately reflect business requirements or whether they need further refinement. In other words are current performance levels, events, alarms and escalation paths sufficient?

The final criterion should be the impact on business processes. If there are any business processes that have sustained unacceptable impact, the logical question is whether you should change provider. Are there alternative providers of the same service? If not, you may also want to perform an extensive analysis into the failure points of outages (network, virtual infrastructure, application) to assess what kind of redundancy can help to address and mitigate the failures.

It is also important to monitor and compare these availability levels not only with the SLA but also with benchmarks and reports from other cloud providers. If your provider is meeting its contractual obligations, but these do not reflect the service levels of its competitors, then you have leverage to renegotiate more favorable terms in the contract.

Access Management

Chapter 18 described the challenge of identity management in a multi-provider world. The impact on service management comes in several forms. On the one hand, federation must be negotiated and managed. For example if there are schema changes, or if attribute semantics change in the corporate directory, then these need to be coordinated with service providers leveraging the identity store.

Changes in access policies and procedures also need to be synchronized. A given transaction that required only first level approval during the initial implementation may now require a second signature. Workflow and business logic may also need synchronization.

The access requirements of the service provider to enterprise resources can also change as a result of service requests. For example, the service provider may require increased integration with the enterprise service desk. The questions for the service manager are who authorizes these and how they are approved. Once the procedural aspect is worked out, then the changes also need to be implemented on a technical level, which may require support from the networking and security departments, for example, in order to implement the necessary proxy and firewall configurations.

Chapter 24

Monitoring

While a great deal of the service delivery may be outsourced in a cloud solution, it doesn't completely remove the continuous responsibility of checking and reporting on service health. The due diligence required in defining key performance indicators and service levels prior to signing the contract is critical. However, someone also needs to take ownership for the stability of the system after it is operational.

The task involves both proactive planning to ensure business/service continuity as well as reactive processes for coping with any problems that occur. This chapter describes some of the principles involved in each. Note that these systems don't necessarily need to be designed from scratch. Established enterprise management frameworks are gradually adding capability to cope with cloud-based services. Some, such as Hyperic, offer plug-ins for Google Apps, Amazon Web Services and other cloud providers.

IT Service Continuity Management

OPERATE

A Business Continuity Plan (BCP) consists of a risk assessment, a business impact analysis and a contingency plan.

Risk Assessment

The first step in ensuring continuity is to identify all risks that may impact the services that are being provided. These should be qualified with an estimate of the probability and impact of each. Based on the overall risk attitude of the organization, it is then possible to categorize the individual threats and decide whether to accept, mitigate, transfer or address them. The concept of risk will be covered in more detail in Chapter 27, so this section will focus on those that potentially have disastrous impact, such as high levels of damage or destruction of a data center.

Business Impact Analysis

The Business Impact Analysis identifies the critical assets such as business processes and business functions and estimates possible damages and losses that could be suffered from disruptions in service. By carefully assessing the value of the assets, it is possible to quantify the cost of downtime and thereby prioritize the sequence for reestablishing service.

It should be clear that while there are practical limits to how fast a service can be restored, it is not always mandatory to take the fastest path since an accelerated restoration may carry additional costs, both directly, as labor and material expenses, and indirectly, in terms of the opportunity costs associated with delaying the restoration of other services.

Contingency Plan

The contingency plan identifies the framework needed to recover from a disruption in service. This may include a sequence of operations, prioritization of applications and escalation paths for obtaining additional resources.

For example, in the case of a disaster recovery there are multiple options, whereby selection may depend on the recovery time objectives set for the applications:

- Gradual recovery (cold standby)
- Intermediate recovery (warm standby)
- Immediate recovery (hot standby)

OPERATE

Which of these has been allocated to a particular service is ultimately a financial decision that should be made based on the business impact analysis and risk assessment. In order to ensure that the disaster recovery plan is complete and functional, it is necessary to test it regularly with fire drills.

For cloud services, IT service continuity is more difficult to verify since outsourced services are largely a responsibility of the providers. Customers are left trying to piece together a picture of dependability based on:

- Limited published information that the provider will share about their internal procedures
- Audits from independent agencies, which tend to reflect only a portion of the entire operations
- Historical track record of the provider and the assumption that the past is a good predictor of the future
- Brand name of the provider
- Contractual agreements, which may, or may not, offer indemnity in the case of data loss

All of these provide some insight into the trustworthiness of the providers; yet it is difficult to quantify or aggregate the metrics, so some degree of subjectivity will always remain.

IT Operations Management

Part of the incentive of moving to a public cloud is to reduce the amount of internal operational activity. However, there may still be some need for internal involvement particularly when the services involve hybrid configurations that also run on internal systems.

In any case, much of the internal infrastructure is local such as the printers, scanners and local network equipment. End-user desktops and mobile devices are also closer to on-site operations personnel. So there is an absolute requirement for some ongoing local operations, which must also be connected with the operational management groups of the service providers.

Backup

One area that is of particular concern to business continuity is backup. Operations personnel are under increasing pressure to meet aggressive backup requirements. Users demand the ability to store more data, yet expect more frequent backups and faster restores. Legal regulations mandate long-term readability. At the same time, virtualization has all but eliminated any scheduled downtime while outsourcing and multi-tenancy have increased the requirement for encryption of the media.

In addition to disaster recovery, backups are used for a variety of reasons, including:

OPERATE

- End-user access to data that has been removed
- End-user access to historical data
- Audits, Troubleshooting, IP retention
- Legal requirements for eDiscovery

However, backup is not the optimal solution to meet these secondary objectives. As described in Chapter 17, an archiving platform can de-duplicate and classify the data to address these functions and can also provide enterprise search. Furthermore, offloading these responsibilities onto an archiving platform relieves the backup function from many of its long-term requirements so that it can focus on offering fast and reliable disaster recovery.

Incident Management

While Operations Management takes a proactive role to maintain system health, Incident Management caters to the reactive side. It revolves around an incident model that describes:

- Steps to handle an incident
- Chronological order of steps, dependencies, co-processing
- Roles and responsibilities
- Timescales and thresholds
- Escalation procedures (contacts)
- Evidence-preservation activities

A standard incident management process involves:

- Incident logging
- Incident categorization
- Incident prioritization
- Initial diagnosis
- Incident escalation
    - Functional
    - Hierarchical
- Investigation and diagnosis
    - Root cause, order, impact
- Resolution and recovery
    - End-user actions
    - Service Desk
    - Specialist support groups
    - 3rd party suppliers
- Incident closure
    - Closure categorization
    - User satisfaction survey
    - Incident documentation
    - Ongoing or recurring problems?
    - Formal closure

The key consideration in a cloud-computing scenario is how to expand this model to include multiple providers. There must be agreement on activities and thresholds that trigger incidents. And it is necessary to enable integration of the incident response systems across firewalls.

Problem Management

Problem Management refers to tracking and resolving unknown causes of incidents. It is closely related to Incident Management but focuses on solving root causes for a set of incidents rather than applying what may be a temporary fix to an incident.

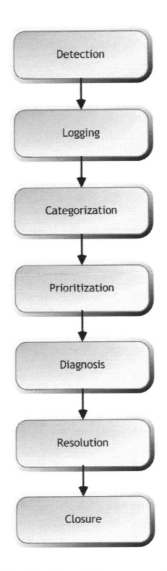

Figure 24-1: Problem Management Process

It follows a similar sequence as was required for incidents (Figure 24-1). As such, in addition to cloud-specific challenges, they also share some commonality including cross-organizational collaboration. It is vital to define roles and responsibilities contractually and to ensure full co-operation in diagnosing and resolving problems even when it is not obvious in which realm the root cause may lie.

Event Management

Event Management tracks discernible occurrences with significance on the management of IT infrastructure or the delivery of IT services. It thereby facilitates early detection of incidents and provides both clues for problem solving and input for capacity planning.

It typically involves both active monitoring/polling tools, which generate alerts when they encounter exception conditions, and passive tools that detect and correlate alerts.

Some of the most common events to be observed include (ITIL, 2007, p. 94):

- Configurations items
- Environmental conditions (fire, smoke)
- Software license monitoring (compliance and optimal utilization)
- Security (e.g. intrusions)
- Auditing use, tracking performance

One set of concerns in the public cloud is the contractual challenge already described above. It is necessary to come to an agreement on the events and thresholds that trigger alerts and on the mechanisms for relaying the information to the destination.

OPERATE

A multi-tenant environment also presents some potential complications. Cotenants may create disruptions, akin to environmental conditions, that need to be signaled. If the multi-tenancy involves sharing of physical resources then it will complicate performance monitoring and projections since performance may be affected by competition for resources.

Chapter 25

Support

One of the biggest challenges of operating a service is the interface to all the humans who are involved in the process. Technical integration can be fully automated but users tend to have requirements that are not as easy to specify. At the same time, they are the most critical elements of the system. It is vital to support them as efficiently as possible so that they can proceed with their business processes.

There is some diversity in the user roles that may require assistance in a cloud solution. We will first focus on the end-users since they are the most varied and numerous of the groups. But, there will also be requirements for support to the IT department and business application owners.

Every technology requires a support model. This is not new with cloud computing. However the heterogeneous, multi-vendor composition of services can complicate support models that had previously been simple and streamlined. On the positive side, the technologies can introduce increased infrastructural stability. However, it is also very difficult to troubleshoot problems that span organizational boundaries, where each player has an incentive to cast the blame on other parties.

OPERATE

Furthermore, the cloud providers will often have a consumer focus by default and may not have the level of expertise required to diagnose problems related to complex enterprise applications. The solution will probably involve integrating service desks, which carries with it additional complexity in terms of passing tickets and defining escalation processes.

End-user Support

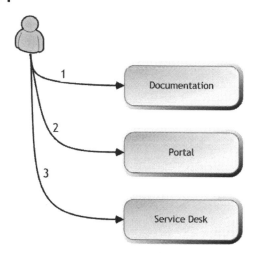

Figure 25-1: End-user Support Path

End-user support should progress in tiers that successively address more difficult and less common problems (Figure 25-1). It begins with simple documentation and on-line help to orient the user and clarify any obvious points of confusion. A self-service portal can then help to trigger an automatic process to fulfill common requests.

These first two levels have the advantage that they don't require any costly human intervention other than that of the affected user. The rest of the support process is then collectively considered the service desk, which may range from desk-side support for common problems to requesting code changes from the developers.

A key pre-requisite to the end-user support process is to test the functionality extensively. This can involve professional testers who typically focus on errors in the code. They may also report unintuitive and complex areas of the interface so that, where it isn't possible to change the software, at least it is possible to prepare the users.

On top of technical testing, it is also vital to obtain some input from typical business users. Selecting a random sample of employees with diverse backgrounds and roles can help to give an advance glimpse of the types of problems and challenges other users will encounter.

Documentation

Documentation is notorious for being ignored. There is little point in giving users volumes of technical information that they are unlikely to use. Instead it is more efficient to focus on the most important questions and concerns and address them clearly.

This might be in the form of an electronic mail message. It might be a printed brochure that is distributed to the users. It can also be an on-line tutorial that is triggered when the user logs on to the application. Ideally, the documentation will not rely on any single communications channel but will include a combination of several mechanisms.

In order to focus the users and avoid overwhelming them it is necessary to study what actually changes for the user and what the user needs to do differently with the new system. If the system involves new functionality, or the user is new to the application, then there should also be some form of Getting Started guide, which walks the user through the initial setup and common processes.

While the information that is thrust on the user should be kept to a minimum this doesn't mean that there cannot be a more complete system of on-line help and documentation available. The users then only need to receive a pointer to the repository and can subsequently choose to investigate some problems on their own.

Portal

A self-service portal can help to automate request fulfillment. Common tasks like provisioning an account or resetting a password may be processed without any call center interaction. This yields a benefit in reduced support costs and may also improve the user productivity since there are no delays associated with logging a call and waiting for a response.

However, for the portal to work effectively, it must be obvious to the users where to go and what to do once they get there. This means that the portal location must be widely communicated and ideally linked to other portals that the users visit regularly, including the application itself.

The portal also needs to cover the right tasks. It may be worth investigating what the most common requests are that the user cannot accomplish in the base applications. This might include subscriptions, unsubscriptions and requests for additional resources.

The business logic of the portal functions depends on the nature of the request. If the functions are universally available, the authorization is simple. For example, it may be the case that any user can subscribe to a service or request a password reset with simple authentication. On the other hand, requests that involve additional costs to the organization and department may require multiple levels of approvals.

Where a cloud service provider is operating the portal there can be connectivity and security ramifications. The portal needs to be able to authenticate the users and the approvers, which may imply federated identity management in order to validate user credentials stored on a corporate directory server. In some cases, the requests may also have cost implications that need to be registered with the enterprise resource planning (ERP) system (for internal charges) or the billing system (for externally provided services).

Super-users

Some organizations have had great success with the role of super-users. It isn't indispensable but can help to add a personal touch to the support process, and some business users may see it as enriching their job if they have the opportunity to gain more familiarity with technology.

The idea is that a group of users is selected who have an interest in the technical aspects of the service and sit in relative proximity to significant groups of (other) end-users. These super-users then receive some additional demonstrations and training on new services so that they are familiar with the most common operations.

They may also be given some access to the support management systems and included on distribution lists for event notifications (e.g. for service incidents and outages). When end-users have questions on the application, they may feel more comfortable approaching someone they know and who can provide desk-side assistance if necessary.

Service Desk

OPERATE

Regardless of the level of infrastructure and automation that is put into place to offload the central IT department, there will always be cases where unanticipated problems arise and the user needs expert resolution. Service desks are the organizational units that are in place to handle these cases.

The term "service desk" often also refers to the actual tool that is used to track tickets, such as questions, problem reports and requests. It is interesting to observe that, like many other management components, there are also SaaS-based ticket-tracking systems, such as ZenDesk (Figure 25-2), for companies that want to minimize internal applications.

Figure 25-2: ZenDesk Ticket Tracking

Support Tiers

A call center is typically organized in a hierarchy of several tiers with 3 levels being the most common (Figure 25-3).

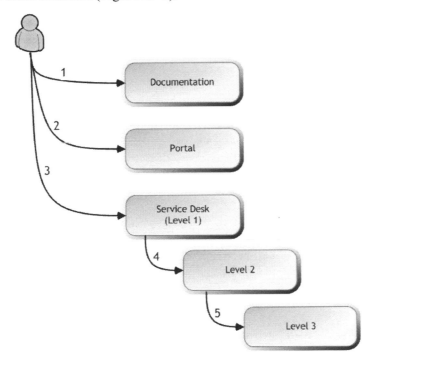

OPERATE

Figure 25-3: Call center Escalation Path

Level 1: The first level of support is responsible for triage and can address simple recurring problems with a scripted response.

Responsibilities typically include:

- Log incident and service request details

- Provide first-line investigation and diagnosis
- Escalate incidents not resolved in time threshold
- Inform users of progress
- Close resolved incidents and requests
- Perform user-satisfaction callbacks and surveys
- Update the Configuration Management System

There may also be an interface with small teams of desk-side support, particularly for larger locations. Where there is no desk-side support, the support requirements increase since it is much more difficult to diagnose many problems remotely, particularly as soon as hardware failures come into play.

While international support has been a concern confined mostly to large corporations in the past, the increasing mobility of users and the development of international trade have made it important for many smaller firms too. Conceptually, this tier must be geographically distributed in order to accommodate all time zones and languages represented by the users. However, this doesn't necessarily mean that the support personnel are also located in those time zones. There are certainly also cases where multiple time-shifts cover worldwide support from the same building by working around the clock.

Level 2: Second-level support is usually much more specialized to certain applications and services. The specialists may not be familiar with the internal design of the products, but they will know how to use advanced features and be aware of the most common product bugs. They will also undertake some research of the internal knowledge management systems to see if they can identify a known problem before escalating it further.

OPERATE

Level 3: If the problem is particularly difficult, or has never been encountered before, then internal knowledge of the products may be required. Third level support should ultimately be able to solve any critical, reproducible problems with debugging tools. If they are not able to find the root cause themselves, they will often have access to the development teams who can step through the code to isolate the problem.

Service Knowledge Management System

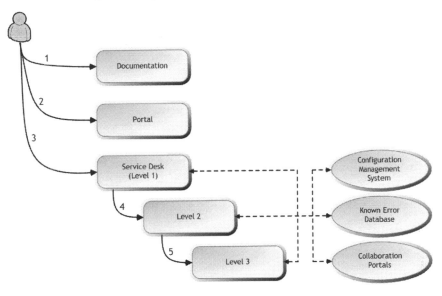

Figure 25-4: Knowledge Management System

A critical factor in keeping support costs down is to expedite problem resolution by leveraging previous solutions and all information that is known about the components related to the problem (Figure 25-4). In order to facilitate these operations, call center personnel (particularly levels two and three) will have access to a variety of tools including:

Configuration Management Database: Listing of the attributes of all configurable entities in the system being supported

Known Error Database: List of common error symptoms along with the root cause analyses and procedures to correct or work around the problem

Collaboration portals: Additional information assembled by the call center that provides background on the technology and products that are being supported

Service Desk Integration

In a cloud delivery model, a starting point is to define which service desk will be responsible for which services at each layer of the support stack. It isn't necessarily trivial to handle calls for additional services. The impact can be calculated by determining the user population for each geographical time zone and support language then estimating the number of calls per user per month as well as the average resolution time. There may also be requirements for advanced training; and specialized skills may make it difficult to overload support of multiple products on individual employees.

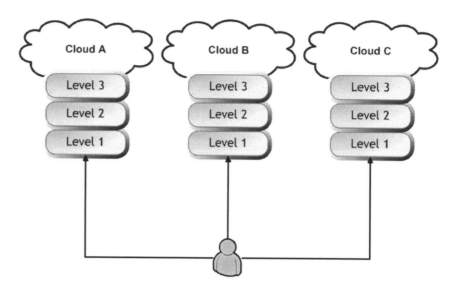

Figure 25-5: Isolated Service Desks

The simplest case involves isolated service desks each supporting their own cloud services (Figure 25-5). Unfortunately, this mechanism is neither efficient nor user-friendly. It duplicates common functionality between providers, and it puts the burden on the user to know which hotline to call for which problem.

To address these problems, it is common that the enterprise, or an outsourcing partner, will take on the first layer of call filtering. This is a difficult function for a provider that is specialized on one service.

OPERATE

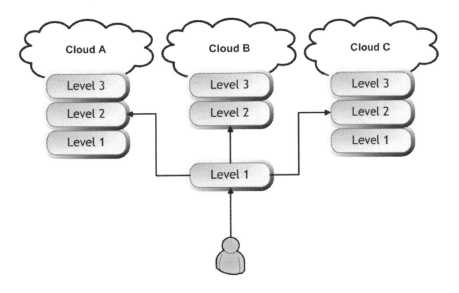

Figure 25-6: Integrated Service Desk

An integrated service desk implies that the support path must fork either at the second or third layer which involves some interaction and connectivity between the teams (Figure 25-6). The KMS, KEDB, CMS should be integrated or interconnected as well as possible and there must be some means of passing tickets.

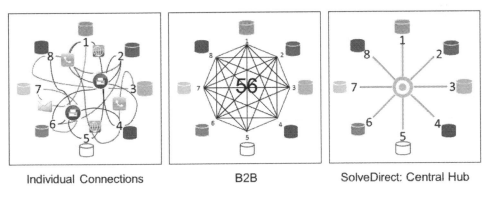

Individual Connections   B2B   SolveDirect: Central Hub

Figure 25-7: SolveDirect Central Hub

OPERATE

As shown in Figure 25-7, B2B integration has laid the foundation for consolidated connectivity. However, point-to-point connections imply the need for an exponentially increasing number of adapters as organizations expand their set of business partners. To address this challenge, SolveDirect offers a central hub that bridges service collaboration across service partners by mapping workflows and data.

This approach facilitates on-boarding of new members in an ecosystem and drives down the overall cost. Automation of the communication process reduces the manual effort for processing service requests between different service partners. It is possible to minimize escalations by virtually eliminating ticket loss and accelerating response time. A single platform for communication also enables service partners to share data and reporting functions for service volume reporting and service-level monitoring.

Although an integrated service desk has many advantages, the interconnectivity challenges don't always demand a technical solution. It is less important whether incidents are raised manually or automatically than it is that there is an agreement in place to solve the problem expeditiously and that providers do not attempt to deflect requests on the pretense that the faults lies elsewhere.

IT Support

In addition to end-users, there is also a requirement for IT and business users to receive assistance from the service providers.

Incident Management Interfaces

The clearest case is where application owners, system administrators, security officers or other stakeholders become aware of a problem that is related to the delivery of a particular service. This problem may not necessarily be visible to end-users but still have an impact on either the service or the local infrastructure. For example, the service may be releasing malware or destabilizing other services. To deal with any potential issues, there must be identified contacts and escalation procedures in place to resolve the issue.

Technical Information

OPERATE

Generally, there must be mechanisms in place for obtaining and sharing documentation and training on all cloud services and technologies. Vendor architecture diagrams and specifications for all technical interfaces can help IT staff as they troubleshoot problems in hybrid systems or trace incidents involving crossover impact between services.

Control

Chapter 26

Compliance

I am not a lawyer nor is it the intent of this chapter to provide any specific regulatory guidance. Rather, it should make it clear that legal counsel will be required and that assessing all facets and ramifications of necessary compliance is not a trivial task, even for a specialized attorney, given the diverse global jurisdictions as well as the rapidly changing pace of IT and the scrutiny to which it is exposed.

To illustrate some of the ambiguity consider the jurisdiction. It may not only apply to the home base of the service but also to anywhere there are operations - or even to where the products should be sold. Indeed, since data travels through a physical medium that may pass through many national boundaries, there is at least a conceptual obligation to adhere to all applicable laws. Given that the Internet may freely re-route traffic, it is feasible that data flowing through a logical connection between two physically adjacent systems could transit the globe to reach its destination. Clearly this is a contrived example, but it highlights the difficulty in trying to assess which laws are applicable to a given service.

That said, some of the most important regulations to consider include:

Sarbanes-Oxley: The Public Company Accounting Reform and Investor Protection Act of 2002, also called Sarbanes-Oxley, Sarbox or SOX, sets standards for all U.S. publicly traded companies defining responsibilities for corporate boards, management and accounting firms. It increases the individual responsibility of senior executives, enhances financial disclosure and limits conflicts of interest. These consequences imply increased internal controls, which must be backed up by extensive auditing.

CONTROL

HIPAA: The Health Insurance Portability and Accountability Act of 1996 attempts to address waste, fraud and abuse in U.S. health care delivery and health insurance with a set of regulations, which collectively improve the effectiveness of the health care system and ensure portability and continuity of coverage. Accountability provisions also set standards, including administrative, physical and technical safeguards protecting private health care information that is exchanged between insurance companies, health care providers, pharmacies, employers and patients in order to minimize the risk of violating patients' privacy.

FDA: The U.S. Food and Drug Administration enforces stringent technical requirements on pharmaceuticals in the area of new drug applications. Title 21 CFR Part 11 of the Code of Federal Regulations defines guidelines on electronic records and electronic signatures including the criteria under which they are considered to be trustworthy, reliable and equivalent to paper records.

FISMA: The Federal Information Security Management Act of 2002 provides a comprehensive framework for ensuring the effectiveness of information security controls over information resources that support U.S. federal operations and assets. It ensures development and maintenance of minimum controls and provides a mechanism for improved oversight of federal agency information security programs.

GLBA: The Financial Services Modernization Act of 1999 – also called the Gramm-Leach-Bliley Act (GLBA) – was passed with the primary objective of increasing the ability of financial institutions to consolidate. Three privacy restrictions were added to the bill in order to enlist sufficient support in the U.S. Congress. The Financial Privacy Rule requires financial institutions to present their policy to each customer on a regular basis. The Safeguards Rule mandates a written information security plan that describes how the institution protects all personal information. Pretexting protection includes provisions for training staff to identify and report suspicious requests and monitoring programs to validate the efficacy of internal controls.

OSHA: The Occupational Safety and Health (OSH) Act of 1970 ensures that employers minimize employee exposure to environmental hazards, such as toxic chemicals, radiation, mechanical dangers, excessive heat, cold or noise, or any unsanitary conditions. Cloud computing is not likely to fall into the category of a hazardous industry, but the data center facility management is an area that needs to be considered. Of relevance is also the requirement for employers to maintain records of job-related injuries and illnesses.

CONTROL

Basel II: The International Convergence of Capital Measurement and Capital Standards, a Revised Framework (2004), also called Basel II Accords, are defined by the Basel Committee on Banking Supervision. The accords are not universally binding, but the U.S. Federal Reserve Bank, and other national agencies, have established guidance that is based on their recommendations. They aim to protect the financial system from the impact of bank failure by imposing deposit requirements that are commensurate with the level of risk that the institution includes in its portfolio. The impact of these requirements on IT and on cloud computing is not direct. However, it is clear that IT plays a large part in the operational risk of any institution. In this case, the risk also has very direct financial consequences in order to ensure compliance.

PCI: The Payment Card Industry Data Security Standard (PCI DSS) governs minimum security standards that are necessary in order to process credit and debit card payments. These do not derive from any national legal requirements. Rather, they are maintained by the payment card industry in order to safeguard their payment system and maintain the trust of their customers. Some of the measures include network security, strong access control, vulnerability management as well as strong information security processes that regularly monitor and test the security of the assets. Most importantly, there are strict provisions for protecting cardholder data, including the encryption of cardholder data passing across public networks.

EU Privacy Directive: The European Parliament Data Protection Directive (officially Directive 95/46/EC) is a European Union directive that regulates the processing of personal data and the free movement of such data within the European Union. One notable provision includes a prohibition preventing transfer of personal data (unless certain stated conditions are met) to third countries that do not provide an adequate level of protection.

US Privacy Act: The Privacy Act of 1974 restricts the collection, use, and dissemination of personally identifiable information by federal agencies. The disclosure of personal information generally requires written consent from the individual, but there are also a set of statutory exceptions, such as collection for use by law enforcement and statistical analysis.

EU Data Retention Directive: The European Union Data Retention Directive of 2006 requires communications providers to retain necessary data to trace and identify the source, destination, time, duration and location of all communications. This would include Call Detail Records (CDRs) of telephony and Internet Protocol Detail Records (IPDRs) of internet traffic, such as emails relayed, web sites visited, files downloaded and various transaction data.

CONTROL

The selection of a cloud service should also consider the fact that national legislation may mandate law enforcement access to any data stored within the reach of organizations based in its territory. In particular, the USA Patriot (Uniting and Strengthening America by Providing Appropriate Tools Required to Intercept and Obstruct Terrorism) Act has received notoriety since it is seen internationally as giving the US extraterritorial powers to retrieve sensitive information that may be accessible to US-based companies.

However, Hogan Lovells (Wolf, 2012) show that the US is not alone in having expansive provisions for legal search and seizure. Confiscation warrants in other countries can also be used to gain access to data stored domestically and belonging to domestic or foreign companies. What's more, within the Western world, cooperation between law enforcement agencies is close enough that legitimate requests for information sharing related to terrorist or criminal activities are usually successful.

This applies not only to cloud resources but also storage of local providers and the organization's own data center. So there is never a guarantee even local data won't end up in any other allied government's hands.

The question to ask isn't so much whether it is feasible that information could fall into foreign hands. Rather, it is a question of how likely such a scenario is and what impact it would have. In other words, it is vital to perform a thorough risk analysis rather than reacting emotionally to an idea that some might find offensive.

Responsibilities

The responsibility for adhering to data-specific regulations varies from country to country and may also depend on the business of the company. Health care and financial services are two industries with specific requirements. Government agencies are also often tightly regulated.

One key concept is the distinction between data owner and data controller. While the customer owns the data, the data controller typically carries more responsibility. It may, or may not, be the case that the customer is considered the data controller for legal purposes since multiple parties may collaborate in the operations of managing, manipulating and maintaining the information.

As mentioned above, the jurisdiction and applicable legal framework may also be unintuitive in a distributed service. The data may span multiple physical countries and it may also span storage providers hosted in multiple different political realms. Laws may even apply to anyone doing business in the country – not just those who store there data there. Even though it might be conceivable to ignore the legislation of remote countries, global companies will not want to jeopardize subsidiaries, clients and business partners in those countries. This fragmentation presents a number of legal conundrums. For example, if a country has a restriction that data of a certain type cannot be exported then, once it enters, it may be difficult to send the information back to the source.

CONTROL

Before you panic, I am not aware of any specific problems of this nature but the point of the illustration is that the convoluted, and currently still very immature, legal environment for cloud computing may harbor risks that are not immediately obvious. In some ways it is fortunate that there has been very little strict enforcement of the most intrusive regulations.

However, the lack of prior consequences is certainly no guarantee that organizations are immune from the potential penalties. In addition to increased responsibility for due diligence on the part of senior management (CEO, CFO, CISO,

Board of Directors), another outcome may be security measures imposed on subcontractors, service providers and outsourcers.

Areas of Concern

Most of the legal provisions that relate to cloud computing fall into one of three categories, which we will look at in a little more detail:

- Data privacy
- Electronic discovery
- Notification

Data Privacy

There are at least three aspects to data privacy. The primary requirement is data protection. There is a need to ensure the data cannot be accessed by unauthorized users. The second is closely related and can be used to help fulfill the first. When the data is no longer needed then there must be a reliable way to destroy it. The third dimension is that of data location. It also helps to supplement data protection by preventing the data from being copied to territories where the protection mechanisms and legal provisions are not guaranteed to be as stringent.

Data Protection

Data protection relies on the principles of separation and encryption to secure personally identifiable information and other sensitive content. The more isolated the data is from other information on the same network, and the stronger the security boundaries between it and other information resources, the better the protection. Multi-tenancy undermines this separation, whereby it is important to differentiate between different levels of multi-tenancy as described in Chapter 18.

In addition to the physical separation of data storage, it is also possible to isolate it logically through encryption. Once encrypted, the risk of co-mingled data in a multi-tenant environment decreases. However, the principal issues remain. The security boundary then takes the shape of the encryption key. So a key management system must ensure that each tenant has a separate key and that there is no means of acquiring a key illegitimately. Alternatively, the customers may manage their own keys and take precautions to prevent compromise.

CONTROL

As noted in Chapter 18, encryption is not a panacea against every threat. The efficacy of encrypting data in a foreign data store depends on the attack. For example if a SQL database is encrypted then a SQL injection will bypass the encryption since the application can decrypt the data and serve back the plain text to the hacker.

It is therefore very important to take an approach of defense in depth, considering all levels of the application stack, to create multi-tiered protection that ranges from the source code through the physical data storage to bonding of cloud provider employees with physical access. Underlying all of these mechanisms is a requirement to classify and label all sensitive data and systems so that the information needing protection is identified and processed accordingly.

Data Destruction

If data is sufficiently encrypted, there should be no need to destroy it. That seems like a logical conclusion. However, it is good practice to destroy data before relinquishing control over any physical media for a couple of reasons:

- Some of the encryption processes, ciphers and key management may be sufficient today, but there is no guarantee that nobody will discover any flaws in them in the future.
- There is always the possibility that the encryption key may be compromised either inadvertently or deliberately.

Once the physical storage is released, there can be no way to retroactively increase or correct the protection on it. If the physical data storage comes into possession of someone with nefarious intent, it may increase future risk exposure.

These reasons make it critical to investigate the cloud provider policies on data retention and destruction, not only at the process level but down to the physical verification of data erasure. Does the mechanism ensure that all residual magnetic traces are gone? For particularly sensitive information this may require rewriting the same sectors many times with various bit-patterns. It is a cumbersome process so it isn't wise to assume the provider is doing this without any incentive on its part.

Data Location

CONTROL

As described above, data location can have significant legal implications. Even though a large territorial spread has benefits to the customer in terms of increased protection against local and regional disasters, it tends to complicate the legal ramifications.

The provider may offer the option to choose between regional data centers so that the customer can balance legal and geographical redundancy requirements. In any case, it behooves the customer to understand, with as great of precision as is possible, where the data may be stored in order to decide effectively which data to store with which provider.

Electronic Discovery

Electronic discovery (also called eDiscovery) presents one of the largest uncontrolled costs for businesses today since they have no adequate records management. These costs may take two forms. There can be penalties for not retaining mandatory records. Alternatively, the inability to offer favorable business records as evidence weakens their case in the event of litigation.

It is critical that data supporting the interest of stakeholders, such as employees, customers, management and investors, can be used in court. To meet this requirement, rules of evidence state that business records offered as evidence must be shown to be both authentic and reliable, which implies very specific data preservation requirements. In addition to the primary information, it is mandatory to keep metadata, log files and other information that serves as an audit trail for any modifications.

There are three aspects of electronic discovery that may be relevant in cloud computing: the procedures in place to comply with a subpoena, the technological process that is used to ensure data will be available and presentable when needed and the ability to obtain the specific information that is requested in an expedient manner.

Procedures

There must be a clear definition of roles and responsibilities of both customer and cloud providers for litigation holds, discovery searches and expert testimonies. A court may order a subpoena for certain information either from the customer or the provider. From the perspective of the customer, these are fundamentally different. If the subpoena is served to the customer, they will require the provider to provide all technical assistance to help them comply with the request.

On the other hand, if the request goes to the provider then the customer will want a provision to be able to fight the request. The provider should give the customer time to challenge the request and exercise its right to protect confidential user data. At a minimum, the cloud service provider should ensure that any request is legitimate and follows correct procedure.

CONTROL

Data Availability

The first step in being able to provide information in the case of a legal request is to make sure that the data has been retained. This means that either the cloud provider performs regular backups and has a tried and tested procedure for recovery, or else the responsibility falls on the customer to ensure all data in the cloud is also replicated to another provider or data center. For important records, a combination of both ensures maximal availability.

It is in the customer's interests to inquire about the provider's support for long-term archiving. A backup doesn't automatically address this need. The data may become inaccessible over an extended period of time due to media degradation and changes in encryption technology.

There is also always a risk that the provider (or customer) may terminate the service agreement. What should happen if a customer defaults on payment or the provider declares bankruptcy? On the one hand, the customer would want the data destroyed for the reasons stated earlier. On the other hand, they may be critically important to a legal case. To address these cases, the customer should ensure that it obtains regular copies of all data. It might extract these though network requests over the Internet, or it may simply obtain physical copies (e.g., on tape media) on a periodic basis.

Data Localization

The fact that the data has been retained doesn't necessarily mean that it is easy to find. A search through all the unstructured data of an enterprise looking for references to a particular customer or project can be very time-consuming.

A comprehensive classification and indexing system can help as well as providing benefits for enterprise search. However, such a system cannot be maintained by a cloud service provider unless the data is not encrypted or else the provider has access to the keys. These are some of the tradeoffs that need to be explored as well as investigating how well the data search and analysis capabilities (of the enterprise or the provider) can cope with data that is often shifted between repositories and storage providers.

Incident Response

One last area of potential legal concern is around incident response. Where customer data is involved, security breach disclosure may be covered by law. Again, there is some ambiguity as to which regional notification laws apply, but it is generally a good recommendation to err on the side of disclosing too much than to be accused of a cover-up.

CONTROL

Technically, intrusion detection systems and application-level firewalls can monitor a number of different attacks such as:

- Malware infection
- Data breach
- Man-in-the-middle discovery
- Session hijacking
- User impersonation

A Security Operations Center (SOC) handles the incident management, which is not simple when there are thousands of application owners. There is a need for a registry of owners and contacts as well as escalation and remediation paths. Even more contentious is the question of when and what must be disclosed. Is it necessary for the provider to tell its customers that an attack took place even if they were able to counteract it? How much detail must they provide on the source, target and nature of attack? These are terms that deserve attention when evaluating the service-level agreement of any cloud provider.

CONTROL

Chapter 27

Risk

In Chapter 8 we looked at some of the risks that cloud computing can help address as well as some new risks that it introduces. We have since seen some security issues in Chapter 18 and concerns around compliance in Chapter 26. This chapter will look more systematically at the risk impact of cloud computing and what enterprises can do to minimize their exposure.

There are several different risk models that you can use to analyze threats. Some of the best known include:

- CCTA Risk Analysis and Management Method (CRAMM)
- Expression des Besoins et Identification des Objectifs de Sécurité (EBIOS)
- Information Security Assessment & Monitoring Method (ISAMM)
- MEthode Harmonisée d'Analyse de RIsque 2007 (MEHARI)
- Metodologia Integrata per la Gestione del Rischio Aziendale (MIGRA)
- ISO/IEC 13335-2: Management of information and communications technology security – Part 2: Information security risk management.
- ISO/IEC 17799:2005
- ISO/IEC 27001 (BS7799-2:2002)

CONTROL

It is not my intention to assess the relative merits of any one of them over the others[1]. They all help to go through parts of a methodology that is roughly composed of:

- Risk assessment
    - Risk identification
    - Risk analysis

---

[1] You can find a high-level comparison from ENISA at:
http://www.enisa.europa.eu/rmra/rm_home.html

- o   Risk evaluation
- Risk treatment, acceptance and communication
- Risk monitor and review

I would stress, however, that it is critical to use a systematic process to analyze all the potential threats as they apply to a given scenario. We already briefly went through a risk assessment in Chapter 8. Next we will look at some of the most apparent risks that are common to many companies and what we can do to mitigate them (Table 27-1). Nonetheless, it is critical to keep in mind that every organization is different. It can be very costly to miss an issue that is unique to a particular business, so it is imperative to conduct a specific analysis.

Threats	Recourse
Data leakage Data loss Non-compliance Loss of service Impairment of service	Encrypt Multi-source Transfer Negotiate service levels Monitor service Audit

Table 27-1: Threats and Recourse

We will then finish off with some words about monitoring and reviewing the risks.

Threats

One of the biggest threats deterring adoption of cloud computing is around non-compliance as discussed more extensively in Chapter 26. Additionally, you need to consider the potential impact of cloud computing on both your data that is stored externally and on the services that are delivered by other providers. Finally, there is the potential that your reputation may be tarnished if either data or services degrade through the cloud model. Let's look at these in more detail.

CONTROL

Data Leakage

The cloud delivery model entails enterprise data physically residing in data centers that are outside the customer firewall. This means that the data is exposed to competitors and hackers. The threat is accentuated through multi-tenancy, and outsourcing.

Multi-tenancy makes the boundaries between the enterprise and the outside more permeable. They lack policy enforcement points and access control points, which the enterprise can enforce and monitor.

Outsourcing by the provider reduces the visibility and control that the enterprise has over hiring policies, role segregation and compartmentalization of job duties, customer assignment and need-to-know information security policies.

Data Loss

The fact that the data is outside the enterprise control also makes it more difficult to impose availability constraints as well as backup and restore procedures. In the event of a disaster, or a human mistake, data can be irretrievably lost.

Multi-tenancy may further exacerbate the threat by exposing the enterprise to denial-of-service and malware attacks that are directed at co-tenants or launched from their platforms.

Loss of Service

Independent of the data risks, there is also a concern about services that enterprises may require for the business processes of their employees or for revenue-generating transactions by customers.

There are several levels of possible service loss:

Service termination: If the cloud provider should declare insolvency, or if there is a fundamental and irresolvable conflict between the customer and provider (for example, unacceptable increase in costs for contract renewal), these may lead to permanent termination of the contract and service.

Service interruption: A less severe problem is when the service is only temporarily unavailable, for example, due to network connectivity loss or technical problems inside the data center.

Partial service interruption: A service may be generally available but only portions may not work as needed. Depending on the criticality of the missing functionality, the severity of this case may vary.

Impairment of Service

CONTROL

Even though a service may technically be available, it could still be suboptimal. If the service-level agreement focuses on availability and neglects performance, service quality, resolution times of non-critical bugs and on-time delivery of new/remediated services, then the enterprise risks employee productivity and customer satisfaction losses.

Similarly, if the provider is physically unable to deliver increases in capacity, or refuses to do so, then the business loses the elasticity benefit of cloud computing. They may even be more restricted than in a fully in-sourced scenario where they do at least have some options to add capacity when it is needed.

Lock-in

The lack of standardization of cloud services can easily lead to a situation where the customer services and data cannot be moved to another service provider without significant effort. There are two drawbacks to this restriction. On the one hand, the provider can hold the customer hostage and force it to accept increasingly disadvantageous terms since it has no viable exit strategy.

On the other hand, if the service does terminate for any of the reasons listed earlier, then the customer has a significant problem in trying to find an alternative. It can take considerable time, cost and effort to find a replacement and migrate all of the data.

Loss of reputation

Data and service problems, if they are visible to the public, can have a cascade effect on the reputation of the company. Customers may be unwilling to do business with a company if they believe their financial, health or other private information is not adequately protected. Similarly they may be disgruntled if their services are not available or are cumbersome to use.

In a multi-tenant scenario, there is also the possibility that co-tenants may unfavorably influence the perception of an organization. If it is publicly known the company shares resources with a high-profile target of attacks, it may reduce the confidence customers have in their services and data; or, if the data centre is known to host services of unsavory businesses or extremist groups some customers may be apprehensive of allowing their information to be co-mingled on the same systems.

Recourse

Fundamentally, there are four options to deal with any risk:

CONTROL

Risk reduction: It may be possible to mitigate the risk by following appropriate processes or obtaining information/research.

Risk transfer: Insurance and contracts both provide mechanisms to transfer the risk to another party. Obviously, there are costs associated with this transfer, but it may be more attractive to the enterprise to pay the expense in order to avoid the risk.

Risk avoidance: If there is no way to reduce the risk and no party willing to accept a risk transfer at an acceptable price, then the organization may want to avoid the risk altogether and forego the opportunity.

Risk acceptance: Particularly where the risk is small or considered unlikely, the firm may be willing to accept the risk without any response at all.

In addition to these options, it is also possible to defer the decision in order to seek better information. However, this is only a temporary remedy. If the deferral is indefinite then it converges with a risk avoidance strategy.

For the issues identified above, we can consider several options to reduce, and potentially transfer, the risks.

- Encryption
- Supplementary backup
- Interoperability
- Multi-sourcing
- Insurance
- Contract negotiation
- Service Monitoring
- Audit

Several of these options will be covered in more detail in Chapter 28 when we will explore the governance of the service provider by negotiating a favorable contract and monitoring its enforcement. In this section we will focus on options that the enterprise can implement.

Encrypt

Encryption of cloud-stored data helps to mitigate the risk that it will be leaked. However, it needs to be clear that this limits the service of the provider. It cannot offer any high-level integrity checking or assist constructively in the case of electronic discovery unless it also has access to the encryption keys.

Generally, an enterprise will prefer the additional responsibility of information management and key management rather than risking the possibility that the key could be compromised. Nonetheless, it is a decision that must be made. Regardless of who performs the encryption, the enterprise must validate that the key management is handled in accordance with its policies and that the ciphers and key-lengths are sufficiently strong.

CONTROL

Supplementary Backup

In addition to any backups taken by the service provider, the enterprise may want a supplementary disaster recovery strategy. The options include

- Co-located system that archives all critical information with the cloud service provider
- Process agreed with service provider to send periodic tape backups of systems to customer
- Replication from within service to another data center or cloud provider

- Customer-activated extraction of data from service through available interfaces

The decision of which approach to use will depend on the availability of each of the options. It is also contingent on the amount of data, the price of bandwidth and the time criticality (both in terms of recovery point objective and recovery time objective) of the data.

Maximize Interoperability

Interoperability is certainly in the interests of the customer. Increased standardization gives the enterprise the flexibility to easily switch from one vendor to another and reduce the risk of lock-in. Unfortunately, the industry is still very immature with regard to standardization particularly related to platforms and services.

This leaves the enterprise with several options, none of which are optimal.

- Encourage open standards. They will probably not reap any short-term benefits but, collectively, enterprises can influence the service providers.
- Prefer interoperability where possible. As vendors begin to incorporate open standards, customers can choose those vendors and options that are as standards-based as possible.
- Investigate service clones that support the same interfaces. For example, Eucalyptus emulates Amazon Web Services and AppScale duplicates an App Engine environment in a private data center.
- Develop contingency plans. Backup strategies might include arrangements with providers of similar functionality and transition plans to migrate code and data.

CONTROL

	Application	Data
IaaS	No	No
PaaS	Yes, based on API and programming language	No
SaaS	Not applicable. User re-training required.	May be accessible via APIs

Table 27-2: Vendor Lock-in by Service Delivery Layer

The amount of lock-in for applications and data varies according to the service-delivery layer (Table 27-2):

IaaS: Uses standard hardware and software. The risk of lock-in is directly related to the lock-in of the virtualization layer. If two providers use the same hypervisor without additional features, it may be possible to move seamlessly between clouds. On the other hand, if they use two different virtualization layers, there will be some effort in porting systems from one provider to the other.

PaaS: The programming languages and APIs may be specific to the platform. It should be possible to extract any data and port it to a neutral format for reloading elsewhere.

SaaS: There is little application lock-in per se. However, any changes in functionality may imply user retraining. The ability to extract data will depend on the SaaS vendor.

Some options to mitigate the risks include:

IaaS: Deploy on an infrastructure with an industry-standard hypervisor and limit cloud-specific items to an abstraction layer. Also, perform your backups in a cloud-independent format and regularly move backup copies out of the cloud.

PaaS: Backup all important data off-cloud and consider similar frameworks and programming languages that might be able to function as suitable replacements. Investigate automatic translation tools or a potential run-time environment that may be able to emulate a given platform.

SaaS: Regularly extract data from the application. This implies a need for programmatic access in a documented format and some resources to implement the extraction. You might also consider other vendors with the same functionality. Unsurprisingly, they often advertize their ability to migrate competitor data.

Multi-source

Another option to reduce the dependency on a single vendor is to design solutions that span multiple providers. It is a sledgehammer approach with the potential to be very complex and costly to manage, but that isn't a reason to rule it out completely. It might be considered where dependency on a single provider is not a viable option.

CONTROL

There are several modes of multi-sourcing applications:

Double-active, replicated: The most efficient, but also most complicated, option is to run both providers in parallel and continuously replicate data between them. This assumes they can both provide the same functionality and there is a means of synchronizing their data.

Double-active, independent: A second option is to segment the application, for example by users or products, so that one provider takes care of one segment and another handles the other. There may be inconsistencies in the functionality but that doesn't need to be a problem. For example, certain user groups may need less functionality than others. In the case that one provider service terminates, there is still a ramp up on the other provider; but an existing agreement and limited experience make it easier than starting back at square one with a search for a new provider.

Active/passive: All services may be provided by a single provider with a second in stand-by position only. This means that the customer already has the agreements in place, and a contingency plan can be invoked to switch to the secondary provider if the case arises.

At a minimum, the enterprise should be constantly vigilant of the viability of its service providers and monitor its service levels while at the same time keeping a careful eye on the competitive landscape to understand both if there are better options and what it would take to move to another one if needed.

Risk Monitoring and Control

In a more general sense, the enterprise should have a process in place to regularly assess the risks and their treatment in the enterprise. Cloud computing is still an immature delivery model, and it entails many very rapidly developing technologies.

It is therefore very likely that new risks and threats will emerge regularly while at the same time existing concerns will eventually be addressed by vendors and service providers. It is necessary for someone to have the responsibility, authority and accountability to:

CONTROL

- Monitor the existing risks to see if they have become more, or perhaps less, acute.
- Establish whether additional safeguards are available.
- Verify whether existing risk-treatment options are working according to plan.
- Test existing safeguards.

Chapter 28

Governance

The principal-agent problem, a common subject of discussion in politics and economics, analyses some of the issues that can arise when a principal hires an agent. The source of the problem is that each party may have different interests. Logically, the principal's interests should prevail, but the agent may behave opportunistically unless it is possible to align the interests or bind the agent.

Governance is the attempt to systematically address this problem. Corporate governance aligns the interests of shareholders and other stakeholders with those of management. IT governance ensures that the information technology strategy of the company is consistent with the objectives of the company and the needs of the business.

In a cloud environment, the customer is the principal and the service provider is the agent. Companies release some of their control over their own operations when they outsource. So, they need a mechanism to minimize the risk and costs of this release.

Conflicting Interests

The conflict of interests between the provider and customer begins with divergent objectives for virtualization. Hosting becomes increasingly cost-effective and lucrative to the provider when resources are shared extensively. On the other hand, enterprises want maximal compartmentalization to reduce their risk exposure.

CONTROL

Cloud providers also attempt to maximize utilization of all their resources since higher use equates directly to more revenue. Customers would be better off, however, if utilization is low since they are less likely to experience bottlenecks and can scale more flexibly.

Customers would like as much information as possible about the internal composition of the services from the hardware and software components to the processes in place to perform the services. Unfortunately, it is to the disadvantage of the provider to release this information since it exposes potential competitive differentiation, increases the attack surface and can be used to put its other customers at risk.

Providers would like to maximize service homogenization in order to achieve the best efficiencies in hardware, software and processes. Enterprises often have specific needs that do not necessarily match the standardized choices.

Finally, it is quite possible that the service provider has a vastly different risk profile than the customer. Neither will welcome a disaster, but while a loss of the data center may only cripple an enterprise temporarily, it may be an event that the provider cannot survive. In such a case, indemnities for a failed disaster recovery become meaningless.

Critical Areas

It is in the best interests of the enterprise to assemble as much information as possible on the cloud provider. The more it knows, the better it can assess risks, try to influence the provider or even weigh a decision on whether to choose a different service delivery model.

The provider's choice of hardware such as switches, firewalls and UPS may reveal vulnerabilities and provides a way to obtain statistics on service availability and error rates. The compartmentalization of systems and networks determine the degree of multi-tenancy and therefore the exposure level to co-tenants. By inspecting key management processes, provisioning procedures and personnel hiring practices, it is possible to derive a picture of how sound the internal controls are and whether they are harmonized. Discovery of other customers can give some insight into the degree of risk of being caught in the cross-fire from an attack against a high-profile target.

The release schedule is a critical part of the equation. If patching is rolled out simultaneously to all tenants, there may be little flexibility in the time frame. There can also be great variation in the processes that are in place for notification, rollbacks and regression testing.

CONTROL

Logging can be critical to enterprises for incident management and reconstructing past events. However, the information is also sensitive since it may be possible for a hacker or competitor to derive patterns of activity that should not be known. It is critical to ask what information is logged, how long it is stored, how it is segmented, and which roles (administrator, user, and audit) are supported. In looking at these areas it is important to consider the likely future requirements as well as only those that are relevant for the current applications.

Cost/benefit Analysis

While there may be many areas where the default offering of the service provider is not optimal from an enterprise perspective, this doesn't mean that each one of them has the same weight. Indeed, some may not be very critical at all.

Ideally, the customer should quantify the value associated with each consideration so that it could be compared to the price which the provider would charge. However, in reality it will be very difficult to estimate the value associated with many of the requirements especially where they serve primarily to reduce risk. It certainly would be feasible to derive and evaluate some formula but the effort expended in the calculation and the degree of accuracy achieved may not speak for it.

Nonetheless, a rudimentary prioritization is necessary so that the effort can be focused where it has the most impact.

Provider Negotiation

The provider may be open to negotiation on some of these points, but since they go against its interests and potentially set a precedent for other customers, the case needs to be compelling. A large customer considering a very lucrative contract is likely to have much more leverage than a small firm looking for a loss-leading opportunity.

As you negotiate, it is useful to have some insight into to motivating drivers of your counterpart. You may be able to reconstruct the value proposition to the provider if you are able to estimate the profit they are likely to extract from your engagement and the costs that it might require to implement your requests.

You should also consider your negotiating position from the point of view of your own options. If the service provider knows that you have no choice but to use their service, then you are in a much weaker position. On the other hand, if there are alternative providers, you can choose the best offer. The provider will be well aware of the possibility that you may opt for a competitor and so may be more willing to compromise.

CONTROL

Other stakeholders may also have a say in the terms of the contract. Local and national governments may impose regulations or informally make demands that need to be considered as part of a multi-party negotiation. Clearly, it is in your interests if they align with your own demands and you can engage them as supporters of your agenda.

Service Contract

Before service delivery can commence, a contract needs to be signed between the provider and the customer. In addition to numerous legal clauses relating to jurisdiction for dispute resolution and contract duration (continuation and dis-continuation terms), it will define provisions for objectives, processes and in-demnities. Although the document is unlikely to be structured along those lines, these are the main conceptual areas to consider.

Performance Indicators

Some of the service-level requirements can be quantified and clearly specified as Key Performance Indicators (KPIs). These might refer to capacity, up-time or data recovery metrics, for example. It is important to identify KPIs that are rele-vant to availability, resilience and performance.

Each indicator will require a metric in order to determine whether or not it is being met. If the provider determines the values, there is an additional trust chal-lenge. Where at all possible, the enterprise should find a means to validate the numbers.

In many cases, it is difficult, if not impossible, to measure end-to-end an SLA in the traditional manner as the tools don't accommodate cloud services. The re-sponse from some providers (such as Microsoft BPOS) is to measure the service at the boundary of their datacenter rather than from a client.

This is a reasonable approach from the provider perspective, as it removes varia-bility in the customer access network as well as Internet latency from the equa-tion. However, it makes the customer task of relating the SLA to business out-comes and expectations more challenging.

Processes/policies

Many of the points of contention between the provider and customer are not nu-meric. There are legal, financial and procedural issues in addition to the tech-nical delivery. The interests may not necessarily be misaligned but the responsi-bilities need to be clear or else it will be difficult to coordinate effectively.

CONTROL

Platform patches and new releases can have an impact on customer applications, so it is useful if the enterprise can be made aware of upcoming updates before they are applied to production systems. This applies for both IaaS and PaaS of-ferings. SaaS is similar in that new functionality or bugs may have an impact on the end-user, but the effects are less likely to be specific to the customer and can therefore be more easily tested by the provider.

Service provider communication to users tends to be ad-hoc and at the conven-ience of provider. This may not be acceptable to an enterprise that needs to have a complete picture of any problems in order to support its own users and prefers defined collaborative processes for remediation.

Application-layer logging frameworks can provide granular narrowing of inci-dents to specific customers based on a registry of application owners by application interface. Application-level firewalls, proxies and application logging can then assist in responding to incidents.

Ideally, the provider's responsibilities include continuous reporting on service incidents, responses and overall site resilience. Data breach notifications are vital if the intrusions were successful. However, even if an attack was thwarted, the enterprise may want to be alerted of dangerous activity beyond certain thresholds.

Security concerns might include cloud provider personnel controls, such as screening processes and logical segregation of duties to reduce the impact of rogue employees. Physical controls might include a wide range of topics, encompassing surveillance, physical access controls, fire protection, back-up generators, battery power, HVAC testing, fences, locks, controlled entry/exit points, emergency procedures, interior movement restrictions, monitoring and immediate response procedures for breaches.

In Chapter 27, we discussed standards adoption as a long-term means to reduce the problems surrounding vendor lock-in. At the time of writing, there are very few standards to which a vendor can subscribe. However, this will probably change in the coming years. As they do appear, it becomes critical that the providers adopt them. This may not be trivial especially without sacrificing backward compatibility with their earlier services. Nonetheless, it is a point that enterprises should investigate, consider in vendor selection and potentially include in their contracts and service levels.

The customer may also be interested in a range of miscellaneous information about the provider. They might request a listing of all 3rd party suppliers with their roles and responsibilities or demand detail on incident response and recovery procedures. Any information about other clients and their workload patterns can be useful in gauging how much competition for resources there might be at peak times. These are very specific questions that may not, in and of themselves, lead to implications for the enterprise. However, they can be used as a starting point for a discussion that can lead in many directions. The more a customer knows about its vendor, the better picture it can paint of where there might be contention or opportunity.

CONTROL

Penalties / Indemnities

The key performance indicators only have meaning if they are backed up with penalties to the service provider for not meeting them. If server performance or network connectivity drops below a defined threshold, then the customer should receive an appropriate indemnity to compensate for the deterioration in service. Similarly, if the provider does not scale resources as requested, the customer will expect some financial settlement for the business growth foregone. If a data breach is attributable to faults by the provider, it is reasonable for the responsible party to be liable for the ensuing damages.

For every performance metric there should be a corresponding formula that defines the compensation that the customer can demand. The amount should be roughly similar to the damages that the enterprise would expect to sustain as a result. This would begin with the direct consequences, such as lost transactions or inability to conduct business. It should also include any indirect losses such as employee dissatisfaction, which might impact productivity, or customer frustration, leading to increased churn. The calculation doesn't need to be exposed to the provider, but it will help in negotiations to have a clear picture of the cost drivers.

Note that financial provisions are only useful if the provider can pay. Many service providers are startups and small companies. If the penalties refer to a disaster recovery and the supplier goes bankrupt during the disaster, the penalties may become irrelevant. If there is any risk at all that a cloud provider may not be financially secure or may be susceptible to catastrophic loss, then this needs to be considered in the risk analysis.

Insurance is another risk transfer technique that may be viable. One option that may be available is for the provider to take out an insurance policy covering its assets. If it reveals the details of this policy to the customer, it may appease some solvency concerns. Another alternative would be for the customer to explore trade credit insurance covering the contract with the provider.

Finally, it should be noted that while your immediate interest in identifying missed indicators may be compensation, in the long term it is much more constructive to work with the provider to resolve whatever obstacles are preventing an acceptable service delivery. The provider may be able to make some technical improvements. There may also be steps that the enterprise can take to alleviate the problem, or they may have information that could help isolate the root causes.

Service Monitoring

CONTROL

Once defined and agreed, you need to continuously monitor the key performance indicators and negotiated policies and procedures to ensure that the provider complies with the service level agreement.

This may entail regular supplier and contract performance reports as well as occasional surveys to end-users and business representatives. These may expose service levels that are not met, but they may also reveal that the agreements have been ill-defined (don't match requirements). In either case, it may be necessary to return to the supplier negotiating table.

The fact that the service is outsourced complicates the process of gathering comprehensive logging information to demonstrate failure to meet service-level agreements. The provider may be able to provide their statistics, but these do not necessarily give the full end-to-end picture and may reflect measuring distortions that are biased toward the providers' interests.

It is therefore important to verify all the statistics from the end-user and enterprise position on a regular basis. It may not be feasible to log every transaction but even spot checks will reveal where the provider's numbers appear suspect or where there may be other causes for concern. For instance, there might also be problems in local network connectivity that need to be addressed.

Statistics are only useful if they measure the right information. End-user surveys can also be a useful tool as they may expose problem areas that were not visible previously and not tied to the right metrics.

Audits

Given the difficulty of an enterprise exhaustively monitoring all provider activity and the practical limitations that a provider cannot offer unfettered access to their operations on a continuous basis, another mechanism to ensure a certain level of reliability is to request audits.

If an enterprise has enough clout with the provider, they may request to perform an audit themselves but it is much more likely that they will insist on regular 3rd party risk assessments and on-site inspections. It is legitimate for any customer to request clear documentation on risk assessments and audit as well as verifying the frequency of assessments.

There are several audit standards that the providers may adopt of their own accord.

SAS 70 Type II certifications are the most common. They are very flexible and, in particular, allow exclusion of critical systems from scrutiny. They are much better than no certification at all, but it is important to carefully examine their scope.

ISO/IEC 27001:2005 can be costly but is more indicative of a systematic analysis. NIST Special Publication 853, FIPS 199/200, WebTrust, SysTrust and SCP also provide standards by which you can measure the depth and efficacy of an audit.

CONTROL

Bear in mind that these are all point-in-time certifications in not only a very dynamic but also opaque and geographically dispersed environment.

CloudAudit[1] is a new initiative promoted through a volunteer cross-industry effort that seeks to provide a common interface for cloud providers (and author-

---

[1] http://www.cloudaudit.org

ized consumers) to automate the Audit, Assertion, Assessment, and Assurance (A6) of cloud environments via an open, extensible and secure set of interfaces.

At the time of writing, it is too early to project whether a specification will converge, and how widely it might be adopted. Nonetheless, the enthusiasm of the working group demonstrates how important reliable auditing is for the successful adoption of cloud computing.

CONTROL

Adapt

ADAPT

Chapter 29

Systematic Refinement

Cloud computing introduces a new model of IT procurement and planning. Once a service has been commissioned, there should be no more need for proactive planning. There may be no new equipment to buy and no capital expenditures to include in the budget. The provider will automatically update the service with the incremental functionality that is in highest demand.

There is the danger that the new approach will lead to purely reactive decision making. The customer only needs to respond to exceptions. When service levels are unsatisfactory, or the service provider suffers an outage, there will be a need to take an active position. Until then, it is possible to refrain from interference in the service.

A reactive approach may sound appealing since it minimizes involvement and therefore reduces your overall management cost. There are, however, two disadvantages to consider:

- The lack of vision and planning may blindside you where a vigilant approach would give you much more advance notice of any problems looming on the horizon.
- It neglects the opportunity cost. Even if the service is running satisfactorily, there may be better options on the market, which you don't leverage. This omission can put you at a disadvantage compared to competitors who are more proactive.

ADAPT

There are three aspects of a proactive approach that are worth considering separately. There should be a continuous analysis of the corporate strategy execution to determine whether it is successful in accomplishing its objectives.

But, in addition, you need to also look at two aspects of the external environment for an assessment of a cloud strategy. On the one hand, the business environment may be changing, which can have a significant impact on your strategy.

It is also very likely that the underlying technologies will be in flux and should be reassessed as you reconsider strategic and technical choices.

Improvement Process

A major part of a systematic improvement process is to perform a continuous gap analysis that tracks execution progress against the objectives.

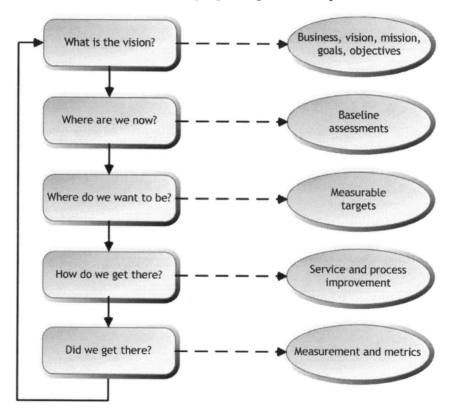

Figure 29-1: Gap Analysis

As shown in Figure 29-1, the idea is to begin by analyzing the vision to determine mission and objectives. The next step is to assess the current status and then to compare it to the desired and expected position.

You then take the gap between these two points and consider how to bridge it. After implementing corrective actions, you need to determine if they were successful and then repeat the whole process for the next cycle of refinement.

A gap analysis is largely a technology-agnostic process. However, there are ramifications from cloud computing that may make the task both easier and harder. The key challenge in identifying a gap is to quantify both the objectives and actual performance. The estimation of direct costs may be made simpler through increased financial visibility and simplified cost allocation. On the other hand, intangible benefits or drawbacks in the areas of productivity, security and risk may be very difficult to measure.

Business Landscape

You need to monitor the external environment for threats and opportunities. There are two levels to consider. At a high level, you should continuously reassess your business strategy to ensure that you are optimizing your competitive advantage, investing in the right products and targeting the right segments. If you change your corporate strategy, it is likely to affect the level of investment that you allocate to IT and the focus that you expect from it. These are implications that are not specifically related to cloud computing, although they may trickle down from the IT budget and objectives.

It is also possible to undertake a more specific analysis. You might assess changes in demand and factor inputs, as well as the competitive landscape, with an eye on the technical alignment of each. For example, if you foresee a reduction in demand of a core product, you can investigate the technical connections that its production and distribution imply.

This data, aggregated over a series of trends, can collectively serve to analyze the entire business portfolio and to model the technical implications of alternative strategies. Given the interdependence of services that may be involved in creating and selling multiple product lines, it would be misleading to assess each in isolation. A portfolio approach has the advantage of providing a composite view.

Technology Evolution

The next chapter will provide a glimpse of some technical changes that may appear over the years and what their effect could be on cloud computing. Regardless of whether those particular changes take place, there is bound to be an evolution of many of the technologies involved in the Internet-based services you use.

The recurring questions that need to be addressed for each development are how it impacts the existing processes and whether it is possible to leverage the changes to your advantage.

ADAPT

For example, new SaaS offerings (such as unified communications) might become available or increase in attractiveness. You may be able to convert some of your IaaS services to PaaS, or convert PaaS services to SaaS and increase your efficiency and cost-effectiveness.

There may be improvements and changes in underlying technologies that you can harness. Increased standardization may enhance your options and reduce the risks associated with services that were previously only marginally attractive. You may also find new or enhanced services on the market that surpass your current selection in risk, cost or quality.

A superior alternative doesn't automatically mean that you should switch. The migration costs and risks may far outweigh the comparative advantage at any point in time. However, it does present a new option that should be highlighted for more careful assessment.

The technologies used by customers, suppliers and partners also require close monitoring. If the processes are to be tightly integrated, changes in a partner product may have an effect on the interfaces and connectivity that is required. Ideally the new product will continue to support the same standards as are already in use, but subtle compatibility problems might crop up.

Even more importantly, the fact that the components interoperate doesn't mean that they are optimized. Every new development carries with it the potential for simplification and fine-tuning. It is worthwhile to investigate if it is possible to use the newest externally induced changes for an additional advantage.

Continual Service Improvement

The ITIL Continual Service Improvement (Figure 29-2) illustrates the nature and importance of feedback from all levels to all other levels. Service Design will uncover some challenges and opportunities to improve the Service Strategy. When the design is actually put into place, it is likely the Service Transition will reveal further areas for fine-tuning, both at the strategic and design level.

Moreover, during on-going operations it is vital to have a process in place to feed back as much as possible into the strategy, design and transition mechanisms, so that future iterations can leverage the experience.

ADAPT

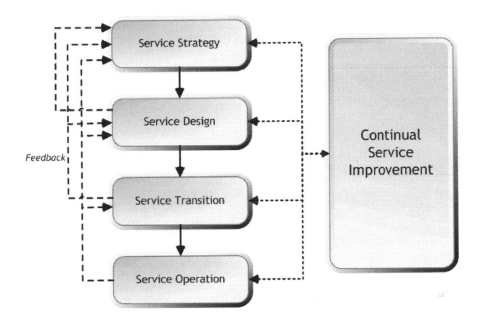

Figure 29-2: Continual Service Improvement

In other words, the output of this chapter should feed into every element discussed in the previous chapters.

Evolve

Chapter 30

Future Trends

Cloud computing is anything but a mature technology. It is growing rapidly and changing shape in the process. While it's mere adoption may have considerable impact on the world in many dimensions of business and technology, these changes are difficult to predict for many reasons. One of them is that we cannot foresee how cloud computing itself will evolve.

Nonetheless there are trends that have already begun, or appear to be imminent, which may be closely related to the future evolution of cloud computing. As such, it is worth taking a closer look at them and monitoring them, and their impact, over the next few years.

In this chapter, we will look at some environmental trends from an economic and cultural perspective. We will then examine some technologies that have the potential to deeply affect cloud computing.

Economic

As described at the beginning of the book, cloud computing may have a dramatic impact on the economy. However, the opposite may also apply. We should monitor the potential for political and economic developments to influence cloud computing.

One area to consider is the increasing globalization of markets. The elimination and reduction of regional boundaries in the physical goods and labor markets mean that it is much easier and more commonly accepted to draw products and services from remote sources.

At the same time, the evolution of the global economy from a manufacturing to services base means that a higher percentage of product will be service-based in the future.

EVOLVE

Both of these trends may facilitate greater adoption of Internet-based services and increase pressure on the resolution of geographical obstacles such as disparate legal compliance or latency-sensitive applications.

A shrinking workforce combined with the ambition of many organizations for increased agility mean that permanent employment numbers are likely to decrease over the coming years. As a result, companies must examine opportunities to automate any repetitive work and integrate a wider variety of productive pools, such as web services and crowdsourcing.

There will be an increased need for unique jobs that combine resources in order to fulfill ad hoc requests and rapidly adapt business processes as requirements change. This requires a broad understanding of both business and technology and the ability to synthesize the two – a skill that is not likely to be common and will be in high demand.

The democratization of the economy is perhaps most visible in the area of printing, with a variety of services that allow easy publication of books, magazines and photo albums. However, the trend is also apparent in software publication with marketplaces that have spawned ecosystems based on a number of platforms from the Apple iPhone to Google.

The fundamental impact of removing entry barriers to these segments is twofold. It enables the so-called "long tail", or distribution of low-volume items, by removing the fixed costs that are associated with each item. By increasing the number of product lines, it enhances the diversity of the market.

The absence of economy-of-scale advantages also puts pressure on larger organizations with higher operational overhead to find creative alternatives for fostering a competitive advantage over their smaller competitors. The result of this indirect influence is unpredictable, but you would expect that it will increase the variety of sources of differentiation.

Cultural

From a cultural perspective, one of the most important trends is that of consumerization. As computing has become a part of life for many people, especially from the younger generations, it has become more difficult (and less desirable) to segregate personal and work activities and tools.

Forcing someone to work with unfamiliar tools can be perceived as akin to enforcing an unpopular dress-code. Many employees will accept it, but some of the brightest and best may choose to work for a competitor instead. As companies strive to retain their top talent, they will need to consider preferred applications and working environments of their employees.

Another personal consideration is the increasing challenge of cognitive overload. As recently as ten years ago, the lack of sufficient information was a common obstacle to achieving business and personal objectives. People didn't know how to perform a given operation and were uncertain how to obtain the required instructions and inputs. Simple functions, such as operating an electronic appliance, might have become impossible if a manual was lost or misplaced.

Of course, it is still possible today to have questions for which it is difficult to find the answer. However, the more common problem is that, while the answer is available and accessible, there is too much information that needs to be filtered in order to obtain an authoritative, or at least reliable, piece of data.

There is a growing need for filtering, sorting, categorization and analytics to help users manage the vast repositories of both structured and unstructured information and to easily find and extract the information that is of interest.

Virtual and Physical Convergence

Cloud computing is primarily a virtual phenomenon. Regardless of the actual operating system that may, or may not, be running on a physical machine, the fact that it is an electronic process means that it is an inherent abstraction of reality and the user's experience.

However, users are becoming more interested in their virtual experiences as these blend with their physical reality. Services, such as Second Life, exemplify the fascination that humans can have with a virtual experience. As virtual reality hardware, from gloves and chairs to goggles and helmets, becomes more advanced, these experiences will only become more compelling.

At the same time, the virtual experience is not limited to entertainment. Even online forums and newsgroups provide a means to establish a virtual persona that may, or may not, reflect the personality and identity of the user. A very rich user experience can also be useful for educational purposes and collaboration in the enterprise.

Tomorrow's virtual world will need to consider a multiplicity of personas, advanced graphic visualization and a plethora of human interface mechanisms. It will also need to be extremely aware of a user's context (location, time, weather, travel direction, businesses or friends nearby) as well as past actions and experiences in order to guide the user and optimize recommendations.

The individual sources of information (maps, traffic, weather-forecasts) are already becoming available as services. The challenge going forward will be to aggregate them and integrate any ancillary information sources that are required to optimize the user experience.

Next-generation Networking

Since cloud computing is fundamentally reliant on networking, any changes or developments in connectivity will have a direct impact on the services and service quality.

EVOLVE

Improved Network Quality

A key aspect of networking to monitor is the quality of the last-mile connection. The Internet connection that users can typically afford from their home, and expect from their hotels and office locations, will dictate the richness of the user experience.

Broadband services in the industrialized countries are approaching the capacity of copper wires, but there is always the potential for additional innovation to increase technical barriers. At the same time, wireless and optical transmission mechanisms may provide a means for dramatic increases that not only enable a richer user experience with high-definition video and high-quality audio, but also facilitate distributed computation on a scale far beyond what is possible today.

Persistent Connectivity

As networks, and network access points, proliferate and users are able to take advantage of them for ubiquitous connectivity, the expectations surrounding a user experience become more demanding.

The challenge is compounded by the fact that users will not necessarily only own and operate a single device. Yet they will expect a consistent experience and unified information view regardless of the location and terminal that they use.

The fact that the network characteristics and machine interfaces may vary considerably makes this objective difficult to achieve. It is further complicated by different client platforms and the lack of awareness each device and application may have of the complete user environment.

There is an increased need for synchronization while respecting authoritative sources of user information. The application also needs to assimilate as much context (e.g. location, user history) as possible in order to minimize the required input of the user while still tailoring the output to the user's expected requirements.

Unified Communications

As the Internet gradually replaces most other forms of networking, service providers are seeking to leverage its versatility to integrate both real-time communication services (e.g. presence, voice and video) and unified messaging services (e.g. voicemail, e-mail and SMS).

EVOLVE

There are also number of collaboration tools, such as Microsoft LiveMeeting, Citrix GoToMeeting and Cisco WebEx, which also facilitate presentation and whiteboard sharing.

While these technologies may ultimately rely on some peer-to-peer protocol for efficient transfer of high-volume data, there will always be a need for central services that provide directory information and are able to broker or proxy connections where direct network connectivity is not possible.

IPv6

3Tera has already demonstrated database replication between applications running in two different datacenters using an IPv6 VPN tunnel created with 3Tera's new VPN catalog appliance (Romanski, 2009). Google offers search services over IPv6 but doesn't support other products over the protocol. So, while there is some activity among the cloud service providers, there is still some way to go before IPv6 becomes ubiquitous, or indeed the protocol of choice.

There has been a substantial amount of discussion about IPv6 in the IT industry over the past ten to fifteen years with many predicting its imminent arrival earlier than was realistic. Unfortunately, this may have encouraged the illusion that it will never be necessary or viable.

It is true that network address translation dramatically increased the potential size of an IPv4 Internet. However, even so, the address space is nearing exhaustion – in some countries more than in others. Beyond merely lifting size limitations, IPv6 also offers numerous benefits in terms of automated management, extensibility, efficiency and mobility.

Nonetheless, the most compelling reason that many organizations will adopt IPv6 is not because of its benefits or any specific limitation that they will encounter with IPv4. Rather, the need to address IPv6 has become urgent in recent years simply because it is already active on most networks. Since it is enabled by default on most common operating platforms it is irresponsible for IT security to ignore it and any threats that may be channeled through it.

Regardless of the reason why an enterprise chooses to evaluate IPv6, it is worth considering that it also includes several benefits that can be relevant to cloud computing. For example, dynamic renumbering and stateless auto-configuration may simplify an automatic deployment. Mobile IPv6 facilitates transfer and load balancing of virtual machines. Furthermore, the increased address space enables direct end-to-end connectivity between end-points in different clouds without any special requirements from the service providers.

Peer-to-peer Networking

Peer-to-peer networking isn't new. The first networks involved peer exchanges. The terms became popular with file and media sharing networks such as KaZaA and later BitTorrent. Skype has become a household term even among the technically illiterate. It is based on peer-to-peer protocols for voice and video over IP.

EVOLVE

Chapter 30: Future Trends

Peer networks are similar to cloud computing in that their attractiveness is highly correlated to the last-mile bandwidth. They are also network-intensive and therefore only very effective on broadband connections.

Unlike cloud computing, peer networks may benefit from the growing power of home PCs. While they are currently an effective complement to data-center-based services, it is quite possible that they will eventually emerge as a competitor to centralized services.

There has already been some interest in volunteer computing (also called peer-to-peer computing, global computing and public computing). For instance, SETI@home, Folding@home, Einstein@home or AQUA@home leverage the collective power of consumer infrastructure. However, the business model is still evolving that would enable any service level beyond best effort. If a proper incentive system is devised, the potential is significant.

Peer networks can accomplish the same purpose as traditional content delivery networks. In small volume they are not sufficiently reliable. But their potential scale with the correct business model could enable massive redundancy and extremely wide coverage – several orders of magnitude beyond what any commercial network can offer today.

There is no reason that the services of a peer network need to be constrained to content delivery. They could also offer models of highly redundant, distributed storage or even distributed computation. If the power of the PC grows beyond the immediate needs of the user, the opportunity becomes more compelling to harness this capacity and offer it to other potential consumers.

Appendix

Cloud Vendors

I have included some brief descriptions of vendors and service providers that are active in cloud computing today. However, I would like to cloak these in a general disclaimer that they are intended only as an introduction and absolutely require further investigation on your part before you adopt or dismiss them.

I have leveraged the official documentation and web materials where they are accessible and have tried to align the terminology and perspective as much as possible. Nonetheless, I cannot guarantee that I have correctly captured the salient technical details.

The appendix is not an exhaustive survey of the products that are on the market. It may exclude important players for no obvious reason. By the same token, given the volatile nature of the cloud landscape, I cannot even imply that companies mentioned in this book will still be in business when you read about them or that they will offer the same functionality.

Finally, this is not an endorsement of any particular offering nor do I attempt to highlight any weaknesses in the solutions. I may omit important information or not characterize and classify the services in the same terms as the vendors.

Nonetheless, I believe that you will get a better picture of what is happening in cloud computing with some actual examples and rough descriptions of the services currently on offer in the market place – if for no other reason than to give you a starting point for your own analysis.

If you do spot any errors or omissions, please let me know so that I can update the text for future buyers and readers of this book.

Amazon

aws.amazon.com

The de facto standard for infrastructure services is Amazon. They are not unique in their offerings yet virtually all IaaS services are either complements to Amazon Web Services (AWS) or else considered competitors to them.

While AWS offers a large number of cloud services, the focus of most users is on the Elastic Compute Cloud (EC2) and its supplementary storage services. EC2 offers the user a choice of virtual machine templates that can be instantiated in a shared and virtualized environment.

Each virtual machine is called an Amazon Machine Image (AMI). The customer can use pre-packaged AMIs from Amazon and 3rd parties or they can build their own. They vary in resources (RAM, Compute units, local disk size), operating systems (several Windows versions and many Linux distributions) and the application frameworks that are installed on them (e.g. JBoss, MySQL, Oracle.).

The Amazon AMIs do not have any persistent storage, but they can be used for logs, results and interim data while the instance is active. Since the locally mounted disks of AMIs are lost between instantiations, Amazon also offers two persistent storage capabilities: The Simple Storage Service (S3) and Elastic Block Storage (EBS).

S3 is accessible through both REST and SOAP APIs. It offers distributed, redundant buckets that are replicated with Amazon's CloudFront content delivery network across Europe, Asia and the United States. S3 can accommodate data sizes from a single byte to 5GB and provides permissions for controlling access based on Amazon Web Services authentication.

The Elastic Block Storage is intended as a high-performance virtual hard disk. It can be formatted as a file system and then mounted on any EC2 instance. The size can range from 1GB to 1TB. Amazon also provides a mechanism to store an EBS snapshot in S3 for long-term durability.

The Amazon Simple DB (SDB) is available for more structured data. It does not use a schema but instead defines "domains" with items that consist of up to 256 attributes and values. The values can contain anywhere from one byte to one kilobyte. It also supports simple operators such as: =, !=, <, >, <=, >=, STARTS-WITH, AND, OR, NOT, INTERSECTION, UNION. So most common queries are possible as long as they are confined to a single domain.

Amazon offers a service called the Simple Queue Service (SQS), which provides an unlimited number of queues and messages, with message sizes up to 8 KB. The customer can create queues and send messages. Any authorized applications can then receive and/or delete the messages. Since the messages remain in the system for up to four days, they provide a good mechanism for asynchronous communications between applications.

Amazon Flexible Payments Service (FPS) is a service for developers that leverages Amazon's sophisticated retail billing system. The customers can use the same identities, shipping details and payment information as they would for ordering directly with Amazon.

Amazon targets corporate customers with more sophisticated offerings. The Virtual Private Cloud provides a means for enterprises to extend their private data center offerings into Amazon's cloud in a secure and reliable fashion.

Finally, it is worth noting that Amazon's services are not necessarily self-sufficient. AWS has spawned a whole ecosystem, which fills in any gaps that Amazon may have left open. Specifically, there are several services that help to managed established infrastructure providers. RightScale and enStratus, for example, offer front ends to managing Amazon EC2 as well as other IaaS offerings.

Appian

www.appian.com

Appian offers management software to design and deploy business processes. The tool is available as a web portal for both business process designers and users. The design is facilitated with a graphic user interface that maps processes to web forms. End-users are then able to access the functionality through a dashboard of forms, while executives and managers can access the same web site for bottleneck analysis, real-time visibility and aggregated high-level analysis (business intelligence).

Appian offers both an on-premise BPM Suite for enterprises and on-demand business process management software to deploy processes. In the case of the latter, Appian Anywhere is a BPM Platform-as-a-Service that delivers the functionality of Appian via a subscription model. Both delivery models provide the same functionality with the same user interface.

The Appian BPM Suite includes several components and features needed to deliver BPM applications:

- Web-based modeling using BPMN and SOA methodologies for deployment and automation of business processes.
- Centrally-managed business rules to automate, enforce and audit policies and practices.
- Portal, dashboard, and forms creation tools that enable users to build collaborative and personalized interfaces.
- Integrated document and content management platform that provides functionality to store, secure, version, search, and manage enterprise content.
- BAM Reporting to track real-time process performance, create reporting dashboards, identify process bottlenecks, and optimize process efficiency flow.
- Identity Management that integrates into the corporate directory and routes tasks and content using skills, roles, or dynamic group structures.
- A repository of re-usable services that accelerate BPM deployment by connecting and integrating data sources.
- Collaboration with threaded discussion boards, targeted content and content sharing.

Appistry

www.appistry.com

The Appistry CloudIQ platform consists of two separate components: The CloudIQ Manager facilitates application management across multiple cloud environments. The CloudIQ Engine is a distributed application container for extreme-scale applications.

The CloudIQ Manager accomplishes two objectives. It unifies application management across a heterogeneous environment, and it also accelerates application deployment.

In addition to a RESTful management API and command line interface, the Appistry console provides a graphical user interface to manage applications across public and private clouds in both a physical and virtual infrastructure. It facilitates the collective administration of similar instances with minimal user interaction.

It includes automated deployment and management that allows existing applications to be packaged without requiring re-architecture. This approach also facilitates portability across multiple private and public cloud environments.

Appistry CloudIQ Engine is a runtime container for Java, Spring, .NET and C/C++ code that provides out-of-the-box scalability and reliability. It facilitates application fault-tolerance without embedded code logic and offers a distributed fault-tolerant memory cache that allows applications to store transient state information in memory.

Its linear scale-out and up helps applications take advantage of all cores available by adding parallelism to non thread-safe applications thereby allowing single threaded code to take advantage of multi-core processors.

It also includes workload management policies that route application requests to the optimal nodes based on user-defined logic and thereby facilitate scale and resource optimization.

Apple

www.apple.com/mobileme
www.iwork.com

Similar to other large technology companies, Apple has several mostly independent initiatives that relate to cloud computing. MobileMe provides users with online storage and a means to synchronize multiple devices. iWork is a service that facilitates online collaboration. The company is clearly a leader in the area of client devices and there are indications that Apple may have plans for additional back-end services.

iCloud provides a means to synchronize favorites, calendars, contacts and mail. The service uses a push technology and can support multiple devices and device types from the PC to the Mac or iPhone. It also offers a photo-sharing web gallery with client applications for the iPhone and iPod touch. Similarly the iDisk service facilitates online storage and file sharing of any other file types. Finally, the "Find My iPhone" service provides device protection with functions to display its map location, remotely set a passcode lock, or wipe the contents or personal information.

iWork allows users to create and edit documents, spreadsheets and presentations online, and store them on central servers that can then be accessed from any computer. The on-line service delivers Apple's iWork suite of computer-based programs through a web interface. It supports collaboration and revision control through time-stamped and color-coded notes that can reference entire documents, spreadsheets or presentations as well as specific text, cells or slides. The feedback is displayed in a threaded discussion and can also be directed encapsulated in email notifications.

There is some evidence that Apple's long-term business plan may reveal additional cloud-offerings. The iPad is positioned to round out the set of client devices from notebooks to iPhones and iPods. The acquisition of Lala.com, a music streaming service may portend intentions to increase its content delivery. At the same time, Apple's new data center in Maiden, North Carolina, demonstrates the huge commitment Apple making to cloud computing. According to Data Center Knowledge, the $1 billion data center is 500,000 square feet in size.

AppNexus

www.appnexus.com

AppNexus is an infrastructure service provider that offers dedicated virtualized servers based on Dell computers running a Xen hypervisor with Ipsilon storage.

Their primary differentiation lies in the degree of visibility they provide on the location of the server with transparency of the data center as well as rack location and position). The location information can be of critical importance in ensuring compliance to local information storage and dissemination laws. But it can also be beneficial to enterprises which have their own data storage policies that they would like to enforce. And it can assist in optimizing latency for critical transactions.

Another feature that AppNexus provides is a private VLAN and configurable firewalls for each customer. Not only do these give the advantage of static IP addresses and reduced exposure to broadcast traffic, but it is also possible to segregate traffic from that of other tenants through the use of Access Control Lists (ACLs).

AppNexus takes great effort in optimizing performance through extensive load balancing both locally and globally. Within the datacenter it uses F5 BIG-IP 6400 Local Traffic Managers (LTMs) for hardware load balancing.

Each AppNexus datacenter also has its own Global Server Load-Balancing (GSLB) server, and each server broadcasts an identical IP address to the Internet. Any request for this IP address is automatically routed to the closer server via BGP. That server then chooses where to direct the user depending on the designated load-balancing ratio. Once a site has been chosen, the server responds to the user's request with the IP address of the local load-balancing pool at that site. If one GSLB server fails, all traffic is directed to the other GSLB server.

Apprenda

www.apprenda.com

Apprenda offers a .NET based PaaS stack that enterprises can deploy onto their own Windows infrastructure. It is not dependent on virtualization or IaaS although it can run in those environments, too.

The basic value proposition of Apprenda is to make developers more productive by removing the need to deal with application management tasks and giving them a new but backwards compatible runtime, APIs and frameworks to build composite cloud applications

The customers thereby receive a platform for modernizing most of their application portfolio to cloud with little effort and can achieve higher efficiency by improving utilization of infrastructure and server licenses. They can also use it to automate application and IT management tasks or to offer self-service application management and deployment to different development teams in the organization.

AT&T

www.att.com/cloud

AT&T's Enterprise Division offers three cloud-related services as part of its Synaptic brand: Synaptic Hosting, Synaptic Storage-as-a-Service and Synaptic Compute As a Service.

AT&T differentiates itself through the global reach of its existing MPLS network as well as networking quality of service (QoS) features that prioritize delivery of data to ensure predictable performance. They also benefit from a reputation for security that some newer cloud computing providers may not have based on AT&T's experience with global network security and embedded defenses against distributed denial of service attacks (DDoS).

Synaptic Hosting provides pay-as-you-go access to virtual servers and storage integrated with security and networking functions. A single service level agreement governs availability and response time of the entire service.

The system uses a web portal to deliver reports and detailed information on the service. It also includes monitoring and management of the network, servers, operating system, web and database layer as well as, optionally, application monitoring and reporting.

Synaptic Storage as a Service provides a policy-based process that places copies of data in one or two geographic locations and automatically replicates them on a predetermined schedule. They offer web services-based access and a unified global namespacc for centralized administration of stored data assets.

Synaptic Compute as a Service offers processing power that can be used for "cloudbursting" of in-house apps or as a testing and development platform. The consumption-priced service can run as a public cloud offering, or in a private cloud on AT&T's infrastructure, connected to a customer data center through AT&T's network. Similar to other infrastructure services, customers use a web portal and API to provision or de-provision new guests and scale your computing, networking and storage resources. The portal also includes the option to view utilization graphs and review metering and billing information. There are several choices of server size and an image library with preconfigured servers. Additionally, AT&T offers one VLAN per customer and firewall services with customer-specific policies.

Binary Tree

www.binarytree.com

Binary Tree is a well-known provider of cross-platform messaging migration and coexistence software, which it has extended to facilitate cloud-based messaging solutions such as Microsoft Office 365, LotusLive and Google Apps.

The migration of productivity software typically involves three phases, which are supported by Binary Tree products. The analysis phase involves taking an inventory of the legacy infrastructure to enable detailed and reliable planning for the subsequent activities. Coexistence ensures interoperability during the migration so that workflow for email, calendar and directory are preserved. The migration of email, tasks, calendar and contacts extracts the legacy data and uploads it into the cloud-based offering.

The tools support the discovery phase with reports that visually depict both usage and complexity of applications. It also identifies obsolete and unused applications as well as redundant replicas and mailboxes that might be candidates for archival. Other preparatory steps that facilitate the deployment include user communication and training.

ZApp, or Zero Touch Application Remediation, is an optional feature of the Coexistence software designed to perform on-the-fly interception and remediation of messages sent from Domino workflow applications to a cloud-based email system.

Binary Tree supports migrations from Lotus Domino to Microsoft Office 365, LotusLive and Google Apps as well as supporting migrations from Microsoft Exchange to LotusLive. These migrations typically only involve messaging, calendaring and contacts but, in the case of a migration from Lotus Domino to a Microsoft BPOS platform, it is also possible to convert standard Notes applications to SharePoint sites.

One particularly interesting offering is Migration-as-a-Service. Companies who don't like the idea of investing in additional infrastructure in order to move to cloud-based services can subscribe to a hosted "Weekend Express" service, which takes care of the entire process.

Box

box.com

Box.net offers an on-demand content management service. It is comparable, in some ways, to Microsoft SharePoint but available purely as a web-based solution.

The service allows users to upload files and folders. It can be used as a synchronization tool - users can put their whole file system on the Box.Net portal and access it from other devices and location.

It can also support collaboration. Multiple users can work on the same documents via the web-based interface. They can also add comments or engage in discussion. The workflow includes the notion of tasks, approvals, reviews and updates.

From a financial perspective, it is interesting to consider that there is no need for end-users to have a license for all the products and file formats which they use. Since they interact through the browser there is no need to download the files. Even the print function acts on a rendered image of the object. This increases the number of file types (Microsoft Office, Adobe Photoshop, Illustrator, etc) that a user can consume without the burden of installation or the license costs.

A premium version of Box.net (Box Business) also provides enhanced functionality including versioning, portal customization, full-text search and activity reporting and user management.

Bungee Labs

www.bungeeconnect.com

Bungee Connect is a platform that facilitates the development of interactive applications, which need to integrate multiple web-based data sources. It is based on a proprietary programming language, which is accompanied by an integrated development environment.

The architectural foundation underpinning the approach is the Model-View-Adapter (MVA) development pattern. It is loosely based on the well-known Model-View-Controller (MVC) pattern which Bungee considers inadequate for handling complex user interactions that have become popular since the advent of Ajax.

While MVC is well suited to full-page-refresh web applications, richer interactions can combine to form an unmanageable set of interrelationships. The MVC pattern is better able to accommodate a scalable array of updates, data transformations and flow-of-control scenarios.

Bungee supplies a proprietary programming language, Bungee Sky, which can be used to connect to multiple different data sources including SOAP and REST services and MySQL and PostgreSQL databases. The language uses a C-style syntax and is conceptually similar to .NET, Java and C++ to ease the developer ramp-up effort.

Developers can use an Eclipse-based IDE that includes a visual form designer with a wide range of Ajax controls and a flexible geometry model. Development is accelerated with automated connectivity for web services and databases, an integrated toolkit for end-user interactivity and integrated source control for developer collaboration. The tool facilitates user-interface integration and binding by automatically binding to controls as represented on forms.

Bungee-powered applications use Ajax to deliver desktop-like interactivity without a plug-in or install and across the most popular browsers (Internet Explorer, Firefox, Safari). Bungee Connect automatically manages the application state between the client and server, view updates as data changes and web service marshalling.

Cisco

www.cisco.com/go/cloud

Cisco is a global supplier of consumer electronics, networking and communications technology and services. The company offers cloud services, such as WebEx. But it also supports cloud computing as an infrastructure vendor selling to public cloud service providers and enterprises setting up their own private-cloud data centers.

The Cisco WebEx Collaboration Cloud is an infrastructure built for real-time web communications that are delivered as Software-as-a-Service. It is architected for large-scale global web communications that may include many types of complex media throughout each session. Some of its key features include:

- Traffic routing is optimized based on location, bandwidth, and availability
- Meeting traffic on the WebEx Collaboration Cloud is globally load-balanced
- The point of presence for each participant is chosen to minimize latency
- All data, audio, and video is backed up
- A multi-layered security model that protects meeting data with data-center facility safeguards, end-to-end encryption, meeting permissions and enterprise policy controls

Cisco WebEx meeting applications that run on the Cisco WebEx Collaboration Cloud include:

- Meeting Center: present information, share applications with customers, partners, and employees
- Training Center: Create, manage, and deliver online training
- Event Center: Share documents, presentations, and applications in real time for online events for such as targeted marketing sessions or all-hands company meetings
- Support Center: Provide remote, real-time IT support to diagnose problems, transfer files, and install patches for employee desktops or unattended servers, computers, desktops, networks, and POS devices

Cisco data-center products provide an infrastructure on which to build both private and public cloud services. The baseline architecture for the Cisco Unified Service Delivery solution consists of network, storage, and compute resources deployed in a uniform fashion to support a range of applications and services across the provider's portfolio. It combines several key technologies from Cisco including:

- The Cisco Nexus Family of unified fabric switches for a single fabric of all traffic within the data center
- The Cisco CRS-1 Family of carrier-class routers for peering and interconnect functions
- The Cisco Unified Computing System to provide a compute-enabled, VM-ready network that is integrated with server virtualization solutions from partners such as VMware
- The Cisco MDS Family of storage networking equipment to facilitate storage consolidation in conjunction with partner solutions from companies such as EMC
- Cisco's Application Networking Services and security portfolios for virtualized, network-based services at Layer 4 and above

Another Cisco offering that is connected with cloud computing is its Virtual desktop infrastructure (VDI) solutions - a form of desktop virtualization that centralizes employee desktops, applications, and data in the data center. Most VDI solutions today run in a virtualized data center environment to further improve the manageability and security derived from consolidating hundreds and thousands of desktops to run on a few powerful servers.

Citrix

www.citrix.com/cloud

Citrix Systems specializes in application delivery infrastructure that can be used as the foundation for both public and private cloud computing. The Citrix Xen hypervisor powers many of the world's largest cloud providers today. NetScaler delivers web applications to a large proportion of all Internet users each day. Building on these technologies, Citrix has extended its offering into the cloud with its Citrix Cloud Center (C3) Solution, an integrated portfolio of Citrix delivery infrastructure products packaged and marketed to the cloud service provider market.

The Citrix C3 solution gives cloud providers a set of service delivery infrastructure building blocks for hosting, managing and delivering cloud-based computing services. It includes a reference architecture that combines the individual capabilities of several Citrix product lines to offer a service-based infrastructure suited to large-scale, on-demand delivery of both IT infrastructure and application services. This architecture consists of five key components: Platform, Desktop Services, Delivery, Bridge and Orchestration.

Platform: XenServer Cloud Edition is a virtual infrastructure solution optimized for service provider environments. It combines the scalability of the Xen hypervisor which powers many of the world's largest clouds, with the virtualization management and dynamic workload provisioning capabilities of the rest of the XenServer product line enabling cloud providers to host and manage a combination of Windows and Linux environments. XenServer Cloud Edition also features a consumption based pricing model for service providers who charge their customers based on metered resource use.

Applications and Desktop Services: XenApp is a Windows application delivery system that manages applications in the datacenter and delivers them as an on-demand service to users anywhere using any device. With Citrix XenApp, service providers can deliver Microsoft Windows applications through the SaaS model. Citrix XenDesktop is a desktop virtualization or virtual desktop infrastructure (VDI) solution that delivers desktops as a service to users by centralizing desktop lifecycle management. Service providers can deliver Windows Desktops as a Service (DaaS).

Delivery: NetScaler delivers cloud-based resources to end-users over the web through its policy-based AppExpert engine. It can optimize end-user application performance and security by dynamically scaling the number of virtual machines

(VMs) or servers available in response to changing workload demands and infra-structure availability. This allows cloud providers to balance workloads across large distributed cloud environments and redirect traffic to alternate capacity on or off premise in the event of network failures or datacenter outages.

Bridge: WANScaler has been designed as an "enterprise bridge" between hosted cloud services and on-premise private services by accelerating and optimizing application traffic between the cloud and the enterprise datacenter, particularly over long distances.

Orchestration: Citrix Workflow Studio provides an orchestration and workflow capability that allows the products in the Citrix C3 portfolio to be controlled and automated, and integrated with customer business and IT policy.

Cloudkick

www.cloudkick.com

Cloudkick is a tool that simplifies cloud server management from a web interface. It allows users to track critical metrics, configure alerts and visualize performance data and trends. A Cloudkick Agent provides on-machine monitoring for cloud servers. It records key metrics, such as disk usage, bandwidth and CPU usage, sending the data to Cloudkick's graphing engine for visualization.

Cloudkick's dashboard unifies management of Rackspace, EC2, Slicehost, GoGrid, Linode and Rimuhosting. Managers can see all the servers in one place and perform administrative tasks such as adding or removing instances.

Key features include:

- Track critical metrics: Users can monitor and set alert thresholds for HTTP, HTTPS, Ping, SSH, Load, CPU, Memory, Disk, Bandwidth, Memcache, or write their own custom plugins. Any metric can be viewed on the graphs page.
- Data visualization: Managers can plot and visualize any metric they have chosen to track. They can overlay multiple graphs and compare series from different sources. Cloudkick also provides data on bandwith and other metrics on servers in easy to use graphs and tables, allowing you a visual snapshot of server activity.
- Alerts: Administrators can set up alerts for critical events. For example, they may elect to receive an email when disk space on a database machine reaches a threshold or an SMS when load average spikes on the web servers.

CloudShare

www.cloudshare.com

CloudShare (formerly IT Structures) allows enterprise technology vendors to "SaaSify" their enterprise solutions by making full-featured virtual enterprise environments available online, on demand, for a variety of applications, such as presales demos, evaluations, technical training, certification and channel enablement.

CloudShare is essentially a collaborative tool for IT environments, allowing users to share, interact and collaborate in enterprise IT environments, for any duration. Organizations can replicate multiple, independent copies of their existing demos or training environments. Users can then do anything with the system that they can do on-premises, including saving records, loading data, and integrating with their local enterprise systems.

Environments for Microsoft SharePoint, Windows Azure, Dynamics CRM and other common tools are pre-configured to include servers, networking, storage and pre-installed operating systems and application licenses. Every CloudShare Enterprise solution includes:

- Complex environments with interconnected VMs and complex networking
- Security features including access control, VPN, secure SSL connections
- Combination of software, virtual appliances and (non-virtual) hardware, if required
- Workflow to support the specific application - inviting prospects to demos, setting up classes for trainees, setting user privileges etc.
- Branded mini-site surrounding the shared application that includes supporting collateral, web conferencing and collaboration
- Multi-tiered hierarchy to support the customer's organizational structure (e.g. manager, customers, instructors and students)
- Analytics and real-time monitoring that provide insight into CloudShare usage.

CohesiveFT

www.cohesiveft.com

CohesiveFT offers two primary products which can be used independently or complementarily. server-cubed represents a platform service while vns-cubed facilitates persistent, secure connections between cloud services.

server-cubed is a web-based console (which may reside in the cloud) that can be used to package application stacks onto virtual machine images. The customer defines the bundles of applications and configuration settings independent of the target provider. After assembling the image from its components, the factory creates a specific image based on the virtualization technology of the chosen cloud destination.

Since bundles can be shared across the CohesiveFT community, there is a small, but growing, ecosystem leveraging the components of other customers. Any individual, team or company can become a software component provider by uploading their software offerings into the platform. They can distribute or sell their finished servers through Elastic Server Sites which allow their customers to customize and download servers in virtualization and cloud-ready formats. A download directory lists the stacks published by other users using a dashboard view, which highlights the most popular components as well as an overall view of community activity.

vns-cubed is a packaged service offering from CohesiveFT that enables customer-controlled security in a cloud, between multiple clouds, and between a customer's private infrastructure and the cloud.

vns-cubed gives customers an encrypted LAN in a single cloud and an encrypted WAN across multiple clouds, allowing cloud-based clusters to appear to be part of one physical network. Using vns-cubed, customers can establish their own security perimeter for their cloud-based assets.

Computer Associates

www.ca.com/cloud

Computer Associates (CA) has acquired several companies that are very active in cloud computing. They complement and extend its Spectrum Automation Manager and Service Assurance and make it appear likely that we will also see a stronger focus on virtual and cloud-based network and systems management tools in the future.

Some important acquisitions that will strengthen CA's offerings in cloud computing include:

- NetQoS - a modular performance management platform including:
- SuperAgent for application response times monitoring
- GigaStor for long-term packet capture and analysis
- ReporterAnalyzer for traffic analysis
- NetVoyant for device performance management
- Unified Communications Monitor for VoIP and video monitoring

Cassatt – Active Response is an automated, dynamic server resource management platform that pools physical and virtual server resources for the most efficient utilization. It supports the automated initial deployment of application and system images, and additionally provides continuous monitoring of server and application health, with the ability to systematically power servers off when not needed and reassign resources dynamically to keep application performance within designated operational levels.

Oblicore provides Service Level Management (SLM) software for enterprises and service providers. It strengthens CA's ability to establish, measure and optimize service levels to meet business expectations across private and public cloud environments and also extends CA's capabilities in cloud vendor management and assurance of cloud service quality.

3Tera AppLogic is not a cloud service, per se, but rather a platform that caters to both service providers and enterprises. It is based on a grid operating system that underpins a catalog of common infrastructure components and software stacks. It also offers a visual interface to design and deploy the application, including the ability to move resources dynamically between infrastructure providers.

Cordys

www.cordys.com

Cordys is a provider of software for enterprise cloud orchestration. The Business Operations Platform (BOP) consists of a suite for Business Process Management (BPM), Business Activity Monitoring (BAM) and SaaS Deployment Frameworks (SDF). It includes an integrated set of tools including Composite Application Framework (CAF), Master Data Management (MDM) and a SOA Grid.

Cordys BOP may run behind both Apache and IIS, as there's only a minor gateway component configured on the web server. That gateway then communicates with the SOA grid where SOAP messages are used when communicating. This stateless nature of the stack makes clustered solutions easier to configure as there's no in-memory state synchronization needed between the nodes.

Cordys Process Factory provides a platform where users can build and execute process enabled situational applications in the Cloud. Business and IT can build new applications from scratch or take readily available services from the web and "mash up" new applications without coding. Cordys Process Factory empowers users to implement new business processes, change organizations or model mergers & acquisitions quickly, at lower cost and without IT involvement.

The most visible element of the Cordys Process Factory is a MashApps Composer that allows users to model and view business processes. As the name implies, they can create mashups of external gadgets and URLs. A visual interface lets them drag and drop components for online data entry. They can define simple workflows including notifications and approvals based on predefined conditions and actions.

It is possible to integrate bi-directionally with other systems. As mentioned above, the gadgets and URLs can be integrated into the user interface. It is also possible to expose the business processes as a web service for external consumption.

Once the process has been completely modeled and organized as forms and tabs, the author can define privileges and access controls for other users and publish the MashApp. It is then possible to monitor the activity of the application with dashboards of charts and reports.

CSC

www.csc.com/cloud

CSC's cloud services consist of a multi-tiered approach in which CSC manages complete ecosystems of cloud service providers, including platform-as-a-service, infrastructure-as-a-service and software-as-a-service. Orchestration helps clients manage data, lower operational costs, and collaborate easily and effectively across public and private networks.

Cloud Orchestration involves service level management, remote monitoring, reporting, auditing and data transparency. CSC provides automated arrangement, coordination, federation, management, security and operation of private, public and hybrid cloud computing environments, supporting industry-specific compliance and auditing services.

Additionally, the Trusted Cloud Services represent a portfolio of desktop, computing, storage and network infrastructure services available on demand. These include

- Microsoft BPOS implementation
- Web performance testing
- Cloud-based Services, such as:
  - Infrastructure: computing storage, PC backup
  - Application Platform: Desktop as a Service, on-demand testing
  - SaaS: BPOS, SAP/Oracle, Email/Collaboration
  - Business Process as a Service
- Cloud adoption assessment

Dell

www.dell.com/cloud

Even though they are not necessarily cloud-specific, Dell's products underpin many large private and public cloud deployments.

For example, Microsoft is working with Dell's Data Center Solutions (DCS), and is using Dell hardware and services, to build-out and power Windows Azure, Microsoft's cloud services platform hosted in Microsoft data centers. DCS offers similar services for many private clouds. Based on an analysis of each customer's compute requirements and physical infrastructure, they optimize the data center environment, from the individual server component to the facility level. The objective is to lower costs through energy efficiency, reduce network infrastructure requirements through virtualization and apply thermal best practices.

The acquisition of Boomi further strengthens their position as cloud providers. Boomi addresses the problem of integrating disparate sources of information to create complex business processes. Some refer to their approach as Integration-as-a-Service (IaaS) or Integration-Platform-as-a-Service (iPaaS).

The foundation of the offering is the AtomSphere platform based on a loose collection of what Boomi calls "Atoms". Each Atom is a federated runtime engine that contains one or more complete integration processes, which can be deployed either in the cloud or behind the firewall for on-premise applications and data sources.

The Boomi Atom is completely decoupled from the Platform from a runtime perspective, which ensures that the data being integrated is never transmitted through the Platform. Instead, the Atom communicates execution activity, such as what integration processes are being executed, the result and how many records were processed.

The platform also includes a library of pre-built connectors, which operationalize an API by abstracting out the technical details and providing a wizard-based approach to access the application, and a centralized, web-based dashboard with a visual tool for building, deploying, and managing integration processes.

Each application or trading partner is considered a connection. Consistent with the utility notion of cloud computing, companies pay by connection on a monthly basis rather than for a license to the software suite.

ElasticHosts

www.elastichosts.com

ElasticHosts is one of very few infrastructure service providers based in Europe as well as the United States. Location may be a critical factor for some European customers not only because of the improved latency and bandwidth but also the fact that data is known to be stored within the EU jurisdiction ensuring compliance with data protection laws.

Another interesting differentiator is the use of Linux KVM as the hypervisor. Companies that have standardized on KVM would obviously see this as a benefit. But some companies that have yet to decide on a hypervisor may find the choice attractive. Since KVM is built into mainline Linux it is able to leverage the full range of hardware virtualization support and directly use the regular Linux scheduler and I/O device drivers – this means that it provides very accurate hardware emulation, and as a result, can offer good performance for any 32-bit or 64-bit PC operating system without modifications.

Other features that characterize the ElasticHosts offering include:

- All storage is persistent
- Static IP addresses are available
- KVM virtualization supports any 32-bit or 64-bit PC operating system (Linux, Windows, FreeBSD, OpenSolaris, etc), including self-installation from CD
- Fully flexible instance sizing rather than a few choices of instance type
- VNC remote desktop available on all servers, including through boot process
- SLA offering attractive credits against downtime incidents
- Five independent availability zones, two in the United Kingdom and three in the North America

EMC

www.emc.com/cloud

Atmos is the first EMC storage solution that optimized for cloud. It is appropriate both for private data centers and public cloud service providers. Some of its key features include:

- Massive scalability: the object-based approach treats each site as single cloud entity. It uses a single interface with one namespace for all locations and is able to accommodate a worldwide spread of multi-petabyte storage.
- Policy-based information management: it is possible to establish rules which define where information should be stored, what actions should be taken as well as information lifetime. For example, a video metadata attribute such as popularity may dictate the number of replicas; an update to the metadata could automatically reduce the number of copies
- Operational efficiency: ability to identify, isolate and remediate failures in all components from the drive to the network interfaces

EMC's new Atmos GeoProtect also introduces a new protection technique called erasure coding. Rather than replicating an entire object (e.g. a television video clip), GeoProtect divides the object into multiple segments and automatically distributes the content across a customer's infrastructure, allowing Atmos to recreate the content in the event of system downtime or a disaster, thereby providing greater resiliency than replication with less storage overhead.

EMC Atmos Online is a cloud storage service based on the EMC Atmos storage product. Atmos Online offers you a multi-tenant, Internet-accessible storage resource that is infinitely scalable and designed for multiple EMC and third-party applications, including solutions for cloud backup, cloud archiving, collaboration, content distribution, and medical imaging.

It is also worth noting that EMC, through its Decho subsidiary, is the owner of Mozy, an online backup tool targeting consumers and businesses.

Enomaly

www.enomaly.com

Enomaly provides a technical foundation for infrastructure services without actually offering their own services through a utility model. Their product, the basic Elastic Computing Platform consists of a management interface with basic functions for infrastructure services such as:

- Start, stop and reboot virtual machines, or groups of machines
- Monitor and audit all jobs and operations
- Provision groups of virtual machines and assign to custom clusters
- Send launch parameters and scripted events to packaged machines
- Create static networks for critical machines
- Create snapshots of virtual machines
- Provision from library of pre-existing VM images
- Add users, create security groups and assign permissions

Additional features vary according to each of the three editions.

- Cloud Service Provider Edition
- Free SpotCloud Edition
- High Assurance Edition

The Cloud Service Provider Edition offers extensions to hosting providers who offer infrastructure services to their customers. It includes a customer self-service interface, integrated load monitoring with trigger-based autoscaling, hard quotas and integration with billing, provisioning and monitoring systems.

The SpotCloud market platform provides public cloud service providers a mechanism to sell unused cloud capacity. With SpotCloud, the provider's capacity is pooled with thousands of regional cloud providers in a structured marketplace, making it much easier for cloud consumers to both discover and buy from them

The High Assurance Edition builds on the feature-set of the Service Provider Edition, adding high-security capabilities to meet the needs of customers who require a higher level of security than that offered by any of the commodity cloud computing services available in the marketplace.

enStratus

www.enstratus.com

enStratus provides a console that displays real-time detail of Amazon and Rackspace infrastructure, among others. The enStratus management interface replaces the cloud vendor's interface while adding a number of features to support:

- User management and activity logging
- Data encryption and key management
- Shell/remote desktop access to cloud servers
- Backup and disaster recovery management
- Automatic replacement of failed servers and services

The product includes four primary components: the Console, Cloud Manager, Cluster Manager and User Manager.

The Console offers detail on the cloud infrastructure and users. This includes cluster information, cloud statistics and user statistics.

The Cloud Manager streamlines the interaction with the Amazon and Rackspace Cloud for typical management actions, such as reserving and reviewing IP addresses, launching and monitoring machine images and reviewing security groups and firewall rules. It also has the facility to track snapshots and volumes across their lifecycle.

The Cluster Manager provides the ability to define dependencies between servers, networking and application components to ensure a self-healing cloud infrastructure.

The User Manager allows customers to keep all encryption and authentication credentials outside the cloud. By removing root access, even the cloud service provider cannot log on to a running instance unless access is specifically granted by the client. The User Manager provides facilities for defining user groups and setting permissions and notification events for each user.

Etelos

www.etelos.com

Etelos targets owners of on-premise technology who would like to move to a SaaS model but do not own the necessary cloud infrastructure, experience or expertise. The benefit of an approach like that of Etelos is that it can provide billing and licensing based on a variety of metrics (CPU, disk space, memory, users, accounts), purchasing mechanisms (credit cards, promotions) as well as bundling and upselling options. This allows you as the application provider to focus on the actual functionality rather than the mechanics of online sales.

The Etelos Platform Suite is divided into four different platforms to address different requirements:

The SaaS Application platform manages the process or packaging the application in the targeted development environment. The solution then moves to a step of enabling automated provisioning, billing, marketing and first-level support. End-users can then try and buy the application through a web interface to the Etelos-hosted service.

The SaaS Marketplace Platform goes one step further in supporting the extension and integration of existing technologies by leveraging the Etelos API which can extend data properties in the application to the account framework.

The SaaS Distribution Platform facilitates private labeling of a marketplace. This involves selecting applications and packaging, installing, supporting and distributing them through a web-based marketplace. The platform caters to distributors of suites of applications which can be provisioned and customized to include value-added service solutions around the core application.

The SaaS Syndication Platform packages SaaS applications and distributes them through a network of web-based storefronts and marketplaces. The approach caters to SaaS providers who wish to significantly grow the number of channels they can use to sell their application.

Flexiant

www.flexiant.com

Flexiant is an infrastructure service provider comparable to Amazon EC2 or Rackspace Cloud. Similar to its competition, the Flexiscale service supports Linux and Windows operating systems and facilitates self-provisioning of cloud servers via control panel or API. Customers can start, stop and delete instances and change memory, CPU, Storage and Network addresses of cloud servers.

They offer extensive firewall rules based on IP addresses and protocols and each customer has their own dedicated VLAN. Unlike some IaaS providers, their virtual machines offer persistent storage, which is based on a fully virtualized high-end Storage Area Network.

In addition to Flexiscale, Flexiant also offers a licensed virtualized platform, called Extility, for hosting providers to build their own cloud or sell cloud services under their own brand. A control panel portal is available to customers, as well as an API, to allow end-users to provision, stop, start and delete virtual dedicated servers, as well as to resize their memory and storage.

GoGrid

www.gogrid.com

GoGrid is an infrastructure service provider that offers preinstalled images of Windows and Linux with Apache, IIS, MySQL and several other applications. MyGSI is a semi-automated process for creating, editing, saving, and deploying a GoGrid Server Image (GSI). A GSI is a Golden Image containing pre-configured and customized applications, as well as the server operating system.

GoGrid Cloud Storage is a file-level backup service for Windows and Linux cloud servers running in the GoGrid cloud. Windows and Linux cloud servers mount the storage using a secure private network and common transfer protocols to move data to and from the Cloud Storage device.

GoGrid Cloud Storage supports other interface mechanisms such as Secure Copy (SCP), FTP, Samba and rsync. For large data sets GoGrid will even perform a manual transfer of a physical hard drive into GoGrid's Cloud Storage – in other words, the customer can transfer data to an external hard drive and mail it to GoGrid.

GoGrid API provides programmatic communication for controlling GoGrid's control panel functionality. Typical API use cases include auto-scaling cloud server networks, listing assigned public and private IP addresses, deleting cloud servers and listing billing details.

F5 Load balancing can spread internet traffic across two or more servers. In the event a server crashes, the load balancer will redirect all traffic to the remaining online servers preventing application downtime. If a web application sees a drastic increase in internet traffic adding additional servers to the load balancer ensures the servers will not crash due to an overload of incoming HTTP requests.

The following load balancing algorithms and persistence settings are supported:

- Round Robin
- Sticky Session
- SSL Least Connect
- Source address

GoGrid Dedicated Servers allow users to connect GoGrid cloud infrastructure with a separate dedicated infrastructure, within a private network. GoGrid Dedicated Servers are available on demand.

Google

apps.google.com
appengine.google.com

Google is one of the most important cloud service providers, with services both in the PaaS (Google App Engine) and SaaS (Google Apps) space.

Google App Engine is a platform service. In addition to a basic run-time environment, it eliminates many of the system administration and development challenges involved in building applications that can scale to millions of users. It includes facilities to deploy code to a cluster as well as monitoring, failover, automatic scaling and load balancing.

App Engine originally supported runtime environments based only on Python. It has since added support for Java Virtual Machines (JVMs) thereby enabling applications written not only in Java but also other JVM languages such as Groovy, JRuby, Jython, Scala, or Clojure. The SDK includes a full local development environment that simulates Google App Engine on the developer's desktop.

Google App Engine includes the following features:

- dynamic web serving, with full support for common web technologies
- persistent storage with queries, sorting and transactions
- automatic scaling and load balancing
- APIs for authenticating users and sending email using Google Accounts
- a fully featured local development environment that simulates Google App Engine on your computer
- task queues for performing work outside of the scope of a web request
- scheduled tasks for triggering events at specified times and regular intervals

Another infrastructural service, used primarily by Google applications themselves is Google BigTable. It is a fast and extremely large-scale DBMS designed to scale into the petabyte range across "hundreds or thousands of machines". Each table has multiple dimensions (one of which is a field for time, allowing versioning). It is used by a number of Google applications, such as MapReduce.

On the SaaS side, Google offers a set of applications under the banner of Google Apps. These are available both as a free service to individuals and a competitively priced service for companies or individuals who may require higher storage limits. They include: Gmail, Google Calendar, Talk, Docs, and Sites:

- Gmail (also called Google Mail in some countries) is a webmail service.
- Google Calendar is a time-management web application.
- Google Talk (GTalk) is a Windows and web-based application for instant messaging and internet telephony.
- Google Docs is a web-based desktop application suite.
- Google Docs serves as a collaborative tool for editing amongst users and non-users in real time.
- Google Sites is a structured wiki.

Hosting.com

www.hosting.com

Hosting.com is a PCI level 3 compliant, SAS 70 type 2 certified and a GSA status hosting provider that serves mid-size and large enterprise companies by offering Dedicated and Co-located Hosting, along with Managed Services.

Cloud Dedicated is a private cluster of highly available, secure and redundant virtualized servers.

The Cloud Hosting options include Cloud VPS (Virtual Private Servers deployed on Hosting.com's cloud) and Cloud Enterprise (isolated virtual, clustered environments with high availability and rapid provisioning).

Cloud Enterprise ensures complete isolation of resources between virtual environments. The service is highly available on both computing and disk infrastructures. Compute resources are implemented within a highly available cluster while the disk environment is protected in a highly available SAN. Automated Provisioning gives customers the power to customize the amount of CPU, memory or disk utilization via the web interface.

vCloud Express, VMware's Infrastructure-as-a-Service (IaaS) solution runs on the Cloud Enterprise infrastructure. It provides instant provisioning and unlimited, dynamic compute resources.

In addition to the hosting options, Hosting.com offers a number of management products and services, such as:

- Dedicated Managed Platforms: customizable dedicated server configurations and server load balancing
- Infrastructure Monitoring: reporting on network connectivity, port activity and resource usage to ensure peak performance
- Storage and Back-Up: storage and backup options including Managed Backups and Server Replication
- Migration: assistance in transferring data and application settings from one server to another
- Network Security: firewalls, patch management, intrusion detection, network scans and penetration testing
- Collaboration: Hosted Microsoft Exchange and SharePoint.

HP

www.hp.com/go/cloud

Hewlett Packard (HP) offers a range of cloud related services that span consumer services, data-center infrastructure offerings as well as consulting and system integration for enterprises adopting a hybrid cloud strategy.

HP offers a number of SaaS-based services targeted at consumers, such as:

- HP ePrint (mobile printing service)
- Snapfish (online photo service)
- Gabble (Web-based service for video conversations)
- MagCloud (online custom-printed magazine service)

At the same time, HP is one of the main infrastructure providers for both private and public data centers, based on a large product portfolio in servers, storage, software and networking. And HP Enterprise Services specializes in securing, sourcing and governing cloud services.

The most recent cloud initiative is HP Cloud a public IaaS offering. HP Cloud Compute and HP Cloud Object Storage are built on HP's hardware and software, with key elements of HP Converged Infrastructure and OpenStack technology.

IBM

www.ibm.com/cloud

IBM's activity in cloud computing ranges from providing hardware and software components of the data center infrastructure for private and public clouds to consulting and integration services targeted at enterprises and cloud service providers. IBM also offers cloud services, such as testing and collaboration.

For those customers who want to leverage the benefits of a public cloud but also have enterprise-class requirements for security, customization and integration with on premise applications, IBM offers both IaaS (SmartCloud Enterprise) and PaaS (IBM SmartCloud Application Services).

These two are closely connected since SmartCloud Application Services (SCAS) automatically deploys virtual resources to SmartCloud Enterprise (SCE). Together they deliver a secure, collaborative cloud-based environment that supports the complete lifecycle of accelerated application development, deployment and delivery.

A core component of SCAS is the IBM Workload Deployer, a hardware appliance that provides access to IBM middleware virtual images and patterns to repeatedly create application environments that can be securely deployed and managed in a private cloud.

Another important module is the IBM PureApplication System, a platform system designed and tuned specifically for transactional web and database applications. It provides 'scale-in' design, integrated provisioning, elasticity and virtualization infrastructure for custom patterns of software, middleware and virtual systems resources.

The Cast Iron acquisition simplifies SaaS integration by delivering Integration as a Service. OmniConnect is its integration platform, which is designed to integrate public and private cloud services with on-premise applications. It targets end-users as well as SaaS service providers with data integration capabilities, such as migration, integration, extraction, cleansing and synchronization.

OmniConnect includes a set of template integration processes (TIPs) for the most common integration scenarios between several enterprise applications and therefore eliminates the need to build common integration elements from scratch.

Intuit

www.intuit.com

Intuit Inc. is a software company that develops financial and tax preparation software, such as Quicken and TurboTax, for consumers, small businesses and financial institutions. Its online services include web-hosting, accounting, payroll and payment solutions.

Intuit Websites allows the user to select a template with relevant pages, images, text and navigation. An embedded website builder provides options to change text, colors, images, fonts, and links. The user can also add a logo or draw on a free library of over 250 000 images.

Intuit QuickBooks Online has tailored onscreen forms to look like familiar checks and invoices, easing the transition to a web-based user interface. It offers options to track sales and expenses or obtain a company snapshot, providing visibility into revenue and spend which can be tracked over time and visualized with charts and graphs. It also provides tools to create, customize and manage invoices. This involves tracking accounts receivable but also providing customer-based access to estimates and contact information.

To help establish a baseline for reference, Intuit Trends provides access to reports on what competitors in the field are spending and making and enables relative comparisons.

Intuit Online Payroll allows users to create paychecks online, providing the W-2 forms and an option for direct deposit. It assists with tax calculations, email reminders to pay taxes and, optionally, electronic payment to the IRS.

Intuits payments solutions include facilities to process credit cards online, accept payment in retail stores with card-swiped terminal rates and process credit cards with a mobile phone, which is useful for anyone doing business away from the office, such as field workers or trade-show representatives.

Intuit also offers a platform service, called the Intuit Partner Platform, IPP. Initially it consisted of an Adobe Flex-based development environment with functions to target the large installed base of QuickBooks users.

It has since expanded into a set of APIs that can be leveraged from any platform, notably including Microsoft Azure, a strong partner of Intuit. The API offer functions such as SAML-based single sign-on, billing and user management as well as common user interface standards and a data API.

Joyent

www.joyent.com

Joyent offers infrastructure services for both public and private cloud deployments as wells as their own web application development platform. For their infrastructure services, they use the term 'Accelerators' to refer to their persistent virtual machines. They run OpenSolaris with Apache, Nginx, MySQL, PHP, Ruby on Rails and Java pre-installed and the ability to add other packages. A feature called "automatic CPU bursting" provides reactive elasticity.

All standard Accelerators come with static IP, persistent storage, and free bandwidth. They use Zeus Software Load Balancers as a traffic manager that can cache several thousands of pages/second in order to increase performance and reduce costs.

Joyent also offers a private version of their framework called SmartDataCenter for enterprise data centers.

Customers use Joyent Cloud Control to create a private cloud within your own data center. Cloud Control is software that runs on top of existing hardware, or on new dedicated machines. Cloud Control manages networking equipment and virtualized compute instances that are hosted within traditional physical servers and storage servers.

Cloud Control gives a web interface and APIs that manage the full lifecycle of application deployment architectures that span virtual and physical machines and even sets of data centers. The interface provides detailed status information including rack diagrams and delivers performance metrics and monitoring data.

LongJump

www.longjump.com

The LongJump Business Applications Platform is a service from Relational Netwoks, Inc, which specializes in web-based business applications.

The platform is built with open source web technologies and is written in Java and HTML. The backend database utilizes MySQL over a proprietary JDBC application and service layer. All requests and responses to the system utilize HTTPS, REST, or SOAP as transport. The policy, data, and session engines are all web-based.

The standard user interface is a browser-based dashboard which provides a view into each of the applications. The initial design is based on a data model which can be constructed through the user interface by defining tabular relationships. LongJump then provides additional automated processing when data is added, changed, or scheduled. The user can specify events that trigger other actions to take place such as validating information, executing a workflow, sending an email, changing data, or custom Java processes.

For more sophisticated application requirements, LongJump provides an Eclipse plug-in which can manage Java or Javascript to handle permissions and forms, manipulate data, run custom processes or actions and write native user interface elements.

LongJump can be installed behind the corporate firewall, inside private data centers, or within an infrastructure provider. This offers organizations the adaptability to use virtualized resources as well as traditional servers to host the platform.

In addition, applications can be packaged for migration from one LongJump deployed instance to another. For example, development can take place in a cloud deployment and be deployed in production in a corporation's data center.

Microsoft

www.microsoft.com/hyper-v-server
www.microsoft.com/windowsazure
www.microsoft.com/online
home.live.com

Microsoft has a strong presence at all layers of cloud architecture. They do not offer any infrastructure services themselves. However, their virtualization technology lends itself to IaaS providers. With Windows Azure they appear to have their sights set on PaaS and Microsoft Online is already a significant player in the SaaS space.

Microsoft offers both a bare-metal hypervisor in the form of Microsoft Hyper-V and also several Type 2 virtual machines such a Microsoft Virtual Server and Virtual PC. While most IaaS providers opt for open source virtualization in order to minimize their costs this is not an absolute rule. Private cloud offerings that rely on Microsoft for the bulk of their infrastructure may find Hyper-V attractive.

The Windows Azure platform is built as a distributed service hosted in Microsoft data centers and built on a special-purpose operating system called Windows Azure. It is implemented as three components: Compute, Storage and a Fabric to manage the platform.

The Compute instances are exposed to the customer as role types that specify tailored configurations for typical purposes.

Azure Storage takes care of three kinds of data storage:

- Blobs
- Tables
- Queue

The Fabric refers to a set of machines running the Azure operating system that are collectively managed and generally co-located in the same region.

Azure also provides a set of services that can be consumed both from the Internet (including the Azure platform itself) and from on-premise applications. They can be loosely categorized as:

- AppFabric

- SQL Azure
- Live Services

SQL Azure provides a cloud-oriented service framework that is available through REST, SOAP, Atom/AtomPub and WS-*.

Live Services provide a set of building blocks that can be used to handle user data and application resources including Identity and Contacts. These include Windows Live Messenger, Live Search and Maps.

Microsoft Online provides distinct SaaS services for consumers and enterprises.

Windows Live includes a number of consumer-oriented modules that cater to some of the most common requirements of home users. Two prominent services include Windows Live SkyDrive, an online file storage and sharing service, and Office Web Apps, a web-based edition of Microsoft Office.

Office 365 caters to enterprises with two editions. The standard offering operates using a multi-tenant model and comes at a very attractive price point for smaller organizations. The dedicated variation involves a higher degree of isolation which is often required by larger enterprises.

Mozy

mozy.com

Mozy offers an online backup solution that allows users to specify folders and files that should be backed up to the cloud on a regular basis. The service automatically detects and backs up new and changed files while the computer is not in use. Scheduled backups can be performed daily or weekly at a specified time of day.

Security is a major concern with cloud-based storage, which Mozy addresses with double encryption. At the beginning of the backup process, all files are locally encrypted with 448-bit Blowfish encryption. The encrypted files are then sent via 128–bit SSL to a Decho–managed data center where they remain in their encrypted state.

The tool backs up common business applications such as SQL, Exchange and includes support for open and locked files, such as Outlook PST files. Mozy only backs up new or changed portions of files, which saves bandwidth. Users can also specify how much bandwidth they want to dedicate to their backups so other high-priority services can run unimpeded.

Users and administrators can restore data via the Mozy software client, through the web, or by ordering a DVD restore. Windows users can also restore data via right-click or through the Mozy Virtual Drive.

The professional version of Mozy adds the role of administrators who can view individual and aggregate account history, reset account password and distribute license keys. They can also create customized email alerts regarding the backup health of their account.

NetApp

www.netapp.com

NetApp is an enterprise storage and data management company. NetApp's cloud strategy is to deliver cost efficient, flexible, scalable solutions that act as the storage infrastructure for cloud environments – both public and private. Rather than offering public services itself, NetApp has partnered with numerous service providers including BT, T-Systems, Terremark, Rackspace and Unisys to design, build, and market cloud services to enterprise customers.

Additionally, NetApp has partnered with technology vendors such as BMC, CA, Cisco, Citrix, Microsoft and VMware, to deliver architectures that enable the end-to-end dynamic infrastructures required by cloud environments.

NetApp and its partners are aligned around the concept of a dynamic data center that enables enterprises, integrators and service providers to deliver IT as a service. A dynamic data center leverages a utility computing model, centralized resource management, and rapid and flexible resource allocation to support a wide range of data center applications.

NetApp's Data ONTAP virtualized storage operating system provides a unified, scalable solution to address NAS, SAN, multi-tier, multi-protocol and multi-tenant virtualized environments. NetApp has combined its preceding operating systems (ONTAP 7G and the high-performance ONTAP GX platform) under a single code base to create a storage platform with both scale-up and scale-out capabilities (ONTAP 8). The newest release offers a foundation for cloud computing that includes secure multi-tenancy, data motion, role-based data management and monitoring tools for service automation, and integrated data protection for backup and recovery.

Secure Multi-Tenancy: Customers can deploy a shared infrastructure across separate user groups or enterprise customers with NetApp's MultiStore technology. Administrators can logically partition storage system, network and disk capacity. They can also provision multi-tenant storage infrastructure, consolidate the functionality of multiple file servers without reconfiguration and move data for disaster recovery, hardware upgrades, and resource balancing. NetApp, Cisco, and VMware jointly built and released the Secure Multi-tenancy Design Architecture, an end-to-end design architecture that helps enterprise customers, systems integrators and service providers develop internal and external cloud services that isolate clients, business units, departments or security zones for enhanced security across the computing, networking, storage and management layers of a unified infrastructure.

Data Motion: Customers can maintain uninterrupted data access during mandatory shutdowns or upgrades and respond quickly to hardware outages across multi-site distributed deployments. Data Motion allows for dynamic data migration among storage arrays, tiers and geographies. Service providers can segment tenants and transparently scale capacity, adjust service levels with on-demand load balancing, redistribute tenants between storage systems or tiers, and refresh infrastructure without the impact of planned downtime.

Service Automation: Customers can leverage a set of role-based data management and monitoring tools to automatically provision storage according to service levels, to meter usage, and to enable a chargeback model. NetApp is working with other service management vendors such as VMware, Microsoft, BMC and CA to integrate its storage management capabilities with management tools that cover other areas of the infrastructure such as virtual machine, physical server, network, etc. These integrated solutions offer control and management over the end-to-end dynamic infrastructure.

Integrated Data Protection: Customers can deploy built-in backup/recovery and business continuity capabilities, which are a necessity for shared infrastructures that must always be on. Integrated data protection allows customers to build a single infrastructure that automatically and efficiently backs up all data regardless of application or workload. NetApp's integrated data protection includes SnapMirror, a data replication solution that provides disaster recovery protection for business-critical data. It also enables a DR site for other activities such as business intelligence, and development and testing without business interruptions. Deduplication and network compression technology improve storage efficiency and reduce bandwidth utilization, thereby accelerating data transfers so that SnapMirror can cover a range of recovery point objectives from zero seconds to hours.

Storage Efficiency: A target of 50% less storage requirement is achieved with a broad set of storage features including space-efficient snapshots, data deduplication, thin provisioning and virtual clones.

NetSuite

www.netsuite.com

NetSuite offers several SaaS services including CRM and ERP.

NetSuite is a popular CRM package. Its base service is called NetSuite while NetSuite ERP and NetSuite CRM+ are the two primary product options. Some of the primary features include:

- Pipeline and opportunity
- Order Management
- Advanced forecasting
- Incentive
- Upsell manager
- Account management

NetSuite Financials supports back-office operations and business processes which are classified as:

- Financial Management
- Financial Planning
- Inventory and Supply Chain
- Order Management
- Services Resource Planning (SRP)
- Human Capital Management (HCM)
- Business Intelligence and Analytics (SuiteAnalytics)

NetSuite has also launched a global business management system called OneWorld which offers on-demand international support to mid-market companies. Multi-national organizations can manage companies with multiple subsidiaries, business units and legal entities in their requirement for homogenous and integrated quotes, forecasts, campaigns and analytics. It can handle all local currencies, taxation rules, and compliance requirements.

As with Salesforce.com, the platform offers very rich support for developers and third parties in an effort to build an extensive ecosystem. The SuiteCloud developer network includes the NetSuite Business Operating System – a set of tools to build, integrate and deliver applications for the NetSuite platform.

SuiteFlex application development platform consists of:

- SuiteBuilder rapid application development builds the user interface online,
- SuiteScript programming environment is a programming language modeled on JavaScript.
- SuiteTalk web services allow access to NetSuite data through a SOAP API.
- SuiteScripte D-Bug interactive debugger facilitates live troubleshooting.

The SuiteBundler application deployment tool allows the developer to productize, package and deliver a solution.

SuiteApp.com is NetSuite's online solution directory which acts as a marketplace for third party developers to sell their NetSuite extensions and layered functionality.

Nirvanix

www.nirvanix.com

Nirvanix CloudComplete is a storage service with an enterprise focus. In addition to working as a virtual mount point for Linux and Windows, it ensures dual/triple replication and allows zone specification (e.g. data should reside in the EU only for compliance or performance reasons).

It maintains storage presence in Europe and Asia as well as several storage pods in the United States. The Storage Delivery Network (SDN) service ensures efficient delivery of static content through an extensive perimeter of edge servers.

The enterprise focus is maintained with aggressive service-level agreements, policy support and hierarchical account management. It also caters to the entertainment industry where it can be used as a source point for CDN media distribution. Additionally, the embedded storage API allows backup and archiving companies to provide co-resident and co-located services.

OpSource

www.opsource.net

OpSource Enterprise Cloud Hosting is a suite of cloud infrastructure services that includes Technical, Application and Business Operations as well as a Services Bus.

The Technical Operations include Bare Metal and Managed Hosting services with high-availability provisions, multi-tier firewalls, load balancers and managed Intrusion Detection Systems that protect against denial-of-service attacks, worms and botnets.

Application Operations include functions for application optimization, roll-out and change management, provisions for SAS 70, PCI DSS and EU Safe Harbor compliance, database management, performance monitoring and optimization and end-to-end service-level agreements.

For potential SaaS vendors using other platforms than Amazon, OpSource offers a Customer Lifecycle Management (CLM) solution which automates customer on-boarding and then manages the customer purchases with facilities to measure usage and invoice the end customer. CLM automates the process of preparing statements, payments and collections of consolidated invoices based on the rules defined by the vendor. The self service feature allows customers to add more users and storage or to upgrade to a different plan.

The OpSource Services Bus exposes an API that allows applications running on the OpSource On-Demand platform to tap web services such as business analytics, onboarding and billing. It facilitates reporting and the visualization of key performance indicators (KPIs) based on data such as: Unit Metrics, Application Events, User Logins, Application Uptime, Bandwidth Utilization, Application Response Time, Monitoring Alerts and Billing Statistics.

The OpSource Connect services extend the Services Bus by providing the infrastructure for two-way web services interactions, allowing customers to consume and publish applications across a common web services infrastructure. This is of particular interest to infrastructure customers who intend to generate revenues from selling the application as a web service.

There are five main components of OpSource Connect:

- Web Services Conductor
- Application Directory

- Connectors
- Certified Integrator Program
- Web Services Enablement Program

A new service from OpSource, called OpSource Cloud, is targeted at companies that seek to combine the availability, flexibility and community of the public Cloud with the security, performance and control that the enterprises traditionally demand.

Its public cloud features include:

- Online sign-up
- Pay by the hour based on usage, with no commitment
- Community resources for sharing and collaboration, third party add-ins and configurations
- Web interface plus complete set of APIs

These are complemented with enterprise features, such as:

- Virtual Private Clouds with user-specified public Internet connectivity
- Customizable security for firewalls
- User-level login/password and access control
- SAS 70 Audited Cloud
- One hundred percent uptime SLA
- Multiple private networks on demand for multi-tier architecture
- Guaranteed sub-millisecond latency between systems
- User selectable server configurations
- Centralized control and billing, with master and departmental management and controls
- Sub-account permissions and budgeting

PingIdentity

www.pingidentity.com

PingIdentity offers both federated identity software (PingFederate) and a single sign-on solution (PingConnect) for heterogeneous web services.

PingOne is an on-demand SaaS single sign-on (SSO) and user account management. It supports Microsoft Active Directory authentication and dozens of SaaS applications for users who either do not have or do not want additional logins to access applications they use on a day-to-day basis. Supported services include Salesforce CRM; Google Apps; ADP; Cisco WebEx; Concur; Rearden Commerce; Success Factors and others.

SaaS User Account Management automates the creation and management of SaaS user accounts. This reduces administrative overhead and improves compliance by replicating access changes to remote SaaS directories and eliminates forgotten "zombie" accounts.

PingFederate is Ping Identity's federated identity software. It provides Internet single sign-on (SSO), Internet user account management and identity-enabled Web Services for all external partner connections including Software-as-a-Service (SaaS) and Business Process Outsourcing (BPO) providers, managed services, trading partners, affiliates, acquisitions and customers. PingFederate's point-and-click connection configuration, out-of-the-box integration kits, and multi-protocol support enable rapid deployment.

Rackspace

www.rackspace.com

Rackspace (formerly Mosso) is an infrastructure and platform provider with three primary offerings: Cloud Servers, Cloud Files and Cloud Sites.

Rackspace is perhaps best known as a founding member of OpenStack, which serves as the technological basis of their offerings.

Cloud Servers cover a number of Linux distributions (such as Ubuntu, Fedora, Centos and RedHat Enterprise Linux) and Windows 2008. They come with a large pool of dedicated IP addresses and offer persistent storage on all instances.

The Cloud Servers API allows programmatic access to create, configure, and control Cloud Servers from within customer applications. The interface uses a REST-based format supporting both XML and JSON data types.

Cloud Files is similar to Amazon S3 with access through a REST API. It provides containers for static content which can be replicated via the Limelight content delivery network to over 50 edge data centers.

Cloud Files is optimized for:

- Backups/archives
- Serving images/videos (streaming data to the user's browser)
- Secondary/tertiary, web-accessible storage
- Scenarios where amount of storage is difficult to predict

Cloud Sites represent fully managed platforms that can host Windows .NET or a complete LAMP (Linux, Apache, MySQL, Perl/Python/PHP) stack and would typically qualify as a PaaS offering. Access to the platform is supported through File Transfer Protocol (FTP) and Secure File Transfer Protocol (SFTP).

RightScale

www.rightscale.com

RightScale is a management platform that supports Amazon Web Services, Eucalyptus Systems, GoGrid and Rackspace as well as many other public and private cloud providers. It provides cloud-ready server templates that come with packaged boot and operational scripts to facilitate automatic deployments and portability between the service providers.

RightScale also provides mechanisms for grouping servers with common input parameters (such as code repositories and databases) so that these can be managed and deployed collectively. This is useful when it is necessary to make systematic changes across very large implementations.

A ServerTemplate starts with a RightImage, a simple base machine image that normally contains only the operating system, and then adds RightScripts, scripts that define the role and behavior of that particular server. RightScripts may run during the boot, operational, and shutdown phases of the server's lifecycle. These servers know how to obtain an IP address, how to access and manage storage, how to submit monitoring data, and how to collaborate with other servers in a cloud deployment.

Deployments bring all the servers associated with an application environment together under unified management. The customer can set global input parameters, monitor the entire deployment, make global updates to upgrade software versions, add applications to multiple servers, and clone the deployment for ongoing development and testing.

Using the Management Dashboard, the user can input deployment-wide parameters that individual ServerTemplates then pick up during boot-time, rather than launching individual servers. RightScale tracks the status of each server as it boots and reports its status in the Management Dashboard.

Salesforce.com

www.salesforce.com
www.salesforce.com/platform

Arguably, the best known SaaS offering comes from Salesforce.com which provides a CRM solution consisting of several modules. It is available in over 20 languages and can be accessed from almost any Internet device including mobile platforms such as Blackberry, iPhone and Windows Mobile.

Some of its modules include:

- Accounts and Contacts
- Marketing and leads
- Opportunities
- Analytics and Forecasting
- Workflows
- Content Library
- Social networking
- Partners
- Recruitment

Salesforce.com also delivers a Platform-as-a-Service which is called Force.com. It is very different from both Google's and Microsoft's offerings in this space. It does also offer hosting services based on its technology with the usual features of redundancy, security and scalability. But Force.com is much more data-oriented than code-oriented.

Force.com exposes all customer specific configurations (forms, reports, workflows, user privileges, customizations, business logic) as metadata which is programmatically accessible.

Force.Com applications are built using Visualforce (a framework for creating graphical user interfaces) and Apex (a proprietary programming language that uses a Java-like syntax but acts much more like database stored procedures).

Apex can run as a stand-alone script on demand or as a trigger on a data event. The language allows developers to add business logic to events, such as (user) button clicks or (data) record updates and Visualforce pages.

The Force.com Integrated Development Environment (IDE) is simply a plug-in to the Eclipse platform which connects directly to the Force.com services in the cloud and acts on the test environment.

Two tools are available for building the user interface for on-demand applications: UI builder and VisualForce.

The UI Builder is the simpler approach. It generates a default user interface based on the data properties of the application. The UI can be modified to change the layout and appearance or to add search functionality. However, it becomes difficult to make changes that involve the business logic.

VisualForce is much more powerful and can be used to create almost any user interface. It implements the MVC (Model: Data, View: User Interface, Controller: Business Logic) paradigm to enforce strict separation of logic from presentation and storage.

Force.com also provides a marketplace, called AppExchange, for buying and selling SaaS services. Once developers have completed and tested their applications they can request publication on AppExchange providing a description of the services along with the details of the pricing and support model.

SAS

www.sas.com

SAS is a software and services provider specialized in business analytics. In addition to general on-demand services for marketing, including campaign management, business intelligence and social media analytics, they offer a range of services that target the pharmaceutical and educational industries.

SAS increased their investment in cloud services in 2012 with the acquisition of rPath, a specialist in automating the assembly, provisioning and updating of diverse operating systems and middleware platforms and application stacks throughout enterprises.

The tool provides automated, policy-based system creation, deep compliance features, and the ability to generate multiple output formats from a single system definition. Its platform ensures complete management and control of deployed applications with capabilities including:

- Automated administration of patches and updates
- Complete system reproduction and rollback capabilities
- Application and systems audit and reporting for compliance management
- A centralized management console for start-up and shutdown across targets

The entire system together with all of its components and dependencies are stored and managed in a version control repository which provides consistent control over the lifecycle of the deployed system.

Savvis

www.savvis.net

Savvis, Inc. is an outsourcing provider of managed computing and network infrastructure for IT applications. Its services include managed hosting, colocation and network connectivity, which are supported by the company's global datacenter and network infrastructure. Savvis offers enterprise customers three primary variants of its Symphony services: Dedicated, Open and Virtual Private Data Center (VPDC).

Savvis Symphony Dedicated is a fully dedicated virtualized compute environment that is hosted and managed in Savvis data centers. The solution can be partitioned into multiple self-contained virtual machines (powered by VMware), each capable of running its own operating system and set of applications. Once deployed, customers can add instances automatically through the SavvisStation Portal.

Savvis Symphony Open is built on a scalable, multi-tenant infrastructure and delivers a secure, enterprise-class cloud environment with built-in high availability and automated resource balancing. It uses a purchase-by-the-instance cost model with flexible month- to-month terms for each instance.

Savvis Symphony VPDC introduces an enterprise-grade virtual private data center solution. Data center provisioning is facilitated through a self-service Web-based drag-and-drop topology designer or through an application programming interface (API). The VPDC supports enterprise-grade security, platform redundancy, and high-performance information lifecycle management (ILM) storage as well as multi-tiered QoS levels with policy enforcement. A VPDC can contain a complete set of enterprise data center services, including compute instances of varying sizes, multiple tiers of storage, redundant bandwidth and load balancing.

Skytap

www.skytap.com

Skytap is a self-service cloud automation solution that provides customers with web-based access to on-demand virtual machines and data centers, while enabling IT to maintain complete control over security policies and usage.

It includes billing and account management tools, a library of application services as well as the physical infrastructure for cloud computing.

The Skytap service allows customers to create virtual servers configured with multiple network adapters, create virtual clusters, add virtual firewalls, routers and gateways and then set up policies to manage those virtual assets on an ongoing basis.

Some interesting features of Skytap include:

- Customers are billed on a usage basis as with most cloud services. To address the unpredictability of costs, management may apply quotas and policies and create reports for charge-back and transaction-level auditing.
- The system supports user access control and the ability to share virtual machines and data based on pre-defined user access rules. Managers can now also determine CPU and memory policies at the VM level.
- A network automation tool can tap into a customer's environment. Once sufficient information is gathered, Skytap presents customers with a visual interface that allows them to either replicate their existing network settings or automate the process of deploying new virtual network adapters.

SOASTA

www.soasta.com

SOASTA is a provider of cloud testing services, which businesses use to verify the real-world performance of their web applications. Customers use SOASTA CloudTest On-Demand services to eliminate web performance issues during development through deployment and into production.

SOASTA CloudTest facilitates tests of any Web application or service from functional/regression testing and load testing to performance testing to Web UI/Ajax testing. SOASTA CloudTest is browser independent and supports common web-based standards such as SOAP, REST, HTTP(S), HTML, Ajax and JSON.

A memory-based analytic service (with persistence to disk) handles large results sets and analytics from distributed tests. The Analytic Dashboard correlates data streams from a distributed test into a single test result on a synchronized timeline providing the ability to drill down to a single event or message to isolate problems.

CloudTest's HTTP(S) Recording feature is a browser-based visual tool that automates the creation of typical usage scenarios by recording and presenting the HTTP(S) message traffic from the target Web application. It captures each HTTP(S) request sent to/from the target. The recording provides visibility into details of the message traffic and parses / presents the HTTP(S) message traffic as it occurs. It can also filter by URL, destination IP address, source IP address, method, duration and count and can include all TCP traffic or record HTTP(S) messages only. For more elaborate requirements it is possible to exclude or include traffic using TCPdump expressions.

A browser-based UI aids in the creation of synchronized test scenarios on a multi-track timeline that allows the user to control the timing, sequence and tempo of each test. By dragging customizable message clips from the message library and dropping them on the multi-track timeline, the user can create a variety of tests and use a Composition Editor to play back, move and resize test compositions interactively.

The interface provides a mechanism to monitor a variety of resources (hardware, network, load balancer, firewall, Web server, database, application server, content management system, etc.) and capture usage information about that resource.

SolveDirect

www.solvedirect.com

SolveDirect provides cloud-based services for multi-organizational IT service management. Its primary selling point is the integration of different service management applications with business-to-business connections. SolveDirect is used as a central service request hub and connects service processes of different organizations.

The integration methods supported include:

- Service request transactions can be sent from a workflow or received by a workflow in various transport formats (SMTP, SOAP, HTTPS Post, FTP, Rosettanet). Flexible data mapping allows the usage of customer specific data formats based on XML.
- Data Ports are used for bulk download or upload of data. Using Time Schedulers, the data can be transferred with SOAP, FTP or SMTP.
- SolveDirect also provides prepared Application Ports for SAP and BMC Atrium CMDB.

At present, SolveDirect offers three solutions:

SolveDirect SD^2 is a SaaS Service Desk Solution that gives service organizations the visibility and actionable intelligence required for service desk, asset management and customer support. Integrated real-time reports track performance against service-level agreements while a workflow engine automates service desk processes.

SolveDirect BRIDGE facilitates B2B integration by connecting leading Service Management Systems, CMDB's, Asset Management Systems, Logistic Systems as well as ERP and CRM Systems. The workflow-based offering supports event processing, notification, alerting, monitoring and collaborative resolution for multi-enterprise processes. It collects operational insights with beginning-to-end visibility into processes and communications.

SolveDirect CUBE combines collaboration and enterprise IT service management. A workflow engine automates service desk processes and a dashboard tracks performance against service level agreements with a real-time view of important KPIs.

SugarSync

www.sugarsync.com

SugarSync is an online backup and file synchronization solution that is provided as a subscription-based service. It is similar to other backup services in providing a mechanism to select files and folders which are transferred and stored securely into cloud-based storage. In the event of a local outage, the files can be retrieved through any web browser after proper authentication.

However, it also has some features that differentiate it from the competition. For example, its real-time backup capability means that it continuously synchronizes all edits and changes to selected files rather than running only as a scheduled task.

It also provides a means to synchronize files between computers and devices. Multiple PCs and Macs can synchronize the same files so that changes made on one automatically replicate to the others. There are also applications for iPhones, Windows Mobile Smartphone and BlackBerry phones to participate in the synchronization.

The next step beyond synchronization is sharing. It is possible to send other users a secure link to specific files. They can view and/or edit them and all changes will be saved and replicated. Inadvertent changes do not necessarily cause a problem. SugarSync automatically saves up to five previous versions of any file so it is possible to revert to earlier copies, whereby only the most recent copy of any file is counted towards the storage quota.

Symplified

www.symplified.com

Symplified extends corporate identity data and policies across the firewall for out-bound Cloud Access Management and in-bound Web Access Management. The solution provides authentication, access control, federated single sign-on, provisioning, auditing and reporting.

Symplified offers two deployment options for access management:

- The Identity Router is a purpose-built appliance with a hardened OS that delivers IAM in a single device.
- The Trust Cloud is a hosted proxy gateway operated in a SAS 70 Type II data center. It integrates with behind-the-firewall directories through SimpleLink web services.

Both enforce who gains access to applications, providing access visibility and termination of user Web and Cloud application access. Centrally monitoring and logging facilitate a unified audit log that reports all authentication, access and authorization events and supports compliance policies.

Supported identity stores include LDAP, Google, Salesforce or simple user databases. The engine can perform strong authentication and can translate between authentication mechanisms, such as username/password, multi-factor, SAML and Kerberos.

Additional functionality available from Simplified includes:

- SinglePoint Studio: a visual policy development and mapping tools that eases a the task of creating and managing role-based compliance policies across their lifecycle
- SinglePoint Identity Vault: hosted LDAP in a secure data center
- SinglePoint Identity Vault Salesforce.com Edition: leverages the Salesforce.com user repository for authentication, authorization and personalization
- SinglePoint Cloud Identity Manager (CIM):user self-service, registration, application requests and user activity reporting
- SinglePoint Sync: automation of user account management and integration with SPML gateways across cloud

Taleo

www.taleo.com

Taleo is a well-known HR software vendor, which also offers its solutions through a SaaS delivery model. Some features include:

Recruitment: Track and manage each job opening with clearly defined ownership. Post opportunities to own career sites or expand to external free and paid job boards. Conduct background checks, pre-screen applicants, and score and rank candidates based on answers to online or phone questions. Ensure hiring system is compliant with federal, state and local regulations and processes.

Performance Management: Establish quantitative and qualitative employee goals, define expectations, and align employee goals to broader company goals. Use configurable templates and business processes to define and monitor the employee review cycle. It includes a behavioral competencies library and facilities to monitor employee self assessments and manager appraisals.

Employee Lifecycle: Taleo OnBoard automates the new hire process by enabling electronic signatures and by supporting the assignment and tracking of key tasks to bring employees up to speed quickly. It can package forms into bundles and then create new-hire packets for various job types and locations. A consistent, reusable onboarding process ensures legal and policy compliance.

Career Management: Career Scenarios motivate and empower top performers to generate career tracks and identify steps for success. The system encourages employees to further their professional development and help them stay on track. It increases inter-departmental cooperation through expanded mentoring and networking opportunities and automatically informs the workforce when new employment, networking, mentoring, education, training or certification opportunities arise.

Succession Planning: scenario planning increases the visibility into a team's capabilities and supports executive decision-making. Succession Plans couple individual career plans with data captured in the performance review processes to create backfill strategies. The notion of Succession Pools represents candidates in the succession short list who are not necessarily officially included in the plan. The system tracks candidate readiness based on skills, competencies and performance and makes it easier to promote top candidates based on relative ranking and composite feedback scores.

Taleo also exposes a SOAP-based Web Services API that developers can leverage to integrate HR function and data in other applications or to build data extracts for backup purposes.

Unisys

www.unisys.com/cloud

Unisys designs, builds, and manages mission-critical environments for businesses and governments. Its primary focus areas include Security, Data Center Transformation, Outsourcing, Support Services and Application Modernization and Outsourcing. The Unisys cloud strategy involves three primary areas: Security, Compliance and Application rewrites/migration. Its primary offerings are marketed as the Unisys Secure Private Cloud and the Unisys Secure Cloud Solution.

Unisys Secure Private Cloud is a pre-integrated, internal private cloud solution that enables organizations to transform their data center operations into a highly automated infrastructure with a self-service portal and storage, network and server virtualization that delivers scale-up or scale-out, virtual or physical machines.

The Unisys Secure Private Cloud is delivered with a management appliance (preconfigured hardware/software solution) and implementation services.

- Unisys Cloud Orchestrator self-service portal
- Unisys uAdapt for physical server management
- Unisys uOrchestate for runbook automation and provisioning
- Unisys uChargeback for metering and billing interaction

The Unisys Secure Cloud solution includes Infrastructure as a Service, Platform as a Service, Software as a Service and also Disaster Recovery as a Service.

- Unisys Secure Infrastructure as a Service (IaaS) provides self-service, on-demand, elastic computing environments consisting of both virtual and physical servers, with the ability to migrate existing virtual and physical workloads into the Secure Cloud without re-installation.
- Unisys Secure Platform as a Service (PaaS) enables a managed computing "stack" with standard middleware, on a subscription basis. The service includes multiple "stacks" (including Microsoft IIS .net and SQL server, IBM Websphere and .NET application servers and Oracle database servers).
- Secure Software as a Service (SaaS) includes several specific offerings:

- o Virtual Office as a Service (VOaaS) provides hosted virtual desktop computing in an "office" environment (including the use of customer's existing PC workstations as thin clients) with centralized control and management.
- o Secure Document Delivery Service (SDD) enables secure electronic delivery of high-volume documents, such as statements and bills, and allows two-way secure interaction with your customers.
- o Secure Unified Communication as a Service (UCaaS) provides hosted Microsoft Exchange mailboxes on a subscription basis. Microsoft SharePoint services and Office Communications Server (OCS) services are also provided.
- Disaster Recovery as a Service (DRaaS) provides comprehensive business continuity/disaster recovery on a subscription basis. Mission-critical business applications and data are protected with replication failover capabilities.

A technology called "Stealth" allows multiple workloads to run together on a shared secure cloud without any changes to the applications. Stealth isolates each workloads data, and ensures that only authorized users and applications can access the data. Even the cloud provider cannot see the data.

Verizon

www.verizonbusiness.com/cloud/

Verizon became a major cloud player with its acquisition of Terremark, a global provider of IT infrastructure services. In addition to collocation, they offer VMware-based infrastructure services, such as utility hosting and enterprise-cloud virtual data centers. Terremark's data centers are built to stringent security standards with one location specialized for serving U.S. federal government needs.

The Enterprise Cloud from Terremark is an enterprise-class, Internet-optimized computing platform. A managed platform gives customers the ability to configure and deploy computing resources for mission-critical applications on-demand. The Enterprise Cloud gives control over a pool of processing, storage and memory resources to deploy server capacity. It's built around Terremark's Infinistructure utility computing platform, top-tier datacenters and access to global connectivity.

Verizon also invested in another acquisition, CloudSwitch, to provide a means to migrate existing enterprise applications to the cloud without re-architecting the application or changing management tools.

CloudSwitch essentially extends the enterprise perimeter into the cloud. It accomplishes this with an appliance that is installed in the virtualization environment (e.g. VMware) of the private data center and a set of CloudSwitch instances that are activated in each of the cloud service providers. All traffic from the corporate data center is bridged (OSI layer 2) to the cloud through an AES-protected connection.

VMware

www.vmware.com/cloud

VMware is a provider of business infrastructure virtualization based on the vSphere platform. Its activity in the cloud comes largely under the umbrella of its vCloud initiative.

vCloud is a set of enabling technologies including VMware vSphere, the vCloud API and additional cloud computing services that are brought to end customers both via internal clouds built on VMware and the vCloud service provider ecosystem. It is a common set of cloud computing services for businesses and service providers – with support for any application or OS and the ability to choose where applications live, on or off premise.

The core components of the vCloud are the ecosystem of VMware Ready vClouds delivered by service providers such as Terremark and Hosting.com, a set of applications delivered as Virtual Appliances and vApps on a foundation of VMware technologies including VMware vSphere and the vCloud API.

VMware vSphere is a cloud-oriented operating system that is capable of managing large pools of infrastructure, including software and hardware both from internal and external networks.

The vCloud API is an interface for providing and consuming virtual resources in the cloud. It enables the deployment and management of virtualized workloads in internal and external clouds as well as interoperability between clouds. The API enables the upload, download, instantiation, deployment and operation of vApps, networks and Virtual Datacenters.

VMware customers have the ability to integrate VMware Ready vClouds provided by service providers directly into their internal VMware infrastructure and management console thus enabling management of on-premise clouds and remote clouds from one interface. This gives them the opportunity to leverage key VMware technology advancements such as VMware VMotion, VMware Storage VMotion, VMware Distributed Resource Scheduler (DRS) and VMware vCenter. For example, users can move virtual machines without downtime. This capability means that applications can be managed, moved and operated in the cloud as they are on-site.

Hyperic, now a division of VMware, provides open source and enterprise monitoring and management software for a variety of web applications. Hyperic HQ is a suite of web application performance management software that is used by many SaaS and consumer web companies. Hyperic's solutions monitor and manage the performance and availability of the application stack from hardware and operating systems to virtual machines, web servers, application servers and databases thereby giving IT and web operations a unified view and control of the performance and health of their entire web infrastructure.

VMware TriCipher is a provider of Identity and Access Management. myOneLogin offers a single sign-on capability that binds multiple authentication and directory options to a range of SaaS providers, including Webex, Salesforce, Citrix, LinkedIn, Google and Basecamp.

The underlying TriCipher Armored Credential System (TACS) offers step-up authentication, with multiple levels of authentication security, including tokens, keys on portable USB devices, smart cards, biometrics, one-time-passwords (via SMS or voice), KBA, OATH tokens, and 'out-of-band' methods.

Workday

www.workday.com

Workday offers a suite of SaaS solutions ranging from Human Capital Management to Financial Management, Payroll and Worker Spend Management.

The Human Capital Management provides functionality including:

- Absence allows visibility of accrued vacation and facilities for registering planned leaves of absence

- Compensation includes salary, equity, benefits and allowances as well as bonuses based on both employee performance and business performance.

- Benefits include health (medical, dental, vision), insurance: (long-term and short-term disability, life), spending accounts (healthcare and dependent care) and defined contribution (401k, 403b) with age validation. There are also options for new hire enrolment, open enrolment and changes based on life events such as marriage and birth.

- Staffing entails functions such as position management, headcount management and job management.

- Development helps to support business performance through talent management with a focus on technical skills, project roles, training and certification as well as tracking awards and accomplishments.

- Performance management involves performance reviews and follow-up management that covers compensation, performance plans and disciplinary actions.

Workday also offers some functionality related to financial tasks such as:

Payroll: pay groups, reporting, tax updates, earnings/deductions, accumulations and balances

Worker spend management: reporting, expenses, reimbursements; onboard contingents

Financial accounting: for investors, creditors, and to ensure Sarbanes-Oxley compliance

Customer accounts: invoicing, accounts receivable

Supplier accounts: all information for vendor management, accounts payable

Cash management: bank statement reconciliation

Procurement: information policies for acquiring goods, services, rights contract labor

It can provide reporting functionality for all of the modules and includes logic to enforce all legal and company-specific accounting rules.

Zmanda

www.zmanda.com

Zmanda is a backup solution based on the Amanda open-source backup software. It provides a central console where administrators can specify hosts, paths and backup destination. Zmanda does not run in a cloud. It is a centrally administered solution that can backup data to disk and tape. However it also provides an option to back the data up cloud-based storage such as Amazon S3.

It caters to enterprises that may need to run in a hybrid environment. The central management server can interact with application agents that cover Microsoft Exchange, Active Directory and SQL Server as Oracle 10g and Oracle 11g.

It does not use any proprietary data formats so it is relatively easy to integrate the solution with other storage solutions. In particular its ZCloud API is publicly documented and can be leveraged by other storage services to become potential destinations of the ever-growing eco-system of backup-to-cloud applications.

Zoho

www.zoho.com

The Zoho offers a collection of browser- based of SaaS applications that generally fall into two categories. Consumers and professionals can use a suite of productivity and collaboration applications. Commercial users can also take advantage of a set of business tools. Zoho applications are currently free for personal use and require a fee for more extensive functionality or professional use.

Zoho productivity and collaboration applications include:

- Mail: Email service as well as calendar, document management, task management, and contact management.
- Writer: Word processor supporting simultaneous editing of multiple users. It supports common formats such as Microsoft Word, HTML and RTF as well as embedded media from hosting sites. Using Google Gears it can also support offline editing.
- Sheet: Spreadsheets application facilitating multi-user collaboration and the abilty to auto-process external data feeds (based on RSS or ATOM).
- Show: Presentation tool supporting collaborative editing and remote presentations
- Docs: Document Management
- Notebook: Note-taking tool that can include text, images, video, and audio with support for sharing the notebook or individual pages.
- Wiki: Collaboration Wiki Site that allows users to create their own site with features like tags, tables of contents and custom appearance
- Planner: Organizer with a calendar, to-do lists, pages and e-mail reminders.
- Chat: An application that supports private instant messaging with integrated access to all the major chat clients. It can also be embedded into web pages, such as blogs.

Zoho business applications include:

- CRM: Customer relationship management application including procurement, inventory and limited accounting functions.

- Discussions: Forums for both internal external user groups. These might include customer support and internal knowledge management.
- Assist: Remote support tool.
- Creator: Platform to create database applications including import templates and drag-and-drop support of script elements.
- Invoice: Invoicing application.
- Meeting: Web Conferencing applications with support for presentations, chat and desktop sharing/control.
- Projects: Project management software with support for creating tasks, assigning ownership, setting deadlines and tracking milestones.
- Reports: Database and reporting application with drag & drop interface to create charts, pivots and other reports.
- Recruit : Applicant Tracking System
- People: Human Resources Information System

Beyond these browser-based services, Zoho also offers a range of plug-ins for browsers and Microsoft Office products. There are also several connectivity options including Gadgets, a mobile device interface, a Facebook applications and an API with a "CloudSQL" extension.

References

Amazon Web Scrivces. (2010, December). Retrieved January 2013, from Amazon Web Scrivces: aws.amazon.com/message/65348/

Armbrust, M., Fox, A., Griffith, R., Joseph, A. D., Katz, R. H., Konwinski, A., et al. (2009, February 10). *Above the Clouds: A Berkeley View of Cloud Computing*. Retrieved January 2013, from UC Berkeley - Electrical Engineering and Computer Sciences: www.eecs.berkeley.edu/Pubs/TechRpts/2009/EECS-2009-28.pdf

Berkeley/Stanford. (2008, September). *The Berkeley/Stanford Recovery-Oriented Computing (ROC) Project*. Retrieved January 2013, from http://roc.cs.berkeley.edu/

BT Global Services. (2009, November). *The challenge for the CIO in 2010*. Retrieved January 2013, from BT Global Services: www.globalservices.bt.com/static/assets/pdf/Insights%20and%20Ideas/BTGS_Enterprise_Intelligence_Research_Report.pdf

Carr, N. G. (2004). *Does IT Matter*. Harvard Business School Publishing Corporation.

Carr, N. (2009). *The Big Switch: Rewiring the World, from Edison to Google*. W.W. Norton & Co.

Cloud Security Alliance. (2011, November). *Security Guidance for Critical Areas of Focus*. Retrieved January 2013, from Cloud Security Alliance: http://cloudsecurityalliance.org/csaguide.pdf

Cloud Security Alliance. (2010). *Top Threats to Cloud Computing V1.0.* Retrieved January 2013, from Cloud Security Alliance: cloudsecurityalliance.org/research/top-threats

Compete, Inc. (2011). *Siteanalytics amazon.com.* Retrieved January 2013, from Compete: siteanalytics.compete.com/amazon.com/

DiNucci, D. (1999). *Fragmented Future.* Retrieved January 2013, from www.darcyd.com/fragmented_future.pdf

ENISA. (2009, November). *Cloud Computing Risk Assessment.* Retrieved January 2013, from European Network and Information Security Agency: http://www.enisa.europa.eu/activities/risk-management/files/deliverables/cloud-computing-risk-assessment

ENISA. (2009, March). *EFR Framework Handbook.* Retrieved January 2013, from European Network and Information Security Agency: http://www.enisa.europa.eu/activities/risk-management/emerging-and-future-risk

Friedman, T. L. (2007). *The World Is Flat 3.0: A Brief History of the Twenty-first Century.* Picador.

Gartner. (2012, September). *Gartner Says Worldwide Cloud Services Market to Surpass $109 Billion in 2012.* Retrieved December 2012, from Gartner, Inc: http://www.gartner.com/it/page.jsp?id=2163616

Gartner, I. (2010, January 13). *Key Predictions for IT Organizations and Users in 2010 and Beyond.* Retrieved March 2010, from Gartner: http://www.gartner.com/it/page.jsp?id=1278413

Gartner, Inc. (2008, December 8). *New Research: Predicts 2009: The Evolving Open-Source Software Model.* Retrieved October 2009, from Gartner Blog Network: http://blogs.gartner.com/mark_driver/2008/12/08/new-research-predicts-2009-the-evolving-open-source-software-model/

Greenpeace. (2010, March). *Make IT Green - Cloud Computing and its Contribution to Climate Change.* Retrieved January 2013, from Greenpeace International: www.greenpeace.org/usa/press-center/reports4/make-it-green-cloud-computing

ISACA. (2009, October). *Cloud Computing: Business Benefits With Security, Governance and Assurance Perspectives.* Retrieved January 2013, from ISACA: www.isaca.org/Knowledge-Center/Research/Documents/Cloud-Computing-28Oct09-Research.pdf

ITIL. (2007). *The Official Introduction to the ITIL Service Lifecycle.* London: UK Office of Government Commerce: TSO.

James, C., & Stolz, M. (2009). *The True Cost of Latency*. Retrieved January 2013, from www.slidesharc.net/gemstonesystems/true-cost-of-latency

Kaufmann, R., & Gayliard, B. (2009, January 13). *http://www.ddj.com/go-parallel/article/showArticle.jhtml?articleID=212900103*. Retrieved January 2013, from Dr. Dobb's: www.ddj.com/go-parallel/article/showArticle.jhtml?articleID=212900103

Knowledge@Wharton. (2005, March). *Why Do So Many Mergers Fail*. Retrieved January 2013, from Knowledgc@Wharton: knowledge.wharton.upenn.edu/article.cfm?articleid=1137

Linthicum, D. S. (2009). *Cloud Computing and SOA Convergence in Your Enterprise*. Addison Wesley.

Mather, T., Kumaraswamy, S., & Latif, S. (2009). *Cloud Security and Privacy*. Sebastopol: O'Reilly.

Meier, R. L. (2000). Integrating Enterprise-Wide Risk Management Concepts into Industrial Technology Curricula. *Journal of Industrial Technology , 16* (4).

Moore, G. A. (2002). *Crossing the Chasm*. Harper Paperbacks.

NIST. (2011, September). *The NIST Definition of Cloud Computing*. Retrieved December 2012, from National Institute of Standards and Technology: csrc.nist.gov/publications/nistpubs/800-145/SP800-145.pdf

O'Reilly, T., & Batelle, J. (2004). Opening Welcome. *Web 2.0 Conference*. San Francisco, CA.

PingIdentity. (2009, September). *Open Source Federated Identity Management*. Retrieved Septemper 16, 2009, from http://www.sourceid.org/content/primer.cfm

Porter, M. E. (1998). *Competitive Strategy: Techniques for Analyzing Industries and Competitors*. Free Press.

Porter, M. E. (1979). How competitive forces shape strategy. *Harvard business Review* , 137-156.

Porter, M. E. (1998). *The Competitive Advantage of Nations*. Free Press.

Raftery, T. (2012). *GreenMonk*. Retrieved 2012, from GreenMonk: http://greenmonk.net

Reese, G. (2009). *Cloud Application Architectures: Building Applications and Infrastructure in the Cloud*. O'Reilly Media, Inc.

Reporter, V. (2008, April). *The Value of a Millisecond:Finding the Optimal Speed of a Trading Infrastructure*. Retrieved January 2013, from TABB Group: www.tabbgroup.com/PublicationDetail.aspx?PublicationID=346

Rhoton, J., & Haukioja, R. (2011). *Cloud Computing Architected: Solution Design Handbook.* Recursive Press.

Ricciuti, M. (2008, September 30). *Stallman: Cloud computing is 'stupidity'.* Retrieved January 2013, from cnet news: news.cnet.com/8301-1001_3-10054253-92.html

Rittinghouse, J. W., & Ransome, J. F. (2009). *Cloud Computing: Implementation, Management, and Security.* Boca Raton: CRC Press.

Roberts, A., & MacLennan, A. (2006). *Making Strategies Work.* Edinburgh: Heriot-Watt University.

Roberts, A., Wallace, W., & McClure, N. (2007). *Strategic Risk Management.* Edinburgh: Heriot-Watt University.

Romanski, P. (2009, October 4). *3Tera Adds IPv6 Support to AppLogic Cloud Computing Platform.* Retrieved January 2013, from Cloud Computing Journal: cloudcomputing.sys-con.com/node/1129095

Ross, J. W., Weill, P., & Robertson, D. C. (2006). *Enterprise Architecture as Strategy.* Harvard Business Press.

Ruth, G. (2009). *Cloud Storage: An Emerging Market.* Midvale, Utah: Burton Group.

Simonds, J. (2009, Dec 21). *Analyst Predictions For 2010.* Retrieved January 2013, from Delusions of Adequacy: johnsimonds.com/2009/12/31/analyst-predictions-for-2010-everyone-is-going-out-on-basically-the-same-limb/

Staimer, M. (2010, March). *Getting started with cloud archiving: Tips for smaller businesses.* Retrieved January 2013, from TechTarget: searchsmbstorage.techtarget.com/tip/Getting-started-with-cloud-archiving-Tips-for-smaller-businesses

Terremark. (2009, October). *Terremark Federal Government Facilities.* Retrieved October 2009, from http://www.terremark.com/industry-solutions/government/facilities.aspx

Vaquero, Rodero-Merino, Cáceres, & Lindner. (2009, January). *A Break in the Clouds: Towards a Cloud Definition.* Retrieved January 2013, from www.sigcomm.org/sites/default/files/ccr/papers/2009/January/1496091-1496100.pdf

Velte, A. T., Velte, T. J., & Elsenpeter, R. (2009). *Cloud Computing: A Practical Approach.* New York: McGraw Hill.

Vogelstein, F. (2009, July 20). *Why Is Obama's Top Antitrust Cop Gunning for Google?* Retrieved January 2013, from Wired Magazine: www.wired.com/techbiz/it/magazine/17-08/mf_googlopoly?currentPage=all

Wardley, S. (2009, July). *Cloud Computing - Why IT Matters*. Retrieved January 2013, from YouTube: www.youtube.com/watch?v=okqLxzWS5R4

Weinman, J., & Lapinski, J. (2009, April). *Why McKinsey's Cloud Report Missed the Mark*. Retrieved January 2013, from GigaOM: gigaom.com/2009/04/21/why-mckinseys-cloud-report-missed-the-mark/#comments

Wolf, C. (2012, May). *A Global Reality: Governmental Access to Data in the Cloud*. Retrieved November 2012, from Hogan Lovells: http://www.hoganlovells.com/hogan-lovells-revealing-study-about-governmental-access-to-data-in-the-cloud-detailed-in-white-paper-released-at-brussels-program-05-23-2012/

Web references

http://reservoir.cs.ucl.ac.uk/twiki/pub/Reservoir/PublicationsPage/CloudDefinitionPaper.pdf

http://code.google.com/appengine/docs/whatisgoogleappengine.html

http://www.rationalsurvivability.com/blog/?p=604

http://www.informationweek.com/news/government/cloud-saas/showArticle.jhtml?articleID=218700118

http://download.boulder.ibm.com/ibmdl/pub/software/dw/wes/hipods/CloudComputingNEDC_wp_28May.pdf

http://people.csail.mit.edu/tromer/papers/cloudsec.pdf

http://www.free-webhosts.com/webhosting-01.php

http://www.free-webhosts.com/user_reviews.php

http://www.pharmacyonesource.com/applications/

http://www.sentri7.com/

http://www.informationweek.com/news/government/cloud-saas/showArticle.jhtml?articleID=218700118

http://wiki.developerforce.com/index.php/DeveloperCoreResources

http://www.saas-showplace.com/saasproviderdirectory/saasapplicationcategory.html

Wikipedia
Found at: http://en.wikipedia.org/wiki/

Amazon_Web_Services
Application_virtualization
Azure_Services_Platform
Bigtable
Business_process_modeling
Call_center
CAPM
Cassandra_(database)
Change_management_(people)
Cloud_computing
Compliance_(regulation)
Data_center
Data_migration
Desktop_virtualization
Dynamo_(storage_system)
Enterprise_application_integration
Enterprise_risk_management
Extract,_transform,_load
FISMA
Force.com
GLBA
GoGrid
Google
Google_App_Engine
Governance
Green_computing
Grid_computing

Hadoop
Hipaa
Information_Technology
_Infrastructure_Library_Version_3
Infrastructure_as_a_service
Ipv6
MapReduce
Microsoft
Occupational_Safety_and_Health
_Administration
Peer-to-peer
Physical-to-Virtual
Platform_as_a_service
Platform_virtualization
Rackspace_Cloud
Rate_of_return
Rightscale
Salesforce.com
Sarbanes-Oxley_Act
Software_as_a_Service
Storage_virtualization
TOGAF
Utility_computing
Virtualization
Vmware
Volunteer_computing
Xenserver

Index

D

E

F

G

H

I

J

L

M

About the Author

John Rhoton is a Strategy Consultant who specializes in defining and driving the adoption of emerging technologies in international corporations. He provides workshops, training and consulting in business strategy and emerging technology around the world.

John has over 25 years of industry experience working for Digital Equipment Corporation, Compaq Computer Corporation, Hewlett-Packard and Symantec where he has led the technical communities and driven the services strategies around a wide variety of initiatives including cloud computing, mobility, next-generation-networking and virtualization.

During his tenure, he has been stationed in several counties in Asia, Europe and North America and is fluent in English, German, Spanish, French and Italian. He holds a Master of Science degree in Computer Science from the University of Missouri-Rolla, and a Master of Business of Administration from Edinburgh Business School (Heriot-Watt University).

You find more details about what John is doing at linkedin.com/in/rhoton, or reach him for any questions or comments at john.rhoton@gmail.com.

Printed in Poland
by Amazon Fulfillment
Poland Sp. z o.o., Wrocław